Ap

Joanne,
Productive once again!

Doug

CONGRESS, THE PRESS,
AND POLITICAL ACCOUNTABILITY

CONGRESS, THE PRESS, AND POLITICAL ACCOUNTABILITY

R. Douglas Arnold

RUSSELL SAGE FOUNDATION   NEW YORK

PRINCETON UNIVERSITY PRESS   PRINCETON AND OXFORD

Library of Congress Cataloging-in-Publication Data

Arnold, R. Douglas, 1950–
Congress, the press, and political accountability / R. Douglas Arnold.
p. cm.
Includes bibliographical references and index.
ISBN 0-691-11710-1 (cl. : alk. paper)
1. Press and politics — United States. 2. United States. Congress —
Press coverage — United States. I. Title.
PN4888.P6A76 2004
070.4′49320973 — dc22   2003055535

British Library Cataloging-in-Publication Data is available

This book has been composed in Electra
Printed on acid-free paper. ∞
www.pupress.princeton.edu
www.russellsage.org
Printed in the United States of America
10 9 8 7 6 5 4 3 2 1

To Alex

Contents _____

Tables and Figures

Tables

Figures

Acknowledgments ⸻

FOR GENEROUS financial support, I am indebted to the Russell Sage Foundation, the National Science Foundation (SBR-9422386; SES-0209609), the Earhart Foundation, the Dirksen Congressional Center, the Caterpillar Foundation, and the Goldsmith Awards Program at the Joan Shorenstein Center on the Press, Politics, and Public Policy at Harvard University. I have also profited from the regular faculty leave program at Princeton University and from research funds available at Princeton's Woodrow Wilson School.

My greatest debts are to Larry Bartels, Tim Cook, and John Zaller, who provided superb advice at various stages of the project, and to a talented group of assistants, including Scott Abernathy, J. J. Balaban, Reggie Cohen, Laura Delanoy, Kimberly Giamportone, Todd Jones, Chris Mackie, Michael Paul, Okiyoshi Takeda, and Helene Wood, who helped create and manage the data sets. I am indebted to Danielle Vinson for sharing data from her own project.

I am grateful to Richard Fenno, Fred Greenstein, Richard Hall, Stanley Kelley, Gregory Koger, Jane Mansbridge, David Mayhew, Robert Merton, Hans Noel, Michael Schudson, Wendy Schiller, Okiyoshi Takeda, and Craig Volden for their critical reactions to various versions of the manuscript. I also profited from suggestions made by seminar participants at Columbia, Harvard, Louisiana State, Michigan, Princeton, Rutgers, Stony Brook, Yale, and the Russell Sage Foundation.

Mere words cannot capture my enormous debt to Alex Quinn.

CONGRESS, THE PRESS,
AND POLITICAL ACCOUNTABILITY

1

Legislators, Journalists, and Citizens

THE MASS MEDIA perform a vital function in democratic systems by reporting what elected officials are doing in office. The media convey not only factual accounts of officials' activities and decisions; they also transmit evaluations of officials' performance, including assessments by other politicians, interest group leaders, pundits, and ordinary citizens. Although the media are not the only source of information about officials' performance, they are by far the most important. Indeed, it is difficult to imagine how large-scale democracy would be possible without a free and independent press to report the actions of governmental officials. Robert Dahl, the democratic theorist, argues that the existence of alternative and independent sources of information is one of seven necessary conditions for the existence of democratic government.[1]

Information about elected officials' performance serves two important purposes. First, it allows citizens to evaluate the desirability of retaining or replacing officials when they run for reelection. Candidates promise all sorts of things when they first run for office. When they run for reelection, however, there is no better guide to their future performance than what they have already done. Second, a regular flow of information about governmental decision making helps keep officials on their toes when they first make decisions. Officials who expect their actions to be featured on the evening news and on the front pages of newspapers may make decisions different from officials who expect their decisions to remain forever hidden from public scrutiny.

How extensively and how effectively do media outlets in the United States cover elected officials? Do they report the kinds of information that citizens need to hold officials accountable for their actions in office? Or is coverage so spotty and incomplete that even the most diligent citizens cannot learn much about who is responsible for governmental decisions? These impor-

---

[1] His exact criterion is that "citizens have a right to seek out alternative and independent sources of information from other citizens, experts, newspapers, magazines, books, telecommunications, and the like. Moreover, alternative sources of information actually exist that are not under the control of the government or any other single political group attempting to influence public political beliefs and attitudes, and these alternative sources are effectively protected by law" (Dahl 1989, 221; 1998, 86).

tant questions are central to the performance of democratic government. Unfortunately, they are not questions to which we know the answers.

Most citizens are exposed to a regular diet of information about what the president is doing in office. The mass media cover presidential activities on an almost daily basis, reporting where the president travels, what he says, what he proposes, how his proposals fare in Congress, what he is doing about various crises, and what innumerable pundits, legislators, politicians, and foreign officials think of his performance in office. Although one can surely raise questions about the adequacy and fairness of the media's coverage of presidential activities and about the depth of citizens' knowledge of presidential performance, two things seem clear. First, presidents know that their deeds and misdeeds will be covered by the press and noticed by the public, so they work hard to produce pleasing records. Second, when pollsters come knocking at their doors, it is reasonable to believe that most citizens have some evidentiary basis for determining whether they "approve or disapprove of the way the president is handling his job as president."

Can one make similar arguments about the way journalists cover members of Congress? Do legislators expect that their individual activities and decisions in Washington will be covered by the press and reported to their constituents? Are citizens exposed to regular information about what their senators or representatives are doing in office? Do citizens have any evidentiary basis for determining whether they approve or disapprove of the way their representatives are performing in office? Here the issues become more complicated, in part because there are 535 legislators to cover. Journalists do not cover all senators and representatives equally well. Citizens in different states and different districts are not exposed to identical flows of information.

Media Outlets

The so-called national press — the networks, newsmagazines, and national newspapers — could not possibly cover the individual activities of every senator and representative. The national press can cover Congress as an institution and report what it is doing about a whole range of problems. It can focus on some colorful or consequential legislators, making Ted Kennedy and Newt Gingrich into household names. The national press could not possibly make 535 legislators into household names. It has neither the time nor the space for such intensive coverage. The typical representative does not appear even once a year in *Newsweek*, *USA Today*, or on the CBS evening news.[2]

[2] Timothy Cook discovered that only 39 percent of House members appeared on any network newscast during a typical year between 1969 and 1986 (Cook 1989, 60).

Local media outlets are better suited to cover individual members of Congress than the national media. Newspapers, television stations, and radio outlets serve geographically defined media markets, and most of these market areas are represented in Congress by only a few legislators. Even local media outlets, however, have constraints on their coverage. The congruence between congressional districts and media markets is far from perfect. A television station in New York City, which has thirty-five representatives within its broadcast area, has no more time in its broadcast day than a television station in Portland Maine, where the broadcast area is essentially congruent with a single congressional district.[3] A small weekly newspaper has to decide whether to devote its meager resources to covering the politics of the several towns it serves or the activities of its representative in Washington. Each media outlet decides what kinds of news it wants to present. No law compels them to cover what representatives are doing in office.

Although local media outlets are better suited to covering individual representatives than are the national media, they are much more difficult to study. The difficulty involves both numbers and access. Four national networks, three newsmagazines, and a handful of major newspapers have been the focus of most previous studies of politics and the press. Once early studies established that coverage patterns were similar among national media outlets, subsequent studies often focused on a single network, newsmagazine, and newspaper. In contrast, 23,000 local media outlets blanket the country in a hodgepodge of overlapping territories.[4] No one knows anything about the similarity of coverage patterns across these thousands of outlets, so one cannot discover much about the universe of outlets by studying only a handful. Studying local outlets requires sampling, but how should one draw a sample that is representative of what citizens see, hear, and read?

The problem of access is even more serious. A research center at Vanderbilt University has recorded and archived network television newscasts since 1968. No one has recorded and archived local television newscasts. Radio newscasts are similarly unavailable. Although most research libraries contain archives of newsmagazines and major newspapers, most local newspapers are found only in the communities where they are published. Given the problems of sampling and access, it is not surprising that few scholars have attempted to study how local media outlets cover members of Congress.

This book is the first large-scale study of how local media outlets cover

---

[3] The best source for information about the overlap between congressional districts and media markets, including information about daily newspapers, commercial television stations, and cable television systems, is Congressional Quarterly 1993a. On the effects of incongruence between media markets and congressional districts on what citizens know about representatives and challengers, see Prinz 1995; Levy and Squire 2000.

[4] These outlets include 1,505 television stations, 9,746 commercial radio stations, 1,567 daily newspapers, and 9,816 weekly and semiweekly newspapers (Census Bureau 1994, 567, 576).

members of Congress. The focus is on local newspapers because it is for them that I have solved the twin problems of sampling and access. No cost-effective solution is in sight for studying local radio or television newscasts.[5] Unlike previous studies, which largely focused on the campaign period, this book explores how local newspapers covered representatives during an entire congressional session, from the first day of 1993 to election day 1994. The longer period is essential for studying political accountability.

Even if it were not the case that studying local newspapers is easier than studying local television, good reasons exist for beginning with newspapers. First, local newspapers have much larger newsholes than do local television stations. Local newscasts are usually fixed at thirty or sixty minutes, so after deducting for weather, sports, and advertisements, the time available for news is quite limited. Newspapers, by comparison, can cover many more subjects and in much greater detail. Second, the constraints in large metropolitan areas, where there are dozens of representatives to cover, are particularly severe for television, whereas large metropolitan newspapers can use regional editions and regional sections to cover representatives. The news hour is fixed; the newspaper is expandable. Third, in many localities, newspapers set the local news agenda and broadcast journalists follow their lead. Jeffrey Mondak found this to be especially true for House campaigns.[6] Finally, two studies of how local media outlets cover Congress found much less coverage on local television stations than in local newspapers (Hess 1991; Vinson 2003).[7]

A full understanding of how the mass media cover representatives requires examination of all types of media — radio, television, cable, daily newspapers, weekly newspapers, and the Web. The arguments for beginning with local newspapers are two. First, local newspapers appear to cover local representatives more intensively than do other media outlets. Beginning with local newspapers allows one to establish a baseline for comparing other types of coverage. Second, the problems of sampling and access are more

[5] Ironically, it is possible to search electronically the archives of the great nineteenth-century mass medium, the local newspaper, whereas there are no similar archives for analyzing coverage by radio and television, the dominant mass media of the electronic age. Both Stephen Hess and Danielle Vinson relied on friends and family to record local newscasts for their studies of how local television stations cover Congress and its members (Hess 1991, 49; Vinson 2003).

[6] Mondak's innovative study during the 1992 newspaper strike in Pittsburgh found that local television stations provided reasonable coverage of the presidential and senatorial campaigns but very little coverage of the three House campaigns. He argued that with newspapers closed, broadcast journalists had no lead to follow on covering House races (Mondak 1995, 65–66). On how local television journalists learn what is news, see McManus 1990.

[7] When answering poll questions, citizens say that they rely on television more than newspapers for national elections like the presidency, newspapers more than television for local elections like mayor or state legislator, and a mix of newspapers and television for senator, governor, and House member (Mayer 1993; Kahn and Kenney 1999, 36).

easily solved for newspapers, thus allowing for much larger sample sizes. It is worth emphasizing, however, that this study is essentially measuring the high-water mark for media coverage of representatives. When local newspapers fail to cover some aspect of a legislator's behavior, it is unlikely that local radio and television outlets are somehow filling the void.

Accountability

The American system does not make it easy for citizens to hold elected officials accountable for governmental decisions. Holding officials accountable is easiest when power is concentrated on a single individual or party team. In a parliamentary system, for example, where two parties compete in regular elections and where the winning party gains complete control over policy making until the next election, citizens need not monitor who is doing what within government. With the executive and legislative functions united, it is reasonable for citizens to assume the in-party is responsible for everything that government does. If citizens don't like what government has been doing, they can throw the rascals out. The incentives for the in-party to produce pleasing outcomes are especially strong when power is concentrated. The rewards are for action and results, not words and excuses.

The American system is one of dispersed power and scattered responsibility. Federalism, separation of powers, and bicameralism make it difficult for citizens to know who is responsible for improving or deteriorating conditions, and therefore whom they should reward or punish. If candidates ran for office and governed as members of strong party teams, citizens could reward and punish the team that controlled the legislative and executive branches, just as they do in parliamentary systems. But candidates run more as individuals than as members of strong party teams, citizens often split their votes among the parties' candidates in separate House, Senate, and presidential elections, and parties do not govern as unified teams. Although the norm was once for a single party to control the House, Senate, and White House, the norm now is for divided control of these three institutions. With weak parties and divided party control, citizens need to know more about what particular officials have been doing if they are to reward and punish the right officials. They need to know who the rascals are before they can throw them out.

A system of dispersed power and scattered responsibility also affects the incentives of elected officials. Whereas members of strong party teams work for the good of the team, often giving up individual glory for team success, elected officials in the American system have a stronger interest in individual glory. Achieving any kind of coordinated action among officials so motivated is difficult. Officials also have strong incentives to blame others for inaction. A president lashes out against a do-nothing Congress; senators complain about the lack of presidential leadership; House members blame a senatorial filibuster. Every participant has a favorite explanation for legislative gridlock.

If citizens are to hold legislators accountable, they need information about what their representatives are doing in office. Where might they find appropriate information? One thing is certain: Most citizens do not have an incentive to search diligently for information about representatives' actions in office. Anthony Downs made the case long ago that information is costly and that few citizens choose to incur substantial costs to become informed voters. Most citizens rely on whatever information comes their way in the course of daily life (Downs 1957, 207–37). Fortunately, many individuals and groups have incentives to inform citizens about representatives' actions in office. They willingly bear the costs so that citizens receive information with little effort. Citizens have at least four sources for information.

Incumbent representatives have the strongest incentives for informing constituents about their legislative activities. If they can shape citizens' views of their accomplishments, they gain an electoral advantage. To that end, they regularly visit their constituencies, speak before labor, business, and civic groups, and attend gatherings of every type. They use their free mailing privileges to shower constituents with newsletters and to target individuals with special mailings. They issue press releases to highlight their positions and accomplishments; they court local reporters and editors. Representatives are assisted in these tasks by press secretaries, legislative correspondents, and caseworkers, some residing in Washington, some in district offices.

Politicians who seek to remove representatives from office are another source for information about representatives' actions in office. Quite naturally, these politicians emphasize different aspects of legislators' records. They may publicize unpopular roll-call votes, complain about the lack of any real accomplishments, or place a different spin on activities that legislators consider to be accomplishments. These politicians include active challengers in primary and general election campaigns, individuals who are considering challenging incumbents, and leaders of the opposite party.

Individuals and groups who care intensely about specific policy problems are a third source for information about representatives' actions in office. Interest group leaders usually monitor what representatives are doing to help or hurt their members' interests and inform either group members or citizens more generally when they observe unfriendly actions. Individual citizens who are very interested in particular problems, policies, or programs—hereafter referred to as opinion leaders—often do the same thing. For example, much of the monitoring of what representatives say and do about abortion is performed by local opinion leaders who care intensely about this issue.

Local newspapers play several roles in conveying information to citizens about what representatives are doing. First, journalists are independent monitors of governmental decision making who actively seek and report information about what elected officials are doing in office. Most journalists consider that reporting the actions of elected officials is one of their central responsibilities. Most media outlets make politics and public affairs an important part of their news coverage. Second, journalists are conveyors of information from all sorts of interested parties. Representatives, challengers, and others who have an interest in publicizing information about representatives' actions do so by encouraging journalists to write stories in ways that further their own goals. This is an efficient way to reach citizens, since stimulating a single reporter to write a single story can reach thousands of citizens. It also increases the credibility of the message because a story published under a reporter's byline seems less promotional than an advertisement. Third, newspapers provide a forum for local opinion leaders to share their views about a representative by encouraging and publishing opinion columns and letters to the editor. Newspapers can make their editorial pages a place for public deliberation about a representative's performance in office.

Citizens

What citizens know about politics and public affairs is largely determined by what the press chooses to cover. Citizens are more likely to learn something if the press covers it intensively than if coverage is sparse. Intensive coverage does not guarantee an informed public. Citizens must be interested in a subject to notice and process the copious information that journalists provide (Zaller 1992). When the press ignores a subject, however, most citizens remain completely uninformed about it. The most interested and attentive citizens may still acquire information through specialized informational networks, but the general public remains in the dark.

Representatives, challengers, interest group leaders, opinion leaders, and journalists play their various roles in creating and transmitting information about representatives' actions in office. How much of this information do ordinary citizens actually receive? How much does whatever information citizens receive affect their evaluations of representatives? Scholars do not have satisfactory answers to these questions.

Determining how much information citizens receive is a difficult task. There are no covert recordings of the messages that citizens actually see or hear. All we have are their own fallible memories. Most citizens do recall receiving communications from or about their representatives. In a survey of citizens who voted in the 1994 House election, 65 percent reported reading about their representative in a newspaper, 61 percent seeing her on television, 33 percent hearing her on the radio, 63 percent receiving mail from her, 14 percent seeing her at a meeting, and 15 percent meeting her personally. Nine of every ten voters recalled at least one of these forms of communications (Jacobson 1997, 100).

We know far less about the content of the information that citizens receive in these communications. Most voters apparently learn their representative's name. In 1994, 51 percent of voters recalled their representative's name from memory, and 93 percent recognized it when offered a list of names (Jacobson 1997, 96). When asked specific questions about their representative, citizens display more modest levels of knowledge. Asked in 1991 how their representative voted on the Persian Gulf Resolution, 19 percent answered correctly and 39 percent guessed correctly. Asked in 1994 how their representative voted on the recent crime bill, 23 percent answered correctly and 28 percent guessed correctly (Alvarez and Gronke 1996; Wilson and Gronke 2000).

Asking citizens to recall specific bits of information about a representative may not be the best way to determine what information citizens actually receive or how the information received affects how they evaluate their representative. Recall of information is most relevant if citizens' decision making is memory based. If citizens make decisions about whether to support or oppose a representative first by recalling all relevant information stored in memory, then evaluating the individual bits of information, and finally combining the individual evaluations into an overall evaluation, then knowing what kinds of information citizens remember would be useful. On the other hand, if citizens process information on-line as they receive it and store only summary evaluations in memory, then knowing what kinds of information citizens remember would not be as helpful.

The jury is still out as to whether citizens' decision making about politics is better captured by memory-based or on-line models. Memory-based models are better at explaining how citizens make decisions about things that they are not expecting to evaluate. John Zaller's account of how citizens answer survey questions about policy alternatives is persuasive (Zaller 1992). In his model, citizens canvass considerations at the "top of their heads" and answer according to the net value of the considerations that come to mind. Since things at the top of the head are often matters that were recently activated, perhaps by recent media stories or perhaps by the survey itself, Zaller can account for how citizens express opinions about a wide range of policy alternatives. Memory-based models seem less satisfactory for explaining how citizens evaluate things that they expect to evaluate.[8] Knowing that

---

[8] The models are not mutually exclusive. Hastie and Pennington (1988) suggest that some citizens may use an "inference-memory-based" process that combines elements from both models. Initially citizens make inferences about candidates when they encounter information about them; later they combine information from various inferences to reach a decision. For

I need to assign grades to students at the end of the semester, I constantly update my evaluations of each student, rather than storing in memory for later evaluation everything they say in class or write in their papers. Knowing that they need to evaluate regularly their senators and representatives, some citizens operate in similar fashion (Just et al. 1996, 21–22).

Milton Lodge and his colleagues offer as an alternative to memory-based models an impression-driven or on-line model of decision making in which citizens react to information as they are exposed to it, storing in memory only summary evaluations.[9] In experimental settings, they show that their on-line model outperforms memory-based models. They conclude that campaign information strongly affects citizens' evaluations of candidates, even though most people cannot later recall the original information (Lodge, McGraw, Stroh 1989; Lodge, Steenbergen, Brau 1995).

If citizens use on-line information processing for evaluating representatives and quickly forget most information they receive, then measures of information recall are poor indicators of citizens' exposure to and reception of politically relevant information.[10] We need more direct measures of the informational environment in which citizens operate. Knowledge about the informational environment is also helpful for understanding what citizens do happen to remember. Observers are often surprised that most citizens cannot recall how representatives voted on specific roll-call votes. It is never clear, however, whether the press featured these votes prominently and citizens failed to notice or remember them or whether the press never spotlighted the votes in the first place. Put differently, are citizens largely to blame for how uninformed they seem about politics and public affairs, or is the press more at fault for failing to report frequently and prominently basic facts about representatives' behavior in office?

Some citizens acquire information about politics and public affairs directly from the mass media. They read newspapers, watch television, or listen to radio newscasts. Many others acquire information indirectly (Huckfeldt and Sprague 1995). They learn from a spouse, friend, coworker, or union leader that their representative voted wrong on the North American Free Trade Agreement. Even when citizens do not acquire information directly from the mass media, the media are generally involved in disseminat-

---

example, jurors make inferences about the credibility of witnesses when they first testify, but jurors postpone judgment until they hear all evidence and receive instructions from the judge. For an excellent discussion of memory-based and on-line models, see Just et al. 1996, 19–24.

[9] A decade earlier Morris Fiorina conceived of party identification in a similar way, with party identification as a running tally of individuals' current attitudes toward the parties (Fiorina 1981).

[10] Doris Graber argues that "the fact that people tend to store conclusions drawn from evidence, rather than the evidence itself, explains why they are frequently unable to give reasons for their opinions" (Graber 1993, 68, 151).

ing political information at earlier stages — for example, to a spouse, friend, coworker, or union leader (Mondak 1995, 101–24). Knowledge about the informational environment is helpful for understanding citizens' decision making no matter whether citizens acquire information directly or indirectly from the mass media. A rich informational environment is more likely to produce an informed citizenry than is an informational wasteland.

Journalists

Journalists need to be selective in what they report about a representative's actions. They could not possibly report everything that a representative did in office — every bill introduced, speech made, position taken, meeting attended, lobbyist met, compromise offered, and contribution solicited. These are the raw materials for good stories, but journalists must select whatever actions seem most newsworthy and write stories that summarize and interpret these actions in interesting and appealing ways.

What kinds of information would be most helpful to citizens? What facts and opinions are most relevant to citizens holding their representatives accountable? At least four kinds of information are especially useful. First, citizens profit by knowing what positions legislators have taken on the important issues of the day. How have their representatives voted on bills that reached the House floor? Where do they stand on various presidential proposals and on bills still in committee? How have representatives explained their positions, especially those that seem contrary to their campaign promises or to citizens' expressed preferences? Position taking is a major part of what legislators do. Knowing what positions representatives have taken helps citizens apportion responsibility for what Congress has done.

Second, citizens benefit by knowing how representatives have contributed to policy making beyond supporting or opposing other legislators' proposals. Nothing happens in Congress unless someone plans for it and works for it. How have individual representatives contributed to legislative action in areas that are important to their constituents or that are part of their committee responsibilities? Are they introducing bills, mobilizing support, and working to solve problems, or are they waiting for other legislators to do the heavy lifting? On any given bill, most legislators are position takers. That is the reality of a legislature with 535 members. But a legislature full of nothing but position takers is an institution that accomplishes little.

Third, citizens benefit by knowing how other people evaluate a representative's performance in office. Ultimately citizens can decide for themselves whether a representative deserves to be reelected or removed. But they are assisted in that task if they first hear a broad range of opinions about a representative's performance. Citizens may find these opinions expressed in news stories, where journalists often seek evaluative comments from representatives, their supporters, and their critics, or on the editorial and op-ed pages, where columnists, editorial writers, politicians, interest group leaders, and opinion leaders debate the accomplishments and failings of Congress and its members.

Finally, citizens gain by hearing about the various candidates running for Congress, including those running in primaries and the general election. Who are the candidates that are challenging the incumbent representative and what are their messages? Do journalists focus on the candidates' past accomplishments and policy differences, or do they feature horse race coverage — who is ahead and who is behind? Do journalists give balanced coverage to incumbents and challengers?

Journalists who report all four types of information increase the probability of citizens acquiring the kinds of information they need to hold representatives accountable for their actions. Journalists who focus on only one or two types of news deprive citizens of the full range of knowledge that contributes to an informed citizenry.

Representatives

Political accountability in the American system is achieved not only by citizens removing from office legislators with disagreeable records but by legislators anticipating what citizens might do and working to forestall unfavorable evaluations. To be sure, the system would not work well if citizens never removed representatives for cause. All that is required, however, is that some representatives fail their reelection examinations some of the time. These failures remind the survivors and instruct the newcomers that anticipating citizens' preferences is the best way to avoid electoral trouble. Defeat at the polls is common enough among career-minded politicians that most representatives have a healthy fear of electoral retribution. They modify some of their behaviors in Washington to remain popular at home (Mayhew 1974; Arnold 1990, 1993).

Representatives may also modify their behavior based on how journalists report news about their Washington activities. Representatives who observe that newspapers regularly feature their positions and actions may make different electoral calculations when they are deciding how to vote or what activities to pursue than do representatives who seldom see news coverage of their Washington activities. When journalists cover a single story assiduously, they increase the probability that citizens will notice what a representative is doing. If a representative believes that the whole constituency is watching, he may adjust his behavior to make it more pleasing. When journalists ignore a story, however, a representative may be less concerned that citizens will ever learn of his actions. In short, the volume and content of press coverage may affect the way in which representatives anticipate and respond to citizens' preferences when they make legislative decisions. Extensive coverage may make representatives more responsive to citizens' policy preferences.

How journalists report the news can also affect the very activities that representatives undertake. If legislators observe that journalists convey little information about legislative activity beyond what legislators reveal in their press releases, they may focus their creative talents on writing press releases rather than writing laws. If legislators notice that journalists monitor carefully what legislators are doing to solve national problems and reform governmental institutions, however, legislators may decide that doing these things well is the best way to attract favorable coverage and impress their constituents. We know that representatives monitor what journalists write about them (Cook 1989, 75, 201). It does not require an enormous leap to imagine that representatives tailor their activities to attract the best coverage.

How journalists practice their profession, then, can affect the behavior of both citizens and legislators. If the press reports nothing about legislators' actions in office, citizens may have insufficient information for determining whether they should renew or terminate representatives' contracts. If legislators know in advance that their actions will go unreported, they may have less reason to make pleasing decisions in the first place. Studying how journalists report news about local representatives, therefore, allows one to make inferences both about how citizens evaluate representatives and about how representatives make legislative decisions.

Informational Environment

The richer the informational environment, the better the two accountability mechanisms work. A rich informational environment increases the chances that citizens will have an evidentiary basis for determining whether they approve or disapprove of a representative's performance in office. A rich informational environment increases the chances that representatives will choose their positions and actions with great care. Of course, local media outlets are only a part of the informational environment in which citizens and representatives operate. Representatives, challengers, and interest groups have other ways to communicate with citizens. Representatives use newsletters and community meetings to communicate directly with citizens. During campaign season, representatives, challengers, and interest groups sponsor events, use direct mail, and purchase advertisements from local media outlets.

An environment in which incumbent representatives and their supporters emphasize their accomplishments while challengers and other critics emphasize representatives' shortcomings can be an informative one for citizens. Just as the adversarial system in trial courts, where attorneys on opposing sides make the best possible cases for their clients, can be an effective way to uncover the truth, so too can an adversarial system in politics demonstrate how well or how poorly incumbents have performed. How informative such a system is for citizens, however, depends on how likely it is that citizens hear both sides. An adversarial system in politics is not necessarily informative for citizens, any more than it is necessarily the best way to uncover the truth in court. If one litigant is represented by the best attorneys that money can buy while the other is represented by a rookie lawyer, jurors may have trouble uncovering the truth. Similarly, if incumbent legislators have ample opportunities to publicize their accomplishments, while challengers and other critics have few opportunities to publicize their criticisms, citizens will be less able to evaluate legislators' fitness for office than they would be if the flow of information were more balanced.

The system works best when lots of citizens notice and read what newspapers publish about representatives. But the system does not break down simply because most citizens are not the ideal citizens that populate democratic theory. Not every citizen needs to be a front-line sentry to keep representatives on their toes. As long as a cadre of individuals and organizations monitor what representatives are doing in office and stand ready to inform other citizens when they see something out of line, representatives know that they are being watched. Much more important is that information regularly flows to those who act as watchdogs, that these watchdogs reflect the diversity of interests in a constituency, and that they have easy ways to communicate with other citizens when they discover representatives doing disagreeable things.

A division of labor is central to any large political system. Yet many observers of American politics fail to appreciate the division of labor between those who actively monitor political actors and those who reward and punish them for their actions. For example, many political scientists once concluded that representatives had little influence over bureaucrats' behavior because they did not systematically monitor what bureaucrats were doing. Mathew McCubbins and Thomas Schwartz changed that view by differentiating between two ways in which principals monitor agents' behavior. They argued that "police-patrol oversight," where a principal actively monitors everything that an agent does, is relatively rare in politics, while "fire-alarm oversight," where other actors do the monitoring and then inform a principal when an agent steps out of line, is more common. Fire-alarm oversight is efficient because it takes advantage of a division of labor (McCubbins and Schwartz 1984).

The discussion in this chapter recognizes a division of labor between professional watchdogs, amateur watchdogs, journalists, and ordinary citizens. Professional watchdogs, including challengers, potential challengers, party leaders, and interest group leaders, have the incentives and resources to ferret out information about a representative's actions even if local journalists ignore what a representative is doing. Amateur watchdogs are local citizens who are intensely interested in politics and publics affairs or in particular problems, policies, or programs. These local opinion leaders rely on journalists for most of their information about a representative's actions. Ordinary citizens may notice regular news coverage about a representative or they may simply wait for professional or amateur watchdogs to sound the alarm when a representative steps out of line.

What would be the consequence if local media outlets ignored what representatives were doing in office? Most representatives would probably be advantaged. Their ability to communicate with citizens using newsletters, meetings, and campaign advertisements would be undiminished, so they could continue to tout their accomplishments. Whether or not challengers and interest groups were able to publicize representatives' shortcomings would depend partly on the seriousness of representatives' shortcomings and partly on their access to financial resources to publicize representatives' transgressions. If a representative made lots of careless choices on major issues, if she repeatedly annoyed powerful interest groups, or if she was indicted for a felony, she would provide powerful ammunition for her opponents. As long as a representative avoided doing these things, however, it would be difficult for another candidate to mount a serious challenge. Accountability would be achieved largely by a representative anticipating what major issues might be used against her and adjusting her behavior accordingly.

When local newspapers cover representatives frequently and thoroughly, however, both accountability mechanisms work better. Extensive coverage allows local opinion leaders and ordinary citizens to monitor contemporaneously what a representative is doing. Citizens need not wait for an angry interest group or a well-funded challenger to inform them during campaign season about a representative's shortcomings; they can read about a representative's positions and actions in the morning paper and judge for themselves. Contemporaneous coverage also encourages a dialogue between a representative and her constituents. Citizens raise challenging questions when a representative attends local meetings; they write letters to the editor complaining about a representative's positions and actions; they send protest letters directly to their representative; they work to mobilize their friends, neighbors, and colleagues to do all these things. Moreover, citizens can monitor their representative for the price of a daily newspaper. They don't need to be represented in Washington by interest groups in order to discover what their elected representative is doing. A final consequence — and a crucial one — is that a representative knows that her actions in Washington are reported regularly to her constituents. Accordingly, she works hard to look good every day of the week. She takes great care when she acts on scores of issues, not just the few issues that would make good campaign issues a year hence.

Standards of News Quality

Extensive coverage of a representative's positions and actions increases the chances for accountable government. But how much is enough? Is there some minimum level of coverage that is necessary to allow citizens to monitor a representative's actions? Can one establish standards for deciding whether newspapers have created an informational environment sufficiently rich to keep representatives on their toes?

John Zaller offers two standards for evaluating the quality of news coverage. According to the Full News Standard, newspapers "should provide citizens with the basic information necessary to form and update opinions on all of the major issues of the day, including the performance of top public officials" (Zaller 2003, 110). In contrast, the Burglar Alarm Standard suggests that newspapers should focus on just a few issues that others have identified as particularly important.[11] Those who might sound the alarm to attract journalists' attention to particular issues include interest group leaders, party officials, the president, and electoral challengers — essentially those I have labeled professional watchdogs. For the case of local newspapers and local representatives, Zaller argues that newspapers should focus on how representatives have voted on bills that were top presidential priorities, on representatives' ethical transgressions, and on any reelection races that appear to be close.

Zaller's distinction between the Full News Standard, which he believes has dominated media studies, and the Burglar Alarm Standard, which he argues is a more appropriate standard, is important and useful. Indeed, I use this distinction throughout the book. But I disagree with Zaller on one point. I believe it is important for local newspapers to meet both the Full News and the Burglar Alarm Standards. Zaller recognizes the need for the elite news media at the national level — the *New York Times*, National Public Radio, the *Newshour with Jim Lehrer* — to meet the Full News Standard, so that politically attentive citizens can form and update their opinions on the important issues of the day and monitor what public officials are doing. He argues that the Burglar Alarm Standard is the more appropriate benchmark for thousands of other media outlets because most citizens are not

[11] Zaller's distinction between the Full News Standard and the Burglar Alarm Standard rests on Michael Schudson's distinction between the Informed Citizen and the Monitorial Citizen. The former is a citizen who gathers extensive information in order to vote rationally; the latter is one who "engages in environmental surveillance more than information-gathering" (Schudson 1998, 311).

sufficiently interested in politics and public affairs to want exhaustive coverage. The basic notion is that opinion leaders use the elite media outlets to keep informed, and once they notice something disturbing, they sound the alarm through mass media outlets. In local markets, however, newspapers are simultaneously elite and mass media outlets. Local newspapers are the only media outlets capable of informing local opinion leaders about what representatives are doing. Local newspapers are also well positioned to broadcast alarms to ordinary citizens when professional watchdogs or local opinion leaders sound the alarm about disagreeable things that representatives have been doing.

When local newspapers do not meet the Burglar Alarm Standard, they seriously impede citizens' ability to hold representatives accountable for their actions. Although well-funded interest groups and well-funded challengers can still communicate directly with citizens about representatives' shortcomings, the resources required for direct communications are so substantial that only the most serious shortcomings are likely to be publicized. When local newspapers meet the Burglar Alarm Standard, they increase the prospects for accountable government. By providing challengers, interest group leaders, and other professional watchdogs with opportunities to sound alarms about representatives' transgressions, without them having to purchase direct coverage, these papers increase the number and variety of transgressions that can be publicized. When local newspapers meet both the Burglar Alarm and Full News Standards, they further increase the prospects for accountable government because they inform and empower local opinion leaders. Representatives are likely to be especially vigilant when they know that a wide range of local opinion leaders, and not just Washington-based interest groups, are monitoring their behavior.

Research Questions

The literature on how the mass media cover politics is large and growing. Most of the literature focuses on how the press covers wars, presidents, election campaigns, and policy issues. Scholars have largely ignored press coverage of Congress and its members. Only ten studies have examined how local newspapers and television stations covered individual members of the House or Senate. These ten studies are best described as pilot studies, rather than systematic studies, because the authors typically chose nonrandom samples of media outlets and studied those outlets for only a few weeks, typically during the campaign period. Most studies focused more on the volume of coverage than on its content.[12]

---

[12] Manheim (1974) examined how 26 papers covered campaigns in 5 congressional districts

This book differs from previous studies by exploring four sets of questions about the volume, content, causes, and consequences of newspaper coverage. First, it seeks to establish how frequently local media outlets cover members of Congress. Do media outlets regularly report information about representatives' actions in office, and do they display their coverage in prominent ways? Or is coverage of representatives infrequent, spotty, or buried in the back pages of newspapers? It is important to determine something about the volume and prominence of political information because both factors affect whether citizens are likely to notice and digest the information.

Second, it examines the content of press coverage of individual legislators. Do the media report the kinds of information that citizens would need to hold representatives accountable for their actions in office, or do they focus on more peripheral matters that entertain, amuse, or enrage citizens without conveying much information about legislators' actual performance? Do they feature bill introductions, roll-call votes, leadership activities, and constituency service? Are the media evenhanded in their stories, or do they offer more extensive or more positive coverage to incumbents than to challengers, or to Democrats than to Republicans?

Third, it seeks to explain why news outlets differ in their coverage of Congress and its members. Why do some media outlets provide exemplary coverage of local representatives while others largely ignore representatives' activities? Do large, well-financed urban newspapers provide better coverage of representatives, or do these papers avoid extensive coverage of local representatives because their primary circulation areas include so many congressional districts? Does press coverage depend on what representatives do in

---

during three months prior to the 1970 election. Hess (1981) studied how 22 newspapers from around the country covered events in Washington during a typical week in early 1978. Tidmarch and Karp (1983) explored how 8 metropolitan newspapers covered 45 House races during the month preceding the 1978 election. Clarke and Evans (1983) investigated how one major newspaper in each of 86 congressional districts covered a local House race during the six weeks prior to the 1978 elections. Goldenberg and Traugott (1984) examined 33 newspapers during three weeks preceding the 1978 elections, searching for all items relating to 43 House races. Tidmarch and Pitney (1985) studied 10 metropolitan newspapers during four weeks in the summer of 1978. Vermeer (1987) examined how 33 small-town newspapers in three rural states covered 11 House races during nine weeks prior to the 1984 election. Westlye (1991) examined coverage in one to four newspapers per state during the three months prior to election day for a dozen Senate campaigns occurring between 1968 and 1982. Hess (1991) examined about 60 hours of local newscasts collected from 57 television stations during late 1987 and early 1988. Vinson (2003) examined newspaper and television coverage of Congress and its members in 8 metropolitan areas during six weeks in 1993 and 1994. In addition to these ten works, there are several studies of media coverage in a single district or state during a House or Senate campaign (Orman 1985; Hale 1987; Goldenberg and Traugott 1987) and one study of media coverage and its effects in a single district outside the campaign period (Larson 1992).

Congress? Do local media outlets cover more extensively legislators who are important participants in congressional policy making—the workhorses—or do representatives attract local press attention by constituency-oriented activities? Does it matter whether media outlets have Washington correspondents?

Finally, it attempts to discover whether differential coverage of local representatives affects citizens' political knowledge. Are citizens who live in areas where media outlets carefully cover representatives more likely to recall or recognize their representatives than citizens who live in areas where media attention is sparse? Does media attention affect the chances that citizens will know something about representatives' records? When the media report extensive information about roll-call votes, are citizens more likely to know where their representative stands on the issues?

Data Sets

Unlike previous studies, which largely focused on the campaign period, this project explores how local newspapers covered representatives during an entire congressional session, from the first day of 1993 to election day 1994. The longer period is essential for studying political accountability. In order to determine what kinds of information newspapers make available to citizens, one needs to collect newspaper articles from a reasonable number of papers, for a reasonable number of representatives, and over a sufficiently long time period. Focusing on how a few newspapers cover a few representatives over a few weeks does not allow one to discover how coverage patterns vary over the cycle of governing, campaigning, and elections, or to generalize with any degree of certainty to the universe of all newspapers and all representatives. Attempting to balance these competing needs, I have selected three samples of newspaper coverage, each sample designed to reveal a different aspect of press coverage.

The first data set is a sample of 25 local newspapers and 25 representatives. It contains every news story, editorial, opinion column, letter, and list that mentioned the local representative between January 1, 1993, and November 8, 1994. My sampling strategy involved first selecting as representative a set of newspapers as possible, and then selecting randomly one House member from each newspaper's primary circulation area.

Selecting the newspaper sample was the greater challenge. At the time the sample was drawn, there were 1,567 daily newspapers in the country with combined circulations of 57 million copies.[13] Eighty-eight of these

---

[13] These figures exclude three papers that did not publish local editions (*USA Today*, *Christian Science Monitor*, *Wall Street Journal*). Circulation data are from Editor & Publisher 1993.

newspapers had publicly available electronic archives for all of 1993 and 1994.[14] The problem was to draw a sample of these 88 newspapers that was a reasonable approximation of the universe of all daily papers. The good news was that the 88 papers included 38 percent of the total daily circulation in the country, despite the fact that they represented only 6 percent of all daily papers. This followed from the fact that a majority of citizens read a newspaper with a daily circulation of more than 100,000 copies,[15] and large newspapers were overrepresented among the 88 papers. The bad news was that smaller newspapers were underrepresented in the electronic archives, and smaller newspapers tend to serve small cities and rural areas.

In order to draw a sample of newspapers that is representative of what the average citizen reads, I rank-ordered the 1,567 papers according to circulation, and then grouped the papers into approximate sextiles so that each group represented about one-sixth of the total daily circulation in the country. I then highlighted the 88 archived papers within the various sextiles.[16] Given that the two lowest sextiles contained only seven of the 88 papers, I combined these two sextiles into a single group. I then randomly selected five papers from each of the five groups. The sample of 25 newspapers includes large national papers like the *Los Angeles Times* and the *Boston Globe*, midsized papers like the *Hartford Courant* and the *Tulsa World*, and small-city papers like the *Rock Hill Herald* (South Carolina) and the *Lewiston Morning Tribune* (Idaho). From each newspaper's primary circulation

[14] The 88 newspapers were available through the DataTimes division of the Dow Jones News Service and the Nexis service of Reed Elsevier's Lexis-Nexis. Today these sources offer several hundred daily newspapers. Although I do not know for sure why these two services chose to include these 88 papers, it seems likely that they sought to include papers that were geographically diverse and that covered business news reasonably well, since both criteria would increase the marketability of the archival services. The first criterion is a plus for my study; the second is not, since it could yield newspapers that were better than average in their attention to politics and public affairs.

[15] This fact is not widely appreciated by those who study local newspapers. One author suggests that "the median newspaper reader is reading a relatively small local paper" (Martin 1996, as quoted in Vermeer 2002, 8). Although the median daily *newspaper* is relatively small (fewer than 20,000 circulation), the median newspaper *reader* reads a paper of greater than 100,000 circulation. The data to support this claim are in the next footnote.

[16] The 88 newspapers are distributed among the sextiles as follows: (*a*) 8 of 11 papers of greater than 500,000 circulation are included, representing 77 percent of the circulation in the highest sextile; (*b*) 24 of 30 papers of between 250,001 and 500,000 are included, representing 81 percent of the circulation in the fifth sextile; (*c*) 33 of 73 papers of between 100,001 and 250,000 are included, representing 51 percent of the circulation in this sextile; (*d*) 16 of 130 papers of between 50,001 and 100,000 are included, representing 15 percent of the circulation in this sextile; (*e*) 6 of 236 papers of between 25,001 and 50,000 are included, representing 3 percent of the circulation in this sextile; and (*f*) 1 of 1,087 papers of fewer than 25,000 is included, representing less than 1 percent of the circulation in the lowest sextile.

area I randomly selected one representative for study.[17] Table 1.1 lists the newspapers and representatives in the first data set.

The 25 newspapers are a diverse lot. Although very small newspapers are necessarily absent, the inclusion of a few small papers should allow one to determine if small newspapers cover House members differently than large newspapers. The sample also contains various types of papers and not just the most celebrated newspapers in the country. It includes tabloids, such as the *Chicago Sun-Times* and *Newsday*, rather than their highbrow competitors, the *Chicago Tribune* and the *New York Times*; it includes the upstart *Washington Times* rather than the *Washington Post*. The sample is also geographically diverse, with newspapers from eighteen states and the nation's capital. The newspapers sell nearly 7 million copies daily—about 12 percent of the nation's total daily circulation. The sample is not as diverse as one would have obtained if one selected a stratified random sample from the complete list of 1,567 newspapers. Taking that route, however, would have required searching most newspapers manually, which would have necessitated a much smaller sample and a much shorter time frame.

The 25 House members are reasonably representative of the whole House.[18] The match in party and seniority was especially good. Fourteen representatives in the sample were Democrats (56 percent), just shy of their actual percentage in the House (60 percent). The median representative in the sample was elected in 1986, as was the median member of the House. Two representatives in the sample, James Bilbray and Larry LaRocco, ran for reelection and lost, exactly matching the percentage for the whole House. Retiring members were underrepresented (only Romano Mazzoli), women were underrepresented (only Barbara Kennelly), and black mem-

---

[17] Matching newspaper circulation with congressional districts is more art than science because newspapers do not disclose circulation data by district. The matching was done with two maps, one identifying the locations of a state's newspapers, the other identifying the locations of a state's congressional districts (Editor & Publisher 1993; Congressional Quarterly 1993a). I first defined, in a fairly mechanical way, the primary circulation area for each of the 88 papers and then matched those areas with all of the congressional districts that overlapped the defined circulation areas. For each newspaper, I identified from one to fifteen districts as being within the primary circulation area by using four decision rules: (*a*) include each district that includes any part of a newspaper's home city; (*b*) include each district that includes a significant portion of a city's suburbs; (*c*) avoid matching a suburban district with a city's newspaper if the suburban area has its own newspaper included among the 88 papers; and (*d*) avoid crossing state lines unless a metropolitan area is heavily concentrated in a neighboring state. These four rules identified 213 districts as within the primary circulation areas of the 88 newspapers; ninety-one districts were within the primary circulation areas of the 25 selected papers. (The number of congressional districts listed in table 1.1 totals 92 because it counts twice Arizona's second district, located within the primary circulation areas of both the Phoenix and Tucson papers.)

[18] For political and demographic data about House members and their districts, see Ornstein, Mann, and Malbin 1996 and Congressional Quarterly 1993a.

TABLE 1.1
Newspapers and Representatives Selected for Study

Newspaper	Circulation	Districts in Area	Selected District		Representative	Party	Year Elected
Los Angeles Times	1,146,631	15	CA	24	Anthony Beilenson	D	76
Newsday (Long Island)	758,358	5	NY	3	Peter King	R	92
San Francisco Chronicle	556,765	8	CA	9	Ronald Dellums	D	70
Chicago Sun-Times	528,324	11	IL	3	William Lipinski	D	82
Boston Globe	508,867	4	MA	9	Joe Moakley	D	72
Houston Chronicle	419,759	6	TX	7	Bill Archer	R	70
Cleveland Plain Dealer	410,237	4	OH	11	Louis Stokes	D	68
San Diego Union-Tribune	373,453	5	CA	50	Bob Filner	D	92
Buffalo News	305,482	2	NY	30	Jack Quinn	R	92
Orlando Sentinel Tribune	285,172	3	FL	8	Bill McCollum	R	80
Seattle Times	239,476	3	WA	7	Jim McDermott	D	88
Louisville Courier-Journal	236,103	2	KY	3	Romano Mazzoli	D	70
Hartford Courant	229,284	1	CT	1	Barbara Kennelly	D	82
Las Vegas Review-Journal	131,769	1	NV	1	James Bilbray	D	86
Tulsa World	127,476	2	OK	1	James Inhofe	R	86
Baton Rouge Advocate	99,444	2	LA	6	Richard Baker	R	86
Washington Times	92,000	5	MD	4	Albert Wynn	D	92
Phoenix Gazette	83,431	4	AZ	4	Jon Kyl	R	86
Norfolk Ledger-Star	57,603	2	VA	2	Owen Pickett	D	86
Bloomington Pantagraph	51,868	1	IL	15	Thomas Ewing	R	91
Tucson Citizen	48,566	2	AZ	5	Jim Kolbe	R	84
York Daily Record	40,525	1	PA	19	Bill Goodling	R	74
Rock Hill Herald	30,495	1	SC	5	John Spratt	D	82
Idaho Falls Post Register	29,799	1	ID	2	Michael Crapo	R	92
Lewiston Morning Tribune	23,105	1	ID	1	Larry LaRocco	D	90
Total	6,813,992	92					

Sources: Circulation data are from Editor & Publisher 1993. Party and year elected are from Congressional Quarterly 1993b.

Note: The newspapers are grouped into the six circulation sextiles discussed in the text.

bers were overrepresented (Ronald Dellums, Louis Stokes, and Albert Wynn). Two of the 25 richest districts in the country made the list (CA24 and NY3); none of the 25 poorest districts did. Although none of these differences are out of line for a sample this small, they are worth noting.

After choosing a sample of newspapers and representatives, I used computerized routines for searching the text of the 16,950 daily newspapers (25 newspapers times 678 days). This search identified and retrieved 8,003 news stories, editorials, opinion columns, letters, and lists that mentioned the 25 local representatives. Three research assistants read the material, coded the articles for their objective content, and summarized the tone and valence of each article. They used 68 variables to code a variety of information, ranging from the size, location, and prominence of each article, to whether an article mentioned a representative's policy positions, roll-call votes, or leadership activities. They also tracked the appearance of 214 policy issues in order to see how journalists portrayed representatives' connections to highly visible issues, such as NAFTA, the budget, crime, and gun control, as well as to less visible issues that Congress handles every year.[19]

One limitation of the first data set is that one cannot determine what accounts for large differences in coverage. Why, for example, did some newspapers cover their representatives more heavily than other papers covered theirs? Did these differences in coverage reflect differences in the newsworthiness of representatives or in the editorial practices of newspapers? The question is unanswerable with a data set in which there is a one-to-one correspondence between each newspaper and each representative. The second and third data sets are designed to overcome this limitation.

The second data set parallels the first. I simply paired six newspapers from the first data set with six newspapers that are published in the same cities. The paired newspapers are from Boston, Chicago, San Francisco, Seattle, Tucson, and Washington.[20] The aim is to determine how pairs of competing newspapers covered the same legislators. My assistants coded the news stories, editorials, columns, letters, and lists in the additional papers according to the same procedures used for the first data set. The second data set contains 2,175 articles — 1,053 from the original six papers and 1,122 from the six comparison papers.

The third data set includes information about the volume and timing of coverage for a much larger sample of newspapers and representatives. This data set shows how 67 local newspapers covered 187 representatives during

[19] In order to guard against the coders becoming too familiar with each newspaper's coverage, and in order to replicate the haphazard way in which most people read newspapers, a coder was assigned a batch of about twenty articles from one newspaper before moving on to the next paper. I arranged the coding assignments so that 4.5 percent of articles were coded twice. Comparing the coding decisions for all double-coded articles revealed a high degree of intercoder reliability. The coders disagreed on 6.4 percent of all decisions. The disagreement rate for the median variable was 3.9 percent. As one might expect, disagreement was minimal for variables that summarized simple facts. Disagreement was greater on matters that required judgment and for which there were several acceptable codes. The high degree of intercoder reliability was achieved by having my assistants spend a week with me practice-coding about 200 articles. Actual coding did not begin until we discussed all differences in the practice-coding of specific articles and agreed how to code tough cases.

[20] The six newspapers — *Arizona Daily Star, Boston Herald, Chicago Tribune, San Francisco Examiner, Seattle Post-Intelligencer, Washington Post* — were chosen randomly from the eight cities that had second newspapers. The two papers not chosen were the *Arizona Republic* (Phoenix) and the *Los Angeles Daily News*.

1993 and 1994, with a total of 242 representative/newspaper dyads. The 61,084 citations — headline, date, section, page, and byline, but not full text — allow one to analyze how the amount and timing of coverage depend on the newsworthiness of individual representatives, the competitiveness of elections, and the resources and constraints of individual newspapers. The third data set is not a random sample of all newspapers; it is closer to the universe of all newspapers that were available for electronic searches in 1993 and 1994.[21] But imbedded in this data set are the 25 randomly selected newspapers from the first data set. By analyzing separately how these 25 newspapers covered the 91 legislators within their primary circulation areas (22,175 citations), I can determine if the larger but less representative sample differs significantly from the smaller but more representative sample.

The fourth data set is designed to determine whether the volume of newspaper coverage affected what citizens knew about their representatives. This data set was constructed by linking information about how extensively the 67 newspapers in the third data set covered particular representatives with information about citizens' knowledge of their local representatives, as recorded in the autumn 1994 survey conducted by the National Election Studies. The unit of analysis is the individual citizen. Added to the usual attitudinal data about each citizen is information about how a local newspaper covered that citizen's representative during 1993 and 1994. The original 1994 NES data set had 1,795 respondents. I have information about local newspaper coverage for 675 of these respondents. Although the fourth data set is not ideal, it is the best that can be assembled, given the original NES survey. The survey contained information about how many times a week a citizen claimed to read a newspaper but not the name of the newspaper that a citizen read. So, I have been forced to assume that the local newspaper for which I have data is the same newspaper that a citizen actually read. The result, of course, is noisy data.[22]

Technology

The main innovation in this study is the use of computerized text searching to locate each mention of a representative's name in a local newspaper between January 1993 and November 1994. Although computerized text searching has been used for studies of the national news media (Fan 1988; Fan and Norem 1992), it has not been used to study how local newspapers

[21] I selected newspapers according to the number of representatives in their primary circulation areas (starting with papers with the most representatives) and continued downloading articles until resources ran out.

[22] The four data sets are available on my website at www.princeton.edu/~arnold. They will eventually be placed in a national data archive.

cover members of Congress. As with any new technology, there are advantages and disadvantages.

The principal advantages of computerized text searching are efficiency and accuracy. It would be extraordinarily expensive to acquire and read paper copies of the 45,426 daily newspapers searched for this study (67 papers times 678 days). It was much less expensive to search through the electronic archives of the same newspapers. Computerized text searching is also more accurate. Computers are very good at finding every mention of a name in millions of lines of text. Human coders are remarkably poor at this mind-numbing task. One of the earliest studies of how newspapers covered members of Congress employed a commercial clipping service (Clarke and Evans 1983). A subsequent audit revealed that the clipping service missed about two-thirds of the articles (Goldenberg and Traugott 1984, 133).

An additional advantage of using electronic archives is that the archives contain articles from all regional editions and neighborhood sections that a newspaper happens to publish. The *Los Angeles Times*, for example, publishes six regional editions, as well as special sections for various neighborhoods. Libraries acquire paper or microfilm copies of only one edition. Searching a library's copies of the *Times* would not be a problem if one were studying a subject that appears in all daily editions—for example, stories about the president or governor. It turns out to be a very serious problem, however, when one is studying how newspapers cover representatives because the editors of the *Times* intentionally place much of the coverage of individual representatives in the various regional editions and neighborhood sections. The editors target constituents with news about their own representatives without distracting them with news about every other representative in Southern California. In order to study how large metropolitan newspapers like the *Times* cover members of Congress, one needs either to acquire all the regional editions and neighborhood sections of these newspapers—something that no library does—or to use the electronic archives that contain material from all editions and sections.

Computerized text searching allows one to analyze very large samples. This is a direct consequence of the technology's twin advantages of efficiency and accuracy. Previous studies limited themselves to a few weeks of coverage. This book includes 97 weeks. Previous studies examined an average of 908 articles. This book examines 61,084 citations and 9,125 full-text articles. The first data set alone is roughly equivalent to the combined sample sizes of the ten previous studies.[23] Large samples allow one to find sub-

---

[23] Ten previous studies examined a total of 9,079 articles about individual members of Congress culled from 260 newspapers and 65 television stations (28 articles per media outlet). My first data set contains 8,003 articles, with an average of 320 articles per newspaper.

tler patterns in newspaper coverage and to generalize with greater confidence to other newspapers and representatives.

Electronic archives have several disadvantages. Some newspapers do not own the electronic rights to everything they publish. As a consequence, information about representatives that appeared in syndicated columns or wire services' reports may not be included in the electronic archives for particular newspapers (Snider and Janda 1998). In addition, some newspapers choose not to include other types of materials to which they do control the rights — for example, letters to the editor and information in tables.[24] Although Nexis and Dow Jones list the types of information excluded for each newspaper, there is no way to estimate the amount of coverage that is actually excluded. My sense is that excluded information is not a serious problem for a study of how local newspapers cover members of Congress, whereas it would be a very serious problem for a study of how local newspapers cover international affairs, since most papers rely heavily on wire services for foreign coverage.

Another problem with computerized text searching is that it is difficult to construct searches that retrieve only articles mentioning the representative. A search that is excessively narrow misses actual coverage of a representative; a search that is too broad finds articles about people who share a representative's name. My solution was to conduct broad searches and then use human coders to discard articles that referred to someone other than the representative.[25]

Another problem is that electronic archives contain duplicate copies of some articles. Twenty-three of the 25 newspapers archived at least some duplicate articles about local representatives. The problem was most common for newspapers that published timed or regional editions. For example, the *San Diego Union-Tribune*, which publishes as an all-day newspaper with up to nine editions over a twenty-four-hour period, archived the most duplicate articles (26 percent).[26] Others newspapers placed nearly identical mate-

[24] All electronic archives exclude advertisements, photos, charts, editorial cartoons, and other nontextual material, although some archives include captions for photos, charts, and cartoons.

[25] The problem was most serious for representatives with common names. In the first data set, the representatives with the most wrong citations were Peter King (19%), Bill Archer (5%), Richard Baker (3%), John Spratt (3%), and Jack Quinn (2%). Although human coders were used to review all articles for the first two data sets, the correction mechanism for the third data set was slightly different. For each representative/newspaper dyad, I first read a sample of the actual articles in search of wrong citations, and then based an adjustment of total citations for each dyad on the errors discovered in the sample. The representatives with the most wrong citations were Bill Young (52%), Dan Miller (48%), Bill Baker (45%), George Miller (44%), and Robert Scott (43%).

[26] The newspapers in the first data set with the most severe rates of duplicates were the *San Diego Union-Tribune* (26%), *Louisville Courier-Journal* (22%), *Los Angeles Times* (15%),

rials in different regional editions, especially when a congressional district was split between two or more newspaper regions. My solution was to use computerized text searching to find all possible articles and then use human coders to discard duplicates.[27] Table 1.2 shows summary information for the four data sets, including details about sampling and error correction.[28]

The advantages of computerized text searching far outweigh the disadvantages. Two of the disadvantages can be overcome by using human coders to discard duplicate articles and articles that refer to someone other than the representative. The other disadvantage — the exclusion of syndicated columns and wire services' reports — is probably not a serious problem when studying how local newspapers cover members of Congress. In any event, this one disadvantage is a small price to pay for obtaining very large samples and for correctly observing the coverage patterns in newspapers that publish regional editions and neighborhood sections.

Description and Analysis

Description is a necessary part of this research enterprise. We know so little about how local newspapers cover members of Congress that one cannot assess the adequacy of newspaper coverage or analyze the causes and consequences of that coverage without first describing the nature of coverage. No doubt each reader of this book begins with some sense of how local newspapers cover members of Congress, perhaps derived from reading a single local paper, perhaps derived from reading papers in several localities where the reader has lived over the years. My first task is to replace whatever impressionistic sense the reader may have about how local papers cover members of Congress with firm evidence from a sample of newspapers.

The descriptive task is complicated by the enormous disparities in newspaper coverage. Some newspapers cover representatives extensively, painting rich portraits of where they stand on the issues of the day and what they are

---

Houston Chronicle (12%), *Rock Hill Herald* (7%), *Newsday* (6%), *Phoenix Gazette* (5%), and *Seattle Times* (5%).

[27] Again, the correction mechanism for the third data set was slightly different. Human coders searched the citation lists for similarly titled articles published on the same day or adjacent days.

[28] Another source of error is that it is difficult to discover when two sister papers are operating as one. Hans Noel, who worked at the *Virginian-Pilot* during the period under investigation, informs me that the *Norfolk Ledger-Star*, one of the papers in the first data set, was essentially the *Virginian-Pilot* with a different front page. Although this type of problem does not affect the content analysis, it does affect the analysis of the volume of coverage in chapter 2, since the real resources behind two papers operating together should be the combined daily circulations of the papers, not the circulation of the one selected for study. No doubt other gremlins appear in the third data set.

TABLE 1.2
Comparison of Four Data Sets

	First Set	Second Set	Third Set	Fourth Set
Unit of analysis	article	article	dyad[a]	citizen
Number of cases	8,003	2,175	242	675
Newspapers	25	12	67	36
Representatives	25	6	187	100
Articles	8,003	2,175	61,084	25,868
Variables	68	68	23	NES + 23[b]
Sample of news-papers	stratified random	random	nonrandom	nonrandom
Sample of repre-sentatives	random	random	complete	complete
Error correction	exhaustive	exhaustive	sampling	sampling
Articles coded for content	yes	yes	no	no

Sources: All information about newspaper coverage (1/1/93 to 11/8/94) was obtained in 1995 from the DataTimes division of the Dow Jones News Service and the Nexis service of Reed Elsevier's Lexis-Nexis. The fourth set is a merger of the third set and the 1994 National Election Study.

[a] Representative/newspaper dyad (one newspaper covering one representative).

[b] All variables from the 1994 National Election Study combined with the volume of coverage during each of 23 months.

doing in Washington. Other newspapers provide meager coverage — meager in both quantity and quality. Throughout this book I convey the nature of these disparities, both with tables that show how each newspaper covered various aspects of the representative's behavior and with occasional summaries of typical, exemplary, or superficial articles. Description of newspaper coverage appears in chapters 2 through 7.

In addition to describing coverage patterns, I assess the quality of newspaper coverage, and particularly whether the information that journalists publish helps citizens hold representatives accountable for their actions. I offer three vantage points for this assessment. Previous work on political accountability shows the importance of particular types of information about legislators' behavior (Mayhew 1974; Arnold 1990, 1993). The current book is partly an attempt to see how much of this information journalists actually provide. A second gauge is provided by Zaller's distinction between the Full News Standard and the Burglar Alarm Standard. Do newspapers provide coverage that allows individuals and groups to monitor what representatives are doing in office? Do newspapers provide opportunities for opinion leaders to communicate with citizens when they discover representatives doing disagreeable things? A third yardstick is provided by journalists themselves. Since journalists often reject outsiders' recommendations about how they should cover the news — what could scholars know about the realities of attracting readers and satisfying advertisers and stockholders? — I treat as a baseline for assessment the actual coverage in the best newspapers in the sample. The best practices of these newspapers — some small, some medium, some large — offer a standard that is more palatable to journalists. Preliminary assessments appear in each of the descriptive chapters (chapters 2 through 7). Assessment takes center stage in chapter 9.

In addition to describing and assessing newspaper coverage, I seek to identify the causal forces that produce particular coverage patterns. For example, chapter 2 first describes the volume of coverage in each newspaper, and then proceeds to test various hypotheses that seek to explain these variations. Other chapters attempt to explain variations in how newspapers cover electoral campaigns, bill introductions, and other topics. I also seek to determine whether variations in newspaper coverage have consequences for what citizens know about representatives. This is the central subject of chapter 8. In short, the book is a combination of description, assessment, and the testing of various hypotheses about the causes and consequences of newspaper coverage.

2

Explaining the Volume of Newspaper Coverage

How EXTENSIVELY do local newspapers cover members of Congress? Why do some newspapers cover representatives more extensively than other newspapers do? Do large urban newspapers or papers with reporters based in Washington provide more coverage than small papers with few resources of any type? Why do some representatives attract more coverage than other representatives? Does press coverage depend on representatives' positions in the congressional hierarchy, on what they do in Washington, or on the competitiveness of their districts? This chapter provides answers to all these questions.

Both the volume and content of newspaper coverage are important if citizens are to learn about their representatives' actions in office. Wonderfully crafted articles that appear once in a blue moon are scarcely more informative for the average citizen than voluminous but vacuous articles that appear frequently. The former are seldom noticed; the latter convey little useful information. When newspapers cover representatives frequently, they increase the chances that citizens will notice and read some of the articles. When newspapers write interesting articles about representatives, filled with relevant facts and balanced opinions, they increase the chances that citizens will profit from the articles that they encounter. This chapter focuses exclusively on the volume of coverage. The next four chapters explore matters of content.

Volume of Coverage

How frequently do local newspapers publish information about representatives' actions in office and their campaigns for reelection? Is newspaper coverage of individual representatives a regular occurrence or a rare event? The two best-known studies of this subject reached very different conclusions. Charles Tidmarch and Brad Karp, who examined how eight metropolitan newspapers covered 45 local House races during the last month of the 1978 campaign, found such meager coverage that they entitled their article "The Missing Beat." The average newspaper published only 1.7 articles per district per month (Tidmarch and Karp 1983). Edie Goldenberg and Michael Traugott, who examined how 33 newspapers covered races in 43 districts during three weeks in the same 1978 campaign, found much greater coverage. The average newspaper in their study published 21.6 articles per district per month (Goldenberg and Traugott 1984). Three other studies of the campaign period found coverage patterns between these two extremes.[1] When one study identifies thirteen times as much coverage as another study — and for the same campaign period — it underscores how little we know about the extent to which newspapers cover House campaigns. We know even less about coverage outside the campaign period.

Figure 2.1 displays the monthly coverage patterns for the 25 newspapers in the first data set. Recall that the first data set contains every article — every news story, editorial, opinion column, letter, and list — that mentioned the local representative between January 1, 1993, and November 8, 1994. The results for September and October, the peak months of the 1994 campaign, are remarkably similar to Goldenberg and Traugott's results. The 25 newspapers published an average of 19.6 articles in September and 24.4 articles in October about their local representative, nicely bracketing the 21.6 items per month that Goldenberg and Traugott identified in their study of the 1978 campaign. The close correspondence is reassuring, given that Goldenberg and Traugott were the only previous scholars who selected a representative sample of newspapers and who used exhaustive methods to locate newspaper articles.[2] The other authors examined the coverage patterns for narrow groups of newspapers, selected their newspapers by nonrandom means, or failed to use exhaustive methods to locate articles.[3]

The principal message in figure 2.1 is that newspaper coverage of individual representatives is a regular event. Political campaigns may stimulate additional coverage, but the increment is relatively small compared to the base

[1] The other studies found 14.2 articles per month in a 1970 campaign study of 26 midwestern papers, 7.4 articles per month in a 1978 campaign study of 71 newspapers, and 6.4 articles per month in a 1984 campaign study of 33 rural newspapers (Manheim 1974; Clarke and Evans 1983; Vermeer 1987). The results for all five studies are expressed as mean citations per newspaper per district per thirty-day month.

[2] Goldenberg and Traugott first selected a random sample of congressional districts and then selected the largest newspaper, and occasionally an additional newspaper, in each district. Their method, like my own, is biased against the selection of very small newspapers. In addition to news stories, editorials, opinion columns, and letters to the editor, their study included political advertisements.

[3] Tidmarch and Karp did not select their newspapers randomly. Clarke and Evans selected a random sample, but they used a clipping service to obtain articles. As mentioned in the previous chapter, a subsequent audit revealed that the clipping service missed about two-thirds of the articles (see Goldenberg and Traugott 1984, 133). Both Manheim and Vermeer selected newspapers randomly, but they did so from restricted sets of newspapers (heavily weighted toward small and rural papers). None of the five previous studies examined more than one edition of each daily newspaper, so they missed the kinds of coverage that newspapers placed in regional editions or regional sections. This last problem was particularly severe for Tidmarch and Karp, who focused exclusively on metropolitan newspapers, and probably accounts for the meager coverage they discovered.

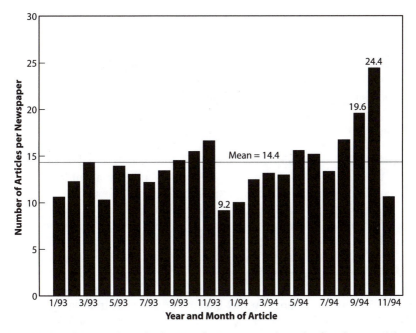

Fig. 2.1 Distribution of Articles by Month. Figures are from the first data set (25 newspapers, 8,003 articles, 22.3 months).

of regular monthly coverage. The average newspaper published 13 articles per month during 1993, 13.7 articles per month during the first eight months of 1994, and 22 articles per month during September and October, the peak months of the 1994 campaign.[4] The incremental newspaper coverage in September and October increased total coverage by only 6 percent.

Newspapers appear to allocate almost a constant-sized newshole to covering local representatives. The focus of newspaper coverage may change over the seasons, from policy making in odd-numbered years to local campaigning in the autumn of even-numbered years, with a blend of the two in between. But the volume of coverage does not fluctuate much from month to month, at least when summed over 25 newspapers. This suggests that most information about representatives to which citizens are exposed is delivered outside the campaign period. If newspaper coverage of representatives is a regular event, it makes sense to examine the content of newspaper coverage in all seasons. This follows even if one were exclusively interested in congressional elections, since it is likely that most of what regular news-

---

[4] The mean of 14.4 articles per newspaper per month in figure 2.1 is based on 22.3 months. The November coverage was for the partial month that ended on election day.

paper readers learn about their representatives is based on information delivered outside the campaign period.

Previous studies discovered that newspapers differed enormously in the
frequency with which they reported information about local representatives
and local campaigns. Goldenberg and Traugott's study of 33 newspapers
found that the *Los Angeles Times* published only 1.4 articles per month
mentioning candidates in California's 39th district, whereas the *Winston-
Salem Journal* published 72.9 articles per month mentioning candidates in
North Carolina's 5th district—more than fifty times as much coverage.[5] Tidmarch and Karp's study of eight metropolitan newspapers discovered that
the *Atlanta Constitution* published the most information about local House
races, with a peak of 9 articles per month devoted to Newt Gingrich's successful campaign for a House seat, whereas both the *Boston Globe* and the
San Francisco Chronicle ignored most of the House races in their core circulation areas.

Table 2.1 shows that the range of coverage for the 25 newspapers in the
first data set was considerably smaller than the range of coverage in previous
studies. The most diligent newspaper published 4.7 times as many articles as
the least active newspaper. At the diligent end of the distribution, the *Tulsa
World* published 27.7 articles per month about James Inhofe and the *Las
Vegas Review-Journal* 26.8 articles per month about James Bilbray. At the
less active end, the *Washington Times* published 5.8 articles per month
about Maryland's Albert Wynn and the *San Francisco Chronicle* 5.9 articles
per month about Ronald Dellums. The median newspaper published 14.9
articles per month.

Articles-per-month is not the only way to measure the volume of newspaper coverage. Table 2.1 offers two alternative measures, the number of
references to a representative's last name in the text of articles and the
number of last-name references in newspaper headlines. Both measures are
highly correlated with articles-per-month.[6] The *Tulsa World* was diligent by
any measure—27.7 articles per month, 86 headline mentions, and 2,158
text mentions—and the *Washington Times* was neglectful by any measure,
at 5.8 articles per month, 4 headline mentions, and 250 text mentions.
Articles-per-month is the most versatile of the three measures because it
allows comparisons with previous studies and with the third data set.

Why did previous studies discover such enormous differences between

---

[5] The citation counts are from the original data set, adjusted to a thirty-day month. The
example is extreme, but only slightly so. Each of the five most diligent newspapers provided 60
or more articles per month about at least one of the representatives in the study, while each of
the five least diligent newspapers provided fewer than three articles per month about at least
one of their representatives (Goldenberg and Traugott 1978, variable 5).

[6] The Pearson correlation between articles and text mentions is .94, and between articles and
headline mentions .70, both significant at the .01 level.

TABLE 2.1
Coverage of Twenty-five Representatives

Newspaper	Representative	Name in Headline	Total Mentions in Text	Mentions per Article	Total Articles	Articles per Month
Tulsa World	Inhofe	86	2,158	3.6	617	27.7
Las Vegas Review-Journal	Bilbray	59	1,692	2.9	598	26.8
Cleveland Plain Dealer	Stokes	34	1,136	2.6	445	20.0
Hartford Courant	Kennelly	25	1,125	2.6	434	19.5
Rock Hill Herald	Spratt	47	1,632	3.9	427	19.1
Buffalo News	Quinn	82	1,301	3.3	421	18.9
Los Angeles Times	Beilenson	59	1,404	3.6	405	18.2
San Diego Union-Tribune	Filner	22	943	2.4	398	17.8
Lewiston Morning Tribune	LaRocco	99	1,591	4.3	393	17.6
Baton Rouge Advocate	Baker	41	1,145	3.3	357	16.0
Phoenix Gazette	Kyl	39	1,118	3.4	341	15.3
Bloomington Pantagraph	Ewing	63	1,053	3.3	335	15.0
York Daily Record	Goodling	67	974	3.1	332	14.9
Orlando Sentinel Tribune	McCollum	30	684	2.4	296	13.3
Norfolk Ledger-Star	Pickett	35	775	2.9	277	12.4
Louisville Courier-Journal	Mazzoli	26	587	2.3	264	11.8
Boston Globe	Moakley	20	637	2.6	255	11.4
Chicago Sun-Times	Lipinski	15	518	2.3	228	10.2
Idaho Falls Post Register	Crapo	34	839	4.0	221	9.9
Newsday	King	8	406	2.1	197	8.8
Houston Chronicle	Archer	8	337	1.8	192	8.6
Tucson Citizen	Kolbe	35	484	3.2	161	7.2
Seattle Times	McDermott	10	316	2.2	147	6.6
San Francisco Chronicle	Dellums	14	287	2.3	132	5.9
Washington Times	Wynn	4	250	2.0	130	5.8
Total		962	23,392		8,003	
Median Representative		34	943	2.9	332	14.9
Median Representative per Month		1.5	42.3			14.9

Coding: Articles include news stories, editorials, opinion columns, letters, and lists. Total Mentions in Text is a count of all references to a representative's last name in the body of an article. Mentions per Article includes both headline and text mentions.

Notes: All counts are from the first data set. Monthly averages are based on 22.3 months. Table is rank-ordered by the number of articles per month. Each median is the median for a single column of data.

newspapers compared with the much narrower differences among the 25 newspapers in this study? One explanation relates to the shortness of their observational periods — three weeks for Goldenberg and Traugott, a month for Tidmarch and Karp — during which time representatives may have differed greatly in their newsworthiness. Over the 97 weeks of this study, many of these differences cancel each other out as representatives drift in and out of the media spotlight. In March 1993, for example, the *Orlando Sentinel Tribune* published four times as many articles about Bill McCollum as the *Rock Hill Herald* published about John Spratt, whereas in October 1994, the *Herald* published twelve times as many articles about Spratt as the *Sentinel Tribune* did about McCollum. In the first instance, Spratt appeared to be doing ordinary things, whereas McCollum was battling to prevent the Navy from closing the Orlando Naval Training Center and working to block the relocation of a new veterans hospital from his district to a neighboring district; in the second instance, Spratt was running for reelection against a strong challenger, whereas McCollum was running unopposed. Averaged over the 97 weeks, the *Rock Hill Herald* published 44 percent more articles than the *Orlando Sentinel Tribune*, not the 1,100 percent more that a study focusing on a single month during the campaign season would have discovered.

The second explanation is that previous authors missed most of the coverage of representatives in large metropolitan newspapers because they examined only a single edition of each newspaper rather than examining all of the regional editions and regional sections that large newspapers use to target audiences within their circulation areas. Tidmarch and Karp found that the *Boston Globe* and the *San Francisco Chronicle* failed to cover most of the House campaigns in their circulation areas, whereas my study shows that in October 1994, the *Globe* published 13 articles about Joe Moakley and the *Chronicle* published 11 articles about Ron Dellums. Goldenberg and Traugott observed that the *Los Angeles Times* published between 1.4 and 5.7 articles per month about the six Los Angeles area representatives in their study of the 1978 campaign, whereas my study shows that the *Times* published 40 articles about Anthony Beilenson in October 1994. Of course, these three comparisons prove nothing, for it is possible that Representatives Moakley, Dellums, and Beilenson were unusually newsworthy in 1994. An examination of how these papers covered all representatives in their circulation areas is necessary before reaching any firm conclusions.

Newspapers and Representatives

Why did the most diligent of the 25 newspapers publish 4.7 times as many articles as the least active newspaper? Did representatives differ in their newsworthiness or did newspapers differ in their editorial practices? It is tempting to search for patterns in the data displayed in table 2.1. Perhaps the *Washington Times* and the *San Francisco Chronicle* offered little coverage of Albert Wynn and Ronald Dellums because the *Times* considers itself a national newspaper, unconcerned with suburban Maryland, and the *Chronicle* considers itself a San Francisco paper, unconcerned with neighboring Oakland. Perhaps the two newspapers avoided heavy coverage of Wynn and Dellums, both of whom are black, because the papers attracted few black subscribers. Alternatively, the explanation could center on the representatives themselves. Perhaps both representatives failed to generate much news for journalists to cover. Although it is fun to play this speculative game, it is ultimately futile. The one-to-one correspondence between 25 newspapers and 25 representatives makes it virtually impossible to separate newspaper-centered explanations from representative-centered explanations.

Determining whether differences in the volume of coverage reflect differences in the newsworthiness of representatives, the editorial practices of newspapers, or both, requires a larger sample. The best sample would include some newspapers that covered two or more representatives and some newspapers that covered exactly the same representatives. Table 2.2 takes the first approach by examining how 18 newspapers in the first data set covered the 85 representatives in their core circulation areas.[7]

Table 2.2 reveals enormous variation in how individual newspapers covered particular representatives. The *Chicago Sun-Times* published 868 articles mentioning Dan Rostenkowski, compared with 53 articles for Harris Fawell. The *San Francisco Chronicle* favored Nancy Pelosi with 294 articles, Tom Lantos with 39. The *Los Angeles Times* had 364 articles on Anthony Beilenson, but only 53 on Matthew Martinez.[8] Clearly the editors of these three newspapers found major differences in the newsworthiness of the various representatives residing in their circulation areas. Other newspapers, however, provided nearly identical coverage of their representatives. The *Tulsa World*, for example, published 566 articles about James Inhofe and 547 about his colleague Mike Synar.

---

[7] Each of the other seven papers had a single congressional district in its circulation area (see table 1.1).

[8] Table 2.1 identifies 405 articles mentioning Beilenson, whereas table 2.2 identifies 364 articles. Similar differences appear for seven other representatives (Archer, Filner, Inhofe, Lipinski, McCollum, Moakley, Wynn). Table 2.1 is based on the first data set, obtained with a more exhaustive search routine, whereas table 2.2 is based on the third data set, where the search routine was less exhaustive. The less exhaustive routine included searches for first name/ last name and nickname/last name references, whereas the more exhaustive routine also included last-name-only references. Although the latter routine produced many more wrong citations, human coders eliminated all incorrect citations and duplicate articles for the first data set. Sampling techniques were used to adjust for incorrect citations and duplicate articles for the third data set (see chapter 1).

TABLE 2.2
Coverage by Eighteen Newspapers with Multiple Representatives

Los Angeles Times		*Houston Chronicle*		*Phoenix Gazette*	
*Beilenson	364†	Andrews	377	*Kyl	341
Berman	334	Green	257	Coppersmith	328
Waxman	306	Washington	251	Pastor	142
Waters	281	Fields	227	Stump	94
Harman	207	DeLay	170		
McKeon	174	*Archer	125†	*Orlando Sentinel Tribune*	
Moorhead	145			*McCollum	245†
Tucker	118	*Newsday*		Mica	205
Horn	98	*King	197	Brown	163
Becerra	94	Ackerman	173		
Dixon	93	Levy	163	*Seattle Times*	
Torres	80	Lazio	156	Cantwell	178
Roybal-Allard	72	Hochbrueckner	148	*McDermott	147
Dreier	62			Dunn	141
Martinez	53	*San Diego Union-Tribune*			
		Schenk	481	*Baton Rouge Advocate*	
Chicago Sun-Times		*Filner	387†	Fields	419
Rostenkowski	868	Hunter	338	*Baker	357
Rush	332	Cunningham	307		
Reynolds	283	Packard	189	*Buffalo News*	
Gutierrez	208			*Quinn	421
*Lipinski	203†	*Washington Times*		LaFalce	393
Hyde	192	Moran	240		
Collins	148	Hoyer	192	*Louisville Courier-Journal*	
Yates	125	Byrne	162	Hamilton	284
Porter	100	Morella	142	*Mazzoli	264
Crane	85	*Wynn	119†		
Fawell	53			*Norfolk Ledger-Star*	
		Boston Globe		*Pickett	277
San Francisco Chronicle		Kennedy	471	Scott	32
Pelosi	294	Frank	281		
Eshoo	136	Markey	266	*Tucson Citizen*	
*Dellums	132	*Moakley	254†	*Kolbe	161
Miller	113			Pastor	119
Stark	90	*Cleveland Plain Dealer*			
Woolsey	60	*Stokes	445	*Tulsa World*	
Baker	60	Fingerhut	400	*Inhofe	566†
Lantos	39	Hoke	387	Synar	547
		Brown	304		

Notes: All counts are from the third data set. Numbers are the number of articles. Median representative had 192 articles (8.6 articles per month).

  * Representative also included in the first data set.

  † Representative with fewer articles identified by the search routine used for the third data set than were identified by the more exhaustive search routine used for the first data set (table 2.1).

The results in table 2.2 put to rest any notion that coverage of representatives by large metropolitan newspapers is a "missing beat" (Tidmarch and Karp 1983). Although large newspapers did not cover individual representatives as extensively as smaller newspapers, they provided regular coverage. The median representative in table 2.2 was mentioned in 192 articles — about 8.6 articles per month.[9] My argument that previous scholars missed most of the coverage in large metropolitan newspapers because they searched only a single edition of each newspaper is now subject to verification. By happy coincidence, Danielle Vinson's excellent study of how local media outlets covered members of Congress included four weeks of coverage by the *Los Angeles Times* during late 1993 and early 1994 (Vinson 2003). Her search of a single print edition found fewer than half as many articles as my own search of the electronic archives that contained all six regional editions.[10] The disparities were greatest for representatives outside central Los Angeles. Vinson identified only 25 articles for representatives Beilenson, Berman, McKeon, Moorhead, and Waxman, whereas my search identified 75 articles during the same four-week period, most of them appearing exclusively in the Valley edition of the *Times*, which circulates in these five districts.

Table 2.3 takes the alternative approach for separating representative-centered and newspaper-centered explanations of coverage. This table examines how pairs of newspapers in six cities — Boston, Chicago, San Francisco, Seattle, Tucson, and Washington — covered the same 33 representatives. The table reveals two striking patterns about the editorial practices of competing newspapers. First, editors tended to agree on the relative newsworthiness of particular representatives. Both Chicago papers provided heavy coverage of Dan Rostenkowski; both San Francisco papers found Nancy Pelosi most newsworthy; both Washington papers provided the least coverage of Albert Wynn. The table is rank-ordered by the volume of coverage in the first newspaper, but the rank order works nearly as well for the second paper. The second finding is that competing newspapers devoted almost identical amounts of space to covering all local representatives in their core circulation areas. The vast differences between newspapers that were so evident in table 2.1 are relatively small for the paired newspapers in table 2.3. The two Chicago papers differed by only 2 percent in their total coverage of eleven representatives, the two Washington papers by 3 percent, the two

---

[9] The conclusion is no different if one focuses on the ten newspapers in table 2.2 with four or more representatives. The median representative in this group appeared in 8.5 articles per month. The coverage is five times greater than what Tidmarch and Karp (1983) found.

[10] For the 15 representatives listed in table 2.2, Vinson found a total of 61 articles; the median representative had 4 articles. My own search of the electronic archives for the same four weeks found 143 articles (after discarding duplicates); the median representative had 9 articles. I am indebted to Danielle Vinson for sharing her data to facilitate this comparison.

CHAPTER 2

TABLE 2.3
Coverage by Pairs of Newspapers in Six Cities

	Articles in Paper #1	Articles in Paper #2		Articles in Paper #1	Articles in Paper #2
1. *Chicago Sun-Times*			1. *Washington Times*		
2. *Chicago Tribune*			2. *Washington Post*		
Rostenkowski	868	745	Moran	240	189
Rush	332	219	Hoyer	192	251
Reynolds	283	249	Byrne	162	168
Gutierrez	208	162	Morella	142	148
* Lipinski	203†	164	* Wynn	119†	121
Hyde	192	222	Total	855	877
Collins	148	121	Median	162	168
Yates	125	102			
Porter	100	245	1. *Boston Globe*		
Crane	85	211	2. *Boston Herald*		
Fawell	53	106	Kennedy	471	207
			Frank	281	152
Total	2597	2546	Markey	266	149
Median	192	211	* Moakley	254†	251
			Total	1272	759
1. *San Francisco Chronicle*			Median	274	180
2. *San Francisco Examiner*					
Pelosi	294	281	1. *Seattle Times*		
Eshoo	136	47	2. *Seattle Post-Intelligencer*		
* Dellums	132	137	Cantwell	178	162
Miller	113	64	* McDermott	147	186
Stark	90	71	Dunn	141	150
Woolsey	60	38	Total	466	498
Baker	60	39	Median	147	162
Lantos	39	40			
			1. *Tucson Citizen*		
Total	924	717	2. *Arizona Daily Star*		
Median	102	56	* Kolbe	161	204
			Pastor	119	117
			Total	280	321
			Median	140	161

Notes: All counts are from the third data set. Numbers are the number of articles. Median representative had 157 articles (7.0 articles per month).

   * Representative also included in the first and second data sets.

   † Representative with fewer articles identified by the search routine used for the third data set than were identified by the more exhaustive search routine used for the first data set (table 2.1).

Seattle papers by 7 percent, the two Tucson papers by 15 percent, and the two San Francisco papers by 29 percent. Only the Boston papers differed significantly, with the *Boston Globe* publishing 68 percent more articles than the *Boston Herald*.

Competition among local newspapers may be intense. Competing newspapers may seek and reach very different audiences. But this competition does not seem to produce radically different views of how newsworthy local representatives are collectively or of which local representatives are most newsworthy. Just as competition between *Time* and *Newsweek* has created two similar newsmagazines, and competition between the television networks has created three almost indistinguishable evening newscasts, so too has competition between local newspapers created convergence in how much total space each paper devotes to local representatives. Unfortunately, the convergence has not been to a high level of coverage. The median representative in table 2.3 was mentioned in only 7.0 articles per month, compared with 14.9 articles per month for the median representative in the random sample of coverage (table 2.1) and 8.6 articles per month for the median representative in the multidistrict newspapers (table 2.2).

The combined data set used for tables 2.1, 2.2, and 2.3 is still not large enough to test alternative explanations for the volume of coverage. It is especially difficult to test newspaper-centered explanations because the sample contains only 31 newspapers. So, I collected data from another 36 newspapers. The third data set contains information about how 67 newspapers covered 187 representatives between January 1, 1993, and November 8, 1994, with a total of 242 representative/newspaper dyads and 61,084 articles.[11]

Newspaper-Centered Explanations

One class of explanations for differences in the volume of coverage across the 242 representative/newspaper dyads centers on newspapers. Newspapers differ on many dimensions, some of which may affect the extent to which they choose to cover local representatives. First, newspapers vary in the total resources available for covering news. Some newspapers are vast organizations with hundreds of reporters and editors; others operate on shoestring budgets. The more resources a newspaper commands, the more extensively it may cover local representatives. Given the lack of reliable data on the number of reporters and editors at each newspaper, I have used daily circulation as a measure of resources. Circulation is a good measure because it

---

[11] Chapter 1 gives full details about the third data set. Each dyad (case) is one newspaper covering one representative for the two-year period. Some newspapers covered more than one representative; some representatives were covered by more than one newspaper.

captures a newspaper's two principal revenue streams, advertising and subscriptions.

Second, some newspapers have fully staffed Washington bureaus, others are part of chains with Washington bureaus, and still others have no Washington-based reporters at all. The more reporters a newspaper has based in the Capital, the more extensively it may cover a representative's actions in office. Washington bureaus differ enormously in size. Eight newspapers in the third data set had ten or more reporters accredited to the House Press Gallery, 22 newspapers had between two and nine reporters, 8 newspapers had a single Washington-based reporter, and 14 newspapers were parts of chains that assigned one or more Washington correspondents to serve a local paper's needs. Only 15 newspapers had no Washington-based reporters at all, and even these papers obtained occasional stories from regional reporters who worked for the wire services. Both the existence of a Washington bureau and the number of reporters in that bureau may be associated with the volume of coverage.[12]

Third, newspapers vary in the number of rival politicians competing for attention, and specifically in the number of representatives from portions of a newspaper's market area. The more representatives a newspaper has within its core circulation area, the less extensively it may cover each legislator. Of course, there is nothing to prevent a newspaper with a dozen representatives from giving each representative as much coverage as a newspaper with only a single representative; but many publishers would be reluctant to devote twelve times as much space to articles about all its local representatives, even with the use of regional editions and regional sections to target readers with information about particular representatives.

Fourth, newspapers may vary their coverage depending on where most of their regular readers reside and on who represents those readers, rather than seeking to cover equally all representatives in their market areas. The *New York Times* sells more copies in Carolyn Maloney's district, centered in midtown Manhattan, than it does in Jose Serrano's South Bronx district. It would not be surprising if the *Times* chose to cover Maloney more heavily than Serrano. Unfortunately, I have not been able to obtain quality data about the circulation patterns of newspapers by congressional district. Instead, I employ a district's median family income as a rough indicator of

[12] For a Washington bureau that served a single newspaper, I used the number of reporters accredited to the House Press Gallery, as listed in the *Congressional Directory* (U.S. Congress 1993, 1074–81). For a newspaper that was part of a chain or that had some other joint arrangement, I used the number of reporters listed in Monitor Publishing (1993) and Bacon (1993) that covered news for a particular locality, assuming one reporter per newspaper if individual reporters were not linked with specific localities.

readership, the argument being that most newspapers sell more copies in richer districts than in poorer ones.[13]

Fifth, newspapers may vary their coverage of representatives because of editorial bias, giving extra coverage to representatives that reporters and editors happen to favor. Many studies have shown that reporters and editors tend to be more liberal than citizens generally (Lichter, Rothman, and Lichter 1990, 20–53). The hypothesis is that the more liberal a representative is, the more extensively reporters cover that representative.

These five hypotheses do not exhaust all possible newspaper-centered explanations for the volume of coverage. Perhaps newspaper bias is more a consequence of a publisher's political views than those of a paper's editors and reporters. Perhaps newspapers that are parts of chains are less attentive to local representatives than are newspapers that are locally owned. Perhaps the long-standing culture of particular newspapers or particular chains explains their attention or inattention to local representatives. No matter how interesting and plausible these hypotheses may be, they are not testable with the data sets that I have assembled. Testing them would require either new information that is difficult to obtain or the creation of even larger data sets.[14]

Representative-Centered Explanations

A second class of explanations for differences in the volume of coverage centers on representatives. Representatives differ in the amount of power they wield in Congress, in their activity levels, in their talent for creating quotable quotes, in their accessability to journalists, and in the extent to which they do things that reporters find newsworthy. All of these things may affect the volume of coverage. One possibility is that local newspapers focus heavily on representatives who occupy influential positions in Congress. Representatives who chair committees, chair subcommittees, or occupy

---

[13] This may not be true in cities with two newspapers, where one newspaper typically attracts more upscale readers than the other. There are hints of this in table 2.3, where Joe Moakley, representing more of a working-class district, attracted more coverage than the other three Boston-area representatives in the tabloid *Boston Herald*, while attracting less coverage than each of the others in the upscale *Boston Globe*. Unfortunately, the third data set does not contain enough newspapers from cities with two papers to explore systematically how the differing audiences of competing newspapers affects their coverage of local representatives.

[14] Daily circulation for each newspaper is from Editor & Publisher 1993. The method for calculating the number of congressional districts within a newspaper's core circulation area is described in chapter 1. Median family income by congressional district is from Congressional Quarterly 1993a. A representative's liberalism is measured as his or her mean ADA score for 1993 and 1994 (Congressional Quarterly 1995b for members who were reelected and CQ's online service, Washington Alert, for members who were not).

leadership positions in their parties are obvious candidates for extra coverage. Members of the majority party and senior representatives may also attract more extensive coverage.

Another possibility is that local newspapers focus more heavily on representatives who perform newsworthy activities. Things that reporters may find newsworthy include introducing bills, holding hearings, obtaining benefits for the district, battling with the president, running for reelection, running for higher office, or getting caught in bed with a thirteen year old. In this study, I employ three measures of newsworthiness. One measure is whether a representative ran for higher office during 1993 or 1994. Eight of the 187 representatives campaigned for governor or senator during this period. A second measure is whether a representative was referred for investigation to the House Committee on Standards of Official Conduct — the Ethics Committee — during this period. Five of the representatives suffered this indignity. A third measure is the number of times a representative was mentioned in the *Congressional Quarterly Weekly Report*, a journal that covers what happens on Capitol Hill for an audience of reporters, lobbyists, and congressional specialists. This last variable is meant to capture activities that Washington insiders found newsworthy in order to determine the extent to which local newspapers reflected those judgments.

A third possibility is that local newspapers cover representatives who are in electoral danger more heavily than those with safe seats. Previous studies of presidential elections have shown that reporters are most interested in the horse race aspects of campaigning — that is, who is ahead and who is behind (Patterson 1980; Robinson and Sheehan 1983; Bartels 1988). Nothing is more boring to the journalistic mind than a campaign for which reporters have already written the final act. Prior to election season the best measure of electoral vulnerability is a representative's percentage in the previous general election. During election season a challenger's fund-raising prowess is a better measure of the competitiveness of a race (Jacobson 1997).

A fourth possibility is that reporters cover more heavily representatives who are distinctive in some way, standing out in an otherwise drab group of 435. Women and minority members of Congress are both candidates for this dubious honor. Reporters often seek them out not just to speak for themselves and their constituents but to speak as representatives of women and minorities generally. Reporters may also seek out representatives who are ideologically extreme. This follows from reporters' attempts to create balanced articles, apparently defined in Journalism 101 as writing articles with equal numbers of quotes supporting and opposing some policy or candidate. Once a reporter has obtained an adequate number of quotes on one side of an issue, the quickest way to obtain the counterbalancing quotes is to call someone who is known to have completely opposite beliefs. Moderate representatives are risky because they might come down on the wrong side of an issue.

The final possibility is that local newspapers cover heavily representatives who have good strategies for dealing with the press. Talented press secretaries, well-crafted press releases, and accessible representatives can combine to produce extensive exposure in the media. Unfortunately, I have not been able to devise a useful measure of news savvy. Future studies may be able to use the recently created electronic archives of congressional press releases. Unfortunately, these archives do not extend back to 1993.[15]

How Newspapers Differ

An analysis of the third data set shows strong support for both the newspaper-centered and the representative-centered explanations. The goal here is to explain the volume of coverage across the 242 representative/newspaper dyads. Regression analysis is the appropriate tool. The full model, containing 18 variables about newspapers and representatives, explains 51 percent of the variance in the number of articles per dyad (equation 2.3 in table 2.4).

The most important newspaper-related explanation for coverage is the number of representatives that a newspaper had in its core circulation area. If a newspaper had more than one representative to cover, it covered each representative less extensively than if it had only one. For each additional representative, a newspaper reduced its coverage of individual representatives by about 23 articles, a reduction of one article per month. Although the difference is small when one is comparing newspapers with one or two representatives, the difference is substantial when a newspaper's responsibilities increase. An increase of one standard deviation in the number of representatives to cover (4.8 districts) resulted in 111 fewer articles per representative. Citizens who happened to read a newspaper that had many representatives to cover found much less coverage of their own representative than citizens who read a newspaper with a market area that was congruent with a single congressional district.

[15] Party, seniority, committee chair, subcommittee chair, gender, and winning percentage for the 1992 general election are from CQ 1993b. Seniority is defined as 1993 minus the year first elected to the House. Party leaders are the top five leaders of the majority and the minority parties (CQ 1993b, 1730–31). House members running for senator or governor is from CQWR 10/22/94, 2995. Referral to the ethics committee is from CQA93, 64–74 and CQA94, 43–55. A representative's total references in CQWR is the number of pages listed in the 1993 and 1994 annual indexes to that representative. A list of minority members can be found at CQWR Special Report 11/7/92, 4. Ideological extremity is measured as the absolute value of 50 minus a representative's average ADA score for 1993 and 1994.

TABLE 2.4
Explaining the Volume of Coverage in Sixty-seven Newspapers

	Equation		
	2.1	2.2	2.3
Resources: Newspaper's Daily	.127**	.094	.112*
Circulation (in thousands)	(.048)	(.055)	(.047)
Washington Resources: Any	−34.019	−1.947	−18.110
Reporters in DC (yes = 1)	(29.628)	(34.046)	(29.317)
Washington Reporters Per			
Number of Districts in Core	−2.623	−4.850	−4.207
Circulation Area	(2.490)	(3.016)	(2.592)
Rival Subjects: Number of			
Districts in Paper's Core	−24.215***	−22.013***	−23.024***
Circulation Area	(3.073)	(3.626)	(3.137)
Newspaper Readership: District's			
Median Family Income	−2.443*	−2.308	−2.356*
(in thousands)	(1.010)	(1.364)	(1.182)
Reporter Bias: Member's ADA	.014	−.570	−.264
Score, 1993–94	(.270)	(.801)	(.698)
Member's Party (Democratic = 1)		103.066	53.523
		(61.257)	(53.109)
Member's Seniority (Total Years		3.688**	.667
in House)		(1.369)	(1.289)
Member Is Chair of a Committee		−28.524	−122.460**
(yes = 1)		(44.022)	(39.804)
Member Is Chair of a Subcom-		−59.613*	−36.742
mittee (yes = 1)		(28.784)	(25.372)
Member Is a Party Leader		158.426**	16.262
(yes = 1)		(55.498)	(52.030)
Member Is a Woman (yes = 1)		3.742	7.237
		(30.905)	(26.616)
Member Is a Minority (yes = 1)		−54.302	−21.170
		(35.641)	(32.240)
Member's Ideological Extremeness		−1.027	−.953
		(.922)	(.810)
Number of References to Member	2.113***		2.516***
in CQWR Index	(.305)		(.410)
Member Running for Senator or	180.848***		169.571***
Governor (yes = 1)	(44.706)		(44.325)
Member Investigated by Ethics	157.128**		135.395**
Committee (yes = 1)	(52.484)		(53.829)

TABLE 2.4 *Continued*

	Equation		
	2.1	2.2	2.3
Member's Percentage in 1992	−2.232**		−1.332
General Election	(.891)		(.958)
Constant	552.277***	452.879***	500.304***
	(77.696)	(70.033)	(82.661)
Number of Cases	242	242	242
Adjusted R^2	.490	.338	.513

Notes: Dependent variable: number of articles in each representative/newspaper dyad (1993–94).
Entries are unstandardized regression coefficients (standard errors in parentheses).
* $p < .05$ ** $p < .01$ *** $p < .001$

Newspapers with more resources at their command tended to cover individual representatives more extensively than did other newspapers. A newspaper that had daily circulation one standard deviation (329,000 copies) above the mean published an additional 37 articles about its local representative. Larger newspapers employ more reporters, and it is clear that they used some of their additional staff to cover local members of Congress. This effect partly counteracted the negative impact of a newspaper having several representatives in its market area, since large newspapers also tended to have many representatives. Even so, the number of representatives was a more important factor than a newspaper's size in explaining the volume of coverage.

Newspapers appear to have varied their coverage according to the income of a district's residents, but the relationship is opposite to my expectation. A district's median family income was meant to be a proxy for newspaper readership. The expectation was that newspapers would cover more extensively representatives from richer districts because they sell more subscriptions in those districts. In fact, newspapers covered more heavily representatives from poorer districts. A representative from a district with a median family income one standard deviation ($10,660) below average attracted an extra 26 articles. This finding may reflect a well-known bias among metropolitan newspapers for covering activities in central cities more heavily than what happens in the suburbs (Kaniss 1991). Their well-off readers may have fled to the suburbs, but newspapers remain firmly anchored downtown. Their editorial practices reflect those roots, even when covering a region's representatives in Congress.

Newspapers with reporters stationed in Washington did not cover representatives more heavily than papers without Washington bureaus. Moreover, both the number of Washington reporters and the number of Washington reporters per coverable representative failed to explain anything about the volume of coverage.[16] As the next chapter shows, newspapers did use their Washington bureaus to cover local representatives; a third of all news stories in the first data set were published with Washington datelines. But articles from Washington appear to displace other kinds of coverage about representatives rather than increasing the total volume of coverage.

A more careful examination of the structure of Washington bureaus is helpful (Monitor Publishing 1993; Bacon 1993). A newspaper with only a single Washington correspondent relies on the wire services to cover national news and employs its lone on-the-scene reporter to cover matters of special significance to local readers. These matters often involve Congress, the only institution in Washington with an organizational structure that corresponds to a newspaper's geographic market. When newspapers create larger Washington bureaus, they employ additional reporters not to multiply their coverage of local representatives but to bypass the wire services and cover national news themselves. Editors with large Washington bureaus assign reporters to cover the White House, State Department, courts, and various agencies; their congressional reporters cover both the national and local aspects of congressional news. Among the largest bureaus, only the *Los Angeles Times*, with forty-four Washington reporters, identified more than two reporters as specializing in covering the local dimension of Capitol Hill news. One reason representatives Beilenson, Berman, McKeon, Moorhead, and Waxman received so much coverage in the *Times* was that the paper assigned one Washington reporter to report news exclusively for the Valley edition that circulates in their districts.[17]

Finally, there is no evidence of any liberal or conservative bias in the way reporters chose representatives to cover. Newspapers gave neither more nor less coverage to representatives whose voting records were admired by the leftward-leaning Americans for Democratic Action (ADA).

How Representatives Differ

Representatives who did newsworthy things attracted more coverage than those who did not. Running for senator or governor resulted in an extra 170

[16] The three equations in table 2.4 include the existence of a Washington bureau and the number of Washington reporters per coverable representative; none of the coefficients are statistically significant. In addition, I have tried a variety of transformations of the number of Washington reporters per newspaper; none of these variables explain anything about the volume of coverage.

[17] The *Times* assigned five reporters to cover Congress as a whole and three reporters to cover news about Orange County, San Diego, and the San Fernando Valley.

newspaper articles (equation 2.3 in table 2.4). Less happily, representatives who found themselves referred for investigation to the House Ethics Committee attracted an extra 135 articles. Despite the fact that few representatives ran for higher office (8 representatives, 10 representative/newspaper dyads) or were referred to the Ethics Committee (5 representatives, 8 dyads), both coefficients were statistically significant.[18] Contrary to expectation, newspapers did not cover more heavily representatives who were electorally vulnerable. The margin of victory in 1992 was unrelated to newspaper coverage in the two subsequent years.

Representatives who did things that legislative specialists found newsworthy also attracted extra coverage. Each mention in the *Congressional Quarterly Weekly Report*, the journal for congressional junkies, was associated with an extra 2.5 articles in the local newspaper. A representative who received one standard deviation more coverage in this weekly (31.3 mentions) received 79 more articles at home. Since this journal specializes in covering legislative activities, the correlation suggests that many of the activities that Washington insiders found newsworthy were also judged newsworthy by local reporters.

Coverage of representatives did not vary with their institutional positions in Congress. Members of the majority party and senior members attracted no more coverage than their minority-party or junior colleagues. Party leaders and subcommittee chairs also failed to attract extra coverage. The one surprise was that representatives who chaired committees attracted less coverage than rank-and-file members. Chairing a committee was associated with 122 fewer articles. Reporters were evenhanded in dealing with representatives who were distinctive in other ways. They were no more likely to cover women, minority members, or representatives whose voting records were ideologically extreme.

The possibility exists that institutional position really did matter but that it was already accounted for by the number of mentions in the *Congressional Quarterly Weekly Report*. Equation 2.2 helps test for this possibility by dropping the four measures of newsworthiness. The new equation shows that both seniority and being a party leader mattered. Each additional year in office was associated with an extra 3.7 articles at home. A representative with one standard deviation more seniority in the House (9 years) attracted an extra 33 articles. Party leaders earned an extra 158 articles. Although committee chairs did not attract additional coverage, neither did they do worse than average as they did in the full model (equation 2.3).

---

[18] Two of the representatives referred to the Ethics Committee, Dan Rostenkowski and Newt Gingrich, also generated lots of other news, the former as chair of the House Ways and Means Committee, the latter as House Minority Whip. Given the small numbers of ethics violators, it is possible that some of the coverage picked up by the ethics variable may reflect these other activities.

Examining the effects of institutional position and newsworthiness, first separately and then together, suggests what drives coverage of representatives in local papers. Equation 2.1, with the four newsworthiness variables, is vastly more successful than equation 2.2, with the eight variables related to institutional position and distinctiveness. The former explains 49 percent of the variance; the latter explains only 34 percent. Quite clearly, representatives need to do something with their institutional positions in order to be covered back home. Coverage is not automatic.

Seniority is probably associated with greater coverage because senior members had more time to stake a claim to some piece of policy turf and become informed and active. Party is relatively unimportant because both parties have plenty of policy experts and policy activists. The lack of partisan differences also reflects the norm of nonpartisanship that is central to journalism. Those committee chairs who did lots of newsworthy things appear to have generated coverage both in CQWR and in their local newspapers. Other committee chairs received below-average coverage. Perhaps this reflects Richard Fenno's observation about the stages of a congressional career. Once representatives are deeply entrenched in their Washington careers, they become less attentive to constituents (Fenno 1978). They travel home less frequently and, perhaps, they do less to cultivate local reporters.

The newspaper-centered and representative-centered explanations are equally successful in explaining the volume of coverage across the 242 representative/newspaper dyads. A regression equation that contains only the six newspaper-related variables explains 27 percent of the variance; an equation that contains only the twelve representative-related variables explains 28 percent. The fact that the full model (equation 2.3) explains 51 percent of the variance suggests that there is virtually no overlap between the two explanations.

Can the results in table 2.4 be generalized to all daily newspapers? One problem in doing so is that the third data set does not contain a random sample of newspapers (see chapter 1). Embedded within this data set, however, are the 25 randomly selected newspapers from the first data set. By reestimating the full model first for the 92 representative/newspaper dyads associated with the sample of 25 papers, and then for the 150 representative/newspaper dyads associated with the 42 newspapers that were not randomly selected, one can determine whether the expansion of the data set has biased the results. Table 2.5 displays the results of these two new regressions. For ease of comparison, the table also includes the results for all 242 dyads (equation 2.3).

The expansion of the data set does not seem to have biased the results. The three equations tell similar stories about what factors affected the volume of coverage. The principal measures of representatives' newsworthiness— running for higher office, ethical problems, and mentions in CQWR—had

TABLE 2.5
Explaining the Volume of Coverage in Three Newspaper Samples

	Equation		
	2.4	2.5	2.3
Resources: Newspaper's Daily	.034	.109	.112*
Circulation (in thousands)	(.076)	(.071)	(.047)
Washington Resources: Any Re-	73.509	−60.926	−18.110
porters in DC (yes = 1)	(44.128)	(39.226)	(29.317)
Washington Reporters Per Num-	2.212	−5.707	−4.207
ber of Districts in Core Circu-	(4.298)	(3.388)	(2.592)
lation Area			
Rival Subjects: Number of Dis-	−11.139	−26.552***	−23.024***
tricts in Paper's Core Circula-	(5.773)	(4.044)	(3.137)
tion Area			
Newspaper Readership: District's	−6.025***	−.821	−2.356*
Median Family Income (in	(1.507)	(1.655)	(1.182)
thousands)			
Reporter Bias: Member's ADA	.517	−1.195	−.264
Score, 1993–94	(.944)	(.933)	(.698)
Member's Party (Demo-	4.161	120.047	53.523
cratic = 1)	(71.587)	(71.152)	(53.109)
Member's Seniority (Total Years	−.740	1.180	.667
in House)	(1.714)	(1.749)	(1.289)
Member Is Chair of a Commit-	−130.413**	−92.229	−122.460**
tee (yes = 1)	(48.855)	(55.857)	(39.804)
Member Is Chair of a Subcom-	19.364	−75.360*	−36.742
mittee (yes = 1)	(33.937)	(34.285)	(25.372)
Member Is a Party Leader	−108.907	72.343	16.262
(yes = 1)	(66.667)	(72.512)	(52.030)
Member Is a Woman (yes = 1)	−8.511	18.247	7.237
	(34.709)	(35.578)	(26.616)
Member Is a Minority (yes = 1)	−131.167**	16.286	−21.170
	(43.601)	(42.584)	(32.240)
Member's Ideological Extreme-	.103	−1.742	−.953
ness	(1.044)	(1.110)	(.810)
Number of References to Mem-	2.079***	2.619***	2.516***
ber in CQWR Index	(.497)	(.579)	(.410)
Member Running for Senator or	118.502*	237.255***	169.571***
Governor (yes = 1)	(56.972)	(61.151)	(44.325)
Member Investigated by Ethics	195.980**	80.330	135.395**
Committee (yes = 1)	(71.448)	(71.150)	(53.829)

TABLE 2.5 *Continued*

	Equation		
	2.4	2.5	2.3
Member's Percentage in 1992	− 1.905	− .020	− 1.332
General Election	(1.280)	(1.331)	(.958)
Constant	525.799***	449.882***	500.304***
	(102.494)	(117.808)	(82.661)
Number of Cases	92	150	242
Adjusted R^2	.513	.563	.513

Notes: Dependent variable: number of articles in each representative/newspaper dyad (1993–94).

Entries are unstandardized regression coefficients (standard errors in parentheses).

* $p < .05$ * $p < .01$ ** $p < .001$

similar effects in all three equations.[19] The principal consequence of the expansion was to allow more precise tests of the newspaper-centered explanations. A data set with only 25 newspapers does not allow one to say much about the consequences of newspapers differing in resources and in coverage responsibilities. Although both circulation and the number of districts in a paper's circulation area mattered when the equation was estimated with a sample of only 25 newspapers (equation 2.4), the standard errors are large. Reestimating the equation with more newspapers allows for greater precision.

The results across the three equations in table 2.5 are similar enough that it makes sense to employ the third data set, with all 242 representative/newspaper dyads, for subsequent analyses of what factors influenced the volume of newspaper coverage. It is worth recalling, however, that this data set is not appropriate for generalizing about how much coverage the typical citizen might find in the local newspaper. Only the first data set, with its random sample of newspapers, is appropriate for that task. The third data sets overrepresents big-city newspapers, and big-city newspapers provided below-average coverage of individual representatives.[20]

---

[19] One oddity in equation 2.4 is that the 25 newspapers covered the 20 minority members much less generously than they covered other representatives (the typical minority representative was mentioned in 131 fewer articles). This pattern does not recur in equation 2.5, which includes an additional 35 minority representatives, nor in the full data set.

[20] The median representative in the third data set was mentioned in 210 articles (9.4 articles per month) compared with 332 articles (14.9 articles per month) for the median representative in the first data set.

Coverage in Election Years

Do newspapers change their coverage patterns with the seasons? Do they cover representatives differently during election years? Reestimating equation 2.3 separately for 1993 and 1994 shows no major differences in how the six newspaper-related variables affected the volume of coverage. The number of representatives a newspaper had within its circulation area was just as much a constraint in an election year as the year before. The added resources that large newspapers enjoyed were equally valuable in election and nonelection years.[21] Similarly, there were no differences in the impact of representatives' institutional positions on the volume of coverage.

The impact of the four variables that measured representatives' newsworthiness did change in 1994. Each of the four regression coefficients was larger for the election year than for the previous year. Running for senator or governor increased coverage by 131 articles in 1994, compared with 39 articles in 1993. Being referred to the Ethics Committee was associated with 89 additional articles in 1994, compared with 46 additional articles the previous year. Each one-point reduction in a representative's winning percentage in 1992 was associated with 1.2 articles in 1994, compared with 0.2 articles the year before. Each mention in CQWR was associated with 1.4 articles the second year, up from 1.1 articles the previous year.[22] The first three increases are exactly what one would expect as reporters turned their attention to covering congressional campaigns. The fourth change probably reflects the fact that CQWR publishes some election-oriented stories, especially about hot races, although its primary emphasis is on legislative activities.

How do newspapers cover intense campaigns? When talented, experienced, well-financed candidates challenge incumbents for reelection, do newspapers respond by increasing their coverage? Do they appear to meet the Burglar Alarm Standard for news coverage? Or do newspapers cover representatives during campaign season just as they do during ordinary

---

[21] For each additional representative in their core circulation areas, newspapers reduced their coverage by 11.3 articles in 1993 and 11.7 articles in 1994. A newspaper that had daily circulation that was one standard deviation (329,000) above the mean published an additional 18.8 articles the first year and 18.1 articles the second.

[22] Rather than using a full-page table to display the two equations, what follows are the unstandardized regression coefficients and standard errors for four newsworthiness variables in the complete eighteen-variable models (first for 1993, then for 1994): Member running for senator or governor 38.827 (21.656), 130.744 (24.186); member investigated by Ethics Committee 45.952 (26.299), 89.443 (29.732), member's percentage in 1992 general election −0.178 (.468), −1.153 (.523); number of references in CQWR index 1.084 (.200), 1.432 (.224). The model explains 46 percent of the variance in 1993 and 54 percent in 1994.

times, giving neither more nor less coverage to representatives who are battling for their political lives against strong challengers compared with those
who are coasting to easy victory against weak challengers? A good case can
be made for either choice. On the one hand, journalists who cover heavily
the most closely contested races are, by the canons of journalism, covering
the most newsworthy campaigns. Reporters know how to write interesting
articles about races in which the outcome is in doubt, and they know how
to make these contests seem consequential. On the other hand, journalists
who avoid covering particular races because they believe that the incumbents are safe practically guarantee that those representatives will remain
safe. They deny citizens information about what challengers have to offer
and about challengers' criticisms of representatives' performance in office.

The evidence in table 2.6 suggests that newspapers did respond to the
intensity of political campaigns. This table is similar in structure to tables
2.4 and 2.5. The differences are three. The new estimates are for the 222
representative/newspaper dyads where the incumbent was running for reelection.[23] The new coverage period is from September 1, 1994, to November 8, 1994, the peak campaign period for most districts. The new equations
include four additional variables about newsworthiness, each focusing on a
different aspect of the campaign.

One of the new variables shows what happened when there was no contest for journalists to cover. A representative who ran unopposed in the
general election received 18 to 21 fewer articles in the local newspaper than
a representative who faced a challenger. Given that the mean level of coverage for these 69 days was 34 articles per representative, coverage was less
than half the usual level for representatives without opponents. The reduction was from one article every two days to one article every four or five
days.

Most experts believe that the best measure of campaign intensity is campaign spending, and particularly spending by the challenger.[24] As equation
2.6 shows, both representatives' spending and challengers' spending were
associated with how extensively newspapers covered representatives during
the peak campaign season. Challengers' spending was three times more
effective in generating news coverage that mentioned representatives than

[23] The twenty cases that are included in table 2.4 but not in table 2.6 include eight representatives who ran for senator or governor (ten dyads), seven who retired, and three who were
defeated in primaries.

[24] Peter Clarke and Susan Evans found that the competitiveness of House races in 1978
affected the amount of campaign coverage that candidates received in local newspapers
(Clarke and Evans 1983, 59). Unfortunately, their measure of competitiveness was based on the
results of the 1978 election, a measure that can also be a consequence of differential press
coverage. Campaign spending is a better measure.

TABLE 2.6
Explaining the Volume of Coverage during Campaign Season

	Equation	
	2.6	2.7
Resources: Newspaper's Daily Circulation (in thousands)	.024**	.025**
	(.009)	(.009)
Washington Resources: Any Reporters in DC (yes = 1)	−11.002	−10.912*
	(5.761)	(5.589)
Washington Reporters per Number of Districts in Core Circulation Area	−1.005*	−1.022*
	(.481)	(.467)
Rival Subjects: Number of Districts in Paper's Core Circulation Area	−4.408***	−4.399***
	(.597)	(.580)
Newspaper Readership: District's Median Family Income (in thousands)	−.509*	−.541**
	(.224)	(.218)
Reporter Bias: Member's ADA Score, 1993–94	.118	.083
	(.133)	(.129)
Member's Party (Democratic = 1)	−9.717	−9.086
	(10.502)	(10.189)
Member's Seniority (Total Years in House)	.311	−.046
	(.232)	(.245)
Member Is Chair of a Committee (yes = 1)	−14.585*	−22.232**
	(7.298)	(7.376)
Member Is Chair of a Subcommittee (yes = 1)	3.849	2.647
	(4.944)	(4.807)
Member Is a Party Leader (yes = 1)	18.157	8.332
	(10.002)	(10.060)
Member Is a Woman (yes = 1)	−.162	−1.029
	(5.053)	(4.907)
Member Is a Minority (yes = 1)	−5.676	−4.231
	(6.179)	(6.007)
Member's Ideological Extremeness	−.197	−.256
	(.157)	(.153)
Member's Percentage in 1992 General Election	.051	.038
	(.202)	(.196)
Member's Campaign Spending for 1994 Election (in thousands)	.011*	.004
	(.005)	(.006)
Challenger's Campaign Spending for 1994 Election (in thousands)	.034***	.037***
	(.007)	(.007)
Member Running Unopposed in 1994 General Election (yes =1)	−18.076*	−21.431**
	(7.419)	(7.254)
Member Investigated by Ethics Committee (yes = 1)	33.012***	23.866*
	(9.776)	(9.801)

TABLE 2.6 *Continued*

	Equation	
	2.6	2.7
Number of References to Member in CQWR		.294***
Index		(.080)
Constant	73.583***	78.503***
	(16.882)	(16.431)
Number of Cases	222	222
Adjusted R^2	.484	.515

Notes: Dependent variable: number of articles in each representative/newspaper dyad (9/1/94 to 11/8/94).

Entries are unstandardized regression coefficients (standard errors in parentheses).

* p < .05   * p < .01   ** p < .001

was representatives' own spending.[25] The average representative in the sample spent $588,000 running for reelection; a representative who spent one standard deviation more than average (an additional $434,000) appeared in an extra 4.8 articles during this period, an increase of 14 percent. The average challenger in the sample spent $214,000 running for election; a challenger who spent one standard deviation more than average (an additional $328,000) produced an extra 11.2 articles mentioning the representative, an increase of 33 percent.[26]

Newspaper coverage did not depend on how well a representative did in the previous general election. A member's winning percentage in 1992 was unrelated to coverage in the 1994 campaign. What mattered was the intensity of the current campaign, not the results of the previous campaign. Representatives who had been investigated by the Ethics Committee continued to attract extra coverage. The typical representative who suffered this indignity was mentioned in an extra 33 articles, doubling the average coverage during campaign season from one article every other day to one article per day.

The principal measure of a representative's newsworthiness in Washington continued to be associated with the volume of coverage back home.

[25] Compare the regression coefficients (.034 and .011) in equation 2.6. Data about campaign spending are from Congressional Quarterly 1995b, 1508–31. I have also tried challenger's spending squared, representative's spending squared, and several other transformations; none of these transformations improve on the simple relationships reported.

[26] Presumably, challengers' spending also increased newspaper coverage of challengers. Unfortunately, the third data set tracks mentions of a representative; it contains no information about whether an article was centrally about the representative, the challenger, both candidates, or neither candidate. Chapter 6 examines how newspapers covered challengers with information that is drawn from the first data set.

Every ten mentions in CQWR yielded an extra 2.9 articles in the local newspaper during campaign season. A representative who was one standard deviation above the norm in CQ coverage (32 mentions) appeared in an extra 9.4 newspaper articles during the campaign period. One consequence of introducing this measure of newsworthiness into equation 2.7 was to eliminate the effect of representatives' own spending that was evident in equation 2.6. Could the editors at CQ be reacting to representatives' own spending? Although this is a plausible explanation, CQ's politically savvy editors surely knew that high spending by challengers was the better guide to incumbents in danger, and challenger spending was equally strong in both equations. A better explanation is that representatives who did news-worthy things in Washington also attracted more campaign contributions. Power in Washington generates lots of valuable things: CQWR coverage, newspaper coverage, and campaign contributions.

Newspapers that had two or more representatives to cover had even greater problems covering them during the campaign period than they did during previous periods. While an increase of one standard deviation in the number of representatives in a newspaper's circulation area reduced coverage of individual representatives by 44 percent in 1993, a similar increase during the height of the 1994 campaign season reduced individual coverage by 62 percent. Perhaps it is inherently more difficult to cover several representatives running for reelection than it is to cover these same representatives when they are participating in Washington activities.[27] A newspaper with several representatives can often use a single reporter to cover many representatives' participation in policy making. In October 1993, for example, a reporter could write about how all local representatives were responding to the intense conflict over the upcoming vote on NAFTA. When covering campaigns, however, this strategy is less helpful. Reporters need to focus on the conflict between an incumbent and a challenger. There are fewer opportunities for writing a single story that recounts useful information about several races.

Newspapers with reporters stationed in Washington did not cover representatives as heavily during the campaign period as did newspapers without reporters on Capitol Hill. A newspaper with a Washington bureau published about a third fewer articles than a newspaper without one. The number of Washington reporters per coverable representative was also associated with below-average coverage of local representatives (table 2.6). Recall that neither of these variables mattered much when the model was estimated for

<hr />

[27] Although this finding is similar to a finding by Edie Goldenberg and Michael Traugott, it is much less extreme. They concluded that "typical urban residents who read newspapers that are inefficient in their congressional districts, usually have available to them very little news about their House races" (Goldenberg and Traugott 1984, 125).

the entire two-year period (table 2.4). What now seems clear is that Washington reporters can be very helpful in ordinary times when newspapers are attempting to cover what representatives are doing in Congress, but they are in a poor position to cover election campaigns. As a consequence, citizens who read newspapers that had Washington bureaus may be exposed to different flows of information about representatives. During noncampaign periods they may read on-the-scene accounts of representatives' activities in Washington. During campaign periods, however, they see less information about the representatives and challengers who are battling for their hearts and minds.

How do newspapers cover primary campaigns? Do newspapers increase their coverage of representatives when representatives face primary challengers? Do newspapers respond to the intensity of primary campaigns in the same way they respond to the intensity of general election campaigns? The evidence in table 2.7 suggests that although contested primaries and campaign intensity matter, the effects are not the same as for general election campaigns. The equation in table 2.7 is similar in structure to the model estimated for the general election (table 2.6). The differences are three. The new equation contains two variables about the 1994 primary — whether the primary was contested and how much the various candidates spent to challenge the incumbent in a primary — and two variables about the competitiveness of the 1992 primary and general election. The model is estimated for 225 representative/newspaper dyads — 222 cases where the incumbent was renominated and 3 cases where the incumbent was defeated. The coverage period is three months — the month in which the primary was held and the two previous months.[28]

A contested primary increased coverage much less than a contested general election. Recall from table 2.6 that a representative who ran unopposed in the general election received 21 fewer articles during the campaign period than a representative with an active challenger. Table 2.7 shows that a representative who ran unopposed in a primary received 9 fewer articles during the three-month primary season than a representative with one or more primary challengers.[29] Put differently, journalists found contested general elections much more newsworthy than contested primaries. The incremental coverage for election campaigns was 2.5 times greater than the incremental coverage for primary campaigns.

The principal reason that contested primaries were lightly covered was

[28] The dates on which primaries were held for the 225 representatives in this model ranged from March 8 to October 1, 1994. The median date was June 7.

[29] Overall coverage was about the same in the two periods. Mean coverage during the 69-day election period was 34 articles; mean coverage during the three-month primary period was 38 articles.

TABLE 2.7
Explaining the Volume of Coverage during Primary Season

	Equation
	2.8
Resources: Newspaper's Daily Circulation (in thousands)	.019*
	(.008)
Washington Resources: Any Reporters in DC (yes = 1)	−1.744
	(5.255)
Washington Reporters per Number of Districts in Core Circulation Area	−.558
	(.435)
Rival Subjects: Number of Districts in Paper's Core Circulation Area	−3.546***
	(.544)
Newspaper Readership: District's Median Family Income (in thousands)	−.587**
	(.198)
Reporter Bias: Member's ADA Score, 1993–94	−.080
	(.120)
Member's Party (Democratic = 1)	14.568
	(9.134)
Member's Seniority (Total Years in House)	−.061
	(.243)
Member Is Chair of a Committee (yes = 1)	−20.107**
	(6.770)
Member Is Chair of a Subcommittee (yes = 1)	−9.323*
	(4.407)
Member Is a Party Leader (yes = 1)	−5.464
	(9.147)
Member Is a Woman (yes = 1)	−1.463
	(4.511)
Member Is a Minority (yes = 1)	−6.002
	(5.449)
Member's Ideological Extremeness	−.243
	(.143)
Member's Percentage in 1992 General Election	−.302
	(.171)
Member's Percentage in 1992 Primary Election	−.069
	(.075)
Spending by All Candidates Challenging Member in 1994 Primary (in thousands)	.017*
	(.007)
Member Running Unopposed in 1994 Primary (yes = 1)	−8.594**
	(3.235)
Member Investigated by Ethics Committee (yes = 1)	13.147
	(9.120)

TABLE 2.7 *Continued*

| | Equation |
	2.8
Number of References to Member in CQWR Index	.528***
	(.070)
Constant	101.550***
	(14.461)
Number of Cases	225
Adjusted R^2	.527

Notes: Dependent variable: number of articles in each representative/newspaper dyad during the month in which the congressional primary was held and during the two previous months. Entries are unstandardized regression coefficients (standard errors in parentheses).
  * p < .05   * p < .01   ** p < .001

that most of them were lightly contested. As with general elections, the best measure of campaign intensity is how much challengers spent during primary season.[30] Whereas the average challenger running in a contested election spent $214,000, the average challenger running in a contested primary spent only $103,000. Surprisingly, the impact of challengers' spending was also less during primary season. A challenger who spent $214,000 in the general election generated an extra 7.9 articles, whereas a challenger who spent $214,000 in a primary campaign generated only 3.6 additional articles (compare the regression coefficients in equations 2.7 and 2.8). In short, most challengers in primary campaigns were not as well financed as challengers in general elections, and even if they were adequately funded, a dollar spent in primary season generated only about half as much newspaper coverage as a dollar spent in election season.

Representatives and Senators

Do local newspapers cover individual representatives more frequently or less frequently than they cover individual senators? Individual senators have a clear advantage in the national media — newsmagazines, network television, and the like. In the most comprehensive study, Timothy Cook examined coverage on network television news between 1969 and 1982 and found that 90 percent of all senators appeared at least once a year on the evening news, compared with 37 percent of all representatives (Cook 1986, 211).

---

[30] Data on campaign spending by all candidates who challenged incumbents in primaries are available at http://www.tray.com/fecinfo/.

Do individual senators also have an advantage in local media outlets? Wendy Schiller's study of how local newspapers covered senators is the best source for comparison because her methods and data sources are nearly identical to my own (Schiller 2000). Schiller investigated how ten newspapers covered senators in ten states during three consecutive two-year periods.[31] The median senator in her study appeared in 19.3 articles per month. The range was from 7.3 articles per month mentioning Alan Dixon in the *Chicago Tribune* during 1987 and 1988, to 61.3 articles per month mentioning Bob Kerrey in the *Omaha World-Herald* during 1991 and 1992. Coverage of Kerrey was inflated during that period because he was running for president; removing articles about his presidential campaign reduced the coverage to 35.5 articles per month. Schiller's findings about senators are remarkably similar to my own findings about House members. Recall from table 2.1 that the median representative was mentioned in 14.9 articles per month, and the range was from 5.8 to 27.7 articles per month.

Why do senators enjoy large advantages in the national media and only small advantages in local newspapers? The most likely explanation rests on the number of legislators clamoring for journalists' attention. For the national media, the competition is between 100 senators and 435 House members. If national journalists paid equal attention to each legislative body, they would provide more than four times as much coverage of individual senators as individual House members. The competition for attention is quite different for local media outlets. The range is from newspapers that have two senators and a single House member representing their readers in Congress to newspapers with two senators and more than a dozen House members representing their readers.

Comparing how Schiller's ten newspapers covered 20 senators over a two-year period with how the same ten newspapers covered 55 representatives in their core circulation areas shows that individual senators attracted more coverage than individual representatives only when newspapers had four or more representatives to cover.[32] The *Atlanta Constitution, Louisville Courier-Journal,* and *Omaha World-Herald,* each of which had three or fewer representatives in their core circulation areas, averaged 26.6 articles per month about each senator and 26.1 articles per month about each representative. In contrast, the *Boston Globe, Chicago Tribune, Houston Chronicle,*

---

[31] The states were California, Florida, Georgia, Illinois, Kentucky, Massachusetts, Minnesota, Nebraska, New York, and Texas. The time periods were 1987–88, 1989–90, and 1991–92. The number of cases was 58 because data were unavailable for the two senators from Kentucky during 1987 and 1988.

[32] Schiller's ten newspapers were also part of my third data set. The monthly estimates for the 20 senators are for 24 months in 1991–92; the monthly estimates for the 55 representatives are for 22.3 months in 1993–94.

Los Angeles Times, Minneapolis Star-Tribune, Newsday, and *St. Petersburg Times,* with between four and fifteen representatives in their core circulation areas, averaged 19.6 articles per month about each senator and 9.5 articles per month about each representative. Since we know from chapter 1 that most citizens read a newspaper with three or fewer representatives in the paper's core circulation area (table 1.1), it seems likely that most citizens do not encounter significantly more articles in local papers about their senators than about their representatives.[33] Only readers of large metropolitan newspapers regularly encounter more articles about their senators.

Do senators enjoy large advantages in other local media outlets? The only evidence on the subject is in Danielle Vinson's study of how eight local television stations covered 20 senators and 68 representatives during four weeks in late 1993 and early 1994 (Vinson 2003). Her data show that the senatorial advantage was modest, at best. The average senator appeared on 1.6 newscasts per month; the average representative on 1.1 newscasts per month.[34] On several television stations, House members attracted more coverage than senators did. The average House member appeared more frequently than the average senator on three stations (Philadelphia, Raleigh-Durham, Santa Barbara) and less frequently on four stations (Atlanta, Charleston SC, Columbia SC, San Antonio). In Los Angeles, not a single senator or representative appeared on a local television newscast during the entire four-week period.

The last finding is a useful reminder that citizens who live in large metropolitan areas face numerous difficulties in finding information about their own representatives. Newspapers in these areas do not feature individual representatives as frequently as newspapers with fewer representatives to cover, although regional sections and regional editions allow for more extensive coverage than would otherwise be possible. Television stations in large metropolitan areas have an even tougher time covering representatives. The news hour in New York and Los Angeles is the same length as the news hour in Albany and Santa Barbara. What differs is the number of representatives clamoring for attention. The surprise was not that KABC failed to feature a particular representative in the Los Angeles area during the four-week period that Vinson examined; the surprise was it did not cover *any* senator or representative during the entire four-week period. This was truly "The Missing Beat."

[33] Mark Westlye also concluded that Senate races were not inherently more newsworthy than House races. What mattered was the intensity of the campaigns. His evidence came from a small state (North Dakota) where a representative attracted more coverage than both the incumbent senator and the Senate challengers (Westlye 1991, 57).

[34] The calculations are my own. I am indebted to Danielle Vinson for sharing her unpublished data.

Summary of Empirical Findings

This chapter employed the first three data sets to measure and explain the frequency with which newspapers cover incumbent representatives. The principal empirical findings are these.

- Newspaper coverage of individual representatives is a regular event. Although coverage increases during political campaigns, the increment is relatively small compared to total coverage during noncampaign periods.
- The median newspaper publishes about fifteen articles per month that mention a local representative — one article every two days. This estimate is from the first data set, the only set that is representative of most daily newspapers in the country (except small dailies). The range is from 6 articles per month to 28 articles per month.
- Large metropolitan newspapers do not ignore members of Congress, as previous studies suggest. These newspapers often use regional sections or regional editions to target coverage of individual representatives.
- In cities with more than one newspaper, competing papers do not differ much in their coverage of local representatives. The editors at competing newspapers tend to agree on the newsworthiness of individual representatives, and they devote similar amounts of space to covering all local representatives.
- Representatives who do newsworthy things attract more coverage than those who do not. Running for senator or governor, being investigated by the House ethics committee, or doing things that legislative specialists find newsworthy generates extra coverage. Institutional position is not associated with extra coverage.
- Newspapers that have two or more representatives in their circulation areas provide less coverage of individual representatives than those that have a single representative to cover. Newspapers that have more resources at their command tend to cover individual representatives more extensively than other newspapers do. Newspapers with reporters stationed in Washington do not provide more coverage than those without Washington corespondents.
- Newspapers show no evidence of bias in the frequency with which they cover particular representatives. They give neither more nor less coverage to liberals, conservatives, ideological extremists, women, or minority members.
- During campaign season, newspapers cover contested races more heavily than non-contested races. They also vary their coverage with the intensity of each race, with spending by challengers generating more incremental coverage than spending by incumbents. Newspapers that have more than one representative in their circulation areas provide

even less coverage of individual representatives during campaign season than during other seasons.

- Newspapers cover contested primaries more heavily than noncontested primaries, although the incremental effects are less than they are for contested elections. Spending by primary challengers also increases coverage, although the effects are smaller than they are for challengers in general elections.

- Most newspapers do not publish more articles about senators than representatives. The exception is that large metropolitan newspapers with four or more representatives in their circulation areas tend to cover senators more extensively than representatives.

Discussion

The volume of information that citizens are exposed to about their representatives depends on where they happen to live. The disparities are greatest between citizens living in large cities and those living in medium-sized cities. In general, large-city newspapers cover each representative less frequently than do papers in medium-sized cities. Moreover, these disparities are reinforced in other sectors of the informational marketplace. Television outlets in large cities cover local representatives much less frequently than do print outlets in the same cities. And candidates in large cities face significantly higher advertising rates than do candidates in small and medium-sized cities.

The differences between the volume of coverage are only partly a function of city size and the number of representatives that a newspaper has within its circulation area. The disparities also reflect differences in the editorial tastes of publishers and journalists. Of course, we have no direct measure of editorial taste. Still it is striking how much the volume of coverage differs for similarly situated newspapers covering many representatives. For example, the median representative in the *Boston Globe* received 52 percent more coverage than the same representatives in the *Boston Herald*—two papers with virtually identical circulation areas. The Chicago area is more populous than the San Francisco area, but the median representative in the *Chicago Tribune* received twice as much coverage as the median representative in the *San Francisco Chronicle* and four times as much as a representative in the *San Francisco Examiner* (see table 2.3). Perhaps these differences reflect the systematic effects of variables that I failed to include in the analysis, but some portion must also reflect the fact that journalists at the *Globe* and the *Tribune* found local representatives more newsworthy than did their counterparts at the *Herald*, *Chronicle*, and *Examiner*.

The effects of such differences are potentially large and important. Scholars have long known that citizens differ widely in their attention to the media. Some citizens read newspapers regularly; some do not. But it now seems that even regular, seven-day-a-week readers are exposed to vastly different amounts of information about local representatives depending on where they live. Newspaper readers in Tulsa and Las Vegas are exposed to much more information about local representatives than readers in San Francisco, Seattle, and Tucson. Chapter 8 shows how these differences in the volume of coverage affect what citizens know about representatives and challengers.

3

How Newspapers Cover Legislators

NEWSPAPERS REGULARLY PUBLISH information about their local representatives. The typical newspaper in the first data set published about 15 articles per month that mentioned the local representative (chapter 2). What kinds of information did newspapers dispense and where did they display it? Did newspapers merely reprint representatives' press releases or did journalists do their own reporting of representatives' actions? Did lists of roll-call votes constitute a large fraction of the coverage of what representatives were doing in office or did journalists write stories about representatives sponsoring bills, working in committees, and building coalitions? Was coverage of representatives confined to the news pages or were representatives featured prominently in editorials, opinion columns, and letters to the editor?

This chapter, the first of four to examine the content of newspaper articles, presents the broad patterns. The next three chapters focus on how newspapers cover representatives as position takers, policy makers, and candidates. The source for these chapters is the first data set—the random sample of 25 newspapers, 25 representatives, and 8,003 articles.

Format

A frequently cited study reports "a third of the members of the House said that newspapers in their districts printed their news releases verbatim, and another third wrote their own columns for the local press" (Green, Fallows, Zwick 1972, 239). I find little evidence in these 25 newspapers that representatives were so successful in getting their prose directly into print. The median newspaper published only two columns or letters written by the local representative during the entire two-year period. Six newspapers never published a single item authored by a local representative.

Only two newspapers published more than six items written by the local representative. Even here the story is more interesting than expected. The *Los Angeles Times* published 12 items written by Anthony Beilenson, the most of any newspaper in the sample. But the *Times* hardly fits the mold of a newspaper reprinting representatives' promotional pieces. It published six unsolicited letters to the editor, in which Beilenson objected to points made in previous editorials or letters. These letters were evidence of some sort of dialogue between a representative and his constituents, not self-promotion.

It also published five columns that he wrote at the request of the editors, on crime, welfare, health care, the budget, and defense policy. The *Times* published these five items adjacent to columns it solicited from his electoral opponent, Richard Sybert, on the same five subjects. Far from being fluff pieces that candidates might submit on their own, these five columns forced both candidates to discuss important issues in ways that allowed citizens to compare their positions directly. Only the *York Daily Record*, which published ten columns and one letter by Bill Goodling, fits the mold of a newspaper offering a representative substantial space for self-promotion.

The impact of a representative's press releases on coverage is more difficult to ascertain, since the best press release stimulates favorable coverage without leaving any trace of its origin.[1] My assistants did record all instances in which news stories were written in the form of press releases (Representative Smith today announced that . . .). Only 3 percent of all stories revealed their origins as conspicuously. Most news stories included either quotations from someone other than the local representative or other signs of independent reporting.

I do not doubt that some newspapers fill their pages with representatives' press releases or allow representatives to write regular columns. A study of weekly newspapers or very small daily newspapers would probably find more evidence of this practice. Most citizens, however, read large daily newspapers, not small weekly newspapers,[2] and the evidence suggests that most daily newspapers, or at least those in the top five sextiles of circulation, do not simply reprint what representatives and their press secretaries send them. To be sure, much of what newspapers report about representatives — or indeed any other subject — is stimulated by the press releases that they receive, but that is a very different matter from printing these releases verbatim.

A second misconception is that lists of roll-call votes constitute a large fraction of what newspapers publish about local representatives. Although some newspapers do publish these lists, and the lists surely convey important information about representatives, they constitute a small fraction of overall coverage. Only 5 percent of the articles in the sample were lists of representatives' positions on roll-call votes.

News stories were the principal vehicle for conveying information about

---

[1] The study of how press releases affect newspaper coverage has been hampered by the lack of an appropriate archive of press releases. The Federal Document Clearing House now collects congressional press releases and makes them available electronically through the Nexis service. Unfortunately, this archive did not begin until the end of my own study. For a study of how press releases affected newspaper coverage during the 1973 gubernatorial race in New Jersey, see Vermeer 1982.

[2] Recall from chapter 1 that a majority of newspaper readers read a paper with a daily circulation of more than 100,000 copies.

representatives. Breaking down the 8,003 articles by format, news stories accounted for 77 percent of coverage, editorials and opinion columns 9 percent, letters to the editor 8 percent, stand-alone lists without any accompanying news stories 5 percent, and representatives' own letters or columns fewer than 1 percent. The total amount of opinion coverage—editorials, columns, and letters—was surprising, given that previous studies had not reported this coverage separately.[3] This opinion coverage was also some of the most informative and valuable. By offering citizens an interpretation of representatives' actions, rather than just a dry rendition of facts, opinion coverage can help citizens evaluate representatives' fitness for continuing to hold elective office. Of course, this assessment of opinion coverage presupposes that newspapers offer readers a balance of opinions and provide representatives with opportunities to respond to criticisms of their actions. In fact, most newspapers were relatively evenhanded in their opinion coverage.[4]

Newspapers differed enormously in the types of coverage they offered. The *Rock Hill Herald*, an exemplar of small-town participatory democracy, published 124 letters to the editor about John Spratt—29 percent of total coverage. The *Tulsa World*, the *Bloomington Pantagraph*, and the *Las Vegas Review-Journal* also published lively exchanges of letters about the achievements and shortcomings of their local representatives. Other newspapers rarely mentioned their representatives on the editorial or op-ed pages. The *Washington Times* published only two editorials and one letter mentioning Albert Wynn, despite the fact that reporters mentioned him in more than 100 news items.[5]

Location

Where did newspapers locate their coverage of representatives? Were articles that mentioned local representatives placed in prominent places where readers might easily notice them, or did newspapers bury information about legislators in the back pages, between the stock tables and the classified ads, where only the most dedicated readers would notice? Newspapers placed most of their articles in reasonably prominent places. Fifteen percent of all articles began on the front page of the main section, 14 percent on the first

---

[3] Few scholars have examined opinion coverage systematically. For studies of letters to the editor, see Hill 1981; Page 1996; Hart 2000. For studies of editorials, see Page 1996; Vermeer 2002.

[4] David Hill's survey of 75 editorial page editors found that 32 percent published all letters received, 31 percent published letters in proportion to the positions they espoused, 4 percent published an equal number of letters pro and con on each issue, and 33 percent used other criteria (Hill 1981, 388).

[5] Table 3.5 near the end of the chapter reports by newspaper the percentage of all articles that were editorials, opinion columns, or letters to the editor.

page of some other section, and 18 percent on the editorial or op-ed pages. In all, newspaper editors placed nearly half their articles in the three most prominent places available to them, locations where space is at a premium. A quarter of all articles appeared in the remaining pages of the main section, and a quarter were scattered throughout other sections.[6] In short, newspapers did not hide their coverage of local representatives; they featured it.

Newspapers differed in how prominently they displayed coverage of local representatives. The *Idaho Falls Post Register*, the second smallest paper in the sample, placed two thirds of its articles about Michael Crapo on one of its first pages, with more than a third on the front page of the main section. Perhaps there is not a lot of competition in Idaho Falls for the newspaper's premier position. The *Hartford Courant* also placed more than half of the articles that mentioned Barbara Kennelly on one of its first pages, with nearly one-third on the front page. The *Courant* had four Washington-based reporters, and they often wove comments from Kennelly into their regular front-page coverage of important issues such as NAFTA, health care reform, and the budget.

In contrast, the *Los Angeles Times*, the largest paper in the sample, placed only a quarter of the articles mentioning Anthony Beilenson on one of its front pages, and only 8 percent on page one. The competition for space on page one was particularly intense for the *Times*, since it had 15 representatives in its core circulation area and many others in its extended circulation area, to say nothing of all the local and regional news that a large metropolitan region generates. Although the *Times* covered Beilenson extensively, it placed three-quarters of the coverage outside the main section, most typically in its Metro section. *Newsday* and the *Chicago Sun-Times*, both tabloids, placed on their front pages only 1 percent of the articles that mentioned Peter King and William Lipinski. Both legislators were probably grateful, since tabloids tend to feature lawbreakers more than lawmakers on their cover pages.[7]

---

[6] None of these calculations include 171 articles that lacked section or page numbers (161 in the *Buffalo News*, 6 in the *Rock Hill Herald*, 3 in the *Lewiston Morning Tribune*, and 1 in the *San Diego Union-Tribune*). Also, there is no easy way to determine which are the editorial and op-ed pages in the electronic versions of some newspapers, so it is possible that a few of the opinion columns or letters appeared elsewhere in these newspapers. For lack of a better alternative, I have assumed that all editorials, columns, and letters appeared on the editorial or op-ed pages.

[7] Neither representative broke any laws to get on the front page. Lipinski made the front page of the *Sun-Times* (*a*) as the only Illinois Democrat to vote against President Clinton's deficit reduction package, (*b*) for surviving a subsequent attempt to purge him of his chairmanship of the Merchant Marine and Fisheries Committee, (*c*) for allegedly telling a local sanitation superintendent to ignore requests from a Chicago alderman with whom Lipinski was feuding, and (*d*) as an example of a once-safe Democrat who was in a tough race for reelection. King made the front page of *Newsday*'s Hempstead West and Hempstead South editions, two of

Centrality

Although most newspapers placed articles that mentioned local representatives in reasonably prominent locations, we also need to know how central representatives were to the articles. Did the articles feature representatives and convey lots of information about them or were representatives incidental players who appeared only briefly? Two approaches are useful for analyzing a representative's importance in an article. First, one can look for objective indicators of centrality. Was a representative mentioned in the headline, the first paragraph, or the first three paragraphs? Did a representative appear in a photo accompanying an article? How many times did a representative's name appear in the text? Second, one can make subjective assessments about how central a representative was to each article. Was a representative the principal subject of the story? Both the objective and subjective approaches are informative.

The three objective measures are relatively straightforward. Appearing in a headline is an excellent measure of centrality, since a headline's purpose is to attract readers by advertising a story's principal message. Twelve percent of the 8,003 articles featured a representative's name in the headline. Appearing in an accompanying photo is a good but less satisfactory measure of centrality, in part because photographs are not always available for breaking stories and in part because editors sometimes use representatives' pictures to highlight articles that would otherwise be difficult to illustrate (i.e., NAFTA). Five percent of the articles were accompanied by a photo with a caption that identified the local representative; 2 percent featured a representative in both headline and photo. The third measure simply counts the number of times a representative's last name appeared in the body of an article. More mentions indicates that an article is centrally about the representative. This measure had an enormous range, from single mentions in those articles where representatives played minor roles, to 51 mentions when the *Phoenix Gazette* published a front-page article that profiled Jon Kyl a week before his election to the Senate (*PG* 11/2/94 A1). The mean for the sample was 2.9 mentions per article; the standard deviation was 3.4.[8]

My assistants also assigned each article to one of four categories: (*a*) the representative was the main subject or one of several main subjects; (*b*) the representative was a secondary subject; (*c*) the representative was mentioned only on a list; and (*d*) the representative was an incidental subject — something that only a computer would notice. They coded the local representa-

---

its fifteen Sunday editions, for agreeing to attend a rally on behalf of Jonathan Pollard, the convicted spy (*CST* 5/28/93 1, 6/10/93 1, 2/17/93 1, 10/19/94 1; *NDAY* 9/26/93 1).

[8] Table 2.1 in the previous chapter breaks down by newspaper the number of appearances in headlines, the total mentions in the text, and the number of mentions per article.

tive as the main subject in 38 percent of all articles, a secondary subject in 51 percent, an incidental subject in 3 percent, and an entry on a list in 8 percent. In order to be included in the first category, a representative had to be mentioned in a story's headline or the first three paragraphs.[9]

Three of the categories — main, incidental, and list — are simple to interpret. Articles of the first type were fundamentally about the local representative. They often conveyed substantial amounts of politically relevant information about what a representative had been doing or where a representative stood on an issue. Lists reported simple facts about several representatives, including campaign contributions, roll-call votes, and interest group ratings. The information in these lists was often important, and the tabular format made it easy for readers to see how their own representative compared with other representatives in a newspaper's circulation area.[10] Incidental articles were the flotsam of a project that employed indefatigable computers to search for every mention of a representative in a local newspaper. They conveyed no messages of political significance about the representative.[11]

What are we to make of the 51 percent of articles in which the representative was a secondary subject? Did these articles convey much information about representatives? Did the information have the capacity to affect citizens' beliefs and opinions about their representatives? Many of these articles did convey important information. For example, nearly three-quarters of the articles in the *Hartford Courant* that mentioned Barbara Kennelly were coded with her as secondary subject. Secondary, perhaps, but like Forrest Gump, she had a talent for showing up at Washington's important events — on the committees that handled NAFTA, health care, and the budget; as a party whip rounding up votes for Democratic programs; at the White House, hobnobbing with the president. In any single article, her role appeared to be secondary, but the picture that emerged, over more than 100 front-page stories, was that Hartford's local representative was a woman of power and

[9] In the analysis of intercoder reliability for the 362 stories that were coded twice, my assistants disagreed about whether a representative was a main or secondary subject on 19 percent of all occasions. This was the fifth highest rate of disagreement for any variable in the study (which was not surprising given that centrality requires a subjective judgment). My assistants did not disagree significantly in the number of times that they used the two categories, only in their application to specific cases near the boundary.

[10] Representatives appeared on 381 stand-alone lists — i.e., lists without accompanying news stories. In addition, there were 223 instances in which, although there was an accompanying story, a representative appeared only on the list.

[11] Examples of representatives as incidental subjects included (*a*) an obituary that mentioned that the daughter of the deceased happened to be a part-time staff member working for James Bilbray, (*b*) a sports story about a local resident, who happened to work for James Inhofe, finishing the New York City marathon, and (*c*) nine articles about the election to fill freshman Bob Filner's recently vacated seat on the San Diego City Council (*LVRJ* 3/7/93 B1; *TW* 12/9/93 S4; *SDUT* 1/6/93 B1).

accomplishment, and that she was centrally involved in the major decisions of the day.

Indeed, many articles in which a representative was a secondary subject were just as informative as those in which the representative was the featured player. Consider a typical month at the *Los Angeles Times*. In June 1993, the *Times* published 23 articles that mentioned Anthony Beilenson. Following are the messages conveyed about Beilenson in nine articles in which he was a secondary subject.

- An op-ed column by a member of the Board of Supervisors argued that the federal government should do more to control illegal immigration. The author closed by praising both Beilenson's bill that would authorize expanding the Border Patrol and Beilenson's resolution that would "amend the Constitution so citizenship will not be granted automatically to U.S.-born children of undocumented aliens" (*LAT* 6/1/93 B5).
- A news story recounted how a class of kindergartners "did chores at home to earn pennies and nickels" in order to buy a flag that had flown over the nation's Capitol. Beilenson "delivered Old Glory to the youngsters" and spoke to the school about the importance of good citizenship. The kids and the flag (but not Beilenson) appeared in two color photos (*LAT* 6/3/93 B2).
- A front-page story recounted the five-year effort to get the National Park Service to purchase Bob Hope's 2,308 acre ranch for the Santa Monica Mountains National Recreation Area. A local environmentalist praised Beilenson and three others for putting together the $17 million deal (*LAT* 6/4/93 A1).
- Bruce Babbitt, the Secretary of the Interior, announced his support for a plan to purchase 248 acres from Soka University to add to the Santa Monica Mountains National Recreation Area. The announcement was made after Babbitt met with Beilenson and another area representative (*LAT* 6/6/93 B1).
- A story by the Washington reporter who was assigned to cover news about the San Fernando Valley chronicled how much Representatives Waxman, Berman, and Moorhead had received for speaking before special-interest groups. The story noted in the second paragraph that Beilenson, the only other Valley representative, "did not take any such trips or deliver any paid talks" (*LAT* 6/12/93 B4).
- A story from Washington announced that a House subcommittee had recommended only $4 million to purchase the 314-acre Paramount Ranch for the Santa Monica Mountains National Recreation Area. Beilenson emphasized that the Recreation Area would get more than 6 percent of the national total for park purchases. "In this budget climate, any amount—no matter how modest—is a victory" (*LAT* 6/16/93 B4).

- Another story from Washington recounted hearings held by a subcommittee of the House Judiciary Committee about establishing a national identification card to verify employment eligibility. The arguments of Beilenson, a proponent, and Jose Serrano (D-NY), an opponent, were used to frame the story (*LAT* 6/17/93 A16).
- A front-page story from Washington reported that the House had voted by a slim margin, 216–215, to build a $25 billion space station. According to the story, Beilenson voted against the proposal, despite last minute lobbying by Vice President Al Gore and despite the fact that he counted many space station workers among his constituents. According to Beilenson, "I don't think it is a wise expenditure of taxes at this time" (*LAT* 6/24/93 A1).
- The headline for a story from Washington about the lobbyist who represented Ventura County said it all: "Looking Out for County Is His Job; Lobbyist Roger Honberger Wins Praise from Local Officials; But Two Area Congressmen Say They Seldom See Him." According to Beilenson's staff, "Honberger has stopped by the office only once to introduce himself" (*LAT* 6/28/93 B1).

Consider the political messages packed into these nine articles. Beilenson was *active* on immigration reform, a hot issue in California (two articles). He was *effective* in obtaining federal funds to buy parkland for the area and he was working to obtain even more (three articles). He was a man of *principle*, voting his conscience on the space station and refusing to accept speaking fees from special interests (two articles). He was *influential* in Washington, meeting privately with the Secretary of Interior and the Vice President (two articles). Despite his importance he was still *accessible*, as evidenced by his visit to an elementary school in the district (one article). Only the article on Ventura County's lobbyist had no overt message about Beilenson, although the subtext of the staff member's observation was that Ventura County needed no lobbyist in Washington as long as Beilenson was there. The objective indicators of centrality would have suggested little of this richness. There were no photos of Beilenson, no headline mentions, and only 19 mentions of his name in the nine articles. But these articles, and many more like them, were painting a portrait of a representative hard at work.

These articles were typical of the way the *Los Angeles Times* covered Anthony Beilenson. There was nothing special about June 1993. Were these articles also typical of the way other newspapers intertwined coverage of representatives with coverage of other subjects? Typical they were, at least in the sense that every newspaper published articles about other subjects that also provided important information about local representatives. Articles about NAFTA revealed representatives' positions. Articles about President

Clinton's health care plan mentioned representatives' objections. Articles about upcoming gubernatorial elections included speculation about whether a local representative might run. The only unusual thing about the articles in the *Times* was the quality of the reporting from Washington. The *Times* was particularly effective at incorporating coverage of Anthony Beilenson into coverage of broader policy issues.

It is even conceivable that these kinds of articles were more informative than those where Beilenson's presence was foreshadowed by headlines and photos. Articles about immigration, national parks, and cute kids may attract more readers than articles that feature an incumbent politician. Readers may absorb more information about a representative when it is fed to them quietly in articles about other subjects than when it is hurled at them in blatantly political articles. Claims of a representative's effectiveness may be more credible when they are made by an environmental leader than when they are made by the representative himself.

When I began this project, I thought the truly informative articles would be the ones in which a representative was the central character. My views have changed. The truly informative articles are the ones that convey politically relevant messages, and these articles come in all sizes and shapes. Headline mentions, photos, and repetition of a representative's name may help convey simple messages, like the name of one's representative, but they do not seem to be associated with more complicated messages. My guess is that far more readers were first attracted by the front-page article headlined "Park Service Will Buy Jordan Ranch from Bob Hope: The Long-Sought Parcel Is Called the 'Crown Jewel' of National Recreation Area," and then happened to learn about Beilenson's role in negotiating the deal, than would be the case if the article headlined Beilenson himself (*LAT* 6/4/93 A1). Bob Hope outdraws Anthony Beilenson any day of the week.

Reporters

Who wrote these stories that mentioned local representatives? Did local newspapers employ one or two reporters who specialized in covering a representative, or did dozens of reporters write about each representative? The question matters because the number of reporters involved in covering any individual can affect the quality and objectivity of news coverage. On the one hand, covering a subject well requires some specialized knowledge; thus, having a few experienced reporters write about each representative has advantages not to be obtained from pulling reporters off the police beat or using general-purpose reporters to cover representatives' actions. On the other, having only one reporter cover each representative has equally unpleasant consequences because a single reporter, in order to maintain easy access, can become excessively sympathetic to a representative.[12]

Most newspapers did not rely on just one or two reporters to cover each representative. Indeed, the tendency was for several dozen reporters on each paper to file at least one story that mentioned the local representative. The number of reporters with at least one published story ranged from 18 in the *Lewiston Morning Tribune* to 87 in the *Cleveland Plain Dealer*. The median newspaper had 45 reporters who mentioned the representative in at least one story during the two-year period. These data provide little support for the notion that a close symbiotic relationship might have developed between individual reporters covering individual representatives. No reporters enjoyed such exclusive arrangements.

Most newspapers did have several reporters who specialized in covering local representatives. The range was from the *Washington Times*, where a single reporter filed 11 percent of the news stories mentioning Albert Wynn, to the *Lewiston Morning Tribune*, where the top reporter filed 47 percent of the stories mentioning Larry LaRocco. The median paper's top reporter filed 18 percent of news stories. The basic message is unchanged if the focus shifts to the top three reporters. The range was from the *Phoenix Gazette*, where three reporters filed 19 percent of the news stories, to the *Lewiston Morning Tribune* where three reporters published 74 percent of the stories. The median paper's top three reporters filed 35 percent of news stories.

Although it is certainly possible for newspapers to provide high quality coverage without selecting a few journalists to specialize in covering individual representatives, newspapers with the least specialization tended to cover representatives poorly. The three newspapers whose top three reporters filed fewer than 25 percent of all stories — the *Phoenix Gazette, Washington Times,* and *Newsday* — provided some of the weakest and most superficial coverage of any newspapers in the sample.[13] Some degree of specialization, therefore, appears to be a minimum condition for covering representatives well.

The principal reason why there were so many reporters in the sample — 1,134 reporters for 6,228 news stories — was that many stories were not centrally about local representatives. Reporters from other beats, whether local, state, national, or international, turned to representatives for information and quotations. Most representatives are known for being accessible and

---

[12] On the trade-offs between specialized and general-purpose reporters, see Gans 1979, 131–44; Robinson 1981, 76; Cook 1998, 94.

[13] Support for overall judgments about the quality of coverage in individual newspapers is provided later in this chapter and in subsequent chapters. The top three reporters filed 19 percent of the stories in the *Phoenix Gazette*, 20 percent in the *Washington Times*, and 22 percent in *Newsday*.

employ press secretaries to make journalists' jobs as easy as possible (Cook 1989). Representatives' quotations often enriched newspaper coverage of other subjects and allowed citizens to learn where their representatives stood on issues that were just beginning to percolate through the system.

Washington Reporters

News about representatives is generated both in Washington and at home. How many newspapers employed reporters in Washington who had the opportunity to observe representatives' legislative activities directly? How many stories did these Washington-based reporters write? Table 3.1 shows that nearly a third of the news stories that mentioned local representatives originated in Washington. The distribution among newspapers, however, was skewed. Nine newspapers published more than four stories per month with Washington datelines, while seven papers published less than one story per month. The median newspaper published 66 stories — about 3 per month.

Newspapers differed considerably in their Washington-based resources. Four newspapers had a dozen or more reporters accredited to the House Press Gallery — the *Washington Times* (74), the *Los Angeles Times* (44), *Newsday* (18), and the *Boston Globe* (12). Seven newspapers had between 2 and 7 reporters stationed in Washington, five papers had a single Washington-based reporter, and four papers were parts of chains, each of which assigned a Washington correspondent to serve a local paper's needs in the Capital.[14] Only five newspapers had no Washington-based reporters, and even these papers obtained occasional stories from regional reporters who worked for the wire services.

It surely mattered whether newspapers had Washington-based reporters. The twenty papers that employed one or more Washington correspondents averaged 91 news stories with Washington datelines, whereas the five that

---

[14] The principal source for information on Washington-based reporters is the Congressional Directory (U.S. Congress 1993, 1074–81). Information on how newspaper chains assigned Washington-based reporters to individual newspapers is available in Monitor Publishing 1993 and Bacon 1993. The *San Diego Union-Tribune* was the dominant paper in the Copley Newspaper chain, accounting for over half the group's circulation. After a brief conversation with the office manager for the Copley News Service in Washington, I counted seven of the chain's ten Washington-based reporters as reporters for the *Union-Tribune*. The *Las Vegas Review-Journal* was part of the Donrey Media Group, which called one of its three Washington reporters the Nevada correspondent. The *Rock Hill Herald* was part of McClatchy Newspapers, which called one of its seven Washington reporters the South Carolina correspondent. The *Tucson Citizen* was part of Gannett Newspapers, which assigned one of its 53 Washington reporters to cover Arizona and two neighboring states. The *York Daily Record* was represented in Washington by the States News Service, which assigned one of its 38 Washington reporters to serve Pennsylvania newspapers.

TABLE 3.1
News Stories with Washington Datelines

				News Stories		
Newspaper	Representative	Reporters Based in Washington	Percentage of Washington Stories by Top Reporter	Total	Washington Dateline	Percentage from Washington
Houston	Archer	6	25	110	64	58
Las Vegas	Bilbray	1*	35	456	248	54
Wash. Times	Wynn	74	16	107	58	54
Hartford	Kennelly	4	55	406	211	52
Cleveland	Stokes	5	28	403	167	41
Newsday	King	18	26	166	66	40
Baton Rouge	Baker	1	87	290	112	39
SF Chronicle	Dellums	1	54	113	43	38
Louisville	Mazzoli	1	44	243	91	37
Boston Globe	Moakley	12	25	225	80	36
Buffalo News	Quinn	2	59	367	133	36
York Record	Goodling	1*	39	274	97	35
Orlando	McCollum	3	31	200	67	34
Tulsa World	Inhofe	1	58	444	141	32
LA Times	Beilenson	44	50	343	95	28
San Diego	Filner	7*	44	279	73	26
Chicago Sun	Lipinski	3	46	149	33	22
Seattle Times	McDermott	1	83	97	18	19
Bloomington	Ewing	0	3	240	34	14
Rock Hill	Spratt	1*	19	279	21	8
Norfolk	Pickett	0	33	216	15	7
Phoenix Gaz.	Kyl	0	15	209	13	6
Idaho Falls	Crapo	0	10	185	10	5
Tucson Citizen	Kolbe	1*	33	142	3	2
Lewiston	LaRocco	0	50	285	4	1
Total		187		6,228	1,897	
Median Representative		1	35	240	66	34
Median Representative per Month				10.8	3.0	

Coding: Top Reporter refers to the Washington reporter who published the most stories that mentioned the local representative.

Notes: All counts are from the first data set. Reporters Based in Washington are those accredited to the House Press Gallery. All reporters represented a single newspaper except for those working for five chains (marked *). Each chain had more than the designated number of reporters available to cover a representative (see footnote 14). Each median is the median for a single column of data. Table is rank-ordered by the percentage of all news stories with a Washington dateline.

had no Washington-based reporters averaged only 15 stories originating in the Capital. Surprisingly, it didn't matter how many Washington reporters a newspaper employed. The four newspapers with twelve or more correspondents averaged 75 stories, the seven papers with two to seven reporters averaged 107, the five papers with a single correspondent averaged 81, and the four papers that used a reporter from a chain's Washington bureau averaged 93 stories. Clearly, one Washington-based reporter was all that was required to file a steady stream of stories about a local representative — even for newspapers like the *Baton Rouge Advocate*, *Louisville Courier-Journal*, and *Tulsa World*, which had more than one representative within its primary circulation area to cover. As noted in the previous chapter, newspapers that built large Washington bureaus used their extra reporters to cover a wider range of stories originating in Washington rather than to deepen their coverage of local representatives.

For Washington bureaus that were sparsely staffed, the chances were high that a single reporter would repeatedly cover a representative's Washington activities. Joan McKinney *was* the Washington bureau for the *Baton Rouge Advocate*, and she accounted for 87 percent of the stories that mentioned Richard Baker. For offices greater than one, however, the overlap was much less severe. The Washington bureau for the Donrey Media Group designated Tony Batt to be its Nevada correspondent, and he accounted for 35 percent of the Washington stories in the *Las Vegas Review-Journal* that mentioned James Bilbray, but the bureau chief, Stephen Tetreault, filed 18 percent of all Washington stories, and several other reporters accounted for the remainder. The enormous Washington bureau of the *Los Angeles Times* assigned a single reporter, Alan Miller, to cover news of interest to the San Fernando Valley, and he filed 50 percent of the stories that mentioned Anthony Beilenson, but seventeen of the bureau's other forty-three reporters filed stories that mentioned Beilenson, including 6 reporters who specialized on Congress, a White House correspondent, and specialists on labor policy, domestic policy, and international trade (Monitor Publishing 1993, 62).

The point is not that close symbiotic relationships could not have developed between Washington reporters and local representatives. I am in no position to know. The point is simply that few reporters dominated the news flow from Washington to local newspapers.[15] The top Washington correspondent in the median newspaper accounted for only 35 percent of the stories originating in Washington that mentioned the local representative (table 3.1). Whether at home or on Capitol Hill, most representatives had to deal with many journalists.

---

[15] For discussions of the relationship between Washington reporters and their congressional sources, see Broder 1987, 233–37; Povich 1996, 92–99.

Messages Delivered

What was the content of these 8,003 articles? What messages about representatives did these 25 newspapers convey to readers? Did newspapers focus heavily on representatives' participation in policy making? Or did newspapers focus more on representatives visiting their constituencies or performing casework for their constituents? How extensively did newspapers cover representatives as candidates for reelection? For each article my assistants coded a representative's principal role. No matter what the main subject and no matter how central or peripheral the representative, the coder was asked what role a representative played in the article. A coder could also assign a secondary role.

Table 3.2 shows that newspapers focused heavily on representatives' connections with policy making. Over half of all articles that mentioned representatives portrayed them as participants in national policy making, defined broadly to include lawmaking and the provision of benefits to their constituencies.[16] Running for reelection was the other major story. One-fifth of the articles portrayed representatives as candidates in past, present, or future electoral contests. Articles that focused on routine interactions with constituents were a small fraction of the total coverage. Only 2 percent of the articles focused on representatives doing casework for individual constituents; 8 to 10 percent of the articles covered representatives visiting their districts or hosting constituents in Washington.

Representatives contribute to policy making in many ways. David Mayhew coined the term *position taking* to capture the various ways in which legislators make judgmental statements about policy goals and policy alternatives (Mayhew 1974, 61). Nearly a third of all articles reported representatives' policy positions (2,382 articles). Half of these articles reported representatives' positions on actual roll-call votes (1,201 articles); the others reported representatives cosponsoring or endorsing bills (268 articles), taking positions on bills that were pending on the House floor (150 articles), or expressing views on bills at some intermediate stage of the legislative process (968 articles).[17] Mayhew argued that position taking is a large part of what representatives do. Position taking is also a large part of what newspapers report about representatives. The median newspaper published 89 articles

---

[16] Chapter 5 examines separately constituency-oriented bills. Also, appearing on a list usually connected a representative to policy making. Sixty-nine percent of the 381 appearances on lists in table 3.2 involved roll-call votes (255 lists) or announced positions on upcoming votes (6 lists).

[17] The total of the four types is greater than 2,382 because 205 articles reported two types of position taking. Table 3.5 near the end of the chapter breaks down by newspaper the percentage of all articles that reported at least one of the four types of position taking.

TABLE 3.2
Representative's Principal and Secondary Roles in Each Article

Type	Principal Role		Secondary Role		Both Roles	
	Number	Percentage	Number	Percentage	Number	Percentage
Participant in Policy Making	4,060	50	290	4	4,350	54
Performer of Casework	141	2	26	0	167	2
Visitor to Constituency	672	8	122	2	794	10
Candidate in Electoral Contest	1,582	20	139	2	1,721	22
Other Role	926	12	—	—	926	12
Incidental Mention	241	3	—	—	241	3
List Only, No Story	381	5	—	—	381	5
All Articles	8,003	100	577	8	8,580	108

Coding: Principal Role: Representative's principal role in article is as: (*a*) participant in federal policy making, broadly defined to include lawmaking and the provision of geographic benefits, (*b*) performer of casework for individual constituents, (*c*) visitor to constituency or host to constituents in Washington, (*d*) candidate in past, present, or future electoral contest, (*e*) other role, (*f*) purely incidental mention in an article on something else, (*g*) list only, with no accompanying story. Secondary Role: Use the first four codes from the list of principal roles.

Note: All counts are from the first data set.

about position taking—four articles per month. Chapter 4 explores coverage of position taking in greater depth.

Coverage of other lawmaking activities was more limited. Five percent of all articles included some discussion of a bill introduced by a local representative (405 articles). Three percent referred to a representative as a participant in some committee activity (216 articles). Two percent showed a representative acting as some kind of leader in Congress, including committee leader, subcommittee leader, party leader, caucus leader, or coalition builder (132 articles). The median newspaper published only 20 articles about one or more of these lawmaking activities—less than one article per month. Representatives were four times more likely to be portrayed as position takers than as active bill introducers, committee members, or leaders. Chapter 5 explores how newspapers covered representatives' participation in policy making.

Coverage of representatives as candidates in electoral contests was extensive, accounting for 20 percent of total coverage. Most of this coverage was about representatives running for reelection, although the sample also contained two representatives running for the Senate. Most newspapers published almost as many campaign articles about challengers as they did about incumbents. Chapter 6 explores how newspapers covered representatives as candidates.

Valence of Coverage

How did these articles portray the 25 local representatives? Did local newspapers praise local representatives, show them performing heroic feats, or otherwise make legislators look good? Or did newspapers criticize local representatives, show them avoiding their responsibilities, or otherwise portray legislators negatively? Previous research has suggested that local journalists cover local representatives with a soft touch. Michael Robinson claimed that local newspapers give "incumbents lots of coverage, most of it favorable" (1981, 90). Charles Tidmarch and John Pitney found a preponderance of neutral coverage, with only modest amounts of positive coverage and virtually no negative coverage. They concluded that "newspapers tend to publish little that will raise doubts about local incumbents in the minds of readers" (1985, 475–76).

Table 3.3 presents a more complex picture of local coverage. One message is that newspapers did publish information that raised doubts about local representatives, but most of this information was contained in opinion coverage, not news coverage. Campaigns were also important for stimulating criticisms of representatives. The last column in table 3.3 shows that 40 percent of all letters to the editor criticized a representative's performance as a policy maker, as did 26 percent of all editorials and opinion columns.[18] In contrast, only 6 percent of all news stories referred to anyone who criticized the incumbent's performance. Summed over all five types of coverage, 10 percent of all articles contained criticisms of a representative's performance. Table 3.3 also shows that criticisms of representatives were concentrated in campaign articles. Twenty-seven percent of the articles about campaigns contained criticisms of a representative's performance, compared to 8 percent in all other articles.[19]

What about the other 90 percent of coverage? Was it full of praise, as Robinson claims, or largely neutral in content as Tidmarch and Pitney maintain? Table 3.3 suggests that neutral coverage predominated, although

[18] The fact that 11 percent of all letters or columns that were written by representatives contained criticisms of their performance reflects nothing more than representatives defending their records by first restating criticisms that had been lodged against them.

[19] Breaking down campaign coverage by type of article: 38 percent of letters, 31 percent of editorials or columns, and 24 percent of news stories contained criticisms of a representative's performance.

TABLE 3.3
Valence of Articles from Representative's Perspective

| Type of Article | N | Percentage of Articles Rated | | | Ratio of Positive to Negative Ratings | Percentage Containing Criticism of Representative |
		Positive	Neutral	Negative		
News story	6,228	25	70	5	5.00	6
List only, no story	381	—	100	—	—	—
Editorial or column	709	32	38	30	1.07	26
Letter to the editor	611	40	16	44	.91	40
Letter/column by Representative	74	95	5	—	—	11
All Articles	8,003	26	64	10	2.60	10
Campaign Articles	1,178	27	52	21	1.29	27
All Other Articles	6,825	26	66	8	3.25	8

Coding: Valence: How would you rate the article from the representative's perspective? Does it appear to contribute to a *positive* impression of the representative (the representative would be happy to have it published on the front page)? Does it appear to contribute to a *negative* impression of the representative (the representative would prefer that the story not run)? Or is the article basically *neutral*, a mix of positive and negative elements, or unclear to the coder (i.e., accurate coding would require a better understanding of the local context)?

Criticism: Did some individual or group cited in the article criticize the representative's performance as a policy maker? Or did the author of an editorial, column, or letter criticize the representative's performance as a policy maker?

Notes: All counts are from the first data set.

Campaign articles do not include 24 articles about three representatives who ran unopposed; these are included in all other articles. See chapter 6 for details on campaign coverage.

the exact valence differed for the various types of articles.[20] News stories were the most neutral in tone. Seventy percent of all news stories were neutral, 25 percent appeared to contribute to a positive impression of the local representative, and 5 percent appeared to create a negative impression of the representative. So, although positive coverage outweighed negative

[20] Unfortunately, I lacked the foresight to create a variable that coded whether some individual or group cited in an article praised a representative's performance as a policy maker. So, I have no direct counterpart to the variable that identified when someone criticized a representative's performance. The rest of table 3.3 is based on a variable called "valence," for which the coders attempted to rate each article from a representative's perspective. The analysis of intercoder reliability suggests that the coders readily agreed on what was a negative article, and they never confused a negative for a positive one. They found it tougher to distinguish between a neutral article and a positive one.

coverage, most news stories lacked any spin at all. Most letters to the editor, however, had a pronounced spin. Forty percent of all letters contributed to a positive impression of the representative, 44 percent to a negative impression, and 16 percent were neutral in tone. Editorials and opinion columns were evenly balanced among the three categories, with about a third each coded as positive, neutral, and negative.

Although negative coverage was surely less prevalent than positive or neutral coverage, it would be a mistake to conclude that newspapers published "little that will raise doubts about local incumbents." Ten percent of all articles contained criticisms of representatives — and 10 percent is far from insignificant when one is on the receiving end. Moreover, many of the negative items were published in prominent places, often with the vivid language of editorialists, columnists, or irate citizens, and frequently during the campaign period.

Which representatives were the objects of this critical coverage? Did all representatives share the pain, or was it concentrated on only a few? Table 3.4 shows that negative coverage was concentrated on about a quarter of the representatives. As the final column indicates, two newspapers, the *Las Vegas Review-Journal* and the *Phoenix Gazette*, published more negative than positive articles about Representatives Bilbray and Kyl. Several other newspapers, including the *San Diego Union-Tribune*, *Lewiston Morning Tribune*, *Tulsa World*, and *Rock Hill Herald*, published nearly as many negative as positive articles. Most of the critical coverage in these six newspapers was located on the opinion pages. The editorial writers and columnists at the Tulsa, Las Vegas, and San Diego papers were unusually critical of their local representatives. In each case, more than 80 percent of the editorials and columns that took a position were critical of the local representative. The letters published in the Las Vegas and Phoenix papers were also decidedly negative, with more than 70 percent of the letters that took a position critical of the representative. In one newspaper, the *Phoenix Gazette*, negative coverage outweighed positive coverage in the news stories themselves. Fifty-five percent of the news stories contained criticism of Jon Kyl.[21]

Why did these newspapers publish so much critical material about local representatives? Was there anything special about these six newspapers, these six local representatives, or the conditions in their districts that might stimulate coverage that was unusually critical of the representatives? Several things stand out. First, two of the representatives, Jon Kyl and James Inhofe,

[21] None of these percentages are based on just a few cases. The total number of editorials and columns that took a positive or negative position was 12 in the *Tulsa World*, 50 in the *Las Vegas Review-Journal*, and 46 in the *San Diego Union-Tribune*. The total number of letters that took a position was 54 in the *Las Vegas Review-Journal* and 21 in the *Phoenix Gazette*. The number of news stories that were coded positive or negative was 67 in the *Phoenix Gazette*. All percentages in table 3.4 that are based on five or fewer cases are marked with an asterisk.

TABLE 3.4
Valence of Articles by Newspaper

Newspaper	Representative	Total News Stories and Opinion Items Coded with a Positive or Negative Valence	Percentage of These Articles That Were Coded Negative			
			News Stories	Editorials/ Columns	Letters to the Editor	Total Articles
Las Vegas	Bilbray	202	27	84	72	53
Phoenix Gaz.	Kyl	130	55	31	81	52
San Diego	Filner	126	15	80	31	41
Lewiston	LaRocco	159	21	62	100*	38
Tulsa World	Inhofe	244	24	100	46	36
Rock Hill	Spratt	228	15	22	54	35
Houston	Archer	35	23	44	—	29
Orlando	McCollum	93	13	65	62	29
LA Times	Beilenson	152	19	50	55	28
Norfolk	Pickett	111	12	38	56	28
York Record	Goodling	127	14	42	67	23
Baton Rouge	Baker	84	19	75*	40*	23
Seattle Times	McDermott	61	11	14	47	23
Newsday	King	76	17	50	25	22
Chicago Sun	Lipinski	56	23	15	25*	21
Wash. Times	Wynn	16	7	100*	100*	19
Bloomington	Ewing	158	5	28	30	17
Tucson Citizen	Kolbe	61	15	25	—	16
Buffalo News	Quinn	148	10	17	59	16
SF Chronicle	Dellums	49	9	11	67	16
Boston Globe	Moakley	86	16	13	—	15
Hartford	Kennelly	143	10	53	—	14
Louisville	Mazzoli	48	8	—	33	13
Cleveland	Stokes	145	9	26	100*	12
Idaho Falls	Crapo	88	10	19	—	11
Total		2826				
Median Representative		111	15	38	47	23

Coding: Coding scheme for valence is the same as in table 3.3.

Notes: All counts are from the first data set. This table does not include the 74 columns or letters written by the representatives or any of the 5,103 articles for which the valence was coded as neutral. Table is rank-ordered by the percentage of all items coded negative.

* Percentage is based on five or fewer cases.

were running for empty Senate seats. Both Kyl and Inhofe were running against other representatives, all four candidates were well-financed, and the campaigns were intense. Second, Representatives Bilbray and LaRocco faced strong, well-financed challengers for their seats; indeed, both representatives lost their battles for reelection. So, intense campaigns, whether for higher office or reelection, appear to be associated with more critical coverage.[22] Policy conflicts can also generate critical coverage. Larry LaRocco introduced a bill that would have changed the land-use regulations for several million acres in Idaho. His reward was 62 articles in the *Lewiston Morning Tribune* mentioning the bill, many of them filled with critical comments.

On the news pages, most journalists adhered to the norm of neutrality. Most negative references to legislators that appeared in news stories consisted of challengers, interest group leaders, or other politicians criticizing representatives, with journalists as their scribes. The most intensely negative coverage of legislators appeared on the editorial pages, where editorialists, columnists, and citizens spoke their minds. The contrast between news and opinion coverage was most vivid in the *Tulsa World*. This paper provided some of the most detailed and objective news coverage of any newspaper in the sample. A total of 444 news stories over the two-year period painted a rich portrait of what James Inhofe was doing in Washington, where he stood on the issues, and how he differed from Dave McCurdy, the other representative vying for the vacant Senate seat. The news coverage was a model of fairness and thoroughness. On the editorial pages, however, Inhofe could do no right. His faults were revealed in everything from a carefully reasoned editorial, entitled "Why We Oppose Jim Inhofe," to a sharply worded editorial, entitled "Tricky Dick Lives," which complained about Inhofe "hiring a professional dirty-trickster" for his campaign (TW 10/23/94 E8; 10/30/94 E8).

Institutional Coverage

Previous research has suggested that journalists cover the institution of Congress with a heavy hand, emphasizing conflict, inefficiency, and scandal, and thereby contributing to citizens' low opinion of the legislature (Robinson 1981; Mann and Ornstein 1994). Although my sample of newspaper coverage is far from ideal for testing this assertion, since it was collected by searching newspaper archives for articles that mentioned the names of local representatives, not Congress as an institution, it is ideal for testing one explanation for why citizens think so poorly of the legislature. Richard

---

[22] Mark Westlye (1991, 51) also found that intense Senate campaigns were associated with more critical newspaper coverage.

Fenno observed some years ago that many representatives run for Congress by running against Congress — polishing their individual reputations by first denigrating Congress and then showing how different they are from other politicians on Capitol Hill (Fenno 1978, 162–69).

Do local newspapers show representatives repeatedly denigrating Congress as an institution? Do they cover challengers doing the same thing? Occasionally they do, but the occasions are few and far between. My assistants found only a trace of this kind of coverage — 41 articles in which representatives attacked Congress as an institution and 21 articles in which challengers attacked Congress.[23] Representatives may assail Congress repeatedly, but local newspapers do not regularly cover these assaults. Perhaps "Representative Bashes Congress" is no longer news. The bashing that did appear was largely a partisan affair. Nine Republican representatives denigrated Congress on 38 occasions; eight Republican challengers did so on 19 occasions. Only three Democratic representatives and two Democratic challengers were guilty of Congress bashing, once each.

Articles that mentioned ethical problems in Congress were even less abundant. Only 18 of 8,003 articles mentioned the general state of ethics in Congress or ethical problems of other representatives. Here is an instance in which newspapers were tougher on local representatives than on the institution. A total of 52 articles mentioned possible ethical problems of local legislators. The point is not that the media do not denigrate Congress; the research is pretty convincing that journalists do not portray the legislature in a favorable light. The point is that press coverage of local representatives does not contribute heavily to the view of Congress as an inept, inefficient, or ethically challenged institution.[24]

The Center and the Range

This chapter has summarized both the central tendencies in how newspapers covered local representatives and the differences among the 25 newspapers. The central tendencies suggest how much information a careful

---

[23] The coding sheet asked the coders to identify any instances in which a representative (or a challenger) attacked or defended Congress as an institution. In addition to the 41 instances of attacks, there were 3 instances in which a representative defended Congress and 3 instances in which a representative offered a balanced critique of Congress (discussing both its strengths and weaknesses). Challengers were associated with 21 attacks, no defenses, and no balanced critiques.

[24] So much for the ability of social scientists to predict what they might find. In the wake of the 1992 House bank scandal, the 1994 indictment of Dan Rostenkowski, and the Republican attacks on Congress in the 1994 election, I allocated 5 of the 68 variables to code information about attacks on Congress and about ethical problems in Congress. Two variables would have done nicely.

reader of a typical newspaper might encounter about a representative during 1993 and 1994. Of course, most citizens are not careful readers of local newspapers and most citizens do not read a typical newspaper. Consider first how citizens differ. The average newspaper reader does not consult a newspaper every day. Although 80 percent of the respondents in a 1994 survey reported that they read a newspaper at least once a week, only 48 percent of these readers claimed a daily habit.[25] Moreover, the average newspaper reader does not scan every page or every section, does not pause to read every item that happens to mention the local representative, and does not notice every reference to a representative in a story about something else. In short, the average newspaper reader who buys a typical newspaper is not likely to encounter anything like 15 articles per month about the local representative.

We can have greater confidence that the median newspaper in the sample resembles the typical newspaper that readers might encounter. Recall from chapter 1 the care that was taken to select a sample of newspapers that would be representative of the range of newspapers that citizens actually read. The only defect in the sample is that it underrepresents very small newspapers—those in the bottom circulation sextile. This is a serious problem that limits one's ability to generalize with any confidence to other small papers. Since it is likely that the excluded newspapers resemble in some respects the five smallest newspapers in the study—the *Tucson Citizen*, *York Daily Record*, *Rock Hill Herald*, *Idaho Falls Post Register*, and *Lewiston Morning Tribune*—it is worth examining in what ways those five papers were distinctive. These papers did not differ significantly in the volume of coverage; they averaged 14 articles per month. The principal differences were these. They were much less likely to employ Washington reporters or to publish stories with Washington datelines (see table 3.1). What they lacked in on-the-scene reporting, however, they compensated for with more intense scrutiny of representatives on their editorial and op-ed pages. Editorials, opinion columns, and letters to the editor accounted for 22 percent of coverage in the five smallest papers, compared with 15 percent in the twenty largest. In effect, they substituted inexpensive opinion coverage for expensive reporters based in Washington.

Of course, most citizens do not read the median newspaper. It is just the midpoint of a distribution with considerable variation. Table 3.5 summarizes the coverage patterns in the 25 newspapers along four dimensions. Total articles and articles per month are the best measures of volume. The range was from 5.8 to 27.7 articles per month. The percentage of all articles that

[25] Seven percent read a paper five or six days per week, 17 percent three or four days per week, and 28 percent one or two days per week (National Election Studies 1995, variable 125).

were editorials, opinion columns, or letters is a useful measure of how much a newspaper helped readers evaluate a representative's positions and actions. The range was from 2 to 34 percent opinion coverage. Valence is the best measure of the direction of evaluative comments from the representative's perspective. The range was from 11 to 53 percent of all evaluative comments having a negative valence. The percentage of all articles that contained information about a representative's policy positions is one indicator of the content of coverage. The range was from 10 to 59 percent of all articles reporting a representative's positions.

Newspapers also differed in the quality of their reporting. A careful reader of an excellent newspaper could learn a great deal about the local representative; an equally careful reader of a weak newspaper might learn very little. In order to give a sense of how much newspapers differed, I offer profiles of two newspapers at opposite ends of the distribution. The *Las Vegas Review-Journal* was one of the best newspapers in the sample; the *Washington Times* was the weakest. Both newspapers were approximately the same size; the *Review-Journal* had a circulation of 132,000, the *Times* 92,000. Both newspapers covered junior Democrats: James Bilbray of Las Vegas in his fourth term and Albert Wynn of Maryland in his first.

The *Las Vegas Review-Journal* covered James Bilbray intensively. It published 598 articles that mentioned him — 27 articles per month — second only to the *Tulsa World*, where James Inhofe was running for the Senate (table 3.5). More than a quarter of the articles appeared on the front page or the first page of another section. Coverage on the opinion pages was also extensive, with editorials, opinion columns, and letters accounting for nearly a quarter of all articles. More than half the news stories originated in Washington, second only to the *Houston Chronicle* (table 3.1).

The quality of the news coverage in the *Las Vegas Review-Journal* was also unusually high. This was one of the three most informative papers in the sample. The *Review-Journal* covered Bilbray as both a position taker and an active lawmaker. Like many newspapers, it reported how its representative had voted on recent roll-call votes (177 articles). Unlike most papers, it explained what was at stake in each vote, summarizing the viewpoints of supporters and opponents. The paper's Washington reporters covered what Bilbray was doing on issues of interest to Nevada, including nuclear waste, Indian gaming, and an empowerment zone for Las Vegas. Seventy-six articles referred to bills he had introduced or to his committee activities, second only to the *Lewiston Morning Tribune's* coverage of Larry LaRocco. Although coverage of Bilbray at home was relatively sparse, it was, like the Washington coverage, heavily oriented toward policy.

The *Washington Times* covered Albert Wynn lightly. It published only 130 articles that mentioned Albert Wynn — 6 articles per month — the least coverage of any newspaper in the sample (table 3.5). Any sense that the

TABLE 3.5
Coverage Patterns in Twenty-five Newspapers

Newspaper	Representative	Total Articles	Articles per Month	Percentage Opinion Coverage	Percentage Negative Valence	Percentage Position Taking
Tulsa World	Inhofe	617	27.7	20	36	26
Las Vegas	Bilbray	598	26.8	23	53	43
Cleveland	Stokes	445	20.0	8	12	22
Hartford	Kennelly	434	19.5	6	14	33
Rock Hill	Spratt	427	19.1	34	35	22
Buffalo News	Quinn	421	18.9	12	16	21
LA Times	Beilenson	405	18.2	14	28	41
San Diego	Filner	398	17.8	22	41	27
Lewiston	LaRocco	393	17.6	28	38	17
Baton Rouge	Baker	357	16.0	6	23	31
Phoenix Gaz.	Kyl	341	15.3	29	52	21
Bloomington	Ewing	335	15.0	28	17	35
York Record	Goodling	332	14.9	17	23	28
Orlando	McCollum	296	13.3	14	29	36
Norfolk	Pickett	277	12.4	21	28	21
Louisville	Mazzoli	264	11.8	8	13	34
Boston Globe	Moakley	255	11.4	11	15	10
Chicago Sun	Lipinski	228	10.2	17	21	37
Idaho Falls	Crapo	221	9.9	16	11	31
Newsday	King	197	8.8	15	22	43
Houston	Archer	192	8.6	7	29	56
Tucson Citizen	Kolbe	161	7.2	11	16	25
Seattle Times	McDermott	147	6.6	33	23	18
SF Chronicle	Dellums	132	5.9	13	16	27
Wash. Times	Wynn	130	5.8	2	19	59
Total		8,003				
Median Representative		332	14.9	15	23	28

Coding: Opinion Coverage includes editorials, opinion columns, and letters to the editor. Percent Negative Valence is from table 3.4. Position Taking includes cosponsoring or endorsing bills, taking positions on roll-call votes, taking positions on bills pending on the floor, and offering views on bills at some intermediate stage.

Notes: All counts are from the first data set. Table is rank-ordered by the number of articles per month. Each median is the median for a single column of data.

Times might have covered Wynn lightly because he represented a suburban Maryland district about which the editors cared little is easily dismissed. They did, after all, publish 46 photos of Wynn, the most photos of any newspaper in the sample. The *Times* covered Wynn largely as a position taker. Fifty-nine percent of the articles focused on position taking. Only 4 articles covered anything related to bills he had introduced or to his committee activities, the least of any newspaper in the sample. Opinion coverage was also the lightest for any newspaper: two editorials and one letter.

Although coverage of position taking is important, the approach the *Times* employed was not very informative. Rather than incorporating coverage of roll-call votes into news stories, editorials, or opinion columns, the *Times* published lists of roll-call votes. The lists seldom had an accompanying explanation of the basic policy conflict. Many of the lists were accompanied by file photos of Albert Wynn and seven other representatives from Maryland and Virginia. It was a nice attempt to draw attention to otherwise drab lists with dull headlines (How Our Representatives Voted), but in addition to attracting attention, the editors might have illuminated the policy conflicts that gave rise to the votes so that readers could evaluate representatives' positions.

The differences between the *Las Vegas Review-Journal* and the *Washington Times* were immense. The former painted a rich portrait of James Bilbray, with nearly an article per day of high-quality journalism. Careful readers of the *Review-Journal* could learn a great deal about what Bilbray was doing to earn his keep. This paper clearly met the Full News Standard. The extensive opinion coverage in the *Review-Journal* suggests that it also met the Burglar Alarm Standard. Those who were dissatisfied with Bilbray had no trouble publicizing their criticism for less attentive citizens. In contrast, the *Washington Times* offered just a rough sketch of Albert Wynn. Readers would have learned very little about what Wynn was doing besides voting. The *Times* failed to meet either the Full News or the Burglar Alarm Standards.

Although the *Las Vegas Review-Journal* was an unusually good newspaper, there were other newspapers in its class, including the *Los Angeles Times* and *Tulsa World*, and other papers that fell just short of this standard, including the *Hartford Courant* and *San Diego Union-Tribune*. Small-town newspapers worthy of note include the *Lewiston Morning Tribune* and *Rock Hill Herald*. The *Washington Times* was in a class by itself; no other newspaper was so uninformative. A step up from the *Times* would be the *Phoenix Gazette*, *Newsday*, and *Tucson Citizen*. Here the problems were not so much the volume of coverage — the *Gazette* was slightly above average in volume — but the amount of information that the articles conveyed. These overall judgments of quality will be sustained as the book presents more evidence about the content of coverage.

Summary of Empirical Findings

This chapter employed the first data set to describe how local newspapers covered representatives during 1993 and 1994. The principal empirical findings are these.

- News stories are the predominant vehicle for conveying messages about representatives. Editorials, opinion columns, and letters to the editor constitute one-sixth of all coverage. Representatives' own writings are a minuscule part of overall coverage.
- Most newspapers publish articles about representatives in reasonably prominent places. Nearly half of all articles appear in the three most prominent locations that newspapers have to offer — the front page, the first page of another section, or the editorial or op-ed pages.
- Representatives are the main subject of 40 percent of the articles. But many of the articles in which representatives are secondary subjects convey substantial amounts of politically relevant information about their positions and actions.
- Most newspapers do not rely on just one or two reporters to cover representatives, although some degree of specialization is common. On the typical newspaper, three reporters write about a third of the news stories that mention a local representative, while several dozen others write the rest.
- Nearly a third of all news stories that mention local representatives originate in Washington. The number of Washington-based reporters that a newspaper employs is unrelated to the volume of coverage from Washington.
- More than half of all articles focus on representatives' participation in national policy making. In these articles, representatives are four times more likely to be portrayed as position takers than as active bill introducers, committee members, or leaders. Twenty percent of articles focus on representatives running for reelection.
- Ten percent of articles contain criticisms of representatives' performance as policy makers. Although most news stories are relatively neutral in tone, 25 percent portray representatives positively and 5 percent negatively.
- Strong opinions abound on the editorial and op-ed pages. Letter writers, editorialists, and columnists are just as likely to criticize representatives as to praise them. A few newspapers publish more criticisms than praise on their editorial and op-ed pages.
- Only rarely do newspapers publish articles that show local representatives denigrating Congress as an institution.
- Newspapers differ enormously in both the quantity and the quality of

their coverage. The range is from newspapers that carefully cover representatives' positions and actions to those that offer superficial coverage
of position taking and legislative activities.

Political Accountability

Citizens are exposed to very different flows of political information depending on where they happen to live. It is not just the quantity of information
in local newspapers that varies from place to place; it is also the nature of
the political information and the way that it is presented that varies from
newspaper to newspaper.

Nowhere are the differences among newspapers in the sample more pronounced than in the way they treated representatives on their editorial and
op-ed pages. Some newspapers featured local representatives in their editorials and opinion columns, most notably the *Lewiston Morning Tribune*
(104 items), *Las Vegas Review-Journal* (76), *Phoenix Gazette* (69), and *San
Diego Union-Tribune* (63). Other newspapers rarely mentioned local representatives in editorials or opinion columns, including the *Washington Times*
(2), *Louisville Courier-Journal* (4), *San Francisco Chronicle* (10), and *Houston Chronicle* (10). The differences among newspapers were equally stark
for letters to the editor. Several newspapers published lively exchanges
among citizens about their local representatives, including the *Rock Hill
Herald* (124 letters), *Tulsa World* (105), *Bloomington Pantagraph* (64), and
Las Vegas Review-Journal (60), while twelve newspapers — half the sample —
published fewer than a dozen letters each that mentioned the local representative.

Opinion coverage can be enormously informative for citizens.[26] Factual
accounts of how representatives voted on various issues are helpful for citizens who already have well-developed preferences about those issues. Most
citizens, however, do not have firm preferences on a range of issues. Editorialists, columnists, and letter writers can help citizens interpret issues on
which representatives have been voting. They also help to interpret other
kinds of activities — for example, policy leadership and coalition building —
that lack any common metric for evaluating and comparing representatives.
Assuming that it is reasonably balanced, interpretative coverage may be especially helpful, compared with news coverage, since citizens are eventually
asked to evaluate their representatives' continued fitness for office and not
simply to describe what representatives have been doing.

---

[26] Newspaper readers clearly value opinion coverage. In one survey, 78 percent of newspaper
readers said they read editorials; 35 percent did so regularly (Bogart 1984, 714). Another study
of readers' preferences found that they ranked editorials and letters to the editor in the top third
of subjects to which they believed newspapers should give a lot of space (Bogart 1981, 214).

Extensive opinion coverage is usually a signal that a newspaper is meeting the Burglar Alarm Standard for coverage. Frequent and thorough news coverage allows citizens who care deeply about politics and who read newspapers regularly to engage in police-patrol oversight of their representative. If these citizens find a representative doing disagreeable things, they can use the opinion pages to sound the alarm and rally citizens who are not so attentive to politics. Viewed this way, the opinion pages are a link between opinion leaders, who practice police-patrol oversight, and ordinary citizens, who practice burglar-alarm oversight. What is not clear is whether the volume of opinion coverage is an indication of how disagreeable are the things that a representative has done, or whether it reflects the extent to which editors welcome opinion columns and letters to the editor. It is probably some of each, although my sense is that editorial taste matters a great deal. Representatives who are rarely criticized on their editorial pages are surely doing things that annoy some of their constituents. Few constituencies are so homogeneous that a representative can please all the people, all the time.

Heavy coverage on the opinion pages may also strengthen the other accountability mechanism — representatives anticipating citizens' preferences or potential preferences and adjusting their behavior in advance of coverage to make it more acceptable to their constituents. We know that most representatives have staff members who clip items about them from local newspapers so that they can monitor how they are being covered (Cook 1989, 75, 201). We know that most representatives are especially sensitive to criticisms about them. The sensitivity comes with the territory for politicians who, according to Fenno, "see electoral uncertainty where outsiders would fail to unearth a single objective indicator of it" (Fenno 1978, 10–11). We know that most criticisms of representatives appear in editorials, opinion columns, and letters to the editor (table 3.3). It follows, then, that some representatives might behave differently in office depending on whether the opinion pages are relatively open or relatively closed to their critics.

4

Legislators as Position Takers

THE RECORDED VOTE is the single most visible and often the most important indicator of what individual legislators have contributed to congressional decisions. Recorded votes have a special status in American politics; they are constitutionally protected. The Constitution requires that the yeas and nays be recorded at the request of one-fifth of those present. For votes to override presidential vetoes, they must be recorded without exception. As one of the framers, James Wilson, put it: "The people have a right to know what their Agents are doing or have done, and it should not be in the option of the Legislature to conceal their proceedings" (Hunt and Scott 1920, 381).

The recorded vote is a superb way to apportion responsibility for specific congressional actions because each representative must stand up and be counted. Each roll call has only two sides — yea or nay — so a representative cannot be all things to all people. Each absence from a roll-call vote creates an electoral liability, so the prudent legislator seldom prefers abstention to choosing sides. Each representative has exactly one vote, so the powerful, the ambitious, and the eloquent play no greater role than the weak, the lazy, and the inarticulate. Each vote requires all representatives to make decisions on the same proposal, thus creating a standardized way for comparing representatives' decisions. Representatives are compelled to take sides on more than 500 issues each year. Their decisions are recorded for posterity.

The current system requires representatives to take firm positions not only on final passage of most bills but also on many important procedural and substantive amendments that shape these bills. At least in theory, this makes it easier for citizens to hold legislators accountable for specific provisions and programs and for the creation or termination of specific costs or benefits. In practice, however, citizens need to know something about the underlying political conflict. The crucial vote on many bills is often not the final vote on ratification but rather some earlier vote — perhaps a procedural vote that determined whether amendments would be allowed or a vote on a "killer amendment" that would have made the bill unacceptable to a majority of representatives or the president. Most citizens do not know these things unless journalists explain them.

Position Taking

Representatives can take positions on policy proposals at any stage in the legislative process. Only at the final stage, when the roll is called, is position taking compulsory. At earlier stages, representatives can choose to declare their positions firmly, express their views with lots of qualifiers, express sympathy for both sides of an issue, or remain uncommitted. The occasions for position taking are also many. Representatives can declare their positions by making statements on the House floor, speaking before constituents or interest groups, issuing press releases, or responding to questions. Representatives can record their support for a bill by asking that their names be listed as cosponsors. Sometimes when an important bill is pending on the House floor, journalists canvass legislators, asking them how they intend to vote.

Roll-call votes are the most reliable measure of where representatives stand on the important issues of the day, and citizens should prefer them to alternative measures. It is nevertheless useful when journalists report representatives' positions at earlier stages in the legislative process. The reasons are four. First, many bills never reach the House floor. Most representatives never had the opportunity to vote on President Clinton's health care plan. If formal votes were all that journalists reported, citizens would never know if their representative favored or opposed the president's plan. Second, many bills spend a long time in the legislative pipeline. The Brady bill was on the congressional agenda for seven years. Citizens should not have to pass judgment in three consecutive House elections before being able to learn where their representative stands on gun control. Third, some citizens have strong views on particular proposals and want to know how their representative plans to vote. An early indication of how representatives were leaning on NAFTA, for example, gave citizens one last chance to urge their representative to switch sides or stay the course. Finally, it makes sense for journalists to report representatives' positions at the height of a legislative struggle because that is when media attention is greatest and when citizens are more likely to notice their representative's positions. If reporters wait until the game is over to announce the score, they may find that citizens have followed the media's lead and shifted their focus to something else.

Position taking can be an empty exercise (Mayhew 1974). A legislature full of representatives making speeches, sponsoring hopeless bills, and taking positions on everything in sight may never get around to enacting legislation or producing pleasing effects. An effective legislature requires that representatives do more than take positions. On any single piece of legislation, however, the principal role of most representatives is to take positions. A few legislators designed the Brady bill; the rest declared themselves for or against. A few legislators drafted health care reform; the rest took positions.

A few legislators negotiated the details of NAFTA; the rest lined up to support or oppose it. It could hardly be otherwise in an institution of 435 members.

Newspapers provide little public service if they print nothing more than roll-call lists that contain titles of bills and representatives' positions. Bill titles are designed to be appealing, not informative. Most citizens need to be informed whether a bill labeled "tax reform" would eliminate or create loopholes, widen or narrow disparities between rich and poor, decrease or increase tax rates. They also need to know whether they would be worse off under something called reform. Newspapers convey information about the content of bills in various ways, ranging from careful coverage of bills as they move through the legislative labyrinth to focused coverage of bills as representatives approve or reject them.

Citizens profit from factual accounts of lawmaking and position taking. They also profit from more opinionated discussions of the advisability of a representative's positions and votes. Editorials, opinion columns, and letters to the editor can help readers understand the pros and cons of particular positions. Critics deserve a chance to publicize their objections to legislators' positions; representatives deserve a chance to explain why they adopted the positions that they did. It is also instructive to know whether a representative's roll-call votes resurfaced during campaign season. Did journalists revisit particular votes when a representative was running for reelection or were citizens largely on their own in recalling past votes? Did a challenger criticize a representative for particular votes? Did journalists report these criticisms?

Volume of Coverage

Frequent coverage of position taking has a number of desirable consequences. It allows newspapers to report legislators' positions on the full range of issues that come before Congress. It increases the number of messages that careful readers encounter and increases the chances that less careful readers might notice at least some of those messages. Frequent coverage in the news pages also encourages editorialists, columnists, and local opinion leaders to evaluate legislators' positions on the editorial and op-ed pages.

How frequently did newspapers cover representatives taking positions on policy issues? My assistants coded four types of position-taking activities. All four types required that a representative take a position on a formal proposal. Vague statements that "taxes are too high," "the government should learn to live within its means," or "there ought to be a law" did not make the cut; a representative must have taken a position on an actual proposal to reduce taxes, an explicit plan to control spending, or a specific bill. Representatives' positions could be vague or contradictory, but each position had to be connected to a specific policy proposal. The four position-taking activities were (a) voting on an actual roll-call vote, (b) cosponsoring or endorsing a bill, amendment, or motion introduced by another representative, (c) making a commitment to vote a certain way on a proposal that emerged from committee and was pending on the House floor, and (d) expressing views on a bill at an intermediate stage in the legislative process.[1] The first two — roll-call voting and cosponsorship — conform with identifiable activities in the House of Representatives that are publicly recorded. The other two categories differentiate between position taking at early and later stages of the legislative process.

The 25 newspapers as a whole covered representatives' policy positions regularly. As table 4.1 shows, nearly a third of the 8,003 articles reported at least one form of position taking.[2] The median newspaper published 89 articles over the two-year period — about 4 articles per month. The most striking finding in table 4.1 is how much the newspapers differed in their reporting of position taking. Given that each representative voted on more than a thousand roll-call votes during this period, cosponsored at least 140 bills, and staked out positions in many other ways, one might have expected greater similarities in newspaper coverage. Yet the newspapers differed markedly in the frequency with which they covered position taking. The most diligent newspaper, the *Las Vegas Review-Journal*, published ten times more articles about James Bilbray's positions than the least diligent newspaper, the *Boston Globe*, did about Joe Moakley's positions. The top five newspapers published five times as many articles as the bottom five.

Of course, these differences in how newspapers covered position taking partly reflect the overall coverage patterns reported in chapter 3. The *Las Vegas Review-Journal* was second from the top in overall coverage; its generous coverage of position taking is no surprise. The *San Francisco Chronicle* was second from the bottom in overall coverage; its meager coverage of position taking is no surprise. But newspapers also displayed varying tastes for covering position taking even when their overall coverage patterns were similar. The *Boston Globe*, which was near the median in overall coverage, mentioned Joe Moakley's policy positions in only 10 percent of its 255 articles. By comparison, the *Houston Chronicle* mentioned Bill Archer's positions in 56 percent of its 192 articles.

Cosponsoring bills is a big business on Capitol Hill. The rules of the

---

[1] Introducing a bill also involves position taking. This activity is examined in chapter 5.

[2] An article that reported more than one position-taking activity was counted only once. It was assigned to the first appropriate code from the following list: actual roll-call vote, firm position on a pending bill, cosponsored or endorsed a bill, or expressed some views on a bill.

TABLE 4.1
Coverage of Position-Taking Activities

Newspaper	Representative	Cosponsor or Endorse Bill	Express Some Views on Bill	Firm Position on Pending Bill	Actual Position on Roll-Call Vote	Total
Las Vegas	Bilbray	25	45	9	177	256
LA Times	Beilenson	24	38	13	90	165
Tulsa World	Inhofe	15	42	10	95	162
Hartford	Kennelly	20	89	14	22	145
Bloomington	Ewing	21	45	7	44	117
Baton Rouge	Baker	8	32	6	65	111
San Diego	Filner	8	34	14	53	109
Houston	Archer	6	24	1	77	108
Orlando	McCollum	4	37	—	67	108
Cleveland	Stokes	10	55	12	21	98
York Record	Goodling	14	46	4	30	94
Rock Hill	Spratt	11	24	3	55	93
Buffalo News	Quinn	7	18	6	58	89
Louisville	Mazzoli	13	20	4	52	89
Chicago Sun	Lipinski	2	9	7	67	85
Newsday	King	7	33	16	29	85
Wash. Times	Wynn	—	17	3	57	77
Phoenix Gaz.	Kyl	5	20	1	44	70
Idaho Falls	Crapo	2	51	2	13	68
Lewiston	LaRocco	3	30	9	25	67
Norfolk	Pickett	3	29	—	25	57
Tucson Citizen	Kolbe	10	12	5	14	41
SF Chronicle	Dellums	3	24	—	9	36
Boston Globe	Moakley	3	13	3	7	26
Seattle Times	McDermott	5	15	1	5	26
Total		229	802	150	1,201	2,382
Median Representative		7	30	5	44	89

Coding: Cosponsor or Endorse Bill refers to an explicit endorsement or cosponsorship of a bill introduced by another representative. Firm Position on Pending Bill refers to a commitment to vote a certain way on a bill that had emerged from committee and was pending on the House floor. Express Some Views on Bill refers to any other mention of a representative's views on a bill. Actual Position on Roll-Call Vote refers to a vote that has already taken place.

Notes: All counts are from the first data set. Table is rank-ordered by the total number of articles reporting position taking. Each median is the median for a single column of data.

House allow a representative to cosponsor a bill from the moment another representative drops it in the hopper until the day a committee reports it for action. Although the 25 representatives in this study sponsored only 308 bills, an average of 12 bills per representative, they cosponsored 7,519 bills, an average of 301 bills per representative.[3] Ronald Dellums, the top cosponsor, added his name to 553 bills; Larry LaRocco, the least active cosponsor, endorsed 148; the median representative cosponsored 265.[4] Cosponsoring legislation serves two functions. Representatives seek cosponsors for bills that they have introduced in order to generate a sense of momentum. Representatives decide to become cosponsors in order to demonstrate publicly their support for particular causes (Campbell 1982; Thomas and Grofman 1993; Koger 2003).

How did local newspapers cover this incessant cosponsoring of bills? They covered it lightly. The 25 newspapers published a total of 229 articles mentioning cosponsorships; the median newspaper published 7 articles.[5] The range was from the *Washington Times*, which published no articles about the 479 bills cosponsored by Albert Wynn, to the *Las Vegas Review-Journal* which published 25 articles about the 283 bills cosponsored by James Bilbray (table 4.1). If representatives hoped to generate news by endorsing lots of bills, their efforts had a poor return — 7,519 cosponsorships yielded 229 articles. Representatives Dellums and Lipinski cosponsored 1,100 bills; the newspapers in their districts published only 5 articles that mentioned any of these cosponsorships. Apparently journalists do not see a lot of news value in this activity.

Sometimes reporters ask representatives to reveal in advance how they will vote on a bill that has emerged from committee and is pending on the House floor. This type of position taking is voluntary; there is no obligation to take a final position until the roll is called. Journalists sometimes work to create a sense of obligation, however, and especially so for important bills in which the outcome is in doubt. By canvassing representatives to determine how they intend to vote, reporters put a local twist on a dramatic legislative

[3] The data are from Congressional Quarterly's electronic service, Washington Alert. The data on cosponsoring include bills, joint resolutions, House resolutions, and concurrent resolutions; the data on sponsoring include bills and joint resolutions but not House resolutions or concurrent resolutions.

[4] The complete list: Dellums (553), Lipinski (547), Filner (531), Wynn (479), McDermott (405), King (392), Baker (380), Quinn (334), McCollum (324), Ewing (312), Bilbray (283), Kyl (278), Beilenson (265), Stokes (263), Inhofe (259), Mazzoli (233), Kennelly (226), Goodling (223), Crapo (218), Spratt (187), Pickett (175), Archer (170), Kolbe (170), Moakley (164), LaRocco (148).

[5] Newspapers do not always use the word *cosponsor*, and they do not always differentiate properly between sponsorship and cosponsorship (there can be only one sponsor but many cosponsors). My assistants searched for "an explicit endorsement or cosponsorship of a bill introduced by another representative."

struggle. Interest groups sometimes canvass representatives too, creating lists of supporters and opponents, and then sending out press releases or writing letters to the editor reporting representatives' intentions. The aim is to inform citizens of representatives' positions and to give them one last opportunity to lobby their representatives.

Newspapers published 225 articles in which reporters asked representatives to take a position on a pending bill. In only 150 instances, however, did representatives make firm commitments to vote yea or nay.[6] The median newspaper published 5 articles of this type. Journalists were most likely to canvass representatives when votes on major national issues were imminent and when the outcome was still in doubt. Fifty-eight percent of the articles that reported firm commitments focused on a single controversial issue, NAFTA. Twenty percent focused on three other controversial issues: crime control, assault weapons, and the FY94 budget. The rest of the articles were scattered across twenty-eight policy issues, with no single issue accounting for more than 4 articles. In short, although journalists did cover representatives' positions on pending bills, they did so mostly for the biggest and most controversial issues of the day.

In addition to cosponsoring new bills and taking positions on pending bills, representatives can choose to express their views on legislative proposals in myriad ways, ranging from unequivocal opposition to a bill just introduced to support for a bill that is conditional on specific amendments, to the kind of vague statement of support or opposition that strategic politicians have made into an art form. Newspapers published 802 articles in this category of position taking. The median newspaper published 30 articles; the range was from 9 articles in the *Chicago Sun-Times* to 89 in the *Hartford Courant*.

This category was not heavily dominated by controversial national issues. Only 26 percent of the articles mentioned representatives' positions on NAFTA, crime control, the FY94 budget, or health care reform. The rest were scattered across 126 issue categories. Here is where representatives had great freedom to express themselves on subjects of their own choosing. Representatives staked out positions on everything from welfare reform, campaign finance, and troops in Haiti to fishing regulation, insurance redlining, and the Vietnam trade embargo. One would be hard pressed to think of any issue from 1993 and 1994 that did not have at least one representative offering an opinion.

The House of Representatives recorded 1,120 roll-call votes during the

---

[6] In 57 cases they offered views on a pending vote without making a firm commitment; in 18 cases they explicitly declined a reporter's request to comment in advance of the roll being called.

study period — the highest two-year total since Jimmy Carter was president.[7] The 25 representatives voted on 96 percent of these occasions.[8] How did newspapers cover these votes? The overall coverage of roll-call voting was about equal to coverage of all three types of advance position taking — 1,201 articles on roll-call votes, 1,181 articles on advance position taking. The median newspaper published 44 articles that mentioned roll-call votes. The range was from the *Las Vegas Review-Journal*, which published 177 articles about James Bilbray's votes, to the *Seattle Times*, which published 5 articles about Jim McDermott's votes.

The evidence is compelling that newspapers differed more in their taste for covering position taking than representatives differed in their position-taking activities. Each representative voted on approximately the same number of roll-calls; the range was from 1,019 to 1,120 votes. Yet newspapers reported representatives' roll-call votes in dramatically different ways; the range was from 5 to 177 articles. Each representative cosponsored lots of bills; the range was from 148 to 553. Yet the number of bills each representative cosponsored was unrelated to the number of articles that each newspaper published about those cosponsorships.[9]

Informational Context

What kinds of information did newspapers provide when they reported representatives' positions? Did they give readers the kinds of factual background they would need to understand what Congress was doing? Or did they merely print lists of roll-call votes, presuming that citizens already had the contextual information to evaluate representatives' positions? Did they cover representatives' positions on their opinion pages? The differences among news-

---

[7] There were 1,122 recorded House votes during 1993 and 1994, but two of these votes took place during a postelection session when the House considered the General Agreement on Tariffs and Trade (GATT).

[8] The voting participation for the sample was virtually identical to that for the whole House, although the range was considerably less. The range for the sample was from the compulsively diligent Bob Filner (100 percent) to Joe Moakley (91 percent); the range for the entire House included Craig Washington of Texas, who voted on 47 percent of all roll calls. Participation rates are from Congressional Quarterly 1994, 31C–35C; 1995a, 11C–12C, 46C–47C.

[9] The best predictor of the number of articles that mentioned bills that were cosponsored by a local representative (Articles, Cosponsor) is the number of articles that mentioned a representative and any other subject (Articles, Other). The number of bills cosponsored by a representative (Bills, Cosponsored) adds nothing to the explanation. Standard errors in parentheses; adjusted R^2 = .31.

$$\text{Articles, Cosponsor} = .906 + .032 \text{ Articles, Other} - .006 \text{ Bills, Cosponsored}$$
$$(4.97) \quad (.010) \qquad\qquad\qquad (.010)$$

papers were stark. Some newspapers made an effort to educate readers with various levels of political interest and attentiveness. Other papers acted as if their readers were already expert enough to evaluate representatives' positions. They sought to inform only the most interested and attentive citizens.

Newspapers had several ways to present factual accounts of representatives' position taking. The news story was the most common vehicle, accounting for 66 percent of all articles (table 4.2). A second option was to attach a list of where area representatives stood on a particular issue to a story that explained what Congress was doing or had just done about that issue. Typically the news story gave readers the background information for understanding the conflict; the list provided representatives' positions in a format that encouraged comparisons among area legislators. This option was frequently used for roll-call votes, accounting for 13 percent of all articles.[10] It was used rarely for advance position taking; only 7 articles were identified. A third option was to publish a stand-alone list of roll-call votes without any accompanying explanation. This option was also employed frequently for roll-call votes, accounting for 21 percent of the articles. It was used only 4 times for advance position taking.

Representatives' positions were also mentioned frequently on the editorial and op-ed pages. Sixteen percent of the articles on position taking consisted of editorials, opinion columns, and letters to the editor. Editorialists and columnists were just as likely to focus on advance position taking as on actual roll-call votes. Put differently, they were equally happy to advise representatives how to vote or to praise or criticize them for votes already taken. Letters to the editor, which were as numerous as editorials and columns, were much more likely to focus on actual roll-call voting than on advance position taking. Citizens who write letters are less likely than those who write editorials or columns to follow congressional happenings in advance of issue resolution on the House floor. Indeed, most local opinion leaders need to see coverage of what positions a representative has been taking before they are prepared to praise or criticize a representative's policy positions.

The *Los Angeles Times* offered some of the most informative coverage of

---

[10] For technical reasons, it is possible that table 4.2 understates how many roll-call lists some newspapers published, especially for the three newspapers that appear to have published none (*Bloomington Pantagraph, Idaho Falls Post Register, Lewiston Morning Tribune*). If a newspaper published roll-call lists as nonsearchable graphics rather than as searchable tables, they would not appear in the electronic archives. In addition, they might not appear in the archives if a newspaper did not own the electronic rights to roll-call lists because they were assembled by an outside news service that retained those rights. There is some evidence that the problem is real. The *Rock Hill Herald*, responding in an editorial note to a letter complaining that the newspaper never published the voting records of South Carolina's senators and representatives, claimed that it published important votes in each Sunday's paper (*RHH* 2/14/94 9A); I was never able to locate these lists in the electronic archives.

TABLE 4.2
Format for Articles Covering Position Taking

Format for Article	Advance Position Taking	Roll-Call Vote	Total Articles	Percentage of Total Articles
News Item				
News Story	1,008	584	1,592	66
List, Not in News Story	7	151	158	7
List Only, No News Story	4	257	261	11
Total News Items	1,019	992	2,011	84
Opinion Item				
Editorial or Opinion Column	90	86	176	7
Letter to the Editor	48	111	159	7
Representative's Column or Letter	24	12	36	2
Total Opinion Items	162	209	371	16
Total News and Opinion	1,181	1,201	2,382	100

Coding: Advance Position Taking refers to the first three types of position taking in table 4.1. List, Not in News Story is used when a representative is mentioned in a list, but not in the story to which the list is appended. List Only, No News Story is used when a representative is included in a stand-alone list.
Note: All counts are from the first data set.

position taking. It is helpful to begin by describing its coverage patterns and then show how other newspapers differed. The *Times* had a two-tier strategy for covering roll-call votes, one for the major issues of the day, another for lesser but still important issues. When the House of Representatives voted on major legislation, reporters frequently covered both House action and the local connection in a single front-page article. The story itself recounted what was at stake in a policy dispute, how the parties and interest groups were aligned, and what a bill's prospects were in the Senate and the White House. The story was accompanied by a list of how each of 52 representatives from California voted, nicely organized into Democrats in favor, Democrats against, Republicans in favor, and Republicans against. This combination of breaking news and individual roll-call votes was an effective way to give citizens a sense of how their representatives contributed to important outcomes; it occurred when citizens' attention was greatest. On at least fifteen occasions, the *Times* offered its readers the national news and the local connection in a single easy-to-digest dose, including votes on the president's economic plan, the president's first budget, NAFTA, family leave, abortion funding, motor voter, public service work, freezing congressional pay, terminating the space station, terminating the super collider, the Brady bill, assault weapons, and three versions of the crime bill.

The *Times* also developed an effective way for covering roll-call votes on more ordinary issues. Every few weeks it ran a story that featured how area representatives voted on several recent issues. The coverage was distinctive in several respects. First, the *Times* displayed roll-call information in a format that helped readers interpret the arcane happenings of Capitol Hill. For each vote, the editors first offered a brief synopsis of the bill and the legislative situation and then summarized the arguments on each side by quoting from at least one proponent and at least one opponent. Second, the *Times* often selected votes that challenged readers to consider the difficult trade-offs among competing values — trade-offs that representatives face daily. Consider its account of a procedural dispute that actually involved a direct conflict between citizens' expressed preferences for a balanced budget and their natural inclination to help the victims of disasters.

> The House refused to allow a Midwest disaster relief bill to be debated under a rule (H Res 220), adding its $3-billion cost to the national debt. This sent the measure back to the Rules Committee, which sets the terms of floor debate. Democrats, who control the House by a wide margin, rarely suffer defeat of one of their rules. Foes of the rule wanted the opportunity to offer an amendment putting the spending on a pay-as-you-go basis. But Democratic leaders noted that the 1990 Budget Enforcement Act permits deficit spending to cope with natural disasters.
>
> Supporter David R. Obey (D-WI) said: "I think it is almost the height of political arrogance to expect even acts of God to comply with mere congressional rules of procedure."
>
> Opponent Timothy J. Penny (D-MN) said: "This is not simply a question of disaster aid. It is a question of leadership. . . . I am convinced that Americans would applaud our leadership in honestly paying for this disaster relief package."
>
> The vote was 205 for and 216 against. A yes vote supported the Democratic rule for debating disaster aid for the flooded Midwest (*LAT* Valley 8/8/93 B5).

A short synopsis like this allowed readers to make up their own minds on a policy dispute and then evaluate how their representative voted. During the period of this study, the *Times* published about 40 stories containing this type of synopsis, with an average of three roll-call votes per story.

The other innovation in the *Los Angeles Times* was the use of regional editions and regional sections to target the reporting of votes on these issues. Most readers would see information on only a handful of legislators — their own representative and several neighboring representatives. Ordinarily they did not confront huge lists enumerating the positions of all representatives

from California (52) or all representatives from the greater Los Angeles area
(15 to 25). Subscribers in the northern portion of Anthony Beilenson's district, for example, received the Valley Edition, which reported the votes of
Representatives Beilenson, Berman, McKeon, Moorhead, and Waxman;
subscribers in the southern portion received the Home Edition, which reported in its Westside section the votes of Representatives Beilenson, Dixon,
Harman, and Waxman.

How did other newspapers cover position taking? Consider first how newspapers reported representatives' positions on a typical issue. The decision to
appropriate $18.3 billion to close nearly a hundred bankrupt federally in-
sured savings and loan institutions is a useful example. Congress had been
deadlocked on the question for seventeen months, while losses continued to
mount. On September 14, 1993, the House finally approved a bill, 214–
208. The issue was typical in several ways. First, although the issue was
clearly important — the editors at Congressional Quarterly (1994, 39C)
called it one of the sixteen key House votes in 1993 — it was not a big,
controversial issue like NAFTA, crime control, or the FY94 budget that had
dominated the headlines. Journalists had no reason to believe that readers
had already been exposed to extensive coverage of the congressional debate
on this bill. Second, the source of the conflict was not immediately obvious.
Readers needed help in understanding why Congress had been fighting this
battle for nearly two years. Third, the vote was covered by a third of the
newspapers — about average for an important issue that newspapers had not
been covering heavily.

Eight newspapers reported how their representatives voted on the savings
and loan bailout. Three newspapers — the *Las Vegas Review-Journal*, *Los
Angeles Times*, and *Louisville Courier-Journal* — gave readers a sense of the
basic conflict. Five newspapers offered no contextual information at all. The
Washington Times, for example, used the following cryptic account to ac-
company a list of how seven representatives from Maryland and Virginia
voted:

> Failed thrifts bill passes. The House voted 214–208 Tuesday to authorize
> $8 billion for the Resolution Trust Corporation to take over failed thrifts.
> A "yes" vote is a vote in favor of the authorization (WT 9/19/93 A13).[11]

Four other newspapers — the *Houston Chronicle*, *Orlando Sentinel Tribune*,
Phoenix Gazette, and *Tulsa World* — offered summaries that were no longer

---

[11] The summary contained three errors: *authorize* should be *appropriate*; $8 billion should
be $18 billion; *authorization* should be *appropriation*. The article was accompanied by seven
photos of the representatives and a headline, "How Our Representatives Voted," both designed
to attract reader attention. The article wins my prize for the largest ratio of fanfare to content
among the 8,003 articles.

and no more informative than what the *Washington Times* published.[12] It is hard to believe that many citizens — or even many readers of this book — would have the contextual information to know whether a yea or a nay vote on this bill advanced or threatened their interests.

The *Louisville Courier-Journal* offered the most useful account. On the day after the vote it published an Associated Press story that summarized the House debate and presented the arguments pro and con; appended to it was a list of how eight representatives from Kentucky and Southern Indiana voted (*LCJ* 9/15/93 A4). The *Los Angeles Times* offered the same type of coverage it provided for the disaster relief bill (*LAT* Valley 9/24/93 B5). The *Las Vegas Review-Journal* took a similar approach, covering in a single article several recent votes; each vote was accompanied by an informative synopsis (*LVRJ* 9/19/93 B3). All three newspapers gave readers a sense of the conflict over the bailout and summarized the arguments for and against the bill. By the way, the dispute was not whether the government should honor its commitment to bailout federally insured institutions; it was whether other programs should be pared or spared as a consequence.

Policy Conflict

How typical was it for newspapers to give readers a sense of the basic policy conflict when they reported representatives' policy positions? The example just discussed, where three out of eight newspapers explained the conflict about the savings and loan bailout, was actually the norm. Whenever my assistants coded an article as reporting a representative's position, either on an actual roll-call vote or on a bill pending on the House floor, they also coded whether the article explained anything about the policy conflict and, if so, whether it explained both sides of the issue, the representative's side, or the opposite side.[13] Table 4.3 reports the findings for all articles that appeared on the news pages. Only 36 percent of the 1,109 articles explained both sides of the conflict. Fifty-three percent explained nothing about the conflict, 8 percent explained the representative's side, and 3 percent the opposite side.

Many newspapers acted as if their readers already had firm preferences on a wide range of policy issues; all citizens needed to know was how their representative voted in order to pass judgment on the representative's behavior. The *Houston Chronicle*, for example, explained the basic policy conflict on only 17 percent of the occasions in which it reported Bill Archer's votes. The *Chronicle*'s standard practice was to report in the Sunday paper how

---

[12] *HC* 9/19/93 A14; *OST* 9/19/93 A22; *PG* 9/15/93 A2; *TW* 9/19/93 D5.

[13] Whether an article explained the basic policy conflict was not coded for cosponsorships or for expressing views at early stages of the legislative process.

TABLE 4.3
Does the Article Explain the Basic Policy Conflict?

Newspaper	Representative	No	Rep.'s Side Only	Other Side Only	Both Sides Covered	Total Articles	Percentage Both Sides Covered
Las Vegas	Bilbray	36	8	1	106	151	70
SF Chronicle	Dellums	1	—	2	6	9	67
LA Times	Beilenson	23	7	2	64	96	67
Cleveland	Stokes	10	4	1	17	32	53
Norfolk	Pickett	6	—	—	6	12	50
Tucson Citizen	Kolbe	3	4	3	8	18	44
Boston Globe	Moakley	4	—	1	4	9	44
Louisville	Mazzoli	24	5	1	23	53	43
Buffalo News	Quinn	19	6	4	21	50	42
York Record	Goodling	7	8	—	9	24	38
Hartford	Kennelly	11	7	1	10	29	35
San Diego	Filner	26	2	2	15	45	33
Bloomington	Ewing	15	10	—	11	36	31
Idaho Falls	Crapo	5	2	—	3	10	30
Newsday	King	23	2	1	11	37	30
Rock Hill	Spratt	10	5	2	7	24	29
Seattle Times	McDermott	2	1	—	1	4	25
Wash. Times	Wynn	41	3	—	15	59	25
Tulsa World	Inhofe	56	7	5	20	88	23
Lewiston	LaRocco	8	3	—	3	14	21
Phoenix Gaz.	Kyl	22	1	1	5	29	17
Houston	Archer	65	—	—	13	78	17
Orlando	McCollum	54	2	—	11	67	16
Baton Rouge	Baker	55	3	1	8	67	12
Chicago Sun	Lipinski	59	3	2	4	68	6
Total		585	93	30	401	1,109	36
Median Representative		19	3	1	10	36	31

Coding: Does the article that reports position taking explain the basic policy conflict: (*a*) no explanation of policy conflict; (*b*) reveals arguments on representative's side of issue; (*c*) reveals arguments on other side of issue; (*d*) reveals arguments on both sides of issue. Position taking here includes taking a position on an actual roll-call vote or taking a firm position on a bill pending on the floor (not cosponsoring a bill or offering views on a bill at an intermediate stage). Articles here include news stories and lists (not editorials, opinion columns, or letters).

Notes: All counts are from the first data set. Table is rank-ordered by the percentage of articles that explain both sides of a policy conflict. Each median is the median for a single column of data.

senators and representatives voted on several bills during the previous weeks, always under the headline "How Texans Voted." Each bill was accompanied by a one-sentence summary in the following format: "National Service: Approved 275–152 a compromise with the Senate on Clinton's national service program offering college aid to young people in exchange for community service" (HC 8/8/93 A21). Other newspapers that followed this basic model are clumped at the bottom of table 4.3, including the *Baton Rouge Advocate, Chicago Sun-Times, Orlando Sentinel Tribune, Tulsa World,* and *Washington Times.*

How reasonable is the assumption that readers already had firm preferences on the issues decided by Congress and needed nothing more than a representative's recorded position? It is a reasonable assumption for only a scattering of issues. For example, most citizens have relatively firm preferences about abortion. Citizens don't need journalists to review the arguments for and against abortion before they are prepared to pass judgment on whether their representative voted as they would prefer. The assumption may also be reasonable for a handful of issues that the media featured prominently in the weeks prior to a roll-call vote. The vote on NAFTA, for example, was preceded by extensive coverage in the print and electronic media. Many citizens may have formed preferences about NAFTA during this period, so that all they needed to know was how their own representative voted.

Unfortunately, these are the exceptions. Most citizens do not have firm preferences about most issues that come before the House. Most citizens do not follow closely what Congress is doing on a particular policy issue. For example, only 5 percent of respondents in a national poll claimed that they were following closely the passage of the National Service Act, the bill mentioned above that the *Houston Chronicle* summarized in a single sentence.[14] Most citizens cannot read a two-line description of a roll-call vote and know whether they would prefer their representative to vote yea or nay. This is especially true because many roll-call votes are not about the black-and-white issues featured in pollsters' questions. Many issues decided on the House floor are in the messy realm of trade-offs; waiving or enforcing a budgetary rule to pay for disaster assistance is more the norm than restricting abortion.

Newspapers that published cryptic accounts of roll-call votes provided valuable information for their most informed readers — the pundits, politicos, policy wonks, and political scientists who follow congressional happenings. Sometimes the information was also helpful for local opinion leaders who had other sources of information about particular policy decisions. It was their average readers who were repeatedly shortchanged. Why

---

[14] The poll, conducted in September 1993 by the Pew Research Center for the People and the Press, is available at http://www.people-press.org/database.htm.

newspapers chose to report roll-call votes this way is not clear. It was not a question of resources. To be sure, the *Los Angeles Times* was the largest and richest paper in the sample. But the *Las Vegas Review-Journal*, with a single Washington-based reporter, published coverage just as informative as the *Times*. Moreover, most of the papers that reprinted uninformative lists employed multiple Washington reporters. They could easily have done better.

Editorials, opinion columns, and letters to the editor were much more likely to explain something about the policy conflict than news items. Sixty-seven percent of opinion items explained at least one side of the policy conflict on which a representative had taken a position, compared with 47 percent of news items. As one might expect, few opinion items explained both sides of the conflict (6 percent). It is not the obligation of the advocate or the critic to explain both sides, although it is the obligation of the editor to publish opinion items on all sides of an issue. Twenty-seven percent of opinion items explained the representative's side and 34 percent the opposite side. In short, the editorial and op-ed pages were an important source of explanation and evaluation. They also helped to counterbalance the pro-incumbent bias on the news pages, where the representative's side of the conflict was nearly three times more likely to be explained than the opposite side.

Unfortunately, opinion coverage of representatives' position taking was concentrated in a few newspapers. The *Las Vegas Review-Journal*, *Lewiston Morning Tribune*, *Rock Hill Herald*, *San Diego Union-Tribune*, and *Tulsa World* contained 53 percent of the opinion items, with an average of 26 items each. The median newspaper published only 7 opinion items; three newspapers did not publish any. In general, it was the small and midsized newspapers that featured representatives' positions on their opinion pages. Newspapers like the *Los Angeles Times*, which found effective ways to cover position taking for multiple representatives on their news pages, did not develop equally effective ways on their opinion pages. The *Times* published only 7 items about Anthony Beilenson's policy positions on its editorial and op-ed pages. Regional editions and sections allowed for targeting news items, but newspapers did not publish separate opinion pages for different regions.

Did newspapers allow representatives to explain their roll-call votes so that citizens would understand why they voted as they did? Both John Kingdon and Richard Fenno argue that explaining is an important part of a representative's job and, indeed, that the need to devise acceptable explanations sometimes influences a representative's decision on how to vote (Kingdon 1973, 47–54; Fenno 1978, 136–70). Newspapers did not regularly feature representatives' explanations. Only 20 percent of the news stories and 12 percent of the editorials and columns that mentioned roll-call votes included representatives' explanations of their votes.[15]

---

[15] There is a conceptual difference between explaining the basic policy conflict and explaining one's roll-call vote. The former involves summarizing the arguments for or against a partic-

Issue Coverage

Not all issues are equally important. Not all votes are equally consequential. Journalists cannot cover every vote; they must choose what seems most newsworthy. What issues did reporters at the 25 newspapers choose to cover when they reported representatives taking positions? How reasonable do their choices seem given expert assessments about the importance of particular issues or particular roll-call votes? What accounts for journalists' choices?

Six issues dominated coverage of position taking in 1993 and 1994.[16] Together they accounted for more than a third of all coverage. As table 4.4 shows, NAFTA accounted for 10 percent of coverage; the Omnibus Crime Act, 8 percent; comprehensive health care reform, 6 percent; the Omnibus Deficit Reduction Act, 5 percent; the FY94 budget resolution, 5 percent; and the assault weapons bill, 3 percent. Actually, the top six issues could just as easily be counted as four. The assault weapons bill, which was originally approved by the House in May 1994, was later incorporated into the Omnibus Crime Act, approved in August 1994. The Omnibus Deficit Reduction Act, approved by the House in August 1993, essentially implemented the congressional budget resolution for FY94, passed in March 1993.

The rest of table 4.4 shows how 25 newspapers covered position taking for every other issue that was mentioned in 25 or more articles. Economic and budgetary issues dominated the list, including President Clinton's economic stimulus package, disaster assistance spending, defense spending, military base closures, terminating the space station, and terminating the supercollider. Three issues of special concern to labor attracted coverage — striker replacement, unemployment insurance, and family and medical leave. The remaining issues include one foreign policy issue (Haiti), a second gun-

---

ular policy; the latter involves giving reasons for a particular vote. In addition to arguments about good public policy, these reasons can include constituency benefits or pressure from constituents, interest groups, party leaders, or the president. Most articles that gave reasons for a vote also explained something about the policy conflict.

[16] A coding scheme, consisting of 214 issue categories, was designed to classify everything from vaguely described bills that had just been introduced to important bills with proper names (Brady bill, Motor Voter bill, NAFTA). The overall list contained all bills that several experts identified as important, as well as many other bills that the *Congressional Quarterly Weekly Report* covered extensively during 1993 and 1994. The list also contained subfield categories that described most areas of congressional action, such as agricultural policy, banking regulation, defense spending, foreign assistance, maritime regulation, and wilderness preservation. These subfield categories were used when my assistants could not find a specific bill on the list that seemed appropriate. The matching of a position mentioned in an article with an actual bill in Congress was easier and more precise for roll-call votes and for positions on pending bills than it was for position taking at earlier stages in the legislative process.

TABLE 4.4
Coverage of Position Taking for Top Twenty Issues

Issue	Cosponsor or Endorse Bill	Express Some Views on Bill	Firm Position on Pending Bill	Actual Position on Roll-Call Vote	Total
NAFTA (trade agreement)	14	39	87	99	239
Omnibus Crime Act	13	20	9	154	196
Comprehensive Health Care Reform	41	93	—	—	134
Omnibus Deficit Reduction Act	2	23	10	94	129
Budget Resolution FY94	4	30	3	82	119
Assault Weapons Bill	3	3	8	47	61
Abortion Policy (any)	2	5	4	42	53
Immigration Policy	15	22	1	10	48
Haiti Policy (any)	2	33	1	12	48
Military Base Closures	—	46	—	—	46
Gays in the Military	2	24	2	16	44
Brady Bill (handguns)	2	1	1	31	35
Defense Spending	—	13	—	19	32
Terminate Space Station	2	4	2	23	31
Disaster Assistance Spending	1	2	—	26	29
Striker Replacements	—	—	1	27	28
Economic Stimulus Package	—	5	—	22	27
Unemployment Insurance	—	2	1	24	27
Terminate Supercollider	—	2	—	23	25
Family and Medical Leave Act	1	—	1	23	25
Total for Top 20 Issues	104	367	131	774	1,376
All Other Issues (152)	125	435	19	427	1,006
Total for All 172 Issues	229	802	150	1,201	2,382

Coding: Position-taking activities are defined in table 4.1. Abortion policy combines three separate codes. Haiti policy combines two separate codes.

Notes: All counts are from the first data set. Table lists all issue categories that were used to code 25 or more articles on position taking. Table is rank-ordered by the number of articles mentioning representatives' positions on a specific issue.

control bill (Brady), and three issues of social policy—abortion, immigration reform, and gays in the military. Not listed in table 4.4 are 152 issues that appeared in between 1 and 24 articles on position taking; these articles accounted for 42 percent of all coverage.

How closely did local newspapers' coverage of position taking correspond with what experts considered the most important issues on the congressional agenda? The first approach is to compare the results in table 4.4 with David Mayhew's list of important laws for the 103rd Congress, a list that is based on journalists' own assessments of importance. At the end of each legislative session journalists at several major newspapers write stories that identify enactments that the Washington community considered to be important, innovative, and consequential. Mayhew sifted through these stories to identify what contemporary observers believed were the 229 most important laws enacted from 1947 to 1994, including 21 that were considered historically important (Mayhew 1991; 1998). Mayhew's list contains 10 laws that Congress passed in 1993 and 1994; 2 of them were considered historically important.[17]

Local newspapers covered heavily representatives' position taking on three of the ten laws: the two historically important enactments, the North American Free Trade Agreement and the Omnibus Deficit Reduction Act, and the important, but not historically so, Omnibus Crime Act. NAFTA was the only issue in which each of the 25 newspapers published at least one article about a local representative's position. Together they published 239 articles. Twenty-four newspapers published at least one article about position taking on the Omnibus Deficit Reduction Act (129 articles) or its precursor, the FY94 budget resolution (119 articles). Twenty-four newspapers published at least one article about representatives' positions on the Omnibus Crime Act (196 articles) or its precursor, the assault weapons bill (61 articles). Only two of the remaining seven issues on Mayhew's list of important laws appeared in as many as 25 articles: the Brady bill and the Family and Medical Leave Act.

Perhaps the greatest surprise was how little attention local newspapers paid to the Brady bill, the first major gun-control legislation to pass Congress since 1968. First introduced in 1988, its passage was a major defeat for the National Rifle Association. With opinions polarized between gun enthusiasts and gun opponents, one might expect that journalists would spread the word about how local representatives voted, that opinion pages would

---

[17] Mayhew's list of major enactments for 1993 and 1994 is based on the year-end wrap-up articles in the *Boston Globe*, *New York Times*, *Wall Street Journal*, *Washington Post*, and *Time*. Actually, his list contains eleven enactments; one of them, the passage of the GATT Trade Accord, took place outside the study period, during a postelection session designed to shield representatives from electoral pressures (Mayhew 1998).

be filled with praise or scorn, and that candidates would revisit the issue in the 1994 campaign. In fact, only 15 newspapers mentioned position taking on the Brady bill in a total of 35 articles. The Family and Medical Leave Act also had a long and tortuous history. Introduced in 1985, fiercely opposed by business lobbyists, derailed first by a Republican filibuster in 1988 and then by presidential vetoes in 1990 and 1992, it became a top priority of the new Clinton administration and its first legislative victory. Ordinarily, one might expect that partisan and interest group conflict of this magnitude would generate extensive news coverage of representatives' position taking. In fact, only 13 newspapers mentioned representatives' positions in 25 articles.

Newspapers paid even less attention to representatives' position taking on the five remaining laws on Mayhew's list: Motor Voter Act (10 newspapers, 20 articles), California Desert Protection Act (8 papers, 12 articles), Goals 2000 Educate America Act (6 papers, 11 articles), National Service Act (5 papers, 7 articles), and reform of college-student-loan financing (5 papers, 6 articles).[18] These were important laws — certified so by journalists at elite media outlets when they were asked to list the important enactments of the 103rd Congress. Yet when journalists at local newspapers were deciding whether to feature either representatives' advance positions or their roll-call votes, they rarely chose these bills. The California Desert Protection Act was not news even in California. Although the *San Diego Union Tribune* published one news story that briefly mentioned Bob Filner's vote, neither the *Los Angeles Times* nor the *San Francisco Chronicle* mentioned anything about the positions of Anthony Beilenson or Ronald Dellums.

Key Votes

A second approach to evaluating coverage of representatives' position taking is to focus on key votes in the House of Representatives rather than important laws. Since 1945, the editors of the *Congressional Quarterly Weekly Report* have selected a series of key votes in the House of Representatives on major issues. Their intent is to select bills that were controversial in Congress and that would, if enacted, produce important policy changes. The

---

[18] Several cautionary notes: First, if an article reported positions on several issues, my assistants coded what seemed to be the most important issue. Although underreporting of less important issues is a logical consequence of this coding rule, my sense is that the actual underreporting of specific issues was relatively small. Second, the reform of college-student loan financing was part of the Omnibus Deficit Reduction Act, so there was no separate roll-call vote on it. Third, although the 214 issue categories contained a code for any position on higher education or student loans (6 articles), there was no exclusive code for the reform of college-student loan financing.

editors selected 16 key votes in 1993 and another 15 in the ten months prior to the 1994 elections. The issues that they chose offer a sweeping view of congressional activity, including everything from bills that eventually became law, to significant bills or resolutions that died in the House or Senate, to important amendments to budget resolutions or appropriations bills.

Nine of CQ's 31 key votes were related to Mayhew's list of major enactments: the Omnibus Crime Act and its precursor (3 votes), the Omnibus Deficit reduction Act and its precursor (2 votes), NAFTA, the Brady bill, the Family and Medical Leave Act, and the California Desert Protection Act (one vote each). These 6 issues and 9 key votes were mentioned in 541 articles on representatives' roll-call votes. Newspaper coverage of representatives' positions on the remaining 22 keys votes was very light (see table 4.5). Twenty-five newspapers published a total of 197 news and opinion items on these issues — an average of 9 items per issue. The total coverage of representatives' roll-call votes on these 22 issues was less than the coverage for the single most-covered issue — the Omnibus Crime Act and its precursor, the assault weapons bill. The message in table 4.5 is crystal clear: Most newspapers did not provide their readers with much information about representatives' roll-call votes on what experts considered to be the major issues of the day.

Some of the most interesting findings in table 4.5 are the issues that newspapers covered most lightly. Despite a widespread sense that there is something wrong with the way Congress does its business, newspapers showed little interest in covering roll-call votes on bills to reform governmental institutions.[19] The House passed by a narrow margin a bill to overhaul the campaign finance system, with strict limits on overall spending, limits on contributions from Political Action Committees, and federal subsidies to make up some of the difference. It would have been the most important change in campaign finance since 1974. Newspapers hardly noticed. Four newspapers mentioned representatives' votes on this bill — two in news stories and two in stand-alone lists. The House also passed by a narrow margin a bill to prohibit members of Congress from accepting gifts, meals, or entertainment from lobbyists and to require greater public disclosure by lobbyists. Most newspapers ignored the bill. Eight newspapers mentioned representatives' votes — three in news stories and five in lists. Newspapers yawned again when the House fell twelve votes short of the two-thirds majority required to pass the balanced budget amendment to the Constitution. This amendment, thought to be popular, would have required that Congress produce a balanced budget within two years of the amend-

---

[19] Mark Rozell found that journalists rarely covered legislative reorganization plans, ethics codes, or other institutional matters. Apparently, they prefer scandals to preventing scandals (Rozell 1994, 111; 1996, 130).

TABLE 4.5
Coverage of Representatives' Positions on Twenty-two Key Votes

			Vote Appears In		
Bill or Amendment	Date of Key Vote	# of Papers	News Item	Opinion Item	Total Items
Domestic Spending					
End Supercollider	10/19/93	10	22	1	23
Terminate Space Station	6/29/94	11	19	4	23
Economic Stimulus Package	3/18/93	14	14	8	22
Penny/Kasich Budget Package	11/22/93	11	12	1	13
Amend Budget Resolution FY95	4/14/94	7	9	—	9
Thrift Bailout Financing	9/14/93	8	8	—	8
Caps on Entitlement Spending	7/21/94	3	3	—	3
Social Issues					
Prohibit Gays in Military	9/28/93	7	15	1	16
Restrict Abortion Funds	6/30/93	13	15	2	17
Abortion Clinic Access	5/5/94	5	3	2	5
Foreign and Defense Policy					
End Bosnia Arms Embargo	6/9/94	10	12	—	12
Withdraw Troops from Haiti	10/6/94	4	4	—	4
Reduce Aid to Russia	6/17/93	2	2	—	2
Reduce Defense Spending FY95	3/10/94	1	—	1	1
Speed Up Somalia Troop Removal	11/9/93	0	—	—	0
Governmental Reform					
Expand Disclosure by Lobbyists	9/29/94	8	10	—	10
Balanced Budget Amendment	3/17/94	7	8	1	9
Campaign Finance Reform	11/21/93	4	4	—	4
Environmental Policy					
Restrict Endangered Species Act	10/6/93	6	6	1	7
EPA to Cabinet Status	2/2/94	3	5	—	5
Industry Regulation					
Telecommunications Reform	6/28/94	2	2	—	2
Mining Law Revisions	11/18/93	2	2	—	2
Total Coverage		25	175	22	197

Notes: All counts are from the first data set. Thirty-one key House votes were identified by Congressional Quarterly 1994, 36C–45C; 1995, 13C–20C. This table does report coverage patterns for nine key votes on eight issues: NAFTA, Omnibus Crime Act (two votes), Omnibus Deficit Reduction Act, FY94 budget resolution, assault weapons bill, Brady bill, Family and Medical Leave Act, or California Desert Protection Act. Coverage patterns for the first seven issues are reported in table 4.4; the last one is reported in the text.

ment's ratification by the states. Seven newspapers mentioned representatives' votes on this amendment.

None of these governmental reforms became law. The balanced budget amendment fell short of the required two-thirds majorities in both House and Senate. The campaign finance bill and the lobbying disclosure bill were derailed by Senate filibusters. Few citizens, however, would learn from newspapers whether their representatives supported or opposed these measures. Fourteen newspapers ignored all three issues. Only five newspapers wrote news stories mentioning roll-call votes on any of the three measures — the *Baton Rouge Advocate*, *Cleveland Plain Dealer*, *Las Vegas Review-Journal*, *Phoenix Gazette*, and *Rock Hill Herald*. Six newspapers published only lists. Newspaper coverage on all three issues combined was exactly equal to newspaper coverage of representatives' votes on an unsuccessful proposal to terminate NASA's space station. So much for governmental reform.

The other surprise was the relatively light coverage of two votes on abortion and one vote reinstituting the ban on gay soldiers in the military. Both of these were hot issues that many representatives preferred to avoid. Although representatives had to stand up and be counted on all three bills, most newspapers allowed them to stand in the dark. Only seven newspapers published anything about the vote on gays in the military. The *Las Vegas Review-Journal* published four stories about James Bilbray; the *Tulsa World* included six items about James Inhofe; and five other newspapers published six items about their representatives' votes. Newspapers barely noticed the contentious debate and vote on safeguarding access to abortion clinics. Five newspapers published two stories, one list, and two letters. The vote on the 1993 version of the Hyde amendment — the annual vote to restrict abortion funding under the Medicaid program — was better covered, with 13 newspapers publishing 17 items on representatives' votes.

The rest of table 4.5 tells a simple story. Newspapers considered roll-call votes about domestic spending to be more newsworthy than most other issues. They provided modest coverage of votes to terminate the superconducting supercollider, to continue the space station, to approve a scaled-down economic stimulus package, to reject the Penny/Kasich package of spending cuts, to reject further cuts in the FY95 budget, to finance the bailout of savings and loan institutions, and to reject ceilings on entitlement spending. Newspapers avoided most votes concerning defense and foreign policy. They seldom covered votes on cutting defense spending, reducing aid to Russia, requiring immediate troop withdrawals from Haiti, or accelerating troop withdrawals from Somalia (although ten newspapers did provide modest coverage of the vote to end the Bosnia arms embargo). Newspapers were equally reluctant to cover votes on complicated regulatory policies, such as the attempts to rewrite the 1872 Mining Law or the nation's sixty-year-old telecommunications law. Votes on environmental issues, such as restricting the Endangered Species Act or elevating the Environmental Protection Agency, were also sparsely covered.

Explaining Coverage Patterns

Why did local newspapers cover roll-call votes on a few issues so extensively, while virtually ignoring many other issues, including those that journalists later identified as important? Recall from table 4.4 that five issues—the Omnibus Deficit Reduction Act, Omnibus Crime Act, NAFTA, FY94 budget resolution, and assault weapons bill—accounted for 40 percent of what local newspapers published about roll-call voting. If journalists were not responding to the intrinsic importance of issues, what was driving their decisions about what roll-call votes to cover?

The first answer is that local newspapers were more likely to cover a roll-call vote when the national media were already covering the issue extensively. A good measure of issue coverage by the national media is how frequently network evening newscasts aired stories about Congress considering an issue. According to the index for the Vanderbilt Television News Archive, the networks broadcast stories about twenty-one of the issues that were later labeled important by Mayhew or Congressional Quarterly.[20] Focusing on the 279 stories that were aired during the four months before the House voted on each of these twenty-one issues, one discovers that two-thirds of the stories were about congressional consideration of five issues—the Omnibus Deficit Reduction Act (76), Omnibus Crime Act (37), NAFTA (34), FY94 budget resolution (21), and assault weapons bill (16). These are the very same issues that local newspapers featured in their roll-call coverage.[21]

Why did the national news media find these five issues so newsworthy compared with all the other alternatives? All five issues were major priorities for the Clinton administration; all five issues had opponents in Congress who nearly scuttled them. For many reporters, intense conflict between president and Congress, where presidential prestige is on the line and the outcome is in doubt, is the very definition of news. Power, conflict, and suspense regularly beat out mere issue importance. Both the Omnibus Deficit Reduction Act and the assault weapons bill were approved by only two

[20] I searched the printed index for any reference to either Congress and a particular issue or the House of Representatives and that issue for the three months preceding a House vote and for the month during which the vote was held (Vanderbilt Television News Archive, 1992–94).

[21] The other third of the stories focused on 16 issues: withdraw troops from Haiti (21 stories), speed up Somalia troop removal (16), Brady bill (15), FY95 budget resolution (10), restrict abortion funds (9), end Bosnia arms embargo (4), Family and Medical Leave Act (4), end superconducting supercollider (3), prohibit gays in military (3), reduce aid to Russia (2), campaign finance reform (2), abortion clinic access (2), expand disclosure by lobbyists (1), California Desert Protection Act (1), Penny/Kasich budget package (1), thrift bailout financing (1).

votes. Representatives blocked action on the Omnibus Crime Act when it first came to the floor; the House later approved a revised version by a margin of 15 votes. The North American Free Trade Agreement, a carryover from the Bush administration, was opposed by a majority of House Democrats; after furious lobbying by the president, the House approved it by a margin of 34 votes. Only the FY94 budget resolution was approved by a comfortable 60 votes; Republicans opposed it unanimously.

By comparison, the other sixteen issues were relatively tame. The administration prevailed on ten of the twelve issues on which it took a position (it failed to save the superconducting supercollider or stop congressional action on the Bosnian arms embargo). Although the conflicts were reasonably intense for most of these issues, many of the conflicts involved interest groups more than the administration. Resolving the conflicts did not require the kind of knock-down-drag-out fights between president and Congress that place presidential prestige on the line. The debates were also much less suspenseful. The margin of victory for the twelve issues averaged 52 votes.

Reporters like a good fight. The biggest fight during 1993 and 1994 was over President Clinton's effort to enact comprehensive health care reform. The reform bill never made it to the House floor, so the roll was never called, but that didn't stop representatives from staking out positions. Local newspapers published more articles about advance position taking on this bill (134) than on any other bill (table 4.4). Some of this coverage was undoubtedly stimulated by the extensive coverage of health care reform by the national media. The television networks aired 73 stories about Congress and health care reform during the four months prior to the bill's demise in August 1994, second only to network coverage in the months before the vote on the Omnibus Deficit Reduction Act (76 stories).

Coverage by the national media creates additional opportunities for representatives to declare their positions. Reporters are much more likely to ask representatives their views on hot issues than on ordinary issues. Washington correspondents often incorporated information about where local representatives stood on NAFTA, the budget, health care reform, and crime control when they were reporting about the prospects for these proposals. Coverage by the national media also stimulates editorial writers, columnists, and local opinion leaders to offer their opinions about representatives' positions, whether those positions are expressed in formal votes or offered in advance of the roll being called.

Information about how the national media covered what Congress was doing about particular issues allows us to revisit a question posed earlier in the chapter about whether citizens have the informational basis to evaluate representatives' votes, particularly votes that local newspapers featured in stand-alone lists that lacked explanations of the basic policy conflict. My argument was that most citizens are incapable of evaluating a representative's position unless the media features an issue prominently in the weeks prior to a vote or the local newspaper provides contextual information when it publishes a representative's position. We now know that the national media feature only a handful of issues that Congress is considering. Thus, when newspapers publish stand-alone lists of roll-call votes on most other issues, they are providing helpful information for only their most informed readers. The vast majority of readers do not have the informational basis to evaluate these lists.

Opinion polls reinforce the argument that most citizens follow congressional consideration of only a few issues. Each month during 1993 and 1994, the Pew Research Center for the People and the Press asked a sample of citizens whether they were following particular news stories closely. Nine of the 126 news stories that Pew investigated were about Congress debating or passing particular bills. Pew found substantial attentiveness to the handful of stories that the national media had featured, but virtually no awareness of important issues that the media had covered more lightly. Following are the percentage of respondents who claimed they were following particular news stories very closely: passage of NAFTA (39), passage of the Brady bill (37), congressional ban on assault weapons (36), debate in Congress about health care reform (32), debate in Congress over Clinton's budget, asked just after passage of the Omnibus Deficit Reduction Act (30), passage of the crime bill (30), Republican opposition to Clinton's economic stimulus package (27), debate in Congress over Clinton's budget, asked just after passage of the FY94 budget resolution (12), and passage of the National Service Act (5).[22]

Newspaper Readers

Did most newspapers share the sense that crime, NAFTA, health care reform, and the FY94 budget were the important issues of 1993 and 1994? Did most regular newspapers readers have reasonable opportunities to learn where their representatives stood on these four issues? Or did it matter where a reader happened to live and what newspaper happened to serve a reader's locality? As table 4.6 shows, it mattered greatly where one lived. Not every newspaper reported representatives' positions even for these four issues. The *Idaho Falls Post Register* never covered Michael Crapo's positions on the Crime Control Act or the assault weapons bill. The *San Francisco*

---

[22] In addition to these nine stories, two items tracked public attention to the NAFTA debate during earlier periods and two items tracked attention to the debate about the General Agreement on Tariffs and Trade, which the House passed after the 1994 election. The 13 congressional items were ten percent of the news stories that Pew tracked during 1993 and 1994. The complete list is available at http://www.people-press.org/database.htm.

TABLE 4.6
Coverage of Representatives' Positions on Four Major Issues

Newspaper	Representative	Crime	Budget	NAFTA	Health	Other	Total
Las Vegas	Bilbray	19	34	7	16	180	256
LA Times	Beilenson	18	18	14	3	112	165
Tulsa World	Inhofe	11	20	16	7	108	162
Hartford	Kennelly	11	15	23	21	75	145
Bloomington	Ewing	25	10	7	8	67	117
Baton Rouge	Baker	5	7	9	10	80	111
San Diego	Filner	7	7	41	2	52	109
Houston	Archer	8	5	7	10	78	108
Orlando	McCollum	14	6	3	—	85	108
Cleveland	Stokes	12	4	7	6	69	98
York Record	Goodling	9	9	5	8	63	94
Rock Hill	Spratt	15	15	10	8	45	93
Buffalo News	Quinn	21	8	8	2	50	89
Louisville	Mazzoli	7	16	3	5	58	89
Chicago Sun	Lipinski	5	28	13	—	39	85
Newsday	King	12	6	24	—	43	85
Wash. Times	Wynn	9	7	4	—	57	77
Phoenix Gaz.	Kyl	23	4	2	7	34	70
Idaho Falls	Crapo	—	5	3	4	56	68
Lewiston	LaRocco	3	11	12	4	37	67
Norfolk	Pickett	7	9	2	2	37	57
Tucson Citizen	Kolbe	9	2	8	1	21	41
SF Chronicle	Dellums	1	—	4	—	31	36
Boston Globe	Moakley	2	1	4	4	15	26
Seattle Times	McDermott	4	1	3	6	12	26
Total		257	248	239	134	1,504	2,382
Median Representative		9	7	7	4	56	89

Coding: Crime refers to votes on the Omnibus Crime Act as well as the separate assault weapons bill that was later incorporated into the crime act. Budget refers to votes on the Omnibus Deficit Reduction Act as well as its precursor, the FY94 budget resolution. Health refers to comprehensive health care reform.

Notes: All counts are from the first data set. Table is rank-ordered by the total number of articles reporting position taking. Each median is the median for a single column of data.

Chronicle never covered where Ronald Dellums stood on the Omnibus Deficit Reduction Act or the FY94 budget resolution. NAFTA was the only issue in which each and every newspaper published at least one article about a representative's position.

Newspapers that did publish articles about representatives' positions on these issues differed considerably in the frequency with which they did so. The *San Francisco Chronicle* published one article about where Ronald Dellums stood on crime control; the *Bloomington Pantagraph* published 25 articles about Thomas Ewing's position. The *Seattle Times* published one article about Jim McDermott's position on the FY94 budget; the *Las Vegas Review-Journal* published 34 items about James Bilbray's position. The *Phoenix Gazette* published two articles about Jon Kyl's position on NAFTA; the *San Diego Union-Tribune* published 41 items about Bob Filner's position. The *Hartford Courant* published 21 articles about where Barbara Kennelly stood on health care reform; five newspapers published nothing about their representatives' positions.[23]

The differences among newspapers are even more dramatic when one examines the content of the articles. The one mention of where Ronald Dellums stood on crime control was in a list of how area representatives voted, which the *San Francisco Chronicle* published the morning after the House vote. By comparison, the *Bloomington Pantagraph*'s 25 articles that mentioned Thomas Ewing's position spanned thirteen months. Some of the articles, credited to the Associated Press, were day-by-day accounts of the crime bill's tortuous path through Congress, with a few sentences inserted in the middle mentioning where Ewing stood. Other articles, with local bylines, gave Ewing an opportunity to explain why he opposed the bill. These stories then generated editorials and letters commenting on Ewing's votes. Later, as the election approached, Ewing's votes on the crime bill were cited in letters and editorials as another reason to support or oppose his reelection. When the *Pantagraph* endorsed Ewing for reelection, the editors first noted that he "hasn't always voted the way you would expect, but he always seems to have a good reason." They then summarized and praised his reasons for voting against the crime bill, and concluded that "he obviously knows the needs of his Central Illinois district" (*BP* 10/16/94 A8). The *Pantagraph*'s initial coverage of the crime bill did not look very different from its initial coverage of other bills. What differed was that news coverage sparked opinion coverage, and opinion coverage eventually became part of the campaign.

Depending on what newspapers happened to serve their localities, readers were exposed to vastly different flows of information about representatives' policy positions, even for the four most prominent issues of the day. Were these differences among newspapers large enough to affect how much citizens learned about representatives' policy positions? A good case can be made that they were. Advertisers know that repetition is the key to communicating commercial messages. Run an advertisement once and a few con-

---

[23] Health care reform never made it to the House floor for a vote, so it is possible that these five representatives never took a position.

sumers notice; run it dozens of times and more people notice; run it hundreds of times and the masses recognize your slogan. It seems likely that repetition of political messages has similar effects. Repetition increases the chances that occasional readers will encounter a message; it also increases the chances that, once encountered, citizens will process and remember a message.

Scholars have yet to investigate how the richness of the informational environment affects what citizens know about their representatives. The two best studies of what citizens know about their representatives explored how various attributes of citizens — their interest, knowledge, attentiveness, partisanship, and ideology — affected whether they knew how their representative voted on the Persian Gulf War Resolution or the Omnibus Crime Act (Alvarez and Gronke 1996; Wilson and Gronke 2000). Both studies took for granted that the media reported how local representatives voted; the puzzle was to explain why some citizens absorbed the available information and some citizens did not.[24] We now know that the puzzle is more complicated. Some citizens are exposed to a rich array of information about representatives' policy positions; others are exposed to little. The next generation of studies needs to sort out how much the informational environment matters.

Effects on Citizens

Most regular newspaper readers had reasonable opportunities to learn where their representative stood on the crime control bill, since the median newspaper published nine articles that mentioned a representative's position. How much of this information did citizens notice, absorb, and retain? Matthew Wilson and Paul Gronke report that when asked in a national survey in 1994 how their representative voted on the crime bill, 23 percent of respondents answered correctly and 28 percent guessed correctly (Wilson and Gronke 2000). It would seem that it takes substantial repetition in the local media before even a quarter of citizens know where their representative stands on a prominent issue.

Survey researchers have not asked citizens whether they know representatives' positions on less prominent issues. The cases examined most recently — the Persian Gulf Resolution, the Clarence Thomas vote, and crime control — were all covered extensively by the mass media. The evidence in this chapter, however, would not lead one to expect that many citizens

---

[24] On the Persian Gulf War Resolution, Alvarez and Gronke wrote: "Thus, while we do not examine media content or media usage by respondents here, it is not unrealistic to assume that information about the congressional debate was widely available." Later they suggest that "in reality, there was substantial variation . . . across newspapers and television stations in how much coverage they devoted to the vote" (Alvarez and Gronke 1996, 106, 124).

would know their representative's positions on less prominent issues. Only 15 newspapers mentioned position taking on the Brady bill (in 35 articles) and only 13 newspapers mentioned position taking on the Family and Medical Leave Act (in 25 articles). Thus, even regular newspaper readers were unlikely to encounter much information about where their representatives stood on these two important bills. Representatives' positions on most other issues were not even reported in a majority of newspapers (table 4.5). Citizens may still be able to guess correctly where their representatives stand on less prominent issues, using partisan and ideological cues and knowledge of a representative's positions on related issues, but actual knowledge about representatives' positions is probably not plentiful.

Asking citizens to recall votes on specific bills is a very tough test. Local newspapers do not cover most individual votes extensively, so it is hardly surprising that most citizens cannot recall specific votes. Local newspapers do cover extensively representatives taking positions on a wide range of policy issues. Recall that nearly a third of all articles mentioned a representative's position on some policy proposal; the median newspaper published 89 articles of this type (table 4.1). Regular newspaper readers, therefore, had substantial opportunities to learn where their representatives stood on at least some issues. This regular coverage of position taking helps explain why nearly half of all respondents in a national survey answered a question about their "general agreement or disagreement with incumbent's votes," whereas only 18 percent answered a similar question about whether they "agreed or disagreed with a vote on a particular bill" (Jacobson 1997, 111). This coverage also explains why citizens who could not recall a representative's vote on the crime bill were nevertheless reasonably successful in guessing a representative's position. All else equal, guessing correctly may be a good measure of exposure to general information on position taking, whereas recalling correctly is a better measure of exposure to more specific information.

Summary of Empirical Findings

This chapter employed the first data set to analyze how local newspapers cover representatives taking positions on various issues that come before Congress. The principal empirical findings are these.

- Most newspapers cover position taking regularly; nearly a third of all articles report at least one form of position taking. The range is enormous, with the most diligent newspaper publishing ten times as many articles as the least diligent paper.
- Most newspapers cover roll-call voting extensively; half of all articles on position taking feature roll-call votes.

- News stories are the most common vehicle for reporting roll-call votes, although lists, editorials, columns, and letters account for half the coverage.
- Newspapers do not offer frequent coverage of representatives cosponsoring bills. The number of bills that a representative cosponsors is completely unrelated to how local newspapers cover cosponsorships.
- Newspapers rarely publish information about how representatives intend to vote on a bill pending on the House floor. The exceptions are for the biggest and most controversial bills.
- Some newspapers are exemplary in the way they explain the essence of a policy conflict when they report representatives' votes. Many newspapers offer only cryptic accounts that do nothing to advance citizens' understanding of the nature of the conflict.
- When newspapers do explain the basic policy conflict they usually cover both sides of an issue. Editorials, opinion columns, and letters are much more likely than news stories to explain something about the policy conflict. Although individually the opinion items are one-sided, collectively they cover both sides of most issues.
- Newspapers feature a handful of issues when they cover representatives' position taking. The issues on which they focus include only some of the issues that experts consider the most important, innovative, and consequential.
- Local newspapers are most likely to cover position taking when the national media feature those same issues in their coverage. These issues tend to be the ones which involve intense conflict between the president and Congress, where presidential prestige is on the line and where the outcome is in doubt.
- Citizens are exposed to vastly different flows of information about representatives' policy positions depending on where they live and what newspapers happen to serve their localities.

Political Accountability

The good news is that most local newspapers covered representatives' positions on President Clinton's four principal priorities: crime, NAFTA, health care, and the FY94 budget. At least for these issues, most newspapers created the kind of informational environment that allowed for both mechanisms of accountability—legislators anticipating how citizens might judge them and citizens actually judging legislators retrospectively. Since the national media had also been covering these issues extensively, many citizens had some sense of what was at stake. Other citizens would learn about these issues if local opinion leaders were sufficiently unhappy with representatives' positions, that they worked to inform citizens generally. Once informed about representatives' positions, ordinary citizens could, if they wished, reward or punish representatives for their votes. Given the intensity of the battles, representatives were probably aware that local newspapers would cover their positions on these issues, so they took special care when deciding which side to support.

The verdict for accountability is much less satisfactory when one considers many other issues that Congress handled in 1993 and 1994. Congress labored strenuously to resolve contentious issues such as abortion, campaign finance, bank bailouts, defense spending, economic stimulus, education, endangered species, gays in the military, handguns, national service, Russian aid, telecommunications, and voter registration. Each was consequential for the nation and for various special interests. Each involved intense ideological, partisan, and group conflict. No doubt some citizens cared as much — or more — about some of these issues as they did about the big four issues. Unfortunately, most newspapers did not cover where representatives stood on most of these issues.

What are the consequences of this type of neglect? The lack of contemporaneous coverage of representatives' position taking does not suggest that they are somehow free to ignore their constituents' strongest wishes. Interest groups that monitor Washington happenings can always sound the alarm if they notice a representative straying far from what they believe a representative's constituents would allow. Moreover, roll-call votes are permanently recorded, so challengers and interest groups can always resurrect a representative's vote on some issue and use it in a future campaign. Although these mechanisms help to keep representatives from straying too far from citizens' preferences, they don't provide the same powerful incentives for representatives that frequent, contemporaneous coverage of an issue does. The lack of contemporaneous coverage also decreases the chances that local opinion leaders — careful newspaper readers who care passionately about politics or about a particular issue — might notice some questionable vote and sound the alarm in opinion columns, letters to the editor, or in some other way. Although many groups with Washington lobbyists monitor representatives firsthand, local groups profit by having local media outlets report how representatives have been voting on issues that concern them.

The evidence in this chapter suggests that some newspapers meet both the Full News Standard and the Burglar Alarm Standard. They regularly report representatives' positions on a wide range of issues, thus serving to inform opinion leaders. They also make their opinion pages available to those who are critical of representatives' positions, thus helping to inform ordinary citizens about legislators' disagreeable positions. Some newspapers meet the Burglar Alarm Standard, but not the Full News Standard. These newspapers cover position taking on a few major issues, both on their news and opinion pages. But they fail to cover position taking very thoroughly. Some newspapers fail to meet either news standard. They fail to cover a wide range of issues; they fail to provide adequate coverage of even the most contentious issues; they seldom make their opinion pages available to those who disagree with representatives' positions.

5

Legislators as Policy Makers

THE RECORDED VOTE is a superb way to apportion responsibility for specific congressional actions because each representative must stand up and be counted. A legislator either supports or opposes a particular bill; no intermediate position is available. The roll-call vote is not an effective way to apportion responsibility for legislative inaction. When Congress does nothing, it is rarely because a majority of representatives rejected a bill on the House floor. Inaction usually stems from other causes. Perhaps no one introduced a bill; a committee never acted; the Senate objected; a conference committee failed to resolve differences between House and Senate; the president vetoed it; time ran out. Those who wished that Congress had approved comprehensive health reform cannot study roll-call votes to discover if their representative contributed to that failure. Death came earlier in the game and without 435 smoking guns.

The roll-call vote also reveals nothing about who is responsible for earlier phases of lawmaking. Walking to the House floor to vote is easy work compared to drafting a bill, orchestrating hearings, guiding it through committee, and building a political coalition. Although it is important for newspapers to report representatives' positions on roll-call votes and upcoming votes, exclusive focus on position taking gives readers a distorted view of who is responsible for the nation's laws. Responsibility needs to be apportioned between entrepreneurial legislators, who propose, energize, and mobilize, and rank-and-file representatives, who reject or ratify bills. Newspapers should cover all phases of the legislative process, not merely votes of ratification.

This chapter moves beyond representatives as position takers to examine how local newspapers cover lawmaking, constituency service, and casework. Lawmaking refers to the myriad tasks that entrepreneurial legislators perform to transform ideas into laws. These tasks include introducing bills, participating in committee hearings, and building coalitions. Constituency service involves representatives working to acquire benefits for their constituencies. Casework refers to representatives helping individual constituents deal with the federal bureaucracy.

Lawmaking

Most of the action on Capitol Hill takes place in advance of counting the yeas and the nays. A roll-call vote is merely the final step in a bill's long and (often) tortuous journey through the House of Representatives. Someone must decide that a condition is a problem and that the problem deserves a governmental solution. Someone must draft a bill and drop it in the hopper. A committee must hold hearings, deliberate, and act. The Rules Committee must establish the conditions for debate and specify whether amendments may be offered. Party leaders must decide whether and when to schedule a bill for floor consideration. Throughout the legislative process, proponents and opponents work to build supporting and opposing coalitions, both within Congress and among affected interests. All these activities take place in the months and years before the House ratifies or rejects a bill in a final flourish of voting.

How do journalists cover these activities? Previous studies suggest that when newspapers cover Congress as an institution they devote substantial space to legislative activities that precede floor consideration. Stephen Hess's study of news stories that were written by Washington reporters and published in 22 local newspapers found that 3 percent of the stories focused on bill introductions, 57 percent on committee or subcommittee activities, 35 percent on floor debates and roll-call votes, and 5 percent on conference committees (Hess 1981, 104). Charles Tidmarch and John Pitney's study of how ten newspapers covered Congress found that 34 percent of all stories focused on committee activities, 32 percent on legislators' statements about pending proposals, and 12 percent on the role of the president. Only 22 percent focused on floor debates and roll-call votes (Tidmarch and Pitney 1985, 477).

None of these studies examined how local newspapers reported local representatives' participation in legislative activities. Their focus was on Congress. Did local newspapers cover the bills that hometown representatives introduced? Did they cover local representatives' participation in committee hearings and deliberations? Did they report on what local representatives were doing to advance or block particular bills? These are important questions. Citizens need to learn what representatives do to earn their keep besides voting and campaigning. Representatives are more attentive to their duties if they know that journalists and constituents are monitoring what they do in Washington (Hall 1996, 60–65).

The activities examined here require journalists to be active reporters. One of the great virtues of roll-call votes is that they are permanently recorded. Even if journalists fail to cover particular votes, enterprising challengers, interest group leaders, or editorialists can unearth them later in an effort to polish or tarnish representatives' reputations. Most other legislative activities do not leave equally permanent marks. Representatives' efforts to build coalitions, forge compromises, or advance a policy agenda do not leave a trail of evidence that future challengers can follow. These activities need to be recorded contemporaneously by journalists who witness the events or interview the participants; otherwise they are entirely lost to view.

These activities are also more difficult for journalists to cover than roll-call voting because there are no standardized measures for comparing representatives' actions. Each roll-call vote requires that each representative make a decision on the same proposal, so that journalists and citizens can easily compare representatives' positions. Drafting bills, forging compromises, and building coalitions allow each representative to paint on a blank canvas, so that comparing representatives' accomplishments requires one to appraise different actions. Each roll-call vote has exactly two sides, so representatives make stark choices. Introducing bills, participating in committees, and building coalitions are multifaceted endeavors that allow representatives to paint with a full palette of shades and hues. Each absence from a roll-call vote leaves a permanent blot on a legislator's record. Each absence from a committee meeting leaves no similar stain because no one keeps systematic attendance records.

Introducing Bills

A bill is a formal proposal to change governmental policy. Only a member of Congress can introduce one. Presidents, interest groups, and citizens can do no more than suggest that there ought to be a law. Representatives introduce bills for many reasons. Sometimes they seek to change governmental policy, and introducing a bill is merely the first step in a carefully orchestrated campaign. Sometimes they seek to demonstrate their convictions or curry favor with interest groups, and introducing a bill is a symbolic gesture that requires no subsequent steps. During the 103rd Congress, representatives introduced 5,739 bills and joint resolutions, an average of 13.2 per representative.[1] The 25 representatives in the sample introduced 308 bills and joint resolutions, an average of 12.3 per representative.[2]

How extensively did newspapers cover these bills? The 25 newspapers

[1] In this chapter, I treat identically bills and joint resolutions — the latter include proposed constitutional amendments — and refer to them collectively as bills. I do not include House resolutions or concurrent resolutions; the former concern matters internal to the House, the latter are used to express nonbinding congressional sentiments. During the 103rd Congress, representatives introduced 5,310 bills, 429 joint resolutions, 589 House resolutions, and 319 concurrent resolutions (CR 12/20/94 D1275).

[2] Lists of these 288 bills and 20 joint resolutions were obtained from Congressional Quarterly's Washington Alert, an electronic database of congressional happenings. In addition, the 25 representatives introduced 86 House resolutions and 17 concurrent resolutions.

published 405 articles that mentioned bills introduced by local representatives, an average of 16.2 articles per representative. Five percent of the 8,003 articles in the sample mentioned legislators' connections with these bills, compared with 15 percent that mentioned roll-call votes and 15 percent that mentioned advance position taking. As with coverage of position taking, newspapers differed enormously in their volume of coverage. Four newspapers accounted for 50 percent of the articles; five newspapers published 3 or fewer articles; the median newspaper published 9 (see table 5.1).

Why did newspapers differ so dramatically in their coverage of bills introduced by local representatives? Did these differences reflect underlying differences in representatives' behavior? Did representatives who introduced lots of bills attract lots of coverage? Table 5.1 suggests that this was not the case. The distribution of bill introductions by representatives was quite different from the distribution of news coverage of these bills. William Lipinski introduced 20 bills; the *Chicago Sun-Times* published one article that mentioned one of them. James Bilbray introduced eight bills; the *Las Vegas Review-Journal* published 57 articles that mentioned them.

A second possibility is that newspapers concentrated their coverage on bills that started to move through the legislative pipeline. Most bills are referred to a committee and never heard from again. Perhaps journalists waited until committees began to consider bills before they decided which ones were worthy of coverage. Table 5.1 offers no support for this hypothesis. Although House committees convened hearings or markup sessions for 59 of the 308 bills, the representatives who were most successful in having their bills considered in committee were not particularly successful in having their bills covered by local newspapers. Representatives Lipinski, Mazzoli, and McCollum, for example, had 20 of their bills considered in committee — one-third of the bills in table 5.1 that reached this stage; the three newspapers in their districts published only 10 articles on all their bill introductions. A third possibility is that newspapers concentrated their coverage on bills that moved through the entire legislative pipeline. Table 5.1 also offers no support for this hypothesis. The representatives who introduced the 27 bills that the House eventually passed were not particularly successful in attracting news coverage.

What did newspapers write about when they covered bills introduced by local representatives? The four newspapers at the top of the list, which together account for half of all coverage, concentrated on a few consequential bills. The *Seattle Times* published 29 articles about Jim McDermott's bill introductions; 24 of them focused on his proposal to replace President Clinton's health care plan with a universal plan financed by a payroll tax. The *Lewiston Morning Tribune* published 80 articles about Larry LaRocco's bill introductions; 62 of them focused on wilderness preservation and forestry regulation in Idaho and, most notably, on a proposal that would have

TABLE 5.1
Coverage of Bills Introduced by Representatives

Newspaper	Representative	Number of Articles on Bills Introduced by Representative	Number of Bills		
			Introduced by Representative	Some Action in Committee	Passed House
Lewiston	LaRocco	80	26	7	1
Las Vegas	Bilbray	57	8	4	2
Tulsa World	Inhofe	38	1	0	0
Seattle Times	McDermott	29	17	2	0
York Record	Goodling	26	24	1	1
Phoenix Gaz.	Kyl	26	15	0	0
LA Times	Beilenson	24	11	0	0
Rock Hill	Spratt	14	11	5	5
Bloomington	Ewing	13	8	2	1
Buffalo News	Quinn	13	2	0	0
Hartford	Kennelly	11	26	2	1
Houston	Archer	9	16	0	0
Newsday	King	9	6	0	0
Tucson Citizen	Kolbe	9	11	2	1
San Diego	Filner	8	11	1	1
Baton Rouge	Baker	7	12	1	0
Idaho Falls	Crapo	6	4	2	0
Louisville	Mazzoli	6	19	8	3
Norfolk	Pickett	5	5	0	0
Cleveland	Stokes	4	6	2	2
SF Chronicle	Dellums	3	10	4	3
Boston Globe	Moakley	3	11	4	1
Orlando	McCollum	3	21	5	0
Chicago Sun	Lipinski	1	20	7	5
Wash. Times	Wynn	1	7	0	0
Total		405	308	59	27
Median Representative		9	11	2	1

Coding: Number of Bills includes bills and joint resolutions. Some Action in Committee refers to a bill that was introduced by a local representative and that was the subject of a committee or subcommittee hearing or markup session.

Notes: All counts are from the first data set. Table is rank-ordered by the number of articles that mentioned bills introduced by the local representative. Each median is the median for a single column of data.

changed land-use regulations for 4.5 million acres in LaRocco's district.[3] The *Las Vegas Review-Journal* published 57 articles about James Bilbray's bill introductions; 46 of them focused on two bills that were enacted into law relating to Nevada's federal lands.[4] The *Tulsa World* published 38 articles about James Inhofe's bill introductions. Most of them focused on two proposals to reform Congress: a bill that would reduce legislators' pay whenever the government ran a deficit and a resolution that would repeal a secrecy rule that had been in force for more than six decades.[5]

The point is not that these were the most important bills introduced by the 25 representatives during the 103rd Congress. The point is that when newspapers decided to focus on bills introduced by local representatives, they focused on a few consequential bills that were moving through the legislative pipeline. Perhaps importance was reason enough for an initial article; movement then created opportunities for additional articles. After regular readers of the *Seattle Times* learned that Jim McDermott had introduced a bill on health care, they were exposed to arguments comparing McDermott's Canadian-style plan with President Clinton's Rube Goldberg–style plan. Readers could even participate in the debate. The *Times* published 11 letters to the editor commenting on McDermott's bill.[6] Readers could watch McDermott's bill falter in the House Subcommittee on Health, attracting only four of the six votes required for approval, and then watch President Clinton's plan suffer the same fate in the same subcommittee.

Regular readers of the *Lewiston Morning Tribune* were almost certain to learn that Larry LaRocco had introduced an important wilderness bill — 62 articles *is* saturation coverage. Once readers became aware of the bill, they could learn from subsequent articles why LaRocco and other politicians from Idaho disagreed about the merits of the bill, where various interest groups stood, and what each side was doing to promote or block the bill. Readers could watch the House Subcommittee on National Parks, Forests,

---

[3] The proposal was known as the Idaho Wilderness, Sustainable Forests, and Communities Act of 1994 (HR3732).

[4] The Spring Mountains National Recreation Area Act (PL 103-63) and the Red Rock Canyon National Conservation Area Expansion Act (PL 103-450).

[5] Newspapers rarely differentiate between the various classes of legislative proposals. Newspapers regularly write about a representative "introducing legislation," when the introduced item was actually an amendment or a resolution. Newspapers also write about a representative "sponsoring legislation" when the reality was cosponsorship of a bill introduced by someone else. I asked my assistants to code all of these instances as the newspapers presented them. Thus, in table 5.1, "the number of articles on bills introduced" includes both the formal bill and the House resolution that Inhofe introduced (as well as several proposed amendments to spending bills), while "the number of bills introduced" refers only to the one formal bill that he introduced.

[6] Opinion coverage of McDermott's bill was greater than news coverage. The *Seattle Times* published 8 news stories, 5 editorials and opinion columns, and 11 letters to the editor.

and Public Lands approve LaRocco's bill and then watch the bill die farther down the road in cross fire from competing interests. Coverage of the wilderness bill also spilled over into campaign season.[7]

Readers of the *Tulsa World* could watch an exciting David-and-Goliath struggle between their own James Inhofe, a junior member of the minority party, and the most senior titans of the House — the committee chairs and the leaders of the majority party. Inhofe proposed amending House rules to make public the names of all representatives who signed a petition to discharge a bill from a recalcitrant committee. This change was designed to put pressure on representatives who claimed that they favored certain popular issues, such as term limits, the line-item veto, or the balanced budget amendment, while they did nothing to liberate these bills from committees and send them to the floor. Before it was over, readers were exposed to a superb editorial putting forth the philosophic case for deliberative democracy over plebiscitary democracy (*TW* 8/15/93 D8), a wonderful set of letters arguing against the editorial and in favor of the cleansing light of public scrutiny, a press conference that yielded a front-page color photo of Representative Inhofe being blessed by Ross Perot, announcement of a strategic alliance between Inhofe and the *Wall Street Journal* that culminated in the *Journal* publishing the secret list of representatives who had not signed the discharge petition and who were therefore not doing their part to liberate Inhofe's proposal from the obstructionist Rules Committee, and, finally, news of the improbable victory of a determined junior Republican over the powers-that-were.

Newspaper coverage of these three proposals by McDermott, LaRocco, and Inhofe was excellent. Most of the coverage was well designed to inform citizens of what their representatives were doing in Washington, presented arguments for and against the proposed legislation, and treated lawmaking as a complicated process with lots of important steps between introducing a bill and enacting a law. This kind of coverage helps citizens monitor legislators' actions and keeps legislators on their toes. Approximately half the coverage of bills introduced by local representatives was of this general character — multiple articles focusing on individual bills.

The other half of the articles consisted of quick snapshots of bills that representatives introduced on 78 different subjects.[8] These quick snapshots — usually one article per bill — served to advertise representatives' positions on issues that they considered important. Readers of the *Baton Rouge*

---

[7] News coverage of LaRocco's bill was greater than opinion coverage. The *Lewiston Morning Tribune* published 45 news stories, 16 editorials and opinion columns, and 1 letter to the editor.

[8] The breakdown by subject area for the entire sample of 405 articles was wilderness preservation (18 percent), health care reform (8 percent), congressional reform (7 percent), national parks (5 percent), immigration (5 percent), historic areas (4 percent), the income tax (3 percent), and 78 other issues (50 percent).

Advocate could learn that Richard Baker introduced a bill to deny federal Medicaid funds for transporting patients who did not have genuine medical emergencies. According to Baker, the Medicaid program had "become a taxpayer-funded taxi service to grocery stores, convenience stores, and shopping malls" (*BRA* 5/9/94 7B). The House never acted on the bill, so no subsequent articles ever appeared, but by introducing a bill, Representative Baker generated a news story advertising his position against waste, fraud, and abuse. Readers of the *Houston Chronicle* could learn that Bill Archer introduced a bill to reform the Supplemental Security Income program. Accordingly to Archer, the program "gives too much money to aliens, to drug addicts, and to children who have claimed disabilities" (*HCH* 5/13/94 A5). It was a safe proposal for a conservative Republican from Houston's richest district. Once Representative Archer introduced a bill, the *Chronicle* was kind enough to spread the word. Readers of the *York Daily Record* could learn that Bill Goodling introduced a bill to prohibit the United States from granting foreign assistance to any nation "whose voting record in the UN General Assembly doesn't coincide with this country's [voting record] at least one-fourth of the time" (*YDR* 5/18/93 B4). The bill was dead on arrival, but the press release announcing the bill's introduction achieved its intended purpose — generating coverage in the local paper that reiterated Goodling's distaste for countries that accepted American money without voting as they were told.

Many of the bills that representatives introduced had no chance of passage. These bills were still excellent vehicles for representatives to proclaim their principles. Journalists do not ordinarily consider it news when representatives declare their policy positions. When representatives introduce bills, however, they create events for journalists to cover, and events help journalists define what is news. Although introducing a hopeless bill may produce only one local story, there is no limit on how many hopeless bills each representative may introduce. Many of the initial articles on bill introductions appear to have been stimulated by press releases, the evidence being not only the style of the stories but the fact that a story appeared within a day or two of when the bill was introduced. Representative Goodling was the most successful at this game. The *York Daily Record* published 26 articles mentioning Goodling's bills on 19 different subjects. Most of the 28 bills that he introduced received at least one mention.

In short, newspaper coverage of bill introductions appeared in two varieties. Approximately half the coverage followed a few consequential bills as they were considered by Congress. This coverage was potentially valuable in informing citizens of representatives' actions in office and in reminding representatives that they were being watched. The other half of the coverage focused more on position taking — the public enunciation of judgmental statements without any associated actions (Mayhew 1974, 61). Although this coverage allowed citizens to monitor whether representatives were taking pleasing positions, it could not have allowed them to determine whether representatives were working to produce pleasing effects.

The most glaring weakness in the coverage of bill introductions was the absence of coverage of other consequential bills that were moving through Congress. The coverage of several bills introduced by Representatives In-hofe, LaRocco, and McDermott was exceptional and exemplary. It was not matched by similar coverage by other newspapers. The *San Francisco Chronicle, Chicago Sun-Times, Louisville Courier-Journal,* and *Orlando Sentinel Tribune* ignored most of the important bills sponsored by Representatives Dellums, Lipinski, Mazzoli, and McCollum. They denied their readers potentially valuable information about their representatives' actions in office.

Committees

More than a century ago, Woodrow Wilson wrote that "the House sits, not for serious discussion, but to sanction the conclusions of its Committees. . . . Congress in session is Congress on public exhibition, whilst Congress in its committee-rooms is Congress at work" (Wilson [1885] 1981, 69). Committees are no less important today. They are the principal gate keepers for all legislation. Committees decide which bills deserve serious consideration, hold hearings to gather information about those proposals, conduct markup sessions where bills are revised and sometimes packaged with other bills, write reports justifying their decisions, and manage the debate on the House floor. During the 103rd Congress, 22 standing committees and 115 subcommittees met 4,304 times. They selected 10 percent of all bills for floor consideration; the House approved 98 percent of the bills that reached the floor (Ornstein, Mann, and Malbin 1996, 119, 159; Takeda 2000, table 1.1).

How do local newspapers cover these committee activities? The literature cited earlier in this chapter suggests that local newspapers focus heavily on committee actions when they cover Congress as an institution. Recall that 57 percent of the articles in one sample focused on committee activities, as did 34 percent in another sample (Hess 1981, 104; Tidmarch and Pitney 1985, 477). My own findings stand in stark contrast. Most local newspapers devoted very little space to what individual representatives were doing in committees. Less than 3 percent of all newspaper articles mentioned local representatives' participation in committee activities.

Table 5.2 summarizes the coverage of local representatives' participation in committee activities. This table includes every article that mentioned, even in an incidental fashion, a representative's connection to a congressional committee. The third column refers to articles that mentioned a repre-

TABLE 5.2
Coverage of Representatives in Committees

Newspaper	Representative	Participant in Committee Activities				Identified as Committee Member
		Hearing	Markup	Other	Total	
Cleveland	Stokes	5	4	19	28	26
Las Vegas	Bilbray	14	—	8	22	15
Hartford	Kennelly	4	2	16	22	37
York Record	Goodling	4	3	11	18	27
Boston Globe	Moakley	1	—	14	15	51
Lewiston	LaRocco	10	3	1	14	2
SF Chronicle	Dellums	3	—	9	12	40
Baton Rouge	Baker	4	—	7	11	11
San Diego	Filner	2	5	3	10	4
Chicago Sun	Lipinski	—	2	8	10	14
LA Times	Beilenson	4	1	3	8	12
Buffalo News	Quinn	5	—	3	8	19
Louisville	Mazzoli	1	1	4	6	8
Idaho Falls	Crapo	2	—	3	5	7
Houston	Archer	2	1	1	4	20
Orlando	McCollum	2	—	2	4	6
Rock Hill	Spratt	2	—	2	4	12
Norfolk	Pickett	1	—	2	3	6
Wash. Times	Wynn	2	—	1	3	6
Bloomington	Ewing	—	—	2	2	5
Tulsa World	Inhofe	—	1	1	2	8
Tucson Citizen	Kolbe	—	1	1	2	5
Seattle Times	McDermott	—	—	2	2	2
Newsday	King	—	—	1	1	3
Phoenix Gaz.	Kyl	—	—	—	0	2
Total		68	24	124	216	348
Median Representative		2	0	3	6	8

Coding: Participant in Committee Activities refers to any participation by a representative in a committee meeting or committee action. Identified as Committee Member refers to any mention of membership on some committee in which neither the committee nor the member is portrayed as doing anything. All categories are mutually exclusive.

Notes: All counts are from the first data set. Table is rank-ordered by the number of articles that mentioned a representative participating in committee activities. Each median is the median for a single column of data.

sentative's participation in a committee hearing, whether as member, chair, or witness. The fourth column refers to articles in which a representative participated in a committee markup—a decision-making session where a committee revises a proposed bill and prepares it for the House floor. The fifth column refers to articles that showed a representative acting as a committee member outside the committee room. Examples include explaining what a committee is about to do, speaking on the House floor about a committee's recommendations, pressuring an agency under a committee's jurisdiction to make a particular decision, or announcing how a committee is dealing with the latest presidential threat. The sixth column is the sum of the previous three. It represents the total number of articles that portrayed a representative as an active participant in committee activities. The seventh column includes all references that merely identified a representative as a member of some committee without giving any details about what the committee or the representative was doing. These incidental references convey no information beyond simple membership.

The 25 newspapers published 216 articles that portrayed representatives as participants in committee activities. The range was from the *Cleveland Plain Dealer*, which published 28 articles about the committee activities of Louis Stokes, to the *Phoenix Gazette*, which published nothing about those of Jon Kyl. The median newspaper published six articles, or about one article every four months. Newspapers provided the least coverage of the most important committee activities—the markup sessions where committees make actual decisions. Eleven newspapers published a total of 24 articles about markup sessions during the two-year period. Other committee activities were slightly better covered. Eighteen newspapers published 68 articles about committee hearings; 24 newspapers published 124 articles about other kinds of activities. This is extraordinarily light coverage of representatives' participation in committee activities. It is light when compared to what previous scholars found about newspaper coverage of committee activities, but light also when compared to the coverage of other activities such as roll-call voting and introducing bills.

The dearth of coverage in some newspapers is astonishing. Jon Kyl won Arizona's open Senate seat in 1994, easily defeating his House colleague, Sam Coppersmith. Kyl had been serving on three committees—Armed Services, Government Operations, and Ethics—and was ranking minority member on an important defense subcommittee. If voters had wondered how effectively Kyl had been performing his committee work, they were unlikely to find answers in their evening newspaper. The *Phoenix Gazette* never once bothered to report on his committee work, not during the campaign and not during all of 1993 and 1994. In 341 articles mentioning Kyl, the attentive reader would find only two articles that casually mentioned his committee memberships, once in the context of an unrelated grant announcement and once in the context of a local conference (*PG* 2/16/93 A8; 6/4/93 D1).

James Inhofe won Oklahoma's Senate seat in 1994, easily defeating his House colleague, Dave McCurdy. Inhofe's activities on the Armed Services, Public Works, and Merchant Marine Committees generated little news coverage. In 617 articles mentioning Inhofe, the *Tulsa World* reported exactly two committee activities, both related to his efforts to obtain funds from the Public Works Committee for widening an interstate highway near Tulsa (*TW* 1/7/94 N1; 5/20/94 N11). Voters in Arizona and Oklahoma elevated Representatives Kyl and Inhofe to the Senate rather than Representatives Coppersmith and McCurdy. Voters could not have determined from their local newspapers, however, whether Kyl and Inhofe were performers or shirkers of their committee work or how effective they were in committee compared with their opponents.

Newspapers not only ignored Representatives Kyl and Inhofe, they ignored much more senior and powerful representatives. The *Houston Chronicle* published only four articles about the committee activities of Bill Archer, the ranking minority member of the Ways and Means Committee, the committee that handled taxes, NAFTA, and health care. The *Orlando Sentinel Tribune* published only four articles about the committee activities of Bill McCollum, a senior member of both the Banking Committee and the Judiciary Committee, and an important leader in the battle to shape the crime bill. The *Seattle Times* published only two articles about the committee activities of Jim McDermott, a member of both the Ways and Means Committee and the Ethics Committee.

A few newspapers did focus on representatives' committee activities. Perhaps the best coverage was in the *Hartford Courant*, which published 22 articles about Barbara Kennelly's committee activities. The *Courant* portrayed Kennelly as an important member of both the Ways and Means Committee and the Budget Committee and an active participant in committee debates about NAFTA, the budget, health care reform, tax withholding for domestic workers, the superfund reauthorization, and trade with China. The *Cleveland Plain Dealer* provided extensive coverage of Louis Stokes's committee activities, with a total of 28 articles. Stokes was a senior member of the House Appropriations Committee and chair of the subcommittee that managed appropriations for veterans, science, NASA, housing, and urban affairs. Stokes's subcommittee handled many important spending programs; the *Plain Dealer* covered what Stokes was doing on more than a dozen separate issues.

Why did I discover such sparse coverage of representatives' committee activities while previous studies found that local newspapers covered committee activities more heavily? The divergent findings have their origins in sample design, but they also reflect an important truth about how local

newspapers cover Congress. Previous studies focused on how local newspapers covered all aspects of Congress. When journalists cover what is happening on important national issues—the budget, NAFTA, health care reform—they focus on congressional committees because that is where the
action is. Committees are newsworthy because they are the loci of decision
making. They are the objects of repeated coverage because bills spend so
long in residence. Most committee stories are written by Washington reporters because reporting what is happening requires on-the-scene observers
to record actions as they occur. Although Washington reporters often feature
individual representatives in their stories about committee happenings, they
feature those representatives who are doing newsworthy things and who advance the story line. Local representatives appear in these stories only when
they sit on the relevant committees and when they are the ones doing newsworthy things.

The meager coverage of local representatives participating in committee
activities has serious implications for political accountability. What happens
in committees is important. Most newspapers recognize this when they
cover Congress as an institution or when they explain the evolution of particular policies. When newspapers ignore what local representatives are doing in committees, however, they deny citizens crucial information about
whether their representatives are leaders or followers, whether they are performers or shirkers of their committee work, and whether they actually work
to implement the policies they espouse. Most representatives probably notice that what they do in committees—indeed, whether they show up—is
not likely to be featured in local newspapers. As a consequence, they have
little reason to believe that their constituents can monitor their individual
contributions to the design of public policy (Hall 1996, 32–34).

When representatives vote on the floor, they do so in the relative sunshine and with the knowledge that recorded votes can always be used against
them. Each vote is a potential smoking gun, just waiting for some future
challenger to unearth and exploit. When representatives act in committees,
however, their actions are hidden from public scrutiny. To be sure, the
committee doors are open, but without journalists to report what individual
representatives are doing, there is little chance that future challengers will
find evidence of truancy, duplicity, or indolence that they can share with
citizens.

Leadership

Every member of the House can be a leader of something. The committee
system offers the largest array of leadership positions. During the 103rd
Congress, nearly half the Democrats chaired a standing committee or sub-

committee; similar numbers of Republicans served as ranking minority members (Ornstein, Mann, and Malbin 1996, 122). The party system also provides numerous leadership positions, ranging from the two or three representatives at the peak of each party's hierarchy to the scores of whips, deputy whips, assistant whips, and regional whips who work to keep the troops in line. Then there are the special caucuses that legislators organize to coordinate strategy and tactics on issues of common concern. Representatives may join and lead one of the thirty formal caucuses, such as the Arts Caucus, the Black Caucus, or the Textile Caucus, or they may affiliate with one of the sixty or so informal caucuses, such as the Copper, Footwear, or Mushroom Caucuses. If existing caucuses fail to match their legislative interests, legislators may organize new ones.[9] Finally, even the most junior representative can work toward building a coalition for or against a bill, no matter who may have proposed the bill in the first place. Coalition building is a group sport that often involves lots of leaders attempting to attract lots of followers. There is no limit on the number of leaders for any coalition as long as a leader is defined as one who gets others to join the parade.

How do journalists cover these various leadership activities? We tracked representatives' leadership activities with five variables. The first four were whether an article showed a representative as (*a*) the chair or ranking minority member of a standing committee, (*b*) the chair or ranking minority member of a subcommittee, (*c*) a party leader within the House, or (*d*) the leader of some congressional caucus. Since my interest is more in leadership activities than in leadership positions, the coders determined whether the story merely *identified* a representative as holding one of these four leadership positions or whether it showed a representative *acting* as a leader. The fifth variable codes whether a representative was portrayed as working actively to build a coalition for or against a bill. Coalition building is something that leaders of committees, subcommittees, parties, and caucuses can do, but it is also an activity for rank-and-file representatives.

The evidence in table 5.3 suggests that newspapers did not cover leadership activities very extensively. Only 85 of the 8,003 articles — 1 percent — showed representatives acting as committee, subcommittee, party, or caucus leaders.[10] When journalists did mention leadership positions, they treated

---

[9] The list of caucuses suggests how easily groups proliferate. The formal caucuses, called legislative service organizations, included the Auto, Border, Hispanic, Human Rights, Space, Steel, and Travel and Tourism Caucuses. The more informal groups included the Beef, Coal, Competitiveness, Corn, Insurance, Maritime, Military Reform, Mining, Olympic, Rural Health, Social Security, Soybean, Tennessee Valley, and Truck Caucuses. For a complete list, see Congressional Quarterly 1991, 536–37.

[10] The coverage was so light that it raises the question of whether my assistants were too strict in how they employed these variables. Did they require that representatives perform extraordinary acts of leadership in order to make the cut? They did not. I have read half the articles that

them more as titles than as subjects to be explored and explained. Three times as many articles identified representatives as committee, subcommittee, party, or caucus leaders as showed them acting in those capacities. Only 37 of 170 articles that mentioned committee leaders[11] referred to actual leadership activities (22 percent); 28 of 68 articles that mentioned subcommittee leaders referred to specific activities (41 percent); and 12 of 70 articles that mentioned party leaders referred to actual activities (17 percent). Mentioning a leadership position without giving any details may have conveyed the message that a representative was an important person. Without additional information, however, citizens were in no position to judge whether a representative had been using the position to do good, do evil, or do nothing.

Among the 25 representatives were several who held important positions in Congress. Joe Moakley was chair of the powerful Rules Committee, which controls the flow of legislation to the House floor. Although the *Boston Globe* referred to his chairmanship in 66 articles, only 15 of them reported anything about what he was doing as chair. Ronald Dellums was chair of the Armed Services Committee. The *San Francisco Chronicle* referred to his chairmanship in 52 articles; only 12 of them reported what he was doing as chair. Jim McDermott was chair of the Ethics Committee. The only mention in the *Seattle Times* of McDermott and the Ethics Committee was a single sentence at the end of a long story about why McDermott decided not to become President Clinton's AIDS Policy Coordinator (*ST* 5/26/93 B2).[12] It was an incidental mention that only a computer — and my diligent assistants — would notice.

Newspapers provided little coverage of caucus leaders. There were only 18 articles that mentioned caucus leaders — 8 articles showing leadership activities and 10 articles mentioning representatives' affiliations. Most of the articles focused on John Spratt, chair of the Textile Caucus, and Louis Stokes, chair of the health panel of the Congressional Black Caucus (even caucuses have subgroups). The coverage of Spratt portrayed him as an active leader working to protect one of his district's major industries. Spratt

---

were coded as showing representatives performing leadership activities; many of the mentions showed only modest evidence of leadership. I also read a quarter of the articles that mention leadership positions without mentioning leadership activities. These also were appropriately coded.

[11] Eleven of the 170 articles reported that a representative was a committee leader when, in fact, he or she was a subcommittee or party leader. Since it was our practice to code all information as newspapers presented it, these were journalistic errors, not coding errors. The misidentified leaders were Beilenson (1), Kennelly (3), McCollum (1), and Stokes (6).

[12] This inattention was during a year in which the committee, known officially as the Committee on Standards of Official Conduct, handled many newsworthy subjects, including the cases of four recently indicted representatives, Dan Rostenkowski (D-IL), Mel Reynolds (D-IL), Joseph McDade (R-PA), and Walter Tucker (D-CA).

TABLE 5.3
Coverage of Representatives' Leadership Activities

Article Mentions Representative as	Shows Acting as	Identified as	Total
Committee Leader — chair or ranking minority member	37	133	170
Subcommittee Leader — chair or ranking minority member	28	40	68
Party Leader — any type	12	58	70
Caucus Leader — any type	8	10	18
Total Mentions — leadership positions	85	241	326
Coalition Builder — working to build legislative coalition	50	—	50
Total Mentions — leadership activities	135	241	376
Less duplicate mentions	3	9	12
Total Articles	132	232	364
Mentions per Representative	5.3	9.3	14.6

Coding: Shows Acting as refers to a representative doing something to advance a cause or attract the support of others. Identified as refers to any mention of a leadership position in which the representative is not portrayed as doing anything. Coalition Builder refers to a representative who is portrayed as working actively to build a coalition for or against a bill. Duplicate mentions arise when two or more positions or activities are mentioned in the same story. Data on committee leaders and subcommittee leaders are also included in table 5.2 under the appropriate committee activities.

Note: All counts are from the first data set.

was shown campaigning against a trade agreement with Caribbean nations, winning passage of an amendment to strengthen enforcement action against illegal textile imports, and meeting with Mickey Kantor, the U.S. Trade Representative, where Spratt threatened to deliver 35 votes against NAFTA if the GATT agreement was not improved (*RHH* 6/16/94 B6; 4/23/94 B4; 7/11/93 A5). The coverage of Stokes showed much less activity. Stokes was shown insisting that health care reform "must have the imprint of the African-American community" and chairing a series of health-care forums during the Black Caucus's annual legislative weekend (*CPD* 6/24/94 A9; 9/17/94 A8).

None of the representatives in the sample held top-tier positions in either party — Speaker, majority leader, minority leader, majority whip, or minority whip. Three representatives were in the next dozen positions: Barbara Kennelly was one of four chief deputy whips for the Democrats; Bill McCollum was vice chair of the Republican Conference; Jon Kyl was one of six deputy whips for the Republicans. Nine representatives held lesser party positions. Only Barbara Kennelly attracted much coverage. Fifty-two of the 70 articles that identified representatives as party leaders focused on Kennelly; 9 of the 12 articles that discussed the activities of party leaders had Kennelly as their subject.

What made Barbara Kennelly so newsworthy? The nine articles showed Kennelly doing what many other whips were doing—attempting to line up votes for important party initiatives, most notably President Clinton's deficit reduction package and the crime bill. What differed was that she was doing so under the watchful eyes of four Washington-based reporters for the *Hartford Courant*. These reporters not only made her party activities part of their coverage of several bills, they paused to explain what a chief deputy whip does and why the position is important. During the debate on President Clinton's first budget, for example, readers were informed that it was Kennelly's "job as a deputy House whip to line up support for the plan," and later that she was "charged with persuading wavering Democrats to support the package" (*HCO* 3/18/93 A1; 5/28/93 A4). During the debate on the crime bill, readers were told that, as a consequence of her position, Kennelly was "one of the people tagged with the most credit or blame when something wins or loses" (*HCO* 8/22/94 A6). The *Courant's* efforts at civic education continued even into the election campaign. An October story, written by one of the Washington reporters, revisited Kennelly's role in rounding up votes for several controversial bills, pointing out the occasional conflicts between her twin roles as representative and as party leader, but also suggesting how she had used her party position to insist on several legislative provisions that were advantageous to home buyers in her district and to the insurance industry headquartered in Hartford (*HCO* 10/17/94 A3).

The final leadership variable, which coded whether a representative was portrayed as working actively to build a coalition for or against a bill, placed every representative on an equal footing. It requires no formal position to ask other representatives to join a coalition. Table 5.3 shows that newspapers provided little coverage of local representatives' efforts at coalition building. Only 50 articles mentioned these sorts of activities. Nineteen representatives were featured as coalition builders in at least one article; four representatives accounted for half the articles: Inhofe (12), Spratt (7), Kolbe (4), and McCollum (4).

Some of these articles we have seen before. The three articles featuring Barbara Kennelly as coalition builder are part of the collection that featured her as chief deputy whip. Seven of the twelve articles featuring James Inhofe discussed how he was building a coalition to end the secrecy of discharge petitions. The five new articles on Inhofe showed him building coalitions on the balanced budget amendment, the "A to Z" spending plan, and a bill designed to limit liability for manufacturers of small aircraft. One of the articles featuring John Spratt mentioned his leadership on a textile issue; the other six articles displayed his coalition-building efforts on Clinton's deficit reduction plan and on a bill dealing with the Catawba Indian land claim.

The most surprising aspect of these 50 articles on coalition building is that they offer so few details about what representatives were doing to attract support. Jim Kolbe was an outspoken advocate of free trade and an important leader in the efforts to enact NAFTA and GATT. The three articles in the *Tucson Citizen* did little beyond delivering summary judgments: "strong leader in the NAFTA fight," "an influential leader in getting the pact approved," and "achieved national prominence for shepherding the North American Free Trade Agreement through the House of Representatives" (*TC* 11/12/93 D15; 12/31/93 D1; 3/4/94 D1). Yes, but what did Kolbe *do* to achieve influence, especially since he held no formal position as committee or party leader? The other surprise was that newspapers failed to cover issues as continuous stories. Only Inhofe's quest to end the secrecy of discharge petitions achieved continuing coverage. More typical was a one-shot story mentioning that a representative was "working hard to attract support" for some proposal, coverage that simultaneously inaugurated and terminated a newspaper's coverage of coalition building.

Overall Patterns

Table 5.4 summarizes how newspapers covered representatives' participation in various law-making activities — introducing bills, participating in committees, and providing leadership. A few newspapers covered these activities with fair frequency. The top four newspapers published an average of 64 articles that described how local representatives were contributing to policy making. As noted above, many of these were informative articles that gave readers a good sense of what representatives were doing. Often the news stories sparked lively debates on the editorial and op-ed pages about the wisdom of representatives' actions. These four newspapers were far from typical. The next five newspapers averaged 33 articles, many of them less informative than those in the top set. The bottom five newspapers published an average of 9 articles about representatives' lawmaking activities — a mere trace.

The articles in the top set demonstrate that journalists are capable of reporting representatives' lawmaking activities. Moreover, journalists need not work for the largest and richest newspapers in the country to do so. Few people would think first of the *Hartford Courant*, *Las Vegas Review-Journal*, *Lewiston Morning Tribune*, or *Tulsa World* if they were asked where one might find exemplary coverage of local representatives' contributions to lawmaking. Why weren't the *Boston Globe*, *San Francisco Chronicle*, and

TABLE 5.4
Coverage of Representatives' Lawmaking Activities

Newspaper	Representative	Number of Articles on				
		Bills Introduced	Committee Activities	Leadership Activities	Minus Multiples	Total
Lewiston	LaRocco	80	14	1	9	86
Las Vegas	Bilbray	57	22	2	5	76
Tulsa World	Inhofe	38	2	12	1	51
Hartford	Kennelly	11	22	10	1	42
York Record	Goodling	26	18	6	10	40
Cleveland	Stokes	4	28	21	18	35
LA Times	Beilenson	24	8	5	3	34
Seattle Times	McDermott	29	2	1	1	31
Rock Hill	Spratt	14	4	12	3	27
Phoenix Gaz.	Kyl	26	—	—	—	26
Buffalo News	Quinn	13	8	3	1	23
Boston Globe	Moakley	3	15	17	15	20
San Diego	Filner	8	10	2	—	20
Baton Rouge	Baker	7	11	1	2	17
SF Chronicle	Dellums	3	12	12	12	15
Tucson Citizen	Kolbe	9	2	4	—	15
Bloomington	Ewing	13	2	—	—	15
Houston	Archer	9	4	4	3	14
Chicago Sun	Lipinski	1	10	1	—	12
Idaho Falls	Crapo	6	5	1	—	12
Newsday	King	9	1	2	—	12
Louisville	Mazzoli	6	6	5	6	11
Orlando	McCollum	3	4	8	4	11
Norfolk	Pickett	5	3	1	—	9
Wash. Times	Wynn	1	3	1	1	4
Total		405	216	132	95	658
Median Representative		9	6	3	1	20

Coding: Bills Introduced are from table 5.1, Committee Activities from table 5.2, Leadership Activities from table 5.3. The next column includes adjustments for 87 articles that included two activities and 4 articles that included three. The final column shows the total number of articles that had any coverage of bills introduced, committee activities, or leadership activities.

Notes: All counts are from the first data set. Table is rank-ordered by the number of articles that mentioned a representative's lawmaking activities. Each median is the median for a single column of data.

Houston Chronicle also providing exemplary coverage? They had reporters based in Washington. Their reporters had important representatives to cover, including the chair of the Rules Committee, the chair of Armed Services, and the ranking minority member on Ways and Means.

What accounts for how particular newspapers chose to cover lawmaking? It surely helped if newspapers had at least one reporter based in Washington to observe representatives' actions, although the *Lewiston Morning Tribune* earned first place in table 5.4 without a single Washington-based reporter. It surely helped if a newspaper did not need to cover many representatives, although the *Los Angeles Times* did its usual good job despite having the most representatives to cover. Beyond that, however, it was probably a matter of editorial taste. Some editors committed the resources to covering local representatives in action. Others looked for easier stories to cover. Unfortunately, most other subjects are easier to cover than what individual representatives are doing to contribute to lawmaking

When they did cover lawmaking, most reporters were attracted to intense political conflict. James Inhofe confronted the most powerful members in the House over the secrecy rule. Jim McDermott challenged President Clinton with an alternative health care bill. Barbara Kennelly was actively involved in several contentious issues, including NAFTA, health care reform, and the budget. Larry LaRocco proposed a wilderness bill that split his own constituents. Journalists were able to write continuing and interesting stories about these subjects because the conflicts were intense and the outcomes uncertain.

Journalists' taste for political conflict is best illustrated by the way the *Chicago Sun-Times* covered William Lipinski. Chair of the Merchant Marine Subcommittee, Lipinski shepherded through subcommittee, committee, and the House five maritime bills bearing his name and several others that were sponsored by colleagues.[13] Only one other representative obtained House passage for as many as five bills (John Spratt, table 5.1). By any measure, Lipinski was a successful legislator. How did the *Chicago Sun-Times* cover these accomplishments? It completely ignored them. It never once mentioned any of the bills that Lipinski guided through the House nor any of his actions as subcommittee leader. It never once portrayed him as working to build a coalition for any maritime bill.[14]

---

[13] The bills that Lipinski guided through the House included a bill providing a billion-dollar subsidy for the shipping industry (HR2151), a bill guaranteeing reemployment rights to workers who left their jobs to serve on merchant marine ships (HR1109), a bill aimed at preventing the introduction of potentially harmful foreign species, such as zebra mussels, into American waters (HR3360), and several bills authorizing funds for existing maritime programs.

[14] Table 5.4 shows one article about a bill introduced by Lipinski; the bill concerned a local public works project. It also shows ten articles about Lipinski's participation in committee activities. Eight of them concerned his other committee assignment, Public Works and Trans-

The *Chicago Sun-Times* sensed a real story, however, when Representative Leslie Byrne (D-VA) circulated a petition among House Democrats proposing to strip Lipinski and ten other Democrats of their subcommittee chairmanships as punishment for voting against President Clinton's deficit reduction package. Between June 2 and June 14, 1993, the *Times* published eleven articles about Byrne's attempt to discipline wayward Democrats. Unfortunately, the *Sun-Times* never explained why a threat to Lipinski's chairmanship merited eleven articles in less than two weeks, while his status as a productive and well-regarded chair did not merit a single mention in two years. Perhaps the editors thought that some Chicago readers had a special interest in learning what punishments awaited those who broke free of party discipline.

Constituency-Oriented Bills

When newspapers report representatives' law-making activities, do they cover representatives working to enact bills of special concern to their districts or do they cover legislators' efforts to enact broader bills designed to ameliorate national problems? Although both kinds of policies deserve advocates, scholars have argued that the incentives are greater for representatives to champion narrow constituency interests rather than broader national interests (Mayhew 1974, 52–61). The principal attraction of constituency-oriented bills is that representatives face no competition for credit. Broader measures are usually the work of many hands, so citizens face "the overwhelming problem of information costs" in sorting out who deserves a share of credit for enacting them (Mayhew 1974, 59).

Newspapers can either reinforce the incentives toward localism, or they can lower information costs and thereby provide incentives for representatives to enact broader measures. If newspapers focus on bills of local concern, representatives have greater incentives to champion narrowly crafted bills. If newspapers focus on more broadly based legislation, they lower the costs of information, make it easier for citizens to know who is responsible for legislative action, and provide incentives for representatives to champion these types of bills.

We have seen examples of newspapers covering representatives championing both types of policies. Representatives earned the top two positions in

---

portation. Only two articles mentioned maritime bills, one a letter objecting to his vote in committee on a provision concerning the importation of polar bear trophies, the other an article mentioning a dispute between Lipinski and Dan Rostenkowski about shipping fees. Table 5.4 also shows one article about his actions as a coalition leader. That article concerned his effort to build a Chicago-based coalition to block expansion of a local sewage treatment facility.

table 5.4 by championing bills of special concern to their constituents. Larry LaRocco concentrated on wilderness preservation and forestry regulation in Idaho, James Bilbray on issues concerning Nevada's public lands. The next two representatives achieved their positions by championing national legislation. James Inhofe worked to reform secrecy rules in the House, Barbara Kennelly to enact NAFTA, health care reform, and deficit reduction. So, both kinds of policies attracted coverage.

The remaining question concerns the frequency of each type of coverage. My assistants found that 36 percent of the articles concerning lawmaking activities showed representatives working either to acquire geographic benefits for their constituents or to block the imposition of geographic costs. The rest of the articles showed representatives championing interests that were not geographically concentrated. In short, although local newspapers cover lawmaking activities for both constituency oriented and nationally oriented policies, the latter predominate.

Constituency Service

All representatives work to acquire geographic benefits for their constituencies and to protect the existing flow of benefits. It is part of the job. Some legislators choose to concentrate on these things and seek committee assignments that enhance their ability to acquire benefits (Fenno 1973). The Appropriations, Natural Resources, and Public Works and Transportation Committees are popular places for those so inclined. Other representatives rely on staff members to handle most aspects of constituency service. Most representatives are eager to claim credit, no matter how acquired, for whatever benefits flow to their districts (Mayhew 1974).

Congress itself decides how some benefits are allocated geographically. When Congress is in charge, a representative who seeks district benefits must work either to pass a free-standing bill or make sure that a favorable provision is included in a large authorization or appropriations bill. Bureaucratic agencies decide how other benefits are allocated. Representatives often help local governments, firms, and organizations when they seek grants and contracts from federal agencies (Arnold 1979, 1981). When representatives do any of these things, I refer to them as local agents.

Newspapers covered extensively representatives acting as local agents. As table 5.5 shows, 14 percent of the 8,003 articles mentioned something about representatives' connections to constituency benefits. Coverage of representatives as local agents was almost as frequent as coverage of representatives taking positions on roll-call votes (1,117 vs. 1,201 articles). Sixty percent of these articles (677) portrayed representatives as working actively either to acquire geographic benefits or to protect an existing flow of bene-

TABLE 5.5
Coverage of Representatives Acting as Local Agents

Newspaper	Representative	Portrayed as Favoring or Opposing a Proposal	Working to Advance or Block a Proposal	Announcing Success or Failure of a Proposal	Total Articles
Las Vegas	Bilbray	8	74	6	88
Lewiston	LaRocco	9	58	16	83
Idaho Falls	Crapo	27	46	7	80
San Diego	Filner	23	41	13	77
Orlando	McCollum	21	45	5	71
Boston Globe	Moakley	22	43	2	67
Norfolk	Pickett	25	39	3	67
Buffalo News	Quinn	19	23	25	67
Rock Hill	Spratt	7	49	9	65
LA Times	Beilenson	11	41	8	60
Hartford	Kennelly	20	31	8	59
Cleveland	Stokes	7	19	11	37
SF Chronicle	Dellums	7	22	5	34
Tulsa World	Inhofe	20	11	2	33
Bloomington	Ewing	14	13	4	31
Tucson Citizen	Kolbe	6	16	8	30
Louisville	Mazzoli	3	26	—	29
Chicago Sun	Lipinski	7	20	1	28
York Record	Goodling	12	12	4	28
Newsday	King	5	22	—	27
Baton Rouge	Baker	9	11	4	24
Wash. Times	Wynn	5	4	2	11
Phoenix Gaz.	Kyl	4	5	—	9
Seattle Times	McDermott	4	3	—	7
Houston	Archer	2	3	—	5
Total		297	677	143	1,117
Median Representative		9	22	4	34

Coding: Each article portrays a representative as a local agent dealing with a proposal to acquire geographic benefits or block the imposition of geographic costs. Geographic benefits and geographic costs are policy effects that are disproportionately concentrated within a representative's district. The proposal may be a legislative bill or a grant or contract administered by a bureaucratic agency.

Notes: All counts are from the first data set. Table is rank-ordered by the number of articles that mentioned a representative acting as a local agent. Each median is the median for a single column of data.

fits, 27 percent showed representatives favoring or opposing proposals that contained geographic benefits or costs for their districts, and 13 percent showed representatives announcing the success or failure of specific proposals.

The most heavily covered issue was the Department of Defense's campaign to close thirty-five major military installations and ninety-five minor ones. Fourteen percent of the articles in table 5.5 concerned this one issue. Congress decided in 1990 to delegate the task of selecting bases for closure first to the Pentagon, to identify superfluous bases, and then to an independent commission for review and decision. Congress reserved for itself the right to reject, but not modify, the final list.

Representatives had three opportunities to protect their districts when the base closing process began in early 1993. First, they could attempt to influence the Pentagon's listing of bases for closure. Second, they could attempt to convince the Base Closure and Realignment Commission that the bases in their districts deserved to remain open. Third, they could work to mobilize the House to reject the Commission's final list. Twenty percent of the articles appeared during the first phase, when the Pentagon was still compiling its list. The coverage was largely of representatives asserting the value of local bases rather than attempting to influence the Pentagon. Seventy-five percent appeared between the date the Pentagon released its list (March 12) and the date the Commission announced its final decisions (July 1). Only 5 percent appeared during the twelve weeks that Congress was considering whether to reject the decisions recommended by the Commission.

Newspapers concentrated their coverage on the middle phase because that was when local communities felt most vulnerable and looked to their representatives for protection. The articles during this period portrayed representatives as actively involved in defending their local bases. For example, Bill McCollum, who faced the potential loss of both the Orlando Naval Training Center and the Orlando Naval Hospital, which together employed more than ten thousand people, appeared in 25 articles between March 13 and July 1. McCollum's initial indignation, "We are dealing with a Navy that has decided to . . . pick on Orlando with no justification" (*OST* 3/13/93 A7), was gradually replaced by a skilled advocate working to prove that some other facility — *any* facility — should be sacrificed in order to preserve Orlando's base. McCollum organized and chaired a local retention committee, gathered comparative data about other bases, hired an economist to crunch numbers, and eventually built a case for how the Navy would save more money by closing the Great Lakes Naval Training Center because, among other things, the Navy ignored "the much higher operating overhead at Great Lakes, which is driven by its huge heating bill" (*OST* 5/16/93 G1). Although he failed to persuade the Commission to spare Orlando, he earned kudos from the editors at the *Orlando Sentinel Tribune*, who wrote that

McCollum "tirelessly pursued the issue and mounted a heroic effort" (*OST* 6/28/93 A8).

During the same period, the *San Francisco Chronicle* published ten articles about what Ronald Dellums was doing to save four bases in his district that employed more than eighteen thousand people; the *Norfolk Ledger-Star* published 18 articles about Owen Pickett's efforts to preserve Norfolk's Naval Aviation Depot, employing fifteen thousand people; the *Louisville Courier-Journal* published 8 articles about Romano Mazzoli's efforts to save the Louisville Naval Ordnance Station, which the Commission added to the Pentagon's list in mid-May. The coverage in these papers paralleled that in the *Orlando Sentinel*. Dellums, who chaired the Armed Services Committee, first reacted by alleging "fraud" at the Pentagon (*SFC* 3/20/93 A17), but before long he was singing the tune of cost-benefit analysis, highlighting the cost advantages of the Alameda base in his district compared with the base in Everett, Washington, that was slated to remain open (*SFC* 4/28/93 A17). Pickett's first reaction was to call the Pentagon's proposal "short-sighted and a grave potential threat to the fleet's readiness" (*NLS* 3/13/93 A1), but by the time he testified before the Commission he spoke of "defective cost data" in the Pentagon's initial analysis (*NLS* 5/18/93 A10).

Representatives had a common script; newspapers produced a common play. The local economy was under attack by bureaucrats in Washington who failed to understand what was unique about a treasured and irreplaceable military installation. Representatives first expressed the collective indignation of local citizens and then adopted a more lawyerly approach of amassing evidence and preparing their cases for trial. Editorial writers were supportive cheerleaders, both for the local base and for the representative who was working assiduously to save it. When the Commission turned down a representative's appeal it was because of ignorance, politics, or both. Representatives said so; editors confirmed it.[15] Representatives were heroes for battling against unbelievable odds.

The congressional phase was another matter. Building a coalition in Congress to block the Commission's recommended slate was a hopeless cause. It had been designed that way (Arnold 1990, 139–41). Few representatives

---

[15] The script was written in 1988 by Senator Phil Gramm (R-TX) when he first advocated a base closing commission: "The beauty of this proposal is that if you have a military base in your district—God forbid one should be closed in Texas, but it could happen—under this proposal, I have sixty days. So, I come up here and I say, 'God have mercy. Don't close this base in Texas. We can get attacked from the south. The Russians are going to go after our leadership and you know they are going to attack Texas. We need this base.' Then I can go out and lie down in the street and the bulldozers are coming and I have a trusty aide there just as it gets there to drag me out of the way. All the people of Muleshoe, or wherever this base is, will say, 'You know, Phil Gramm got whipped, but it was like the Alamo. He was with us until the last second'" (Deering 1996, 164).

made any public effort to persuade Congress to block the Commission's entire slate. Although the *Orlando Sentinel* mentioned several times that Bill McCollum might file suit against the decision, it was silent on any efforts McCollum might be making to convince Congress to reject it. Ronald Dellums, chair of Armed Services, was statesmanlike in defeat and never mentioned that Congress still had a role to play: "Based on everything that I can determine, the current commission discharged its responsibilities with great sensitivity to local concerns and in a thorough and professional manner" (*SFC* 6/28/93 A1).

The potential loss of a military installation was not the only threat that stimulated coverage of representatives' actions. Coverage was also heavy when a district was threatened with the loss of other types of federal benefits or the imposition of large geographic costs. The *Rock Hill Herald* published more than 40 articles about John Spratt's efforts to keep the Catawba Indians from suing sixty-three thousand landowners in Spratt's district for unlawfully occupying land that was taken from them nearly two centuries ago. The threat was real; the potential harm for Spratt's constituents great. Spratt stage-managed the negotiations and persuaded all parties to accept a settlement just before the deadline set by the tribe. He was a local hero. The *Idaho Falls Post Register* published more than 30 articles about Michael Crapo's attempt to preserve the Integral Fast Reactor at the Idaho National Engineering Laboratory. Although his efforts were not successful, blame was clearly assigned to President Clinton and the Democrats who controlled Congress. The *San Diego Union Tribune* published more than a dozen articles about Bob Filner's successful effort to kill a proposed binational airport on the border between San Diego County and Mexico.

Newspapers were much less likely to publish continuous stories when representatives were working to acquire new benefits for their districts. Although the *San Diego Union Tribune* published a dozen articles about Bob Filner's successful attempt to obtain federal funding for a sewage treatment plant for San Diego, and the *Orlando Sentinel Tribune* published nearly a dozen articles about Bill McCollum's unsuccessful attempt to have the Veterans Administration build a hospital in his district rather than a neighboring one, these were the exceptions. Typically newspapers published only one or two articles about a representative's efforts to acquire this or that constituency benefit.

The real prospect of losing geographic benefits made for a better continuing story than the mere possibility of acquiring new benefits. The prospect of termination gave journalists all the raw materials for compelling narratives. Current beneficiaries were the victims, politicians and bureaucrats in Washington the villains, and local representatives the knights in shining armor doing battle to protect constituents from harm. Risk, drama, and uncertainty kept journalists writing and constituents reading. The possibility of a representative acquiring benefits offered journalists less rich materials. The prospect of a representative bringing home the bacon was good for a story or two, but lacking victims, villains, and drama, there was little to keep these stories going.

Representatives attracted extensive coverage of their activities as local agents in two ways. Some representatives attracted heavy coverage because their districts were under siege. They had no choice but to defend their constituencies against the potential loss of geographic benefits. As previously discussed, Representatives Crapo, Dellums, McCollum, Pickett, and Spratt found themselves in this unfortunate position. Other representatives attracted heavy coverage because being a local agent was a central part of their representational style (Fenno 1978, 101–13). Surely that was the way the *Boston Globe* portrayed Joe Moakley. Despite his chairmanship of the House Rules Committee, which made him one of the most powerful members of Congress, the *Globe* focused more on his efforts to obtain federal funds for Boston than on his role in national affairs. Indeed, comments about his power in Washington were usually in reference to his ability to bring home the bacon. Representatives Filner, LaRocco, and Quinn also had a healthy taste for pork, although newspapers in their districts did not portray them as unidimensionally as the *Globe* portrayed Moakley. Representatives who attracted extensive coverage in this way did so by actively pursuing a wide variety of constituency benefits.

One surprise was that newspapers concentrated far more on what representatives were doing to retain or obtain constituency benefits for their districts than on representatives announcing actual decisions or claiming credit for their success. Despite the fact that representatives regularly issue press releases announcing federal grants, contracts, and appropriations for their districts (Cook 1989, 39), newspapers seldom published anything about these outcomes. The median newspaper published only 4 articles announcing a representative's success or failure in acquiring constituency benefits, compared with 22 articles about representatives' active efforts to serve their constituencies (table 5.5).

Casework

Representatives also help individual citizens deal with the federal bureaucracy. Citizens turn to their representatives for assistance in dealing with myriad problems, including veterans benefits, immigration problems, student loans, agricultural assistance, small business loans, and lost Social Security checks. Representatives employ specialized staff in their Washington and district offices to perform casework, but the work is always performed in the name of the representative.

Although only about 20 percent of citizens report that they have contacted their representative for assistance, most citizens acknowledge that they expect their representative would be helpful if they did seek assistance (Jacobson 1997, 110). How do citizens learn to expect helpfulness from their representative when they have no direct experience? One possibility is that they hear from friends about how a representative helped them. Some evidence supports this surmise. About 20 percent of citizens report hearing about a friend's experience in dealing with his or her representative (Jacobson 1997, 110). A second possibility is that citizens learn about a representative's accessibility and helpfulness from newsletters and other mass mailings that a representative distributes. A third possibility is that the mass media report what a representative has been doing to help individual citizens.

The evidence shows that newspapers do not report much about casework performed by representatives and their staff members. The median newspaper published 5 articles about casework; the range was 0 to 17 articles. Most of the newspapers that did feature casework were from small cities — Bloomington (IL), Norfolk (VA), Rock Hill (SC), and York (PA). In most cities, newspapers were not an important vehicle for transmitting messages about representatives' helpfulness in dealing with the federal government.

Summary of Empirical Findings

This chapter analyzed the first data set to determine how local newspapers cover representatives taking active roles in policy making. The principal conclusions are these.

- Newspapers provide modest coverage of bills that local representatives introduce. The amount of coverage is unrelated to the number of bills a representative introduces and to how far bills advance through the legislative process.
- Newspapers provide even less coverage of representatives participating in committee and subcommittee activities. Although references to committee membership are reasonably common, connections to committee activities are usually lacking.
- Newspapers provide only occasional coverage of representatives acting as leaders, including leading committees or subcommittees or acting as party leaders, caucus leaders, or coalition builders.
- Editorial taste, rather than the actions of representatives, is the better explanation for why some newspapers cover lawmaking more extensively than others. When reporters do cover lawmaking, they are most attracted to intense political conflict.

- Although newspapers sometimes cover representatives working to enact bills of special concern to their districts, they also cover legislators' efforts to enact broader bills designed to ameliorate national problems.
- Newspapers cover extensively representatives acting as local agents — that is, working to acquire or protect constituency benefits. They rarely cover representatives announcing actual decisions or claiming credit for outcomes.
- Representatives are more likely to attract continuing coverage when they are working to protect an existing flow of federal benefits than when they are working to acquire new constituency benefits.
- Although representatives and their staff members devote substantial resources to casework, newspapers rarely report anything about those activities.
- Newspapers are far more likely to report representatives working to acquire or protect constituency benefits than to report their active participation in lawmaking.

Political Accountability

Local newspapers published extensive information about representatives' actions as policy makers. Twenty-one percent of the 8,003 articles portrayed representatives as participating in one or more of the policy-making activities featured in this chapter.[16] The information published, however, was highly skewed. Newspapers emphasized some policy-making activities and largely ignored others. Newspapers were far more diligent in reporting a representative's actions as a local agent, where the median newspaper published 34 articles about a representative's attempts to attract or retain constituency benefits, than they were in reporting leadership or committee activities.

Senator John Culver (D-IA), who had a superb reputation in Congress for legislative leadership, once complained about the media: "They only focus on the things that make news. Leadership doesn't make news" (Fenno 1996, 130). The evidence in this chapter strongly supports his claim. The median newspaper published only three articles over the two-year period about what a local representative was doing as a committee, subcommittee, party, caucus, or coalition leader (table 5.4).

Committees are the very heart of the legislative process. Most of the suspense about what Congress will do each year centers on committees, which approve 10 percent of the bills that are introduced, rather than on the

---

[16] Articles reporting multiple activities are counted only once. This count excludes articles that merely identified a representative as a committee member or as a committee, subcommittee, party, or caucus leader (see tables 5.2 and 5.3).

whole House, which approves 98 percent of the bills that reach the floor. Unfortunately, committees do not play an equally prominent role when local newspapers write about local representatives. The median newspaper published only six articles over the two-year period about representatives' participation in committee activities (table 5.2).

Although most of the action on Capitol Hill takes place in advance of counting the yeas and the nays, and most newspaper coverage of Congress as an institution reflects the importance of prefloor activity, newspapers reversed the emphasis when they covered how local representatives participated in lawmaking. Most newspapers covered representatives' participation in the final flourish of voting more heavily than they covered the months of prefloor activities. To put these findings in perspective, the typical newspaper published nine articles about all of a representative's leadership and committee activities over a two-year period and nine articles about a representative's position on a single bill—crime control (table 4.6).

The implications of these findings for political accountability are two. First, citizens are far more likely to see their representative as a position taker and a local agent than as a legislative leader or craftsman. Citizens are far more likely to know their representative's position on crime control than they are to know whether their representative is a leader or a follower, a heavyweight or a lightweight, a credit or an embarrassment to the district. Second, representatives are far more likely to be concerned with their records as position takers and local agents—things that are done in the relative sunshine—than with their records in the darkened committee rooms or the corridors of Congress.

These generalizations do not apply universally. Some newspapers came close to meeting the Full News Standard. They painted rich portraits of what representatives were doing in Congress. The *Hartford Courant*, *Las Vegas Review-Journal*, *Lewiston Morning Tribune*, *Los Angeles Times*, and *Tulsa World* published frequent and informative articles about representatives' lawmaking activities. Citizens in those communities had ample opportunities to learn what their representative was doing across the entire range of legislative activities. Representatives from those communities knew that their lawmaking activities were becoming part of the public record.

Most newspapers do not even come close to meeting the Full News Standard. They largely ignore what, if anything, representatives are doing to advance causes they espouse. By failing to meet the Full News Standard, they also fail to meet the Burglar Alarm Standard. Since local opinion leaders have no real alternatives to learn about representatives' lawmaking activities, if local newspapers fail to provide information about those activities, opinion leaders are unable to monitor what representatives are doing other than voting and campaigning. Thus, they are unable to spread the word when representatives neglect to work for things they claim to favor.

Three decades ago, David Mayhew argued that although the electoral connection encourages representatives to emphasize position taking and constituency service, it provides few incentives for representatives to become leaders within Congress (Mayhew 1974, 115–21). The problem is that it is very difficult for representatives to gain credit for leadership activities unless someone is watching them closely. Interest groups have the potential to monitor representatives' leadership activities, and even to provide selective incentives in the form of campaign contributions. The incidence of interest groups doing these things is not known. Local newspapers also have the potential to monitor leadership activities and to provide coverage that enhances a representative's reputation at home. The incidence of local newspapers doing this is now known to be highly variable, but centered around a relatively low mean. In short, most local newspapers do not provide most representatives with incentives that encourage them to do the heavy lifting required in lawmaking.

6

Legislators as Candidates

How do newspapers cover representatives running for reelection? Do they focus on representatives' past performance or their promises about the future? Do they review what representatives have been doing in office — their leadership activities, votes, and accomplishments — or do they assume that citizens need no prompting before deciding whether representatives deserve reelection? Are issues that were resolved a year or more ago, such as NAFTA and gays in the military, featured as prominently as issues of more recent vintage, such as crime control and health care reform? Do newspapers publish more frequent or more positive coverage of incumbents than of challengers? This chapter explores these and other questions about how newspapers cover representatives as candidates.

Most representatives start running for reelection within days of their election to Congress. With two-year terms, they have no time to spare. As a consequence, no sharp line exists between periods when representatives are legislating and periods when they are campaigning. There is also no sharp divide between coverage of representatives as lawmakers and coverage of them as candidates. Still, there is a difference between a representative meeting with constituents who are unhappy with her position on the upcoming NAFTA vote in autumn 1993 and publicly debating an opponent about the wisdom of her actual vote a year later. The former is principally about policy making, the latter about campaigning. This chapter examines articles that focused specifically on the 1994 primary and general election campaigns. It does not examine articles that were largely about policy making, even if they were published in the fall of 1994. These articles have been examined in previous chapters.

Representatives differed in the electoral challenges they experienced. Some representatives in the sample faced talented, well-financed challengers. Others were entrenched incumbents who seemed immune to serious challenge. No matter where citizens happened to live, however, they deserved to find information in their local newspapers about both incumbents and challengers. Editors and reporters who assumed that representatives battling for their political lives deserved copious coverage while other incumbents and their opponents deserved minimal coverage denied some citizens the opportunity to make informed decisions. By their actions, they contributed to the safety of incumbents.

Two representatives, James Inhofe and Jon Kyl, ran for the Senate. My assistants coded information about the Senate races, not about the contests to fill their House seats. Romano Mazzoli retired from Congress after twenty-four years in office. No information was collected about the race to succeed him. Eight representatives faced challengers in both the primary and general election. Information was collected about the races at both stages. Ten representatives ran unopposed in the primaries but had challengers in the general election. One representative, Richard Baker, won the open primary in his district by a simple majority, thus avoiding a general election. Three Republicans ran unopposed at both stages: Bill Archer, Bill Goodling, and Bill McCollum.

Voters defeated two representatives in the general election: James Bilbray attracted only 48 percent of voters and Larry LaRocco 45 percent. Three representatives had very close calls. William Lipinski was reelected with 54 percent of the vote, John Spratt with 52 percent, and Anthony Beilenson with 49 percent (in a three-person race). Three other incumbents won with less than 60 percent of the vote: Filner (57), King (59), and Pickett (59). Both candidates for the Senate were elected—James Inhofe with 55 percent, Jon Kyl with 54 percent. The eleven other representatives were renominated with more than 70 percent of the vote and reelected with more than 60 percent.

Volume of Coverage

How frequently did newspapers publish articles about the various campaigns? Approximately one-sixth of the articles in the 24 newspapers were about the 1994 House and Senate campaigns (1,202 of 7,739 articles).[1] As figure 6.1 shows, campaign coverage began in the early months of 1993, usually with speculation about who might challenge a representative. Campaign coverage gradually increased in early 1994, as primary season began, and it reached a crescendo in the ten weeks before election day. In contrast, noncampaign coverage was nearly constant across the 22.3 months of the study.[2]

Table 6.1 displays the differences in campaign coverage across the 24

[1] The alert reader may notice that table 3.2 identifies an additional 380 articles in which a representative's principal role was as a candidate in an electoral contest. The broader category includes articles about various 1992 House races and about the 1994 House races to succeed Representatives Inhofe, Kyl, and Mazzoli, as well as articles about one representative, Bob Filner, who resigned from the city council in San Diego to serve in Congress, and about several representatives who were considering running for other offices, including Barbara Kennelly for governor.

[2] Figure 6.1 disaggregates the monthly coverage data in figure 2.1 according to an article's connection to the 1994 campaign. Figure 2.1 includes coverage of Mazzoli; figure 6.1 excludes it.

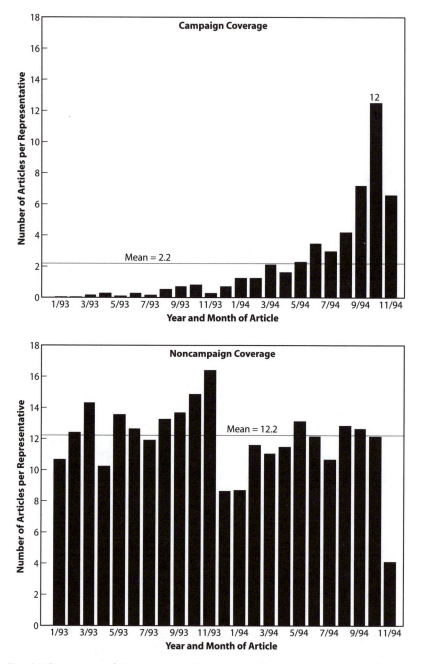

Fig. 6.1 Campaign and Noncampaign Coverage by Month. Figures are from the first data set (24 newspapers, 7,739 articles, 22.3 months). Campaign coverage includes 1,202 articles; noncampaign coverage, 6,537 articles.

TABLE 6.1
Campaign Coverage of Representatives

Newspaper	Representative	About Own Party's Primary	About Other Party's Primary	About General Election	Total Campaign Articles	Campaign Articles as Percentage of All Articles
		Running for the Senate				
Tulsa World	Inhofe	38	2	114	154	25
Phoenix Gaz.	Kyl	20	21	98	139	41
		Running for Reelection				
Rock Hill	Spratt	1	3	142	146	34
Lewiston	LaRocco	3	31	98	132	34
LA Times	Beilenson	4	30	90	124	31
Buffalo News	Quinn	—	40	39	79	19
Las Vegas	Bilbray	5	7	61	73	12
Bloomington	Ewing	1	10	55	66	20
Norfolk	Pickett	—	9	31	40	14
Boston Globe	Moakley	4	10	19	33	13
San Diego	Filner	—	1	32	33	8
Tucson Citizen	Kolbe	8	3	18	29	18
Hartford	Kennelly	—	—	28	28	7
Idaho Falls	Crapo	—	1	21	22	10
Baton Rouge	Baker	18	—	2	20	6
Cleveland	Stokes	5	—	13	18	4
Chicago Sun	Lipinski	—	—	16	16	7
Newsday	King	5	—	8	13	7
Seattle Times	McDermott	3	—	3	6	4
SF Chronicle	Dellums	—	—	4	4	3
Wash. Times	Wynn	1	—	2	3	2
		Running Unopposed				
Orlando	McCollum	—	1	9	10	3
York Record	Goodling	1	2	5	8	2
Houston	Archer	4	—	2	6	3
Total		121	171	910	1,202	15
Median Representative		2	2	20	29	9

Notes: All counts are from the first data set. Romano Mazzoli did not run for reelection. Richard Baker won a majority in the open primary on 10/1/94, thus avoiding a general election. Table segments are rank-ordered by the number of campaign articles. Each median is the median for a single column of data.

newspapers. Both Senate races were heavily covered. Each race included a pair of experienced, well-financed candidates sacrificing their House careers for a chance to serve in the Senate. The *Tulsa World* published 154 articles about James Inhofe's race against Representative Dave McCurdy. The *Phoenix Gazette* published 139 articles about Jon Kyl's race against Representative Sam Coppersmith. Campaign coverage in the *Gazette* was surprisingly large. It constituted more than 40 percent of all articles about Kyl over the two-year period.

Three House races attracted about the same volume of coverage as the two Senate races. The *Los Angeles Times* published 124 articles about the race between Anthony Beilenson and Rich Sybert. The challenger spent $1.7 million on the race — nearly three times as much as Beilenson — and nearly toppled him. The *Lewiston Morning Tribune* published 132 articles about the race between Larry LaRocco and Helen Chenoweth. Each candidate spent about $800,000 on the race; the challenger won, 55 to 45. The *Rock Hill Herald* published 146 articles about the race between John Spratt and Larry Bingham. Although the challenger spent only $200,000 on this race — one-third of Spratt's war chest — Bingham reduced Spratt's 1992 winning margin from 61 percent to 52 percent.

Three other House races attracted more than 50 campaign articles. The *Las Vegas Review-Journal* published 73 articles about the race between James Bilbray and John Ensign. The challenger, who spent $700,000 to the incumbent's $900,000, defeated Bilbray by fewer than fifteen hundred votes. The *Buffalo News* published 79 articles about Jack Quinn's quest for reelection; the *Bloomington Pantagraph* published 66 articles about Thomas Ewing's race. Both incumbents won easily, attracting two out of three voters. Coverage of thirteen other contested elections was sparse; the median newspaper published only 20 articles about each race; the range was from 3 to 40 articles. Three uncontested elections averaged 8 campaign articles each.

What accounts for the vast differences in campaign coverage? Chapter 2 examined several factors that appear to affect the volume of coverage during the primary and campaign seasons, including the incumbent's spending, the challenger's spending, and the margin of victory in the previous general election. Although the data set examined in chapter 2 was large, consisting of 225 representative/newspaper dyads, no information was available about whether an article focused on policy making or campaigning, or about whether the subject was the primary campaign or the general election campaign. Primary season was simply defined as the three months preceding the primary, and campaign season as the period from September 1, 1994, to November 8, 1994. How closely do the coverage patterns in table 6.1, where articles are known to be about campaigns and coded by a campaign's stage, correspond with the findings of chapter 2?

As chapter 2 demonstrated, a representative's previous electoral margin explains little about the volume of coverage in subsequent campaigns. Representatives King, Baker, and Quinn were the only legislators running for reelection who had been elected in 1992 with 55 percent or less of the vote (50, 51, and 52 percent, respectively). How much campaign coverage did they receive in the 1994 electoral cycle? The races involving Richard Baker and Peter King attracted coverage that was considerably below average. The race involving Jack Quinn attracted coverage that was above average, but more than half of it focused on the other party's primary. Although at first it seems surprising that the question of who would challenge Representative Quinn was considered more newsworthy than David Francyk actually challenging Quinn in the general election, the lateness of New York's primary is surely relevant. A primary held on September 13 expands the primary season and compresses the general election campaign to a mere eight weeks.

As previously shown, a challenger's spending affected campaign coverage. Three challengers spent more than $500,000 on their campaigns — namely, the three Republicans who challenged Representatives Beilenson, Bilbray, and LaRocco. These three campaigns were among the top five in overall campaign coverage (table 6.1). A challenger's spending did not guarantee campaign coverage, however. Four other challengers spent more than $250,000 each. Two of the four campaigns attracted coverage that was slightly above the median (Pickett and Filner); the other two attracted little campaign coverage at all (Lipinski and King). *Newsday* did not find Peter King very newsworthy in or out of campaign season. Despite his failure to win a majority of votes in 1992, and then his encountering both a challenger in the 1994 Republican primary and a challenger who spent more than $400,000 in the general election, King's race did not interest *Newsday*'s editors. His was fourth from the bottom among the 19 representatives running in contested elections (table 6.1). In short, how much a challenger spent mattered, but only when editors were predisposed to cover representatives and campaigns.

The impact of incumbent spending on newspaper coverage is less clear in this small data set than it was in the larger data set examined in chapter 2. Two types of representatives spent a lot of money. Three representatives who faced well-financed challengers spent more than $500,000 on their campaigns (Beilenson, Bilbray, LaRocco). Their races were heavily covered. Other representatives spent lots of money because their institutional positions made fund-raising a cakewalk. Joe Moakley, chair of the powerful House Rules Committee, spent $980,000 in a race against a poorly financed challenger. Barbara Kennelly, member of the Ways and Means Committee, spent $580,000 to her opponent's $25,000. Both races received average amounts of coverage. Clearly, challenger spending is a better measure of campaign intensity than incumbent spending. It is also a better predictor of campaign coverage in local newspapers.

The most striking finding in Table 6.1 is how infrequently newspapers covered congressional primaries. Eight incumbents faced challengers in both primary and general elections (Beilenson, Bilbray, King, Kolbe, McDermott, Moakley, Stokes, and Wynn). Their eight primary races together attracted only 35 articles, with a median of 5, whereas their eight election races attracted 214 articles, with a median of 16. Only the Senate primaries and the primaries to select who would challenge Representatives Beilenson, LaRocco, and Quinn in the general election attracted much coverage.[3] Most primary challengers are not well financed; most primary campaigns are not very intense; most newspapers pay scant attention to primaries.

The conclusions here largely support the findings of chapter 2. Competitive races for the House and Senate are covered extensively; less competitive races are covered more lightly; uncontested elections and primary campaigns are hardly covered at all. A challenger's spending is a better measure of competitiveness than either an incumbent's spending or an incumbent's previous electoral margin. The volume of information that newspaper readers are exposed to about congressional campaigns depends very much on a challenger's success in raising the resources required for a viable campaign. In short, challenger spending not only buys coverage in the form of paid political advertisements; it stimulates coverage in the so-called free media—the news and editorial pages of local newspapers.

John Zaller suggests that, according to the Burglar Alarm Standard, the news media "should ignore races in which the opposition party mounts no serious challenge, while paying close attention to those in which it does" (Zaller 2003, 125). Did local newspapers meet this standard? The editors at Congressional Quarterly provide a convenient measure of "serious challenge." For the 383 House races where an incumbent was running, the editors identified 282 as safe for the incumbent, 37 where the incumbent was favored, 39 that leaned toward the incumbent, and 25 with no clear favorite (CQWR 10/22/94 3005–10). For the 19 contested races in the first data set (table 6.1), they identified 12 as safe, 4 where the incumbent was favored (King, Lipinski, Pickett, Quinn), 2 that leaned toward the incumbent (Bilbray, LaRocco), and 1 with no clear favorite (Beilenson).

How did the 19 newspapers cover these races? In the aggregate, the newspaper behaved as Zaller would like. The median newspaper covering the 3 most competitive races published 90 articles about the general election, the median paper covering 4 other competitive races published 24 articles, and the median paper covering 12 noncompetitive races published 19 articles.

[3] The open primary in Louisiana includes candidates from both parties on a single ballot. There was no general election in 1994 because Richard Baker won the open primary by a majority.

Clearly, newspapers differentiated between very competitive races, which received extra coverage, and moderately competitive races, which were covered more like noncompetitive races. There was, however, much variance within the three categories. Two newspapers with noncompetitive races provided extensive coverage of the Spratt (142 articles) and Ewing (55 articles) races, while two papers with competitive races provided meager coverage of the King (8 articles) and Lipinski (16 articles) races.[4]

These patterns also remind us that extensive coverage of congressional races can affect election outcomes. Two weeks before the election, the editors at Congressional Quarterly called the race in New York's Third District competitive and the race in South Carolina's Fifth District as safe for the incumbent. The election outcomes were just the opposite. John Spratt was reelected in a squeaker, with 52 percent of the vote, while Peter King coasted to victory with 59 percent. Could it be that the *Rock Hill Herald*, which published 142 articles about Spratt's race, helped make the race competitive, whereas *Newsday*, which published 8 articles about King's race, helped to guarantee his reelection? The evidence in chapter 8 suggests that the level of coverage does have consequences like these.

Representatives and Challengers

How frequently did local newspapers mention the candidates who were challenging incumbent representatives in primary or general election races? Did newspapers cover incumbents more heavily than challengers? Although the first data set is not ideal for answering these questions, it is nevertheless revealing. For each campaign article, my assistants determined whether it mentioned a primary or general election challenger. If it did, they determined how central the challenger was in the article and whether it portrayed the challenger in a positive, negative, or neutral way. They also counted how many times the challenger's last name appeared. All three measures

---

[4] Zaller codes the races differently. He focuses on the outcomes of the twenty-two races where the incumbent was running (including three who ran unopposed) and finds that "in the five cases in which voters clearly faced a real rather than a nominal contest, local newspapers produced an average of 81 articles focusing on the general elections," whereas "in the remaining 17 races, coverage averaged about 18 articles on the campaign" (Zaller 2003, 125). He defines a real race as one where the incumbent was defeated (two cases) or won with less than 55 percent of the vote (three cases). The Congressional Quarterly ratings are a superior measure of competitiveness than the outcomes themselves, in part because these ratings rely on information that was available to newspaper editors when they were deciding how to cover particular races, and in part because outcomes can be a consequence of media coverage. Zaller's method, for example, includes the Spratt race, which attracted the most coverage of any race in the sample, whereas the editors of Congressional Quarterly had (wrongly) called it safe for the incumbent.

are identical to the ones used for coding a representative's centrality, valence, and last-name mentions (chapter 3).

More than three-quarters of the campaign articles mentioned challengers.[5] Coverage of challengers was much more frequent than one would expect from the literature, which regularly repeats the generalization that press coverage of congressional campaigns heavily favors incumbents over challengers (Herrnson 2000, 216). Moreover, my count of challenger mentions is almost certainly an undercount because the data set includes articles about challengers if and only if they mention incumbents. So, although it is possible to have representative-only articles in the sample, it is not possible to have challenger-only articles. Representative-only articles were particularly common on the opinion pages, where editorials, columns, or letters criticized or praised a representative without mentioning the challenger. It seems likely that the editorial pages also contained some items that criticized or praised a challenger without mentioning the incumbent. Unfortunately, these items had no chance of being included because the search routine was representative-driven.[6]

How central were incumbents and challengers in the articles that mentioned both candidates? The coders identified the incumbent as a main subject in 62 percent of the articles and a secondary subject in the rest. They also identified the challenger as a main subject in 62 percent of the articles and a secondary subject in the rest.[7] In short, challengers were just as central to these campaign articles as representatives. For those who prefer objective indicators of centrality to my coders' subjective assessments, the message is essentially the same. Representatives were mentioned a total of 4,922 times, challengers a total of 4,723. Twenty-one representatives were mentioned between 1 and 51 times in each article, with a mean of 5.5 mentions per article. Twenty-one challengers were mentioned between 1 and 45 times, with a mean of 5.3 mentions per article.

How did these articles portray incumbents and challengers? Contrary to expectations, they treated challengers more kindly than representatives. Twenty-three percent of the articles appeared to contribute to a negative impression of the incumbent, whereas only 18 percent did so for the challenger. Twenty-three percent appeared to contribute to a positive impression

[5] Challengers appeared in 893 of 1,178 campaign articles (76 percent). The denominator does not include 24 articles about three representatives who ran unopposed (Archer, Goodling, McCollum).

[6] On the news pages it was much more common to mention both representatives and challengers, if only to identify one candidate as the other candidate's opponent.

[7] Forty-six percent of the articles were coded with both candidates as main subjects, 22 percent with both candidates as secondary subjects, 16 percent with the representative main and the challenger secondary, and 16 percent with the challenger main and the representative secondary.

of the incumbent, whereas 27 percent did so for the challenger.[8] Although the advantage to challengers was slight, it was surprising, given the conviction in the congressional literature that press coverage is just one more arena where incumbents are advantaged.[9]

Table 6.2 shows how newspapers portrayed the 21 representatives and 21 challengers. The advantage for challengers was not the result of a few deviant races. Indeed, the advantage was most pronounced in the nine most heavily covered races, which together accounted for 83 percent of campaign articles. Each of nine incumbents in these races appeared in fewer articles that portrayed them positively than did their challengers (153 vs. 211 articles). Eight of nine incumbents appeared in more articles that portrayed them negatively than did their challengers (180 vs. 136 articles).[10] Only in the lightly covered races did newspapers cover representatives more positively than challengers.

What accounts for the small advantage given to challengers? There is no evidence that the advantage reflected editorial bias. Editorial endorsements during campaign season are the best indicator of whether editors and publishers preferred specific candidates. On the editorial pages, they regularly preferred incumbents. In contested House races, newspapers endorsed twelve incumbents but only two challengers (Ensign against Bilbray, Acevedo against Filner).[11] In short, although editors preferred incumbents, they covered challengers about as frequently as they covered incumbents, and they covered challengers somewhat more favorably than they did incumbents.[12]

The small advantage given to challengers probably arises because incumbents are more likely to be the objects of criticism than challengers. Repre-

---

[8] See table 3.3 for the rules used to code valence from the representative's perspective. The same rules were used to code challenger valence.

[9] This finding support's John Zaller's hypothesis (and evidence from presidential elections, 1948–96) that press-initiated criticism of candidates in general elections is positively associated with political strength (Zaller 1999, 96–100).

[10] Table 6.2 classifies Representatives Inhofe and Kyl, the two legislators in the study who were running for open Senate seats, as incumbents, and their opponents, Representatives McCurdy and Coppersmith, as challengers. None of the generalizations reported in the text depend on this arbitrary distinction.

[11] Local newspapers did not endorse any candidates in the races involving Representatives Baker, King, LaRocco, Spratt, and Wynn. In the two Senate races that involved pairs of incumbent representatives running against each other, the *Phoenix Gazette* endorsed the candidate arbitrarily coded incumbent (Kyl) and the *Tulsa World* endorsed the candidate arbitrarily coded challenger (McCurdy).

[12] Previous studies differ on whether editorial endorsements are correlated with news coverage. A study of 47 newspapers during the 1992 presidential campaign found no relationship between newspapers' formal endorsements and news coverage of the campaigns (Dalton, Beck, and Huckfeldt 1998). A study of 67 contested Senate elections between 1988 and 1992 found that information on the news pages was slanted in favor of the candidate endorsed on the editorial page (Kahn and Kenney 2002).

TABLE 6.2

Valence of Articles from Representative's and Challenger's Perspectives

Representative	Positive Valence		Negative Valence		Total Articles
	Representative	Challenger	Representative	Challenger	
Inhofe	29	31	32	19	121
Spratt	35	45	35	31	116
LaRocco	23	26	24	30	115
Beilenson	20	39	24	17	112
Kyl	16	17	24	22	91
Bilbray	9	19	17	5	58
Quinn	8	13	6	3	56
Ewing	8	10	8	7	41
Pickett	5	11	10	2	32
Kolbe	10	5	4	6	24
Moakley	4	2	7	1	22
Filner	1	5	3	3	22
Crapo	6	5	4	2	18
Kennelly	14	7	—	1	18
Lipinski	3	2	3	3	12
King	1	2	1	1	10
Baker	1	—	—	7	10
Stokes	6	1	—	1	9
McDermott	3	2	—	—	3
Wynn	—	2	—	—	2
Dellums	—	—	—	—	1
Total	202	244	202	161	893
Median	6	5	4	3	22

Coding: See table 3.3 for coding rules for positive, negative, and neutral valence.

Notes: All counts are from the first data set. Total articles include those coded positive, negative, and neutral. Neutral articles for individual candidates can be calculated from the included data. Neutral from the perspective of the representative totaled 489; neutral from the perspective of the challenger totaled 488. Table is rank-ordered by the number of campaign articles that mentioned both candidates. Each median is the median for a single column of data.

sentatives have records to defend. Even the typical freshman has introduced a dozen bills, voted on hundreds of roll-call votes, and received campaign contributions from scores of Political Action Committees that represent special interests. Each of these actions has the potential to create enemies as well as friends. The enemies frequently use the campaign period to peddle their criticisms, with their criticisms showing up in news stories, editorials, opinion columns, and letters. Most challengers do not have extensive records to defend. They are less likely than representatives to be the objects of criticism.

Campaign coverage of representatives and challengers is best explained as a consequence of two interrelated causes. First, journalists like to cover close races. When challengers raise substantial campaign funds, they make representatives appear vulnerable and they create a conflict worth covering. Journalists respond by covering both incumbents and challengers. When incumbents appear invulnerable, however, journalists don't perceive a real conflict or a story worth covering. They provide scant campaign coverage of both candidates. Second, journalists are guided by professional norms of fairness and impartiality. During campaign season, this means that neither candidate deserves more coverage than the other. On the editorial pages, it is acceptable for editors to endorse one candidate over another. On the news pages, professional journalists do not believe it is acceptable to take sides or to provide inordinate coverage of a single candidate. In short, a campaign's intensity drives the overall volume of coverage, while norms of fairness and impartiality guarantee similar amounts of coverage for incumbents and challengers.

Representatives do enjoy enormous advantages in news coverage compared with challengers. Their advantage is in noncampaign coverage. Month after month, newspapers cover their actions as representatives, both in Washington and at home. As figure 6.1 suggests, this coverage is nearly constant across the study period and continues unabated throughout the campaign period. The volume of noncampaign coverage is more than five times greater than the volume of campaign coverage. Over the entire two-year election cycle, therefore, citizens see much more information in local newspapers about incumbents than about challengers.

National Policy Issues

What kind of role did national issues play in congressional campaigns? Did campaigns feature issues that dominated the 103rd Congress, or did they focus on issues that were primarily of local concern? Did representatives and challengers revisit the big issues of 1993, or did they concentrate on issues that were being featured by the news media during the campaign period? How much could citizens learn about representatives' and challengers' connections with national issues by reading about campaigns in their local newspapers?

My assistants tracked seven national issues that were prominent during 1993 and 1994. For each article in the first data set they determined whether it mentioned any proposal related to abortion, crime control, gun

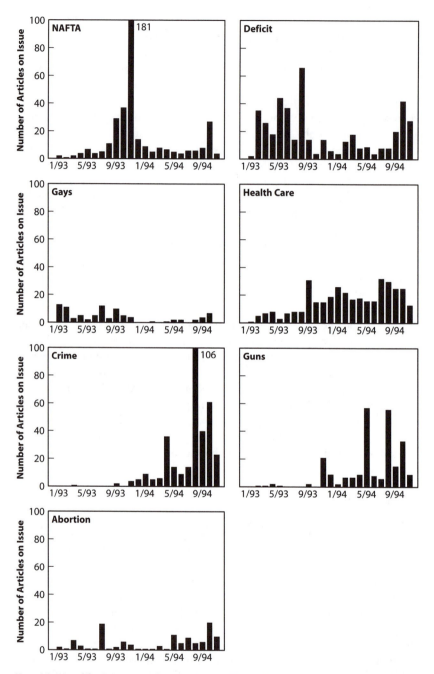

Fig. 6.2 Monthly Coverage of Seven Issues. The coding is the same as for table 6.3. Each bar shows the number of articles mentioning an issue during a particular month. The figure includes all 21 representatives running in contested elections (6,919 articles). Exact counts for two months that are off-scale are indicated for NAFTA (11/93) and crime (8/94).

TABLE 6.3
Campaign Coverage of Seven Policy Issues

	Crime	Deficit	Guns	Health	Abortion	NAFTA	Gays	Total
Article								
Campaign	118	97	74	72	51	46	12	470
Noncampaign	217	345	172	295	69	340	80	1,518
Total	335	442	246	367	120	386	92	1,988
% Campaign	35	22	30	20	43	12	13	24
Representative								
Kyl	13	10	13	11	19	3	—	69
Spratt	19	15	5	10	3	6	—	58
Beilenson	17	13	9	4	4	5	—	52
Inhofe	13	6	10	2	2	2	8	43
Ewing	11	5	3	10	2	2	—	33
LaRocco	2	8	3	5	11	1	1	31
Bilbray	6	7	6	7	1	3	—	30
Quinn	11	1	8	2	1	3	—	26
Pickett	6	5	5	4	4	—	1	25
Kolbe	5	4	4	3	—	7	—	23
Filner	3	4	1	1	2	7	—	18
Kennelly	4	7	2	4	—	1	—	18
Crapo	2	5	3	5	—	1	—	16
Stokes	3	2	—	2	—	1	—	8
King	2	—	1	—	1	2	1	7
Lipinski	—	2	1	—	1	1	—	5
McDermott	—	2	—	2	—	—	—	4
Wynn	—	1	—	—	—	1	—	2
Moakley	1	—	—	—	—	—	1	2
Baker	—	—	—	—	—	—	—	0
Dellums	—	—	—	—	—	—	—	0
Total	118	97	74	72	51	46	12	470
Median	3	4	3	2	1	1	0	18

Coding: Does the article mention any proposal related to crime control, balancing the budget or reducing the deficit, banning or regulating guns, comprehensive health care reform, abortion, the North American Free Trade Agreement, or gays in the military? Each article could be coded for multiple mentions.

Notes: All counts are from the first data set. Does not include three representatives running unopposed. The 470 issue mentions appeared in 286 of 1,178 campaign articles; the 1,518 mentions appeared in 1,301 of 5,741 noncampaign articles. Table is rank-ordered by the total number of issues mentioned (rows) and by the volume of campaign coverage for each issue (columns). Each median is the median for a single column of data.

control, NAFTA, gays in the military, comprehensive health reform, or deficit reduction. Articles could be coded for multiple issues. Nearly a quarter of all articles in the first data set mentioned at least one of these issues.[13] Figure 6.2 and table 6.3 show how 21 newspapers covered these seven issues. Figure 6.2 displays the monthly coverage patterns for each issue throughout the study period and provides a baseline for analysis. The top section of table 6.3 compares the volume of issue coverage in campaign articles with the volume in noncampaign articles. The bottom section shows how frequently each issue appeared in articles about various campaigns.

Campaign coverage did not ignore national issues. Indeed, these seven issues were featured more prominently in campaign articles than in noncampaign articles.[14] A quarter of all campaign articles mentioned at least one of these issues, with an average of 1.6 issues per article. The range was from no issue mentions in the *San Francisco Chronicle* (Ronald Dellums) to 69 in the *Phoenix Gazette* (Jon Kyl). The median representative appeared in articles that mentioned these seven issues on 18 occasions (table 6.3). Issue coverage was most extensive in competitive races. The five most competitive races (Beilenson, Bilbray, Inhofe, Kyl, and LaRocco) averaged 45 articles that mentioned these issues.

The two biggest stories of 1993 were NAFTA and the effort to reduce the budget deficit. Coverage of the controversial North American Free Trade Agreement was unusual in that 47 percent of articles appeared during November, the month Congress approved it. The NAFTA story began slowly. During the first eight months, while President Clinton was deciding what to do about this holdover issue from the Bush administration, newspapers published only 36 articles, an average of 5 per month. Newspapers increased coverage during September and October, after President Clinton endorsed it, publishing an average of 33 articles per month. Then came an explosion of coverage during November 1993. Every newspaper published at least 2 articles; the median newspaper published 8; one newspaper (*Newsday*) published 19. The total for the month was 181 articles — the heaviest monthly total for any issue in the study. Then quietude returned. Despite the sense in late 1993 that how representatives voted on NAFTA could have electoral repercussions a year hence, few campaign articles referred to the trade

---

[13] Of the 8,003 articles, 1,479 mentioned one of the seven issues, 271 mentioned two, 53 mentioned three, 20 mentioned four, 6 mentioned five, and 1 mentioned six, for a total of 1,830 articles and 2,296 issue mentions. Although I selected these issues for special tracking before coding began, these seven codes happened to include nine of the top twelve issues on which representatives took positions (there were two gun-control issues and two deficit-control issues among the top twelve). The other three issues in the top twelve were military base closures, immigration, and Haiti (see table 4.4).

[14] The typical campaign article mentioned 0.40 issues (470/1178); the typical noncampaign article mentioned 0.26 issues (1518/5741).

agreement. Only four representatives appeared in as many as five campaign articles that mentioned NAFTA; the median representative appeared in one (table 6.3). In short, although NAFTA was heavily covered as a policy issue, it was lightly covered as a campaign issue.

Moving from statistical to textual analysis, NAFTA seemed to play a role in only two races. Seven campaign articles about Jim Kolbe in the *Tucson Citizen* portrayed his strong support of NAFTA in the most favorable light. Even his opponent, Gary Auerbach, praised Kolbe for his efforts to enact the trade pact, before suggesting, "now that NAFTA has passed, I don't think Kolbe presents a clear agenda for the future" (*TC* 1/10/94 C1). In contrast, campaign articles about Bob Filner in the *San Diego Union-Tribune* portrayed his opposition to NAFTA as contrary to his constituents' true interests. The *Tribune* published four editorials in the month before the election that criticized Filner for his opposition, including one that endorsed his opponent, Mary Acevedo, largely on the basis of her support for NAFTA and GATT. The closest Filner came to praise on this issue was when Mickey Kantor, the president's trade representative, visited San Diego and endorsed Filner, but this news item was followed by an editorial entitled "Strange Bedfellows" that highlighted the "exquisite irony" of Kantor praising Filner when it was Acevedo who shared Kantor's and the president's views on trade (*SDUT* 10/29/94 B6).[15]

Newspapers covered the effort to reduce the deficit much more as a continuing story. Although newspapers concentrated heavily on the seven-month battle of the budget in early 1993, publishing 240 articles that mentioned deficit reduction between February and August, coverage continued throughout the 103rd Congress as the House considered the Penny-Kasich spending plan, the balanced budget amendment, the FY95 budget resolution, and innumerable amendments to cut spending.[16] Coverage also carried over into the campaign period. Ten representatives appeared in five or more campaign articles that mentioned deficit reduction; median coverage was greater than for any other national issue (table 6.3).

Deficit reduction made a better campaign issue than NAFTA because it was a continuing story and because candidates differed so much on what

---

[15] Two other newspapers published five or more campaign articles about NAFTA. The *Rock Hill Herald* published six letters that mentioned John Spratt's support of NAFTA, including two that praised him, two that were critical, and two that were neutral. The *Los Angeles Times* published five articles that mentioned Anthony Beilenson's support for NAFTA. One suggested that Ross Perot's followers were looking for a candidate to challenge Beilenson; another stated that a local union refused to endorse him because of his vote; the others merely reported, without passing judgment, his support for the trade pact.

[16] Deficit reduction was such a prominent issue in the 103rd Congress that Congressional Quarterly selected seven votes about it for inclusion in its biennial list of thirty-two key votes. See *CQA93*, 36C–45C; *CQA94*, 13C–20C, 48C–53C.

was the best remedy. The vote on NAFTA was showdown at high noon — a single climactic event that was eagerly anticipated, sure to attract a large crowd, and guaranteed to leave only one side standing. Newspapers covered it heavily. But once it was over, it was over. Congress was not about to unravel a multinational trade pact, no matter what happened in the next election. In contrast, controlling the deficit was the ultimate continuing story. It had dominated congressional politics for more than a decade and seemed certain to occupy center stage for as long as politicians could imagine. Moreover, most candidates differed in how they would achieve budget balance. Some would slash defense spending, some domestic spending, some both. Some candidates pushed for new revenues; others claimed taxes were already too high. All incumbents had votes to defend; all challengers were prepared to exploit at least some of those votes. In short, deficit reduction was a superb issue for candidates seeking to differentiate themselves. It was an issue for all seasons.

President Clinton's initial proposal to allow gays to serve in the military and the compromise "don't ask, don't tell" policy was the least covered of the seven issues. Only 12 campaign articles and 80 noncampaign articles mentioned it (table 6.3). The issue was visible in only one campaign, the Senate race between Representatives James Inhofe and Dave McCurdy. Ironically, both candidates voted for the compromise. Nevertheless, Inhofe attempted to portray McCurdy as a closet supporter of the president's original proposal, while Inhofe advocated returning to the previous absolute ban (TW 9/24/94 N16). Although the evidence on what each candidate truly believed was thin, the charges and countercharges generated four news stories, two editorials, one opinion column, and one letter. Perhaps the issue failed to take root in other campaigns because most representatives had voted with majority opinion in their districts — the compromise was approved, 301–134 — thus depriving challengers of a good campaign issue. Ordinarily, candidates need to take opposite positions in order to create good campaign issues.

Coverage of health care reform was unusual in that the volume was virtually constant, month after month (figure 6.2). From its formal unveiling in September 1993 until election day 1994, monthly coverage averaged 22 articles, essentially one article per representative per month. Although health care reform dominated coverage in 1993 and 1994, it did not dominate coverage of most congressional campaigns. No reform bill ever reached the House floor, so the roll was never called. Incumbents had no votes to defend; challengers had none to attack. The best that representatives and challengers could do during campaign season was to declare how they would reform health care or attack the president for his failure to develop a consensus. Coverage was actually more informative in the summer of 1994, when representatives were taking positions for or against President Clinton's proposal. One of the virtues of a formal proposal is that it forces politicians to consider both the costs and benefits of reform. Once the president's proposal was dead, no single proposal existed to focus debate among candidates or to keep them from favoring lots of incompatible ends.

More campaign articles focused on crime control than on any other issue (table 6.3). The virtues of crime as a campaign issue were three. First, the issue was of recent vintage. In August 1994, when the House defeated the rule that would have allowed consideration of the conference report on crime control, it handed President Clinton a major defeat. Journalists covered heavily both the defeat and the bill's resurrection ten days later. Second, the conflict in Congress was intensely partisan and ideological. Candidates had no trouble taking opposing positions on an issue framed with colorful ideological language about the virtues of midnight basketball programs, additional prisons, tougher sentences, the death penalty, or banning assault weapons. Third, the House took more than forty roll-call votes on various aspects of the bill. Incumbents had extensive records to defend and challengers had ample opportunities to attack them. Most newspapers that had competitive races to cover featured crime control. Six newspapers published more than ten campaign articles that mentioned it (table 6.3).

Regulating guns was the third most popular campaign issue. Gun control appeared more regularly in campaign articles than either NAFTA or health care reform (table 6.3). Although the House passed two gun control measures during this period, the Brady bill in November 1993 and the assault weapons bill in May 1994 (the latter was incorporated into the Omnibus Crime bill three months later), it was the assault weapons ban that attracted the most campaign coverage. The Brady bill appeared in only two campaign articles. An article in the *Buffalo News*, which focused on how Jack Quinn and his opponent, David Franczyk, had completely opposite views on gun control, mentioned that Quinn had voted in favor of the Brady bill, the assault weapons ban, and the crime bill (*BN* 10/22/94 L1). An article in the *Las Vegas Review-Journal* mentioned that, although James Bilbray had supported many of the president's proposals, he had opposed both NAFTA and the Brady bill (*LVRJ* 8/22/94 B1). Campaign coverage was remarkably scant for the first major gun control bill enacted in twenty-six years.

What made the assault weapons ban more newsworthy than the Brady bill? First, the House enacted the ban by a tiny margin, 216–214, so each supporter was pivotal. If a single proponent had switched sides, the outcome would have changed. By comparison, the House enacted the Brady bill by a much larger margin, 238–189. Second, the assault weapons ban was more consequential than the Brady bill. It prohibited the sale or possession of various semiautomatic weapons, whereas the Brady bill merely required a five-day waiting period before someone could purchase a handgun. Although the National Rifle Association strenuously opposed both bills, it opposed the assault weapons ban more fiercely. Opponents began working to rescind the ban on assault weapons the moment it was enacted. Third, the assault weapons bill was incorporated into the omnibus crime bill in the middle of campaign season. As with the crime bill, Washington politics spilled over into campaign politics for the assault weapons bill. The Brady bill was long since forgotten — at least in local newspapers.

The sense in Washington is that abortion is a dangerous political issue and that representatives need to be especially careful when walking through this legislative minefield. Dangerous, perhaps, but most local newspapers did not cover abortion in ways that contributed to electoral peril. In non-campaign articles, abortion was covered less frequently than any other major issue (table 6.3). As noted in chapter 4, most newspapers did not cover extensively the two key House votes on abortion, the Hyde amendment prohibiting federal funds for abortions (6/30/93) or the bill protecting access to abortion clinics (5/5/94). One unusual aspect of abortion was that the volume of campaign coverage was almost equal to the volume of noncampaign coverage. This was a result not of the proximity of legislative action to the campaign period, as it was for crime control and gun control, but of the role that abortion played in two campaigns. Abortion was an important campaign issue in the races involving Jon Kyl and Larry LaRocco. Coverage in the *Phoenix Gazette* and the *Lewiston Morning Tribune* accounted for 60 percent of abortion-related articles (table 6.3).

The analysis of how local newspapers covered seven national issues supports two generalizations. First, national issues played an important role in most newspapers' campaign coverage. The newspapers that published little coverage of national issues were largely the ones that published minimal campaign coverage of any type (compare tables 6.1 and 6.3).[17] Second, the issues that newspapers featured in campaign coverage tended to be those of recent vintage. Gays in the military and NAFTA, the hot issues from 1993, were covered much less frequently than either crime control, gun control, and health care reform, the hot issues of late 1994, or controlling the deficit, an important issue in both 1993 and 1994. Even within issue categories, temporal proximity mattered. The assault weapons ban was covered much more heavily than the distant Brady bill.

Representatives often attempt to dispose of the most controversial issues on the congressional agenda long before the start of campaign season, hoping that on election day people will forget what Congress did long, long ago.

---

[17] Two previous studies of how newspapers covered issues in House campaigns reached opposite conclusions. Clarke and Evans concluded that issue coverage was light and disappointing, while Tidmarch, Hyman, and Sorkin found that nearly half the articles about House races had substantial issue content. Neither set of authors was explicit about how they coded for issues (Clarke and Evans 1983; Tidmarch, Hyman, Sorkin 1984).

This section provides strong evidence that journalists facilitate that task, behaving largely as incumbents prefer. During campaign season newspapers focus on recent issues more than on distant issues. Presumably, part of this focus reflects what issues representatives and challengers are featuring during their campaigns. But it also reflects what journalists choose to emphasize. Journalists chose to remain silent about the Brady bill during the campaign, an issue that they had previously warned would be politically dangerous for some representatives.

Party, Ideology, and the President

Candidates run for office as individuals (Mayhew 1974). Representatives defend their individual records in office and attempt to show why they deserve reelection; challengers attempt to show that they would make better legislators than current incumbents. But candidates are also linked to larger political forces. Most candidates run as members of party teams. Individual candidates may choose to emphasize or deemphasize their party links. Candidates may also be linked to the incumbent president or portrayed in ideological terms. This section explores how newspapers portrayed representatives as supporters or opponents of the president, as supporters or opponents of a party, and as adherents to a particular ideology. It also examines the way newspapers reported a unique element of the 1994 election, the common platform under which most Republican candidates ran, the Contract with America.

How frequently did newspapers portray representatives as supporters or opponents of their own party in Congress? Who portrayed them this way?[18] Was support or opposition a badge of honor that representatives wore proudly, or was party support a nasty label that challengers attached to incumbents? Party was not a central feature of campaign coverage; only 3 percent of all campaign articles portrayed representatives as party supporters or opponents (32 of 1,178). Nor was party support a badge of honor. Challengers and their friends were seven times more likely to portray representatives as party supporters than were representatives and their friends (21 vs. 3, with 5 portrayals by neutral sources). Portrayals of representatives as party opponents were extremely rare (3 articles). In short, party was not a central element of

[18] Coding for party support: "Is the representative portrayed as a supporter or opponent of his or her own party in Congress. The portrayal should be fairly obvious to the casual reader." Coding for party portrayal: "Who portrayed the representative as a supporter or opponent of his or her own party in Congress: (a) the representative, (b) someone who clearly approves of the representative, (c) a neutral source or mixed sources, (d) someone who clearly disapproves of the representative, or (e) an electoral challenger." Similar questions were used to code for presidential support, presidential portrayal, ideology, and ideological portrayal.

campaign coverage, but when it was used in campaign articles, it was used more to disparage representatives than to praise them.

Newspapers were much more likely to portray representatives as supporters or opponents of President Clinton than as supporters or opponents of their parties. Nearly 10 percent of campaign articles portrayed representatives in this fashion (111 articles). Most candidates did not consider President Clinton to be an electoral asset. Representatives and their friends were three times more likely to portray a representative as an opponent of the president than as a supporter (25 vs. 8 articles). Challengers and their friends were ten times more likely to portray a representative as a supporter of the president than as an opponent (57 vs. 6 articles).[19] References to connections with the president were heavily concentrated in a few districts. Representatives LaRocco and Spratt were tarred with being Clinton supporters on 35 occasions (LaRocco 12, Spratt 23). Representative Inhofe and Kyl proclaimed their firm opposition to the president on 18 occasions (Inhofe 11, Kyl 7).

Newspapers portrayed representatives in ideological terms in 7 percent of campaign articles (82 articles). Seldom did representatives refer to themselves with ideological language, and when they did it was to proclaim that they were moderate (5 articles) or conservative (10 articles). Challengers and their supporters regularly referred to representatives in ideological terms, tarring them as liberals (42 articles) or conservatives (15 articles), never moderates.[20] The representatives most likely to be portrayed in ideological terms were Spratt (16), Inhofe (14), Kyl (12), Beilenson (10), LaRocco (10), and Pickett (10).

The most striking finding about party support, presidential support, and ideology is how negative were the connotations in campaign articles. Representatives and their friends seldom emphasized how much a representative supported a party, the president, or a recognizable ideology. In contrast, challengers and their friends frequently argued that a representative excessively supported the party or the president, or possessed some unacceptable ideology. In short, representatives really did campaign as individual candidates, and newspapers really did cover them that way. It was challengers who attempted to tar and feather representatives as ideologues or as blind supporters of party leaders or the president. Whatever association representatives had with team sports was portrayed more as vice than virtue.

The surprise in 1994 was that most Republican candidates — incumbents and challengers alike — chose to run under a team platform, the Contract

---

[19] In addition, neutral sources portrayed representatives as presidential supporters twelve times and as presidential opponents three times.

[20] In addition, neutral sources portrayed representatives as liberal (2), moderate (1), and conservative (7).

with America, that promised a ten-point program, including term limits, a balanced budget amendment, welfare reform, and congressional reform (Gimpel 1996). How frequently did local newspapers mention the Contract with America in their coverage of congressional campaigns? Did coverage focus on this unusual attempt to nationalize congressional campaigns with a detailed plan for action? Coverage was sparse. More campaign articles mentioned distant issues like NAFTA or abortion than mentioned Republicans' agenda for the future. Counting even the most incidental mentions, only 40 articles mentioned the Contract. Seven newspapers never mentioned it once; the median newspaper mentioned it twice; the *Rock Hill Herald* mentioned it seven times.

How frequently did local newspapers cover congressional campaigns as horse races? Scholars have long noted that when journalists cover presidential campaigns, they feature horse race stories above all else, telling citizens more about who is winning and who is losing than about the candidates, their platforms, and their accomplishments (Patterson 1980; Robinson and Sheehan 1983; Bartels 1988). Journalists who cover House campaigns do not suffer from this affliction. Only 7 percent of campaign stories focused on the horse race. One reason for the difference is that the outcome in most congressional contests is not in doubt.[21] More than 70 percent of horse race stories were concentrated in the six most competitive contests, the two Senate campaigns (Inhofe, Kyl), the two where the incumbents lost (Bilbray, LaRocco), and the two where the incumbents won with less than 53 percent of the vote (Beilenson, Spratt). A second reason for the difference between presidential and congressional campaigns is that journalists who cover House races do not have access to myriad polls, focus groups, and expert prognosticators to fuel their supposedly natural instincts to cover campaigns as horse races. This is true even when the outcome is in doubt. In the six most competitive races, horse race coverage was only 8 percent of total campaign coverage.[22]

Criticizing Representatives

Democracy functions best when those in power are subjected to regular doses of public criticism. The fear of criticism inspires executives and legislators to do their best. The practice of criticism helps citizens decide

[21] The impact of competitiveness on horse race coverage is clear by comparing presidential, Senate, and House campaigns. Horse race coverage is greatest for presidential campaigns, considerably less for Senate races, and much less for House races. On Senate campaigns, see Westlye 1991, 53; Kahn 1991, 360; Kahn and Kenney 1999, 125.

[22] The coding for horse race coverage was conservative in that my assistants were asked to determine the principal focus of a campaign article.

whether they approve or disapprove of what elected officials have been doing in office. A free press is essential to democracy because it keeps incumbent politicians from suppressing public criticism of their actions.

We know that the media regularly report criticisms about the president's performance as a policy maker. We know very little about whether the media report criticisms about representatives' performance. How frequently do local newspapers publish criticisms about representatives? Who are their main critics? How frequently do newspapers publish the criticisms of challengers, other politicians, interest group leaders, editorial writers, or citizens? On what kinds of policy-making activities do these critics focus? Do they concentrate on leadership activities, roll-call votes, or other activities? How much are these criticisms concentrated in the campaign period?

Newspapers published criticisms of representatives' performance as policy makers in 11 percent of articles. The median representative was criticized in 23 articles — one article per month. The range was from 3 articles for Albert Wynn to 86 articles for James Inhofe. The criticisms were heavily concentrated in the campaign period. Twenty-six percent of campaign articles contained some sort of criticism, compared with 8 percent of noncampaign articles (table 6.4). As a consequence, representatives who faced weak, inexperienced, underfinanced challengers were far less likely to be criticized in print than representatives running against strong, well-financed challengers.[23] Competitive races stimulated campaign coverage, and campaign coverage was inherently more critical of representatives than noncampaign coverage.

Representatives were criticized most frequently for the positions they took (table 6.4). Forty-nine percent of criticisms focused on position taking, with half focusing on actual roll-call votes (177) and half on cosponsored bills (29), upcoming votes (15), or basic positions (147). Representatives were criticized much less frequently for their actions in office. Only 14 percent of criticisms focused on representatives' actions, including bills introduced (71), committee activities (12), costs that critics traced to specific actions (16), or a poor attendance record (4). Nine percent of criticisms focused on representatives' inactions, including lack of accomplishments (39), failure to keep promises (3), or being out of touch with constituents (22). Eight percent of criticisms suggested that representatives had a conflict of interest (18) or had allowed campaign contributions to affect their decisions (41). Twenty percent of articles contained several different criticisms (54) or miscellaneous criticisms (104) that did not fall within the classification scheme.

The things for which representatives were criticized were largely the

---

[23] Representatives who ran unopposed were even less likely to be criticized in print. Only 6 percent of articles contained criticisms of Representatives Archer, Goodling, or McCollum. Five percent contained criticisms of Romano Mazzoli, who was retiring. Table 6.4 does not include articles about these four representatives.

TABLE 6.4
Criticism about Representative's Performance as a Policy Maker

Criticism Focused on	Noncampaign Article	Campaign Article	Total Articles	Percent in Campaign Articles
Position Taking				
Actual Vote	108	69	177	39
Bill Cosponsored or Endorsed	20	9	29	31
Upcoming Vote	14	1	15	7
Basic Positions	97	50	147	34
Total about Position Taking	239	129	368	35
Actions				
Bill Introduced	58	13	71	18
Committee Activities	9	3	12	25
Costs Traced to Some Action	11	5	16	31
Poor Attendance Record	0	4	4	100
Total about Actions	78	25	103	24
Inactions				
Lack of Accomplishments	18	21	39	54
Failure to Keep Promises	2	1	3	33
Out of Touch with Constituency	10	12	22	55
Total about Inactions	30	34	64	53
Conflicts				
Conflict of Interest	9	9	18	50
Campaign Money Affected Decision	21	20	41	49
Total about Conflicts	30	29	59	49
Other Criticisms	63	95	158	60
GRAND TOTAL	440	312	752	41
Total Articles in Category	5,741	1,178	6,919	17
Percentage with Criticism	8	26	11	

Notes: All counts are from the first data set. Includes articles from 21 newspapers. Does not include articles about three representatives who ran unopposed or about Romano Mazzoli, who did not run for reelection.

things that newspapers covered in their news pages. Newspapers covered roll-call votes and other forms of position taking more heavily than they covered any other policy-making activities; critics followed their lead. Newspapers largely ignored what representatives were doing in committees; critics did the same. Newspapers provided modest coverage of bills that representatives introduced, and so did critics. These patterns are largely what one would expect if the actual division of labor between journalists and local watchdogs is the one described in chapter 1. Journalists observe what representatives are doing and report their findings in newspapers. Local politicians and local opinion leaders learn about representatives' positions and actions in these papers and sound the alarm when they discover representatives doing disagreeable things. The things about which local watchdogs sound the alarm are necessarily the things that journalists choose to report.

Position taking was the only thing for which every single representative was criticized. The median representative was criticized in 14 articles. The range was from 1 for Ronald Dellums to 47 for John Spratt. Representatives running in the seven most competitive races were much more likely than others to be criticized for their policy positions: Beilenson (30), Bilbray (45), Inhofe (28), Kyl (38), LaRocco (24), Lipinski (7), and Spratt (47). How much representatives were criticized for things other than position taking was affected by both electoral competitiveness and by the extent to which representatives had done controversial things in office. Three-quarters of the criticisms about bill introductions were lodged against Representatives Inhofe (10), Kyl (12), and LaRocco (30). Larry LaRocco introduced a bill that would have changed land-use regulations for 4.5 million acres in his district. James Inhofe proposed repealing a secrecy rule in Congress that leaders of the majority party wanted to preserve. Jon Kyl proposed moving Tax Day to Election Day, so that citizens would better understand the consequences of their electoral choices. Half the criticisms about committee activities were lodged against Bob Filner (6), who used his influence in committee to kill a proposed binational airport on the Mexican border.

Electoral challengers were the leading critics of representatives' performance as policy makers, accounting for 27 percent of all criticisms (table 6.5). Some challengers were highly successful in getting their criticisms of incumbent representatives in print, including the candidates opposing Representatives Kyl (29), Beilenson (28), Inhofe (21), LaRocco (21), Spratt (17), and Bilbray (15). Other candidates failed completely. The challengers to Representatives Baker, Dellums, Filner, Lipinski, and McDermott failed to get a single criticism in print; the candidates opposing Representatives King and Wynn managed one criticism each. Experienced, well-financed challengers were more successful in having their criticisms of representatives published. Candidates in less competitive races were much less successful.

TABLE 6.5
Who Criticized Representative's Performance as a Policy Maker?

Critic	Noncampaign Article	Campaign Article	Total Articles	Percent in Campaign Articles
Electoral Challenger	11	189	200	95
Obvious Supporter of Challenger	8	13	21	62
Member of Congress	34	1	35	3
Other Politician	16	11	27	41
Interest Group Leader	88	15	103	15
Constituent	139	52	191	27
Columnist or Editorial Writer	141	29	170	17
Multiple Critics	3	2	5	40
Total	440	312	752	41

Notes: All counts are from the first data set. Includes articles from 21 newspapers. Does not include articles about three representatives who ran unopposed or about Romano Mazzoli, who did not run for reelection.

The median newspaper published only eight criticisms lodged by challengers.

Constituents were also frequent critics of representatives as policy makers, accounting for 25 percent of all criticisms. Ninety percent of their criticisms appeared in letters to the editor. With one major exception, constituents' criticisms were not concentrated in the campaign period. The exception was the *Rock Hill Herald*, a small town daily with a lively letters page, which published 52 letters criticizing John Spratt's performance, 80 percent of them in the summer and fall of 1994. Constituents' criticisms in other newspapers were more evenly spaced, with February 1994 as the median date of publication. Constituents were most critical of representatives' positions (122) and least critical of their actions (8). Undoubtedly, they reacted to what they were reading in news stories, which focused heavily on position taking and lightly on representatives' actions. Newspapers with more congressional districts in their core circulation areas published fewer criticisms by constituents. Newspapers with one or two districts averaged 13.5 criticisms per representative; newspapers with three or more districts averaged 4.2 criticisms per representative. Newspapers with multiple districts did not expand their letters pages to allow citizens equal chances to criticize their representatives, whereas they did expand their news pages to allow reporters to cover multiple representatives.

Columnists and editorial writers accounted for 23 percent of all criticisms. Most representatives had little to fear from the editorial pages of their local newspapers. Although 20 of 21 representatives were criticized in at least one editorial or column (not Moakley), the median representative was criticized only three times in two years. Five representatives were not so fortunate and suffered frequent criticisms on the editorial pages: Bilbray (36), Filner (31), LaRocco (24), Inhofe (21), and Kyl (12). Although four of these representatives were involved in competitive races (not Filner), heavy editorial criticism predated campaign season, with half occurring in 1993 (60) and half in 1994 (64). Since representatives in other competitive races attracted few criticisms on the editorial pages — Spratt (3), Beilenson (2), Lipinski (1) — it appears that a representative's electoral vulnerability was not the driving force behind editorial criticism. A close examination of editorials suggests that editorial writers at three newspapers — the *Las Vegas Review-Journal, San Diego Union Tribune,* and *Tulsa World* — strongly disagreed with just about everything that Representatives Bilbray, Filner, and Inhofe did.[24]

Criticisms lodged by columnists and editorial writers were distinctive in two respects. First, columnists and editorial writers frequently critiqued representatives for what they were about to do, and not just for what they had already done. Clearly, they were attempting to influence representatives' actions on important matters like the budget, NAFTA, and crime control. Second, the criticisms were relatively evenly spaced throughout 1993 and 1994. The criticisms followed the pace of congressional decision making, peaking in the late summer and early fall of 1993, much more than the pace of congressional campaigns.

The forces that contributed to regular doses of public criticism were four. Newspapers published more criticisms when (*a*) newspapers carefully covered representatives' positions and actions on their news pages, (*b*) representatives were running in competitive races against well-financed challengers, (*c*) editorial writers or columnists disagreed strongly with representatives' positions and actions, or (*d*) newspapers welcomed and published lots of letters from opinionated citizens. Any two of these factors resulted in extensive criticism, as exemplified in the coverage of Representatives Inhofe (86), LaRocco (84), Spratt (84), Bilbray (83), and Kyl (83). One of these factors was often enough to produce above-average amounts of criticism, as in the coverage of Representatives Beilenson (50) and Filner (47). When all four factors were absent, however, newspapers published little criticism of representatives' performance as policy makers. Few citizens would notice the sporadic criticisms of Representatives Wynn (3), Dellums (6), McDermott (10), or Kolbe (11).

---

[24] In 157 editorials in these three newspapers, the valence from the perspective of the representative was overwhelming negative (17 positive, 49 neutral, 91 negative).

Editorial Endorsements

Most newspapers endorse candidates in congressional elections. As previously noted, editorial writers preferred incumbents by a wide margin. In nineteen contested House races, they endorsed twelve incumbents (Beilenson, Crapo, Dellums, Ewing, Kennelly, Kolbe, Lipinski, McDermott, Moakley, Pickett, Quinn, Stokes) and two challengers (Ensign against Bilbray, Acevedo against Filner), while remaining neutral in five races (Baker, King, LaRocco, Spratt, Wynn). Newspapers also endorsed three representatives in contested primaries (Kolbe, Moakley, Stokes). In the Senate races, the *Phoenix Gazette* endorsed Jon Kyl and the *Tulsa World* endorsed James Inhofe's opponent, Dave McCurdy. In uncontested races, the *York Daily Record* endorsed Bill Goodling, while the *Houston Chronicle* and the *Orlando Sentinel Tribune* were editorially neutral on the inevitable reelection of Bill Archer and Bill McCollum.[25]

How did editorial writers justify their choices in the twenty instances in which they endorsed a candidate? Did they carefully review the performance of incumbents, evaluate the promise of challengers, and make reasoned choices? Or did they simply announce their choices with no more justification than "trust us, we know what is best for you"? Did editorial writers evaluate aspects of representatives' behavior that reporters had been covering on the news pages, or did they introduce new information that reporters had not bothered covering? Did they focus exclusively on the favored candidate or did they also evaluate other candidates?

The arguments that editorial writers use to justify their choices are important to an educated citizenry, perhaps more so than the choices that editors recommend. Well-reasoned editorials help citizens think about the kinds of standards that are important in evaluating candidates for Congress, encouraging them to consider aspects of representatives' behavior that are not featured in campaign advertisements. Editors can contribute to informed decision making by highlighting relevant facts, suggesting criteria for judgment, and weighing the advantages and disadvantages of competing candidates. Editorials can be helpful even for citizens who do not share editors' core values. For example, a citizen who reads that editors prefer a representative because she voted for NAFTA, the Brady bill, and President Clinton's bud-

---

[25] The citations for the editorial endorsements and quotations in this section are Beilenson (*LAT* 10/26/94 B6); Bilbray (*LVRJ* 10/23/94 C2); Crapo (*IFPR* 10/28/94 B10); Dellums (*SFC* 10/30/94 P1); Ewing (*BP* 10/16/94 A8); Filner (*SDUT* 11/2/94 B6); Goodling (*YDR* 10/26/94 A8); Inhofe (*TW* 10/16/94 E8; 10/23/94 E8); Kennelly (*HC* 10/23/94 C2); Kolbe (*TC* 9/10/94 A5; 10/5/94 A8); Kyl (*PG* 10/28/94 B8); Lipinski (*CST* 10/16/94 41); McDermott (*ST* 11/6/94 B10); Moakley (*BG* 9/12/94 18; 10/30/94 74); Pickett (*NLS* 11/2/94 A20); Quinn (*BN* 10/23/94 E8); Stokes (*CPD* 3/29/94 B6; 9/26/94 B6).

get bill may have learned just enough to vote knowledgeably *against* the editors' recommendation. The information would be adequate if the citizen happened to believe that NAFTA is an abomination to American workers, the right to bear arms is fundamental to a free society, and President Clinton is the devil incarnate.

Most newspapers attempted to persuade readers that editors' choices were sound. Only five of twenty endorsements lacked any arguments to support the recommended candidates. The *Tucson Citizen* endorsed Jim Kolbe's renomination, with a single sentence: "In District 5, Republican incumbent Jim Kolbe has only token opposition from professional candidate Joseph Sweeney, whose candidacy isn't worth discussing further." The *Boston Globe* twice endorsed Joe Moakley, first for renomination and then for reelection, but offered no reasons for either recommendation.[26] The *Seattle Times* listed Jim McDermott among 72 individuals it supported for various national, state, and local offices. The *San Francisco Chronicle* listed Ronald Dellums among 106 individuals or propositions it supported.

All other editorials advanced arguments to buttress their recommendations. Most editorials were reasonably comprehensive assessments of representatives' performance. Only two editorials focused on a single dimension of a representative's behavior. The *San Diego Union-Tribune* opposed Bob Filner's (and Lynn Schenk's) reelection solely because they "placed the political interests of organized labor ahead of the economic interests of San Diego by casting votes against the North American Free Trade Agreement." The *Chicago Sun-Times* emphasized William Lipinski's pork-barrel prowess, calling him "good for Chicago and the region. Lipinski has represented the interests of his Southwest Side district well, as evidenced by his leadership in opposing the expansion of the McCook Reservoir." Other newspapers painted more complete portraits of representatives, often discussing both the accomplishments and the shortcomings of representatives.

Editorial writers clearly valued things that were not a central part of newspapers' ordinary coverage of representatives. Among these were leadership, independence, experience, committee service, and seniority. The *Idaho Falls Post Register* praised Michael Crapo for his leadership on gay rights, congressional reform, term limits, and wilderness preservation. The *York Daily Record* commended Bill Goodling for his leadership on the National Literacy Act, child nutrition, and vocational education. Barbara Kennelly won kudos from the *Hartford Courant* for rounding up the votes to pass the

---

[26] The text of the two endorsements: (*a*) "In other congressional primaries, incumbents Joseph Moakley, Barney Frank, and Gerry Studds deserve renomination over token opponents" and (*b*) "In other districts, we believe the incumbents deserve reelection. In particular we support Representative Joseph Moakley of South Boston, although he should be more willing to debate Republican Michael Murphy."

1993 deficit-reduction plan and for sponsoring legislation to make compliance with the "nanny tax" easier. The *Tucson Citizen* applauded Jim Kolbe for his leadership on the North American Free Trade Agreement.

Editors valued independence in their representatives, especially independence from party leaders. The *Buffalo News* claimed that Jack Quinn displayed "commendable independence on several critical national issues—the family leave bill, for example, and this year's anticrime measure, both of which he supported—requiring him to cross party lines." The *Cleveland Plain Dealer* argued that Louis Stokes was "unafraid to buck party-line positions, as he did this year when he voted against the crime bill because of his opposition to the death penalty. He also opposed a U.S. invasion of Haiti, a position that set him at odds with many members of the Black Caucus." The *York Daily Record* appreciated that Bill Goodling "stood up to his own party leaders when they tried to cut child nutrition programs." Editors at the *Bloomington Pantagraph* were not complaining when they wrote that Thomas Ewing "hasn't always voted the way you would expect, but he always seems to have a good reason." Editors at the *Idaho Falls Post Register* seemed unusually broad-minded about Michael Crapo, writing that "we don't agree with the congressman on many issues, but we find him always open to hearing new ideas and adept at defending his own."

Once representatives had served in Congress for a while, editorial writers emphasized the risks of sacrificing representatives' experience, seniority, and committee positions. The *Cleveland Plain Dealer* claimed that Louis Stokes, "who has served in Congress for 26 years, is not only the most senior member of the state's congressional delegation. He also is arguably the most powerful—at least when it comes to federal dollars." The *Norfolk Ledger-Star* worried that "with so much at stake in the base-closing and realignment process next year, especially with Oceana Naval Air Station at risk, Hampton Roads needs all the clout and seniority it can get on the Armed Services Committee. For that reason, we endorse Representative Owen Pickett for another term." The *York Daily Record* forecast that "if, as expected, the Republicans become the majority party, Congressman Goodling's influence in education legislation should be even greater during the 104th Congress." Experience seemed to count even for freshman Michael Crapo. The *Idaho Falls Post Register* argued that "unless you've elected a dud, you don't retire a member of Congress just as he's starting to really get going. And Representative Mike Crapo is far from a dud."

Editorial writers assessed roll-call voting, position taking, and ideology, but they emphasized these matters much less in editorial endorsements than reporters, columnists, and citizens did in ordinary news and opinion coverage. Most editorials were forgiving of a few wrong votes: "Mrs. Kennelly was wrong to vote against the North American Free Trade Agreement in 1993. But one wrong vote does not cancel many right votes." The rejection of Bob

Filner for a single vote on NAFTA was an exception. Representatives who disagreed fundamentally with editors' values were not so fortunate. The *Las Vegas Review-Journal* endorsed John Ensign after reviewing unfavorably James Bilbray's "penchant for social engineering and Washington activism" and his favoring of "tax hikes, burdensome regulation, and larger bureaucracies." In contrast, Ensign "is a moderate who favors local, market-oriented solutions to problems, rather than an expansion of federal hegemony."

Editorial writers were uneven in their attention to challengers. The *Hartford Courant* merely listed the names, ages, hometowns, and occupations of Barbara Kennelly's two challengers. The *Chicago Sun-Times* and the *Norfolk Ledger-Star* were equally sparse in their treatment of the candidates opposing William Lipinski and Owen Pickett. Most newspapers reviewed challengers' qualifications, often focusing on their positions on major issues, occasionally on their experience. The *Bloomington Pantagraph* summarized Paul Alexander's views on NAFTA, health care, the budget, and defense spending. The *Tucson Citizen* analyzed Gary Auerbach's positions on crime control and entitlement programs. The *Cleveland Plain Dealer* revealed that James Sykora's campaign against Louis Stokes was based "almost entirely on the abortion issue." The *Buffalo News* was particularly impressed with David Franczyk's experience on Buffalo's Common Council, although favoring Jack Quinn "in a close call." The *Idaho Falls Post Register* found Penny Fletcher "a refreshing candidate" who "waged an inspiring campaign." The editors hoped that "we haven't seen the last of her in Idaho politics." Most editorial writers did not ignore challengers. They merely preferred incumbents. They valued incumbents especially for their leadership, seniority, and institutional positions, three things that were beyond the reach of challengers.

The most detailed editorials focused on two Senate races. They were also the most partisan and vitriolic. The *Phoenix Gazette*'s 1,676-word editorial reviewed the records of Representatives Kyl and Coppersmith, finding much to praise about Kyl and little to admire about Coppersmith, who apparently suffered from an affinity for President Clinton. The *Tulsa World* required two editorials to make its case, the first, a 630-word item entitled "For Dave McCurdy," reviewed favorably McCurdy's experience and record in the House, while the second, a 1,435-word item entitled "Why We Oppose Jim Inhofe," criticized everything from Inhofe's character, business acumen, and social graces to his fierce partisanship, ideology, and campaign techniques. Faced with the choice between two representatives, each with established records in the House, the editors of the two papers portrayed the favored candidates as nearly faultless, the disfavored ones as virtueless.

The editors also believed that the two Senate races would be unusually consequential. The *Phoenix Gazette* argued that partisan control of the Senate was on the line: "The stakes are not just high, they are monumental. The midterm elections of 1994 have become a referendum on the Clinton administration and its sometimes stealthy, often fumbling but clearly blatant attempts to impose a leftist social agenda on the federal government in America." The *Tulsa World* characterized James Inhofe's fierce partisanship as so extreme that he was the only committee member "to be excluded from the annual picnic thrown by the chairman." The editors concluded that "Congress needs Republicans and Democrats who will put partisanship aside to work for the good of all. Jim Inhofe, the partisan, the loner, the true believer, is not a likely candidate for that movement."

Eight newspapers used a single editorial to endorse several candidates, so the space devoted to individual candidates was necessarily small.[27] Writers responded to the challenge by using language economically. The *Los Angles Times*, which endorsed fourteen House candidates in a single editorial, wrote the following about Anthony Beilenson (199 words):

> Substantive, smart, and honest, Anthony C. Beilenson (D-Woodland Hills) deserves to be reelected. Beilenson has been enormously thoughtful on the deficit and other spending issues, independent on immigration, and supportive of the Santa Monica Mountains National Recreation Area. After the Northridge earthquake he helped gain an immediate infusion of federal funds for his hard-hit district, which includes parts of the San Fernando Valley and eastern Ventura County. He also deserves credit for his successful amendment to the crime bill, a provision requiring the federal government to reimburse states for part of the cost of incarcerating illegal immigrants who have been convicted of felonies. With bipartisan support, his amendment got $33.4 million for the state. His Republican challenger, Richard Sybert, an articulate lawyer and a former Wilson Administration official, favors welfare reform, like most candidates regardless of party affiliation, but, alas, offers only vague ideas on the topic. He dismisses as "industrial welfare" the defense conversion money the bipartisan California delegation worked so hard to deliver to a state devastated by defense/aerospace cutbacks. And he pans the crime bill as an ineffective piece of legislation, even though it will put more police officers on our streets. The *Times* endorses Beilenson.

Most of the editorials were both thoughtful assessments of incumbent representatives and fair, though much shorter, evaluations of challengers' qualifications for office. They helped to frame electoral choices in a way that news coverage could not. Editorial endorsements also encouraged at-

---

[27] In five editorials that focused on single-district races, the median editorial was 495 words; the range was 416 to 585 words. The median text for an individual endorsement in editorials that covered multiple districts was 259 words; the range was 73 to 614 words.

tention to aspects of representatives' behavior that were seldom covered in the news pages, including leadership, independence, seniority, and experience. Only a few editorials were completely one-sided, most notably the two editorials that recommended replacing Representatives Bilbray and Filner and the two in which editors were choosing between experienced representatives running for open Senate seats. In all four cases, editors believed the outcomes would be especially consequential, not just for the district but for the balance of power in Washington. Party control and partisanship, largely absent in campaign coverage, took center stage in the editorials about Representatives Bilbray, Inhofe, and Kyl.[28]

Quality of Newspaper Coverage

Newspapers varied in both the quantity and the quality of their campaign coverage. The two newspapers that offered the best coverage of House campaigns were the *Los Angeles Times* and the *Lewiston Morning Tribune*, the largest and the smallest papers in the sample. Each newspaper published more than 120 articles about the campaign, covered the challenger extensively, appeared scrupulously fair, and provided analysis and guidance on its opinion pages.

The Idaho campaign was a nasty one. Larry LaRocco and Helen Chenoweth insulted each other frequently; the *Morning Tribune* gave each candidate nearly equal space for their charges, countercharges, and rebuttals. Taken together, however, the news stories gave a good sense of what LaRocco had been doing in office and how the incumbent and challenger differed. Editorially neutral, the paper employed three opinion columnists: the first a LaRocco admirer, the second relatively neutral, the third hostile, repeatedly calling the incumbent "Beltway Larry." The California campaign was hard fought but civil. Although the *Times* endorsed Anthony Beilenson near the end of the campaign, the news and opinion pages were equally open and equally generous to both candidates. The *Times* commissioned five columns from both the incumbent and challenger, one each on crime, welfare, health care, defense, and the budget, and then published the paired columns together. The intent was to force Beilenson and Sybert to discuss important issues in a manner that allowed readers to compare their positions directly. The *Times* and the *Morning Tribune* had different strategies

---

[28] The results in this section support one finding in a previous study of endorsements in House elections but stand in stark contrast to another. Peter Clarke and Susan Evans found that more than 90 percent of editorial endorsements favored the incumbent, not significantly different from the 86 percent in this study. They also suggested that "the bulk of editorials make dull reading," which was not my experience. Perhaps they had higher standards; perhaps overall quality has improved (Clarke and Evans 1983, 74, 85).

for covering House campaigns, but both newspapers were informative and fair.

It was not surprising that the quality of campaign coverage in the *Times* and the *Morning Tribune* was impressive, since both newspapers were impressive in their coverage of Beilenson and LaRocco prior to the start of the 1994 campaign. The quality of coverage in other newspapers, however, changed dramatically once campaigns were launched. For one newspaper it was a change for the good. If 1993 was the standard for judgment, the *Phoenix Gazette* was one of the least impressive newspapers in the sample. Every few weeks the *Gazette* published an item entitled "Write to Your Elected Officials" that listed the names and addresses of state legislators and House members who represented the greater Phoenix area. Unfortunately, the *Gazette* published so little information about Jon Kyl's positions and actions in 1993 that it was not clear what matters citizens might raise with Kyl. Perhaps the editors thought readers should write Kyl and inquire what he had been doing. By comparison, the *Gazette* covered the Kyl-Coppersmith battle for the Senate rather well. The news articles were extensive and even-handed. Editorially, the newspaper strongly preferred Kyl, but most pro-Kyl editorials were followed a day or so later by anti-Kyl letters. Still there was an odd disjunction between campaign and noncampaign coverage. The *Gazette*'s endorsement applauded Kyl for his knowledge of foreign and defense policy. As one of my assistants quipped, "The editors must read another paper, because Kyl's expertise was not otherwise conveyed."

For some newspapers, campaign coverage was much weaker than noncampaign coverage. The change was most dramatic in the *Hartford Courant*. This paper provided extensive coverage of Barbara Kennelly's Washington activities. More than half of all news stories had a Washington dateline, and many of these stories showed Kennelly heavily involved in national issues such as NAFTA, health care, and the budget. By comparison, campaign coverage was much lighter. The *Courant* was scrupulously fair to the principal challenger, Douglas Putnam, reporting his views clearly and without bias. But campaign coverage was only 7 percent of total coverage, giving Kennelly an extraordinary edge over the poorly financed challenger. The shift was similar in the *Cleveland Plain Dealer*. Coverage of Louis Stokes's Washington activities was extensive. Coverage of the 1994 campaign was paltry, with only nine articles mentioning James Sykora, the challenger.

The quantity and quality of campaign coverage depended both on journalistic habits that were developed outside the campaign season and on how much challengers spent. Newspapers that covered representatives superficially outside campaign season did not suddenly become strong newspapers just because well-financed challengers happened to appear. Long Island's *Newsday* and the *Chicago Sun-Times* did not change their spots when Peter King's opponent spent $416,000 and when William Lipinski's opponent spent $278,000. The transformation of coverage in the *Phoenix Gazette* was the only exception to this rule, an exception fueled by the $6 million battle for Arizona's open Senate seat. On the other hand, newspapers that covered representatives comprehensively outside campaign season did not continue these habits in campaign season if there was no real battle to cover. Not even strong newspapers, such as the *Hartford Courant* or the *Cleveland Plain Dealer*, wrote extensively about quiet campaigns in which challengers spent less than $25,000.

The best campaign coverage appeared in quality newspapers with competitive races. The *Las Vegas Review-Journal, Lewiston Morning Tribune, Los Angles Times*, and *Tulsa World* set the standard here, with the *Bloomington Pantagraph, Buffalo News*, and *Rock Hill Herald* as runners-up. The worst campaign coverage appeared in weak newspapers with uncompetitive races. The *San Francisco Chronicle, Seattle Times*, and *Washington Times* occupied the cellar; the *Tucson Citizen* was only slightly better than the cellar dwellers.

Summary of Empirical Findings

This chapter employed the first data set to analyze how local newspapers cover representatives campaigning for reelection. The principal empirical findings are these.

- The intensity of a campaign drives the overall volume of campaign coverage. Newspapers cover competitive races heavily, less competitive races lightly, and primary campaigns hardly at all.
- Newspapers publish almost as many campaign articles about challengers as they do about incumbents. Challengers and incumbents are equally central in the articles that mention both candidates.
- Campaign articles tend to portray challengers somewhat more favorably than they do incumbents. This is especially true in the most competitive races.
- National issues are an important part of campaign coverage. Indeed, newspapers feature national issues more prominently in campaign coverage than in noncampaign coverage. When newspapers discuss national issues, they feature issues of recent vintage more frequently than they feature issues resolved in the previous year.
- Newspapers frequently portray representatives as supporters or opponents of the president or as adherents to some ideology. They rarely portray representatives as supporters or opponents of their party in Congress. Most references about a representative's connection to party, ide-

ology, or the president are made by challengers and are negative in their connotations.

- Although horse race stories are common when newspapers cover presidential campaigns, they are not common when newspapers cover congressional campaigns.
- When representatives run in competitive races against well-financed challengers, newspapers tend to publish regular criticism of them. Representatives are much more likely to be criticized for their positions than for their actions.
- Most newspapers endorse incumbents for reelection. Editorial writers often emphasize things that are not part of their regular news coverage, including leadership, independence, experience, committee service, and seniority.
- Representatives enjoy enormous advantages in news coverage compared with challengers. Their principal advantage, however, is not in campaign coverage, but in all the noncampaign coverage that they receive over the entire two-year election cycle.
- The quantity and quality of campaign coverage depend both on journalistic habits that are developed outside campaign season and on how much challengers spend. Some newspapers provide exemplary coverage of campaigns, some abysmal, and some in between.

Political Accountability

Before campaign season, local newspapers and representatives are the principal sources for information about what representatives are doing in office. Representative use newsletters and community meetings to communicate directly with citizens. Newspapers report some of what representatives are doing and some of what various critics are saying about their performance in office. Ordinarily, the flow of information from these two sources is either positive (from the representative's perspective) or neutral. The criticisms that newspapers publish constitute a small fraction of newspaper coverage.

During campaign season, the sources of information about representatives' performance change, as the paid media become increasingly important. The tone of coverage also changes. Challengers, representatives, and interest groups use direct mail and paid advertisements to communicate directly with citizens. These paid messages tend to contain more criticisms than do news stories. How much information citizens happen to receive from the paid media depends on whether a local race is competitive. When challengers raise lots of money, they are able to communicate messages about representatives' shortcomings and their own virtues. When challengers raise lots of money, they also stimulate incumbents, and sometimes interest groups, to raise and spend substantial sums to neutralize challengers' messages. Of course, these changes in the flow of information occur in only some districts, since most challengers are unable to raise enough money to mount competitive races.

How much does the flow of information change in the free media during campaign season? Do newspapers reinforce the patterns in the paid media, or do they counteract them? The evidence suggests the former. Most newspapers do not cover challengers extensively unless they have already proven their prowess by raising lots of money. Most newspapers do not cover incumbents heavily unless challengers have raised enough money to threaten incumbents' electoral security. To be sure, newspapers would have nothing much to cover if challengers were unable to craft appealing messages about representatives' shortcomings and their own virtues. Indeed, some challengers fail to pass this threshold. But there is also a group of talented challengers, with powerful messages to convey, who merely lack the wherewithal to communicate directly with citizens.

Most local newspapers appear to be fair during campaign season. They provide comparable amounts of information about challengers and incumbents. They do not seem to be biased in favor of incumbents, at least on their news pages. But the consequence of this fairness is to cover extensively only those races where challengers raise lots of money. Accordingly, most campaigns are effectively over before they start. Citizens are exposed to a barrage of largely favorable information about representatives during non-campaign season, some directly from representatives, some reported in the newspapers. During campaign season, citizens are exposed to a barrage of information only if challengers are superb fund-raisers. If challengers can't raise money, most citizens won't hear much, either in the paid media or the free media, about incumbents' shortcomings or challengers' virtues. The few exceptions to this rule involve representatives who violate ethical rules or make other spectacular errors. For example, newspapers covered Dan Rostenkowski's (D-IL) 1994 indictment for embezzlement and fraud so heavily that Michael Flanagan, his Republican challenger, coasted to victory with minimal expenditures.

Incentives still exist for representatives to be careful about their positions and actions in advance of campaign season. The best way for challengers to raise money is to identify serious mistakes that representatives have made, and use these mistakes to jump-start their campaigns. The best way for incumbents to deny challengers such issues is to be careful about what they say and do in Washington, especially on prominent and conflictual issues. The incentives for representatives to be careful about their positions and actions would be more powerful, however, if challengers had more opportunities to communicate with citizens. It is not a healthy sign for democracy that so few incumbents have to defend vigorously their records against challengers who see the world differently. In order to survive, representatives need to be good enough to keep talented candidates from deciding to challenge them, and good enough to keep challengers from raising substantial sums of money. Ordinarily, they do not need to be good enough to survive a fair battle between two candidates, each of whom has reasonable opportunities to communicate their messages to voters.

7

How Newspapers Differ

NEWSPAPERS DIFFER GREATLY in how they cover local representatives. They differ both in the frequency with which they cover representatives and in what kinds of messages they convey about legislators. That much is clear from the evidence presented in chapters 2 through 6. But it is still not clear how much these dissimilarities reflect differences in the newsworthiness of particular representatives and how much they reflect differences in newspaper markets or in the practices of individual editors. This chapter examines what makes newspapers distinctive.

The principal source for this chapter is the second data set. As discussed in chapter 1, this data set reveals how pairs of newspapers in six cities — Boston, Chicago, San Francisco, Seattle, Tucson, and Washington — covered the same representative. It contains 2,175 news stories, editorials, opinion columns, letters, and lists that mentioned six local representatives, including 1,053 items from six papers in the first data set and 1,122 items from six comparison papers. The second data set allows one to hold constant the newsworthiness of representatives and thereby isolate what is distinctive about particular newspapers. The chapter also employs the first and third data sets for several broader comparisons.

Does Competition Matter?

Does it matter whether a city has more than one daily newspaper? Many commentators believe that it does. There is much mourning when a city that once had competing daily papers is reduced to a single newspaper. But it is far from clear whether competition among local newspapers stimulates good journalism.

Some experts argue that rival newspapers compete for readers by devoting more resources to news gathering than do monopolistic local newspapers that have little reason to fear their readers' defection (Bogart 1981, 264; Bagdikian 1987, 129). Several studies offer empirical support for this proposition. For example, one study found that competitive newspapers had larger newsholes than noncompetitive newspapers (Everett and Everett 1989). A pair of studies found that competitive newspapers were more likely than noncompetitive papers to subscribe to multiple news services (beyond the ubiquitous AP and UPI), such as the services run by the *Los Angles Times*,

New York Times, Washington Post, or Dow Jones (Weaver and Mullins 1975; Lacy 1990). One of the few studies to examine the quality of coverage found that competitive newspapers were more likely than noncompetitive papers to win Pulitzer Prizes, the industry's badge of journalistic excellence (White and Andsager 1990).

Other scholars argue that market structure has no significant effects on news and editorial content (Compaine 1982; Picard 1989). Several studies offer support for this proposition. For example, Robert Entman analyzed coverage in ninety-one newspapers during ten days in 1974 and found that competitive and noncompetitive newspapers were equally likely to publish serious, in-depth articles and editorials, offer a diversity of views on public issues, and present political controversies fairly (Entman 1989, 92–97). Another study found no differences in content between a matched set of thirteen competitive and noncompetitive newspapers (Nixon and Jones 1956). A longitudinal study found no differences in one newspaper's content after its longtime rival folded (McCombs 1987).[1]

A third view is that competitive market pressures actually diminish the quality of news. John Zaller argues that the norms of the profession inspire journalists to produce high quality news about politics and public affairs whenever they can. Doing so makes them feel like professionals, not hired hands, and gives them the independence to produce what they and their colleagues value most. After all, journalists win awards and professional recognition by producing high quality news, not by maximizing circulation. As competitive pressures increase, however, journalists are forced to lower the quality of news and do more things to attract larger audiences (Zaller 1999, 30–53).

Zaller offers various types of cross-sectional and time-series evidence to support his argument. Among other things, he shows that the television program *60 Minutes* produced many high quality stories about politics and public affairs when it was the only national newsmagazine, but when NBC and ABC also began producing newsmagazines, their programs offered fewer high quality stories than *60 Minutes*, and soon *60 Minutes* joined the race to the bottom. Similarly, the BBC, which for two decades enjoyed a monopoly in national television news, produced higher quality newscasts than did the three American networks that competed with each other, but when two commercial news programs were introduced in Britain in the 1980s and 1990s, they both offered lower quality news coverage than the BBC, which itself lost market share. He also shows that the quality of local television newscasts in the United States was lower in the most competitive media markets and that news quality declined over time as competition

---

[1] For additional citations to the literature on the impact of competition on editorial practices and newspaper content, see Lacy and Simon 1993, 91–129.

among stations increased. Although Zaller also examined the effects of competitive market pressures on the quality of news coverage in local newspapers, his evidence was too thin either to support or to refute his basic proposition.

The data sets collected for this book are ideal for determining whether competition stimulates or impedes the production of high quality news about politics and public affairs. Admittedly, these data sets are restricted to the way local newspapers cover House members, so one cannot generalize about how newspapers cover other aspects of politics and public affairs. But they are better quality data sets — and more relevant to the basic question — than most of the data sets that have been used heretofore to test propositions about the impact of competition on news coverage. The third data set is appropriate for examining the effects of competition on the volume of coverage. The second data set is ideal for exploring the impact of competition on newspaper content.

Volume of Coverage

The purest form of competition occurs when two or more daily newspapers are published in the same city by separate firms. By this standard, New York City, with four daily newspapers in 1993, was the most competitive newspaper market in the country. Its largest paper, the *New York Times*, had 44 percent of the weekday market, compared with the *New York Daily News* (29 percent), *New York Post* (17 percent), and *New York Newsday* (10 percent). Other varieties of competition also exist. Some cities have daily newspapers, owned by separate firms, that have merged one or more of their business functions, including printing, advertising, or circulation (e.g., *Detroit News* and *Detroit Free Press*).[2] Other cities have newspapers that are owned by the same firm but that continue to publish separate newspapers with separate editorial staffs (e.g., *Phoenix Gazette* and *Arizona Republic*). Still others have newspapers that are owned by the same firm and produced by the same group of editors, typically a morning paper under one name and an afternoon paper under another (e.g., *Harrisburg Patriot* and *Harrisburg Evening News*). Here I consider that two newspapers are competitors if they are published in the same home city and produced by separate editorial staffs.[3] Under this definition, shared ownership, shared business func-

---

[2] The *Detroit News*, owned by Gannett, competes vigorously with the *Detroit Free Press*, owned by Knight-Ridder. On Saturday and Sunday, they produce a combined edition that contains sections independently edited by the two papers. The Detroit Newspaper Agency, jointly owned, handles printing, advertising, circulation, and accounting for both papers.

[3] In addition, separately owned newspapers from neighboring cities sometimes compete with

tions, or any other joint operating agreement does not count against being competitors as long as separate editorial staffs produce the news and opinion pages.[4]

Cities that have competing daily newspapers tend to be more populous than those that have a single daily newspaper, although there are lots of exceptions. For example, according to the definition used here, Sacramento, Salt Lake City, Tucson, and York had competing newspapers in 1993, while Atlanta, Baltimore, Dallas, Minneapolis, and New Orleans had monopoly papers. Since more populous cities also tend to have more local representatives for journalists to cover, it is important to control for the number of districts in a newspaper's core circulation area. This helps to guarantee that we don't confuse the effects of competition on news coverage with the effects of rival subjects. Controlling for each newspaper's daily circulation is also important, since circulation is known to be associated with both competition and the volume of coverage.

Table 7.1 contains three tests of Zaller's hypothesis that competition impedes the production of news about local representatives. All tests are conducted with subsets of the third data set. The first equation is for the 31 newspapers that were chosen randomly and includes a total of 125 representative/newspaper dyads. This group includes all 25 newspapers from the first data set, which were selected as a stratified random sample from all available newspapers, and the six additional newspapers from the second data set, which were chosen randomly from the list of available same-city newspapers. The second equation is for the 36 newspapers that were not chosen randomly and includes an additional 117 representative/newspaper dyads. The third equation is for the union of all 67 newspapers in the third data set.

Table 7.1 supports the hypothesis that competition among local newspapers impedes the production of news about local representatives. A newspaper with at least one competing daily paper published 70 fewer articles about its local representative than did a monopoly newspaper. The negative effect of competition on the volume of news is apparent despite controls for circulation, which appears not to matter, and for the number of representatives in a newspaper's core circulation area, which matters a great deal. The effect of competition on coverage is statistically significant in both the equa-

---

each other. For example, the *Los Angles Times* competes on the home turf of the *Orange County Register* and the *San Diego Union-Tribune*. I avoided this form of competition when assembling the four data sets, since one of the decision rules for matching newspaper circulation with congressional districts was to "avoid matching a suburban district with a city's newspaper if the suburban area has its own newspaper included among the 88 papers" (see chapter 1). I continue to avoid this form of competition in order to keep the analysis manageable.

[4] Information about ownership, joint operating agreements, and editorial staffs is from Editor & Publisher 1993.

TABLE 7.1
Effects of Newspaper Competition in Three Samples

	Equation		
	7.1	7.2	7.3
Competing daily newspaper in the same city (yes = 1)	−79.856* (35.664)	−3.713 (44.493)	−70.181** (26.528)
Resources: Newspaper's Daily Circulation (in thousands)	.025 (.064)	−.005 (.064)	.047 (.044)
Rival Subjects: Number of Districts in Paper's Core Circulation Area	−6.853 (5.608)	−27.403*** (4.846)	−18.375*** (3.498)
Constant	320.696*** (28.640)	459.251*** (26.929)	396.795*** (19.374)
Number of Cases	125	117	242
Adjusted R^2	.097	.412	.284

Notes: Dependent variable: number of articles in each representative/newspaper dyad (1/1/93–11/8/94).

All results are from the third data set. Equation 7.1 is for the 31 newspapers that are also in the first and second data sets; equation 7.2 is for the 36 newspapers that are only in the third data set; equation 7.3 is for their union.

Entries are unstandardized regression coefficients (standard errors in parentheses).

* $p < .05$ ** $p < .01$ *** $p < .001$

tion based on the random sample (equation 7.1) and in the full sample (equation 7.3), although not in the middle equation. Seventy percent of the newspapers that had local competitors are concentrated in the first and third equations.

Table 7.2 adds the new variable on competition to the two large models that were developed in chapter 2 to explain the volume of coverage in 67 newspapers. Equation 7.4, which is a one-variable revision of equation 2.1, demonstrates that the effect of competition on the volume of coverage in 1993 and 1994 is virtually the same as in the simple model reported in table 7.1. A competitive newspaper published 72 fewer articles about a local representative than did a similarly situated monopoly paper. Equation 7.5 shows that the effects of competition are also strong when the dependent variable is the volume of coverage during the ten-week campaign season (11 fewer articles). Most of the other relationships reported in chapter 2 are unchanged in the expanded model, with the exception of those involving rival subjects and newspaper circulation, both of which are attenuated (see tables 2.4 and 2.6).[5] It is now clear that although newspapers published

---

[5] In addition to the two equations reported in table 7.2, the new variable on competition was added to all the other equations reported in tables 2.4 and 2.6. The results were no different from those that are reported in table 7.2.

TABLE 7.2
Effects of Newspaper Competition on the Volume of Coverage

	Equation	
	7.4	7.5
Competing daily newspaper in the same city (yes = 1)	−71.958** (23.163)	−11.341** (4.308)
Resources: Newspaper's Daily Circulation (in thousands)	.094* (.048)	.022** (.009)
Washington Resources: Any Reporters in DC (yes = 1)	−24.095 (29.263)	−10.252 (5.591)
Washington Reporters per Number of Districts in Core Circulation Area	−1.345 (2.479)	−.510 (.446)
Rival Subjects: Number of Districts in Paper's Core Circulation Area	−18.587*** (3.519)	−3.521*** (.653)
Newspaper Readership: District's Median Family Income (in thousands)	−2.151* (.996)	−.470** (.183)
Reporter Bias: Member's ADA Score, 1993–94	.097 (.267)	−.053 (.051)
Number of References to Member in CQWR Index	2.186*** (.300)	.233*** (.063)
Member Investigated by Ethics Committee (yes = 1)	145.475** (51.664)	21.337* (9.452)
Member Running for Senator or Governor (yes = 1)	188.693*** (43.964)	
Member's Percentage in 1992 General Election	−1.986* (.878)	.044 (.189)
Member's Campaign Spending for 1994 Election (in thousands)		.006 (.005)
Challenger's Campaign Spending for 1994 Election (in thousands)		.040*** (.007)
Member Running Unopposed in 1994 General Election (yes = 1)		−16.792* (6.986)
Constant	528.807*** (76.654)	66.316*** (15.749)
Number of Cases	242	222
Adjusted R^2	.509	.510

Notes: Dependent variable (7.4): number of articles in each representative/newspaper dyad (1/1/93–11/8/94). Dependent variable (7.5): number of articles in each representative/newspaper dyad (9/1/94–11/8/94).
   Entries are unstandardized regression coefficients (standard errors in parentheses).
   * p < .05   ** p < .01   *** p < .001

fewer articles about a local representative when they had other representatives to cover, the reduction was much less when a newspaper enjoyed a local monopoly than when it had at least one competitor.

Competing Newspapers

Newspapers that compete with each other publish fewer articles about local representatives than do similarly situated newspapers that enjoy local monopolies. That much is clear. But do competing newspapers differ in what news they choose to report? Does one paper specialize in reporting political news while its main competitor features other types of stories? Do competing papers portray a representative in similar ways or do they paint very different portraits of what a representative has been doing in office and where he or she stands on the issues? Does competition induce convergence or divergence in how newspapers cover local representatives?

Newspapers can differentiate themselves in many ways. They once differentiated themselves according to partisan and factional affiliations. Partisan affiliation affected both news coverage and opinion coverage; or, perhaps more accurately, newspapers had yet to develop the distinction between news and opinion coverage that we recognize today. Partisan affiliation was often displayed proudly and prominently as part of a newspaper's name. Although some newspapers retain vestiges of these partisan affiliations in their names, both the need to attract broader audiences and the evolving norms of journalism have driven blatant partisanship from the news pages of most papers (Cook 1998, 20–37). Of course, partisan and ideological preferences are still visible on many editorial pages. Few students of politics would have trouble determining whether a stack of editorials came from the rightward leaning *Washington Times* or the leftward leaning *Washington Post*. It remains an open question, however, whether preferences expressed strongly on a newspaper's editorial pages affect how its reporters cover political news.

Newspapers can also aim for different types of audiences. Some cities harbor competition between a broadsheet and a tabloid, the former aiming more for an upscale, educated audience, the latter for a downscale audience, often by featuring stories about crime, violence, and scandal (Entman 1989, 91–95). Whether tabloids and broadsheets cover legislative and electoral politics in distinctive ways has yet to be determined. Perhaps broadsheets emphasize politics more than tabloids do. Perhaps tabloids publish similar quantities of information about local representatives but differ from broadsheets in the kinds of news that they choose to cover about representatives. Or perhaps newspaper competition is better captured by a Downsian model where local newspapers converge and provide nearly identical coverage, just as *Time* and *Newsweek* publish similar newsmagazines, and ABC, CBS, and NBC produce similar newscasts.

Table 7.3 shows that competing newspapers did converge and provide similar amounts of information about six local representatives.[6] Recall from table 2.1 the great diversity in how much information 25 local newspapers published about 25 representatives, with the most active paper publishing nearly five times as many articles per month as the least active paper. Table 7.3, which is identical in format to table 2.1, is a story of competing newspapers converging — and converging at a low level. Whether the measure is articles per month or headline mentions, the *Boston Globe* and the *Boston Herald* provided virtually the same volume of coverage. The same was true for the *Washington Times* and the *Washington Post*. The convergence was not quite as tight in Chicago, San Francisco, Seattle, and Tucson, but the differences between articles per month for competing newspapers were small compared to the differences in table 2.1. The more active paper in each of these four pairs published between 25 and 38 percent more articles per month than the less active paper.

The two tabloids had no trouble keeping up with their broadsheet competitors. The *Chicago Sun-Times* and the *Boston Herald*, the only tabloids among the twelve papers, either matched or exceeded the volume of coverage in their competitors. The *Sun-Times* published 38 percent more articles per month about William Lipinski than did the *Tribune*; the two Boston papers published nearly identical amounts about Joe Moakley. The tabloids accomplished this despite the fact that each paper published much shorter newspapers than its competitor.[7]

Position Taking

Position taking is one of the easiest legislative activities for journalists to cover (see chapter 4). Roll-call voting is especially easy to report, since representatives voted on more than a thousand roll-call votes during the study period, all of them readily available for local newspapers to use, whether as part of regular news stories or in stand-alone lists. Were competing newspapers equally likely to grab this low-lying fruit and report representatives'

[6] The attentive reader may notice that the total number of articles reported for several newspapers in table 7.3 is greater than what was reported for the same newspapers in tables 2.2 and 2.3. The reason is that table 7.3 is based on the second data set, obtained with a more exhaustive search routine, whereas tables 2.2 and 2.3 are based on the third data set, where the search routine was less exhaustive. See chapters 1 and 2 for further details.

[7] The consumption of newsprint per reader is a convenient measure of a newspaper's average size. The *Boston Herald* consumed 136 tons of paper annually per thousand daily circulation, compared to 228 tons for the *Globe*. The *Chicago Sun-Times* used 218 tons annually per thousand daily circulation, compared to 276 tons for the *Tribune* (Editor & Publisher 1993).

TABLE 7.3
Volume of Coverage in Paired Newspapers

Newspaper	Representative	Name in Headline	Total Mentions in Text	Mentions per Article	Total Articles	Articles per Month
Boston Globe	Moakley	20	637	2.6	255	11.4
Boston Herald	Moakley	23	766	3.1	251	11.3
Chicago Sun-Times	Lipinski	15	518	2.3	228	10.2
Chicago Tribune	Lipinski	7	382	2.4	164	7.4
San Francisco Chronicle	Dellums	14	287	2.3	132	5.9
San Francisco Examiner	Dellums	14	458	2.6	182	8.2
Seattle Times	McDermott	10	316	2.2	147	6.6
Seattle Post-Intelligencer	McDermott	24	534	3.0	186	8.3
Tucson Citizen	Kolbe	35	484	3.2	161	7.2
Arizona Daily Star	Kolbe	32	569	2.9	204	9.1
Washington Times	Wynn	4	250	2.0	130	5.8
Washington Post	Wynn	5	399	3.0	135	6.1
Median (above 12 newspapers)		15	471	2.6	173	7.8
Median (other 19 newspapers)		39	1,118	3.1	357	16.0

Coding: Articles include news stories, editorials, opinion columns, letters, and lists. Total Mentions in Text is a count of all references to a representative's last name in the body of an article. Mentions per Article includes both headline and text mentions.

Notes: All counts are from the second data set. Monthly averages are based on 22.3 months. Each median is the median for a single column of data. The medians for the other 19 newspapers in the first data set are calculated from the counts in table 2.1.

positions to their readers? Table 7.4 shows that competing newspapers, despite their convergence in overall levels of coverage, reported position-taking activities in diverse ways. In four of the six cities — Chicago, San Francisco, Seattle, and Washington — one newspaper published between two and two-and-one-half times as many articles about position taking as the competing paper. The divergence was especially great for the reporting of roll-call votes, where one paper in San Francisco published six times as many articles as its competitor.

TABLE 7.4
Coverage of Position Taking in Paired Newspapers

Newspaper	Representative	Cosponsor or Endorse Bill	Express Some Views on Bill	Firm Position on Pending Bill	Actual Position on Roll-Call Vote	Total
Boston Globe	Moakley	3	13	3	7	26
Boston Examiner	Moakley	5	25	7	6	43
Chicago Sun-Times	Lipinski	2	9	7	67	85
Chicago Tribune	Lipinski	2	5	1	29	37
San Francisco Chronicle	Dellums	3	24	—	9	36
San Francisco Examiner	Dellums	4	28	2	55	89
Seattle Times	McDermott	5	15	1	5	26
Seattle Post-Intelligencer	McDermott	15	21	—	15	51
Tucson Citizen	Kolbe	10	12	5	14	41
Arizona Daily Star	Kolbe	15	25	4	21	65
Washington Times	Wynn	—	17	3	57	77
Washington Post	Wynn	—	7	2	23	32
Median (above 12 newspapers)		4	16	3	18	42
Median (other 19 newspapers)		8	34	6	52	98

Coding: The four position-taking activities are defined in table 4.1.

Notes: All counts are from the second data set. Each median is the median for a single column of data. The medians for the other 19 newspapers in the first data set are calculated from the counts in table 4.1.

One reason for the disparities in coverage of position taking is that three newspapers — the *Chicago Sun-Times, San Francisco Examiner*, and *Washington Times* — regularly published lists of how area representatives voted on recent roll calls, while their competitors did so infrequently. The decision to publish roll-call lists is a policy decision that strongly affects the volume of coverage on position taking. But this simple editorial choice is only half the story. Newspapers had differing tastes for covering where representatives stood even in their regular news coverage. The *Chicago Sun-Times* discussed William Lipinski's controversial positions on NAFTA and the FY94 budget in 41 articles; the *Chicago Tribune* did so in 15 (see table 7.5). The *Arizona Daily Star* declared Jm Kolbe's position on NAFTA newsworthy on 16 occasions; the *Tucson Citizen* declared it so only 8 times. The *Seattle*

TABLE 7.5
Representatives' Positions on Four Major Issues in Paired Newspapers

Newspaper	Representative	Crime	Budget	NAFTA	Health	Other	Total
Boston Globe	Moakley	2	1	4	4	15	26
Boston Examiner	Moakley	1	9	11	3	19	43
Chicago Sun-Times	Lipinski	5	28	13	—	39	85
Chicago Tribune	Lipinski	4	10	5	—	18	37
San Francisco Chronicle	Dellums	1	—	4	—	31	36
San Francisco Examiner	Dellums	5	5	3	1	75	89
Seattle Times	McDermott	4	1	3	6	12	26
Seattle Post Intelligencer	McDermott	5	1	3	15	27	51
Tucson Citizen	Kolbe	9	2	8	1	21	41
Arizona Daily Star	Kolbe	3	3	16	1	42	65
Washington Times	Wynn	9	7	4	—	57	77
Washington Post	Wynn	2	3	5	1	21	32
Median (above 12 newspapers)		4	3	5	1	24	42
Median (other 19 newspapers)		11	9	7	6	63	98

Coding: Crime refers to votes on the Omnibus Crime Act as well as the separate assault weapons bill that was later incorporated into the crime act. Budget refers to votes on the Omnibus Deficit Reduction Act as well as its precursor, the FY94 budget resolution. Health refers to comprehensive health care reform.

Notes: All counts are from the second data set. Each median is the median for a single column of data. The medians for the other 19 newspapers in the first data set are calculated from the counts in table 4.6.

Post-Intelligencer covered Jim McDermott's position on comprehensive health care reform in 15 articles; the *Seattle Times* reported it in 6.

Tables 7.4 and 7.5 are the best evidence so far about the extent to which editorial tastes vary across newspapers. Each of the paired newspapers had the same representative to cover, had access to the same objective record of roll-call votes, and presumably received the same supply of press releases from representatives, their supporters, and their opponents announcing, defending, or criticizing a representative's positions. Nevertheless, the editors at each paper choose to cover position taking in very different ways. Put differently, the objective reality was identical for each representative; but the news that competing papers chose to report was very different. Citizens who subscribed to one paper learned different things about a representative's policy positions than did their friends and neighbors who subscribed to the other paper.

Other Political Activities

How did newspapers report other legislative and electoral activities? We know that some representatives are active lawmakers; others choose to invest their energies elsewhere. Some legislators are energetic local agents, working to acquire constituency benefits; others delegate this task to staff. Some representatives face tough electoral opponents and campaign ceaselessly for reelection; others face weak challengers. The question is whether competing newspapers recognize these distinctions. Does one paper cover a representative as an active lawmaker while its competitor concentrates on the legislator working as a local agent? Does one paper heavily cover a representative's reelection campaign while the other paper largely ignores the campaign?

Table 7.6 shows how the six pairs of newspapers covered three important activities. "Lawmaking" refers to a representative introducing bills, participating in committee or subcommittee meetings, or acting as a party leader, caucus leader, or coalition builder — in short, doing just about anything related to lawmaking except for taking positions on other people's proposals. "Local agent" refers to a representative working to acquire geographic benefits for his or her constituency or working to block the imposition of geographic costs. "Campaign" refers to a representative running for reelection, including at the primary and general election stages.

The six paired newspapers gave representatives' lawmaking activities similar amounts of coverage. Both Seattle papers published an above-average number of articles about Jim McDermott's lawmaking activities; both San Francisco and Tucson papers were close to average in their coverage of Ronald Dellums and Jim Kolbe; both Boston papers were a bit below average for Joe Moakley; and both Chicago and Washington papers were well below average for William Lipinski and Albert Wynn. The paired newspapers also gave similar amounts of coverage to representatives acting as local agents, and they largely agreed about the relative importance of representatives' activities as lawmakers and local agents. The Boston, Chicago, and Tucson papers portrayed their three representatives more as local agents than as lawmakers; the Seattle papers portrayed Jim McDermott more as lawmaker than local agent; and the Washington papers portrayed Albert Wynn as not particularly active in either role. Only the San Francisco papers were inconsistent in their ranking of relative importance, although the differences were small. The volume of campaign coverage was similar in four pairs of papers — Chicago, San Francisco, Seattle, and Tucson — but divergent in the other two. The

TABLE 7.6
Coverage of Other Political Activities in Paired Newspapers

		Number of Articles on		
Newspaper	Representative	Lawmaking Activities	Local Agent	Election Campaign
Boston Globe	Moakley	20	67	33
Boston Examiner	Moakley	12	47	11
Chicago Sun-Times	Lipinski	12	28	16
Chicago Tribune	Lipinski	9	20	20
San Francisco Chronicle	Dellums	15	34	4
San Francisco Examiner	Dellums	25	24	2
Seattle Times	McDermott	31	7	6
Seattle Post-Intelligencer	McDermott	55	7	5
Tucson Citizen	Kolbe	15	30	29
Arizona Daily Star	Kolbe	26	49	21
Washington Times	Wynn	4	11	3
Washington Post	Wynn	9	9	16
Median (above 12 newspapers)		15	26	14
Median (other 19 newspapers)		23	59	12

Coding: Lawmaking activities include bill introductions, committee activities, and leadership activities (see table 5.4). Local agent refers to dealing with a proposal to acquire geographic benefits or block the imposition of geographic costs (see table 5.5). Campaign coverage includes the primary and the general election (see table 6.1).

Notes: All counts are from the second data set. Each median is the median for a single column of data. The medians for the other 19 newspapers in the first data set are calculated from the counts in tables 5.4, 5.5, and 6.1 (except for campaign coverage which is based on the 13 representatives in table 6.1 who were running in contested elections).

Washington Post published five times as many campaign articles about Albert Wynn as the *Washington Times*, and the *Boston Globe* three times as many about Joe Moakley as the *Boston Examiner*.

Overall Patterns

What are we to make of these overall patterns of coverage among the six pairs of competing newspapers? The lead story is one of convergence. Most competing newspapers portrayed individual representatives in similar ways. It was not the case that one paper covered a representative as a diligent lawmaker, while the other portrayed the representative as an active pork barreler. Despite these similarities, competing newspapers diverged in many important ways, most notably in their coverage of position taking and re-election campaigns. Some newspapers reported much more carefully where a representative stood on the issues than did their competitors; some newspapers covered campaigns more diligently than did other same-city papers. Finally, most competing newspapers covered the representatives in their local coverage areas much less assiduously than did monopoly papers. The convergence was at a low level, and the level was only partly a consequence of these newspapers having multiple representatives to cover.

These generalizations still do not get to the heart of the matter. It is still not clear if local citizens would perceive a representative in different ways depending on which of two competing local newspapers they happened to read. Did newspapers such as the *Washington Post* and the *Washington Times*, so far apart on their editorial pages, convey different messages about local representatives like Albert Wynn? Knowing that the *Post* covered the campaign more extensively, while the *Times* covered position taking more heavily, tells us only part of what we seek to learn.

The rest of this chapter examines more closely how each of the six pairs of newspapers covered a local representative. My focus is on what messages each newspaper conveyed about a representative and on whether there were significant differences between competing papers. The approach is a combination of qualitative and quantitative analysis. Although the quantitative approach has been necessary for examining the coverage patterns of the 31 newspapers in the first and second data sets, a qualitative approach is feasible for comparing two papers at a time.

Boston Papers

Joe Moakley chaired the House Rules Committee, the gatekeeping committee that controls the flow of bills to the House floor. He was a major player in Washington politics. Few readers of the *Boston Globe* or the *Boston Herald* would ever learn much about what role this committee leader played in Congress. Although his chairmanship was often mentioned in the two Boston papers (BG 66, BH 61),[8] Moakley was rarely shown doing anything as chair (BG 15, BH 9). Journalists treated the position in the same way they routinely identify party and state when they mention a politician, "Joe Moakley, (D-MA), chair of the House Rules Committee, today declared . . ." It was a title, nothing more.

Both newspapers emphasized Moakley's efforts and successes as a local

---

[8] These brief notations should be read "*Boston Globe* 66 articles, *Boston Herald* 61 articles."

agent, attracting money for his district, city, and state. It was not just the number of articles (*BG* 67, *BH* 47), but the tone and prominence of the coverage. My assistants quickly noted that Moakley's home style was probably that of servicing the district (Fenno 1978, 101–13). Although both newspapers covered national issues with some frequency, the *Herald* was more informative. More of its stories had a Washington dateline (*BH* 102, *BG* 84) and more of them mentioned something about the three major issues before the 103rd Congress—NAFTA, crime control, and the deficit (*BH* 57, *BG* 35). Neither paper did a very good job at covering the local campaign. Although the *Globe* published more campaign stories than the *Herald* (table 7.6), the coverage was not particularly informative.

The biggest difference between the two Boston papers was the tone of the coverage. The *Globe* usually portrayed Moakley in a favorable light; the *Herald* was much more critical. This pattern was most obvious on the editorial pages, where the *Globe* had seven times as many positive pieces as negative ones, while the *Herald* had ten times as many negative pieces as positive ones. Positive coverage was also more common in the news pages of the *Globe* than in the *Herald*.[9] Consider the difference in how the papers covered Moakley's refusal to debate his Republican opponent. Although the *Globe* mentioned in several news stories that Moakley was unable to agree to terms for a debate, it was silent on the editorial page. The closest the *Globe* came to a critical reaction was when it endorsed Moakley's reelection with just one reservation: "In particular, we support Representative Joseph Moakley of South Boston, although he should be more willing to debate Republican Michael Murphy" (*BG* 10/30/94 74). In contrast, the *Herald* wrote a scathing editorial:

> The two U.S. Senate candidates and every incumbent Massachusetts congressman except one already has debated or accepted debate offers against their challengers. The lone holdout, Rep. Joseph Moakley (D-South Boston), should get off his high horse and debate 9th District Republican nominee Michael Murphy. Moakley insists that Murphy must sign a virtual unilateral disarmament—a so-called "clean and fair campaign practices pledge"—before any encounter. Rightly, Murphy refuses to sign. The pledge contains vague bans on "personal attacks" and exacts a promise from the challenger not to "spend a penny of campaign funds promoting unsubstantiated attacks and politically motivated charges." Come on, Joe. Do you get to define "unsubstantiated?" Does that mean news reports criticizing your free rides to Boston aboard a Federal Express jet are off limits? . . . You don't owe it to Murphy. You owe it to your constituents. (*BH* 10/26/94 32)

[9] In the opinion pieces for which my assistants coded valence, the *Globe* published 14 positive and 2 negative pieces, the *Herald* 2 positive and 20 negative. On the news pages, the corresponding figures were 59 and 11 for the *Globe*, 29 and 11 for the *Herald*.

The critical coverage in the *Herald* was, in my view, much more informative than the excessively laudatory coverage in the *Globe*.

Boston was fortunate to have two daily newspapers. Unfortunately, neither paper was very good at covering the legislative activities of Joe Moakley. The *Boston Globe* was clearly one of the least informative papers in the entire study. One assistant who helped code the 25 newspapers in the first data set wrote that "the *Boston Globe* was one of the most superficial papers we read." Another assistant, who read all articles in the second data set, ranked the *Globe* as eleventh out of twelve papers in informativeness (beating out the *Washington Times* for last place).[10] Although the *Boston Herald* was somewhat more informative (ranked eighth out of twelve), it was far from being a model paper. It was merely the better paper in a weak pair.

Both newspapers surely had the resources, both in Washington and Boston, to do better. Moreover, Moakley was doing plenty of newsworthy things. James Inhofe, the junior Republican from Oklahoma, attracted superb coverage in the *Tulsa World* when he mounted a campaign to change the rules of the House so that the names of all representatives who signed a petition to discharge a bill from a recalcitrant committee would be made public (see chapter 5). Since Inhofe's successful battle was waged largely against Joe Moakley and the party leaders, one might have thought that the Boston papers would cover the story at least as comprehensively as did the much smaller *Tulsa World*. They did not. The *Boston Globe* covered the national story, but it never informed Moakley's constituents why he was opposed to the cleansing effects of sunshine. The closest the reader got to an argument was Moakley's assertion that reformers were "peddling snake oil" or that reform would give "fat cats and special interests a road map on who to go after" (*BG* 9/9/93 9). The *Boston Herald* published more articles on the subject, including a column by Moakley that made a case for the status quo, several articles that discussed the tensions between Moakley and area representatives who favored reform, and a postmortem analysis of why Moakley lost and what the loss said about the decline of his type of power in the modern House (*BH* 8/29/93 28; 8/29/93 14; 9/19/93 11). An editorial in the *Herald* even took aim against the *Boston Globe* for supporting Moakley's efforts, suggesting that the *Globe* was "a newspaper opposed to debate — now there's one for 'Ripley's Believe It or Not!'" (*BH* 9/27/93 20). The quality of coverage in these three papers was inversely correlated with their resources.[11]

Why the two Boston papers were so weak is far from obvious. Perhaps Moakley, elected in 1972, was such a well-known fixture to Boston journal-

---

[10] This assistant, who was not involved in coding the articles and who did not have access to the coded data, was asked to read the articles in the second data set and rank the twelve papers according to how informative they were for citizens.

[11] Daily circulations were *Tulsa World* (127,476), *Boston Herald* (330,614), *Boston Globe* (508,867).

ists that they believed there wasn't much new to report about him. But such a view was not very helpful to citizens who do not follow politics carefully, to new residents of Moakley's district, or to first-time voters. In short, it was not very helpful to most South Boston readers.

Seattle Papers

The two Seattle papers were considerably more informative than the two Boston papers. The *Seattle Post-Intelligencer* was the better of the two. Indeed, my assistant ranked it the most informative of the twelve newspapers in the second data set. Although the *Seattle Times* had many virtues, it was much less thorough and comprehensive than the *Post-Intelligencer.*

The lead story in both papers was comprehensive health care reform. Jim McDermott was a major player in health care reform, both as author of one reform option, a Canadian-style single-payer approach, and as coalition leader working to attract support for various reforms. Thirty-four percent of the articles that mentioned McDermott in the *Post-Intelligencer* mentioned health care reform (64 articles), while 27 percent of those that mentioned him in the *Times* mentioned health care (40 articles). Coverage of health care reform in the *Post-Intelligencer* was considerably more thorough and nuanced than coverage in the *Times.* Although both papers were excessively laudatory in their coverage of McDermott's role in health care reform, this pattern probably reflected local pride in having its representative centrally involved in an important national debate and hobnobbing with the president. It was not apparent in the papers' coverage of McDermott and other issues.

The *Post-Intelligencer* covered McDermott's connection with other national issues reasonably effectively, including 29 articles that mentioned something about NAFTA, crime control, and the deficit. Although the volume of coverage on these issues was smaller than in many other papers, the articles were more informative than average. Coverage of these issues in the *Times* was less frequent (21 articles) and less informative. One reason for the superior coverage in the *Post-Intelligencer* was its greater use of Washington-based reporters. Nearly a third of the articles in the *Post-Intelligencer* had a Washington dateline (58 articles), compared with 14 percent in the *Times* (20 articles). Articles from Washington-based reporters in the *Post-Intelligencer* were particularly effective at discussing what was happening on some national issue, with journalists incorporating information about where McDermott stood and how he saw Congress resolving the issue. Both papers portrayed McDermott's home style as a specialist on national issues, not local issues (Fenno 1978, 91–99). In fact, few articles mentioned him acting as local agent (*SPI* 7, *ST* 7).

Neither paper seemed interested in McDermott's chairmanship of the

Committee on Standards of Official Conduct, better known as the House Ethics Committee. The *Post-Intelligencer* did mention that "Representative Jim McDermott, D-Wash., was named head of the House Ethics Committee," but those thirteen words were all the paper had to say about his chairmanship during the two-year study period (*SPI* 2/5/93 A3). The *Times* was no more forthcoming. Its only mention was in an article discussing why McDermott took his name out of the running for AIDS Policy Coordinator in the Clinton administration, where the reporter noted that "the position came up at a time when McDermott is beginning to work his way into a position of leadership in the House. He is a regional whip and earlier this year Speaker Tom Foley appointed him chairman of the House's ethics committee, known as the Committee on Standards of Official Conduct" (*ST* 5/26/93 B2). The failure of the two papers to mention anything about McDermott's leadership of the committee, during a time when it handled many high profile cases, including the cases of four recently indicted representatives, Dan Rostenkowski, Mel Reynolds, Joseph McDade, and Walter Tucker, is puzzling, although it is probably not a serious problem for accountability. Unlike the House Rules Committee, where Joe Moakley routinely acted on issues of concern to his constituents, the Ethics Committee acted on issues that were more central to the integrity of Congress. It would be more worrisome if the local papers that served districts represented by those accused of unethical behavior ignored the committee's actions.

Regular readers of the *Post-Intelligencer* and the *Times* would learn quite a bit about Jim McDermott, what he was doing on health care reform, and where he stood on various important issues. Readers would be badly informed, however, if they relied on just the campaign coverage. The two papers provided neither frequent nor detailed coverage of the campaign. Surely one of the problems was that McDermott was the presumptive winner. He had attracted 78 percent of the vote in the previous election, and he was so confident of victory in 1994 that he gave the state Democratic Party a $118,000 contribution from his own campaign treasury (*SPI* 11/3/94 B3). But when newspapers fail to cover challengers' campaigns effectively, they give incumbents one more advantage, especially incumbents like McDermott, who were well covered during the noncampaign season.

Washington Papers

Chapter 3 reported that the *Washington Times* was the least informative newspaper in the first data set. It achieved the same dubious honor in the second data set. There is no doubt in my mind — or that of my assistants — that the *Times* was the least informative of the 31 papers. Before comparing its coverage with that of the *Washington Post*, it is useful to recall what made its coverage so abysmal. In chapter 3 I wrote:

The *Washington Times* covered Albert Wynn lightly. It published only 130 articles that mentioned Albert Wynn — six articles per month — the least coverage of any newspaper in the sample. Any sense that the *Times* might have covered Wynn lightly because he represented a suburban Maryland district about which the editors cared little is easily dismissed. They did, after all, publish 46 photos of Wynn, the most photos of any newspaper in the sample. The *Times* covered Wynn largely as a position taker. Fifty-nine percent of the articles focused on position taking. Only 4 articles covered anything related to bills he had introduced or to his committee activities, the least of any newspaper in the sample. Opinion coverage was also the lightest for any newspaper: two editorials and one letter. Although coverage of position taking is important, the approach the *Times* employed was not very informative. Rather than incorporating coverage of roll-call votes into news stories, editorials, or opinion columns, the *Times* published lists of roll-call votes. The lists seldom had an accompanying explanation of the basic policy conflict. Many of the lists were accompanied by file photos of Albert Wynn and seven other representatives from Maryland and Virginia. It was a nice attempt to draw attention to otherwise drab lists with dull headlines (How Our Representatives Voted), but in addition to attracting attention, the editors might have illuminated the policy conflicts that gave rise to the votes so that readers could evaluate representatives' positions.

Perhaps some readers of this book should admit that when they first read this assessment of coverage in the *Times* they assumed the consequences were relatively minor, since the *Post* is the dominant paper in the Washington metro area, and the *Post* is known to be one of the country's best papers. Unfortunately, the *Post*'s coverage of Albert Wynn was only marginally better than the *Times*. The *Post* is a great paper, well known for its national coverage, investigative reporting, and columnists, but the *Post* chose not to invest much talent or space in covering the freshman representative Albert Wynn.

The *Washington Post* published 135 articles that mentioned Wynn. Only two papers published fewer articles than the *Post* — the *Washington Times* and the *San Francisco Chronicle*. The *Post* was much less likely to cover position taking than the *Times* (WP 32, WT 77), but it was much more likely to give readers some information about the nature of the policy conflict when it did report his positions. The *Post* portrayed Wynn as heavily involved in local politics in Prince George's county, including his unsuccessful effort to obtain for a friend the Democratic nomination for county executive. The paper also portrayed him as reasonably active in constituency service. Like the *Times*, it wrote little about what Wynn was doing in Congress other than taking positions. Campaign coverage was more plentiful in the *Post* than the *Times*, but it was not very informative compared to that in other papers.

Why did the *Post* and the *Times* have so little to say about Albert Wynn's activities in Congress? Perhaps there wasn't much news to report about a freshman legislator. One problem with that argument is that other papers found plenty to report about their freshmen legislators. The *Las Vegas Review-Journal*, one of the best newspapers in the sample, covered extensively what James Bilbray was doing in Congress (see chapter 3), as did the *San Diego Union-Tribune* and the *Buffalo News* for Bob Filner and Jack Quinn. Perhaps Albert Wynn, unlike the other freshmen, did not do very much worth reporting. That is the line that a *Post* reporter took in an excellent article entitled, "Wynn, After Making History in '92, Toiled Quietly through First Term" (WP 10/29/94 B8). But a representative who is doing little in Congress while meddling endlessly in county politics should be the subject of news coverage too. The *lack* of effort and accomplishment is news, and it is highly relevant for citizens who need to pass judgment on their representative. The most telling quote in this article was by Ben Sheffner, assistant editor of the *Cook Report*, who claimed "I can't remember reading anything positive or negative about what he's done in the past Congress." Finally, even if Wynn had done nothing more than take positions, journalists missed the opportunity to interview Wynn and show how he reasoned about complicated votes on crime, the deficit, and NAFTA, or what he thought about health care reform. These were tough issues for many legislators. Many papers helped readers understand why legislators took the positions they did by reporting how they balanced the trade-offs among competing goals and why they voted as they did. The two Washington papers did little to help their readers understand how Wynn approached difficult issues.

Tucson Papers

The *Arizona Daily Star* was much more informative than the *Tucson Citizen*. The volume of coverage was only 27 percent greater in the *Star*, but the information packed into those 204 articles was vastly greater than in the *Citizen*'s 161 articles. The *Star* painted a reasonably rich portrait of Jim Kolbe; the *Citizen* offered just a hazy sketch. Although the sketch and the portrait were clearly of the same man, the sketch was a poor guide for citizens who wondered what their representative was doing in office or where he stood on a range of issues.

The *Star*'s portrait emphasized three things about Kolbe. First, readers would learn that Kolbe was a strong and active supporter of NAFTA. He chaired a bipartisan House task force on free trade and worked actively to build a winning coalition for the trade pact. An article headlined "Arizonans

Dare Perot to Debate" announced that Kolbe and John McCain had challenged Ross Perot to a debate on NAFTA whenever or wherever Perot might like (ADS 6/18/93 3A). When Perot visited Arizona without agreeing to a debate, Kolbe was his chief critic. Second, readers would learn where Kolbe stood on most national issues. He came across as a free-thinking Republican, economically conservative but more moderate on social and cultural issues. For example, he was one of twelve Republicans to vote against the amendment that codified the long-standing policy about gays in the military.[12] Third, Kolbe was very active as a local agent, working to acquire benefits for his district, including advocating that the Saguaro National Monument become a national park. The *Star* covered most of these things in their day-to-day coverage. Campaign coverage was not nearly as informative.

The *Tucson Citizen* touched on many of these same themes, but the themes were poorly developed. Readers could learn that Kolbe was somehow active on NAFTA, but the paper published virtually no details of his activism. The *Citizen* reported Kolbe's positions on some national issues, but it missed many important issues. The only place that coverage in the *Citizen* resembled coverage in the *Star* was in depicting Kolbe's actions as local agent, although even here, the stories in the *Star* were much richer. Campaign coverage in the *Citizen* was abysmal, mostly focusing on the horse race.

Chicago Papers

Both the *Chicago Sun-Times* and the *Chicago Tribune* painted similar portraits of William Lipinski. Although the *Sun-Times* published more articles that mentioned Lipinski than the *Tribune* (CST 228, CT 164), the *Tribune's* coverage was more comprehensive, balanced, and informative. Both papers portrayed Lipinski principally as an influential leader in Chicago politics. In addition to representing the Third District in Congress, Lipinski was the Democratic committeeman for the Twenty-third Ward. He was one of the last old-style ward bosses, repeatedly able to deliver large margins for almost any candidate. In early 1993, Lipinski ordered James Laski, the alderman for the Twenty-third Ward, to vote for Mayor Daley's proposed property tax increase. When Laski refused, Lipinski ordered him to vacate his aldermanic office in Democratic headquarters (CT 2/10/93 1). Both papers covered the ensuing battle in great detail — indeed, in more detail than they covered anything Lipinski did in Washington during 1993 and 1994. Li-

---

[12] This vote occurred three years before Kolbe announced that he was gay, an announcement triggered by an impending article in a gay magazine.

pinski was the only representative in the study whose home style — at least as portrayed by the 31 newspapers — appeared to be that of local political leader (Fenno 1978, 113–124).

The biggest difference between the two Chicago papers was the tone of the coverage. The *Sun-Times* portrayed Lipinski very positively, often stressing how hard he was working for his constituents and how much he had accomplished for them and for all of Chicago. In contrast, the *Tribune* offered a more balanced view of Lipinski, considerably less positive and much less connected to local affairs. Although the difference between the two papers' coverage is reflected in the coding for valence — the *Sun-Times* published 47 positive and 12 negative pieces, the *Tribune* 24 positive and 20 negative ones — it is even more evident if one simply reads at one sitting the nearly 400 articles in the two papers. Journalists at the *Sun-Times* clearly liked Lipinski; those at the *Tribune* covered him more objectively.

The *Sun-Times* published more articles that mentioned Lipinski's positions on the issues before Congress (table 7.4), but the *Tribune* provided more informative coverage of position taking. The *Sun-Times* was more likely to publish a stand-alone list of how area representatives voted on some issue; the *Tribune* was more likely to incorporate coverage of position taking into its coverage of national political issues. Neither paper was very good at covering Lipinski's lawmaking activities, except when those activities had a direct connection with Chicago politics. This was surprising, since Lipinski was actually a very productive legislator (see chapter 5).

Lipinski faced difficult reelection campaigns twice in a row. In 1992 redistricting forced him into a bitter primary with another Democratic incumbent. In 1994 Lipinski made peace with Alderman Laski, who was considering challenging Lipinski, and then battled a well-funded Republican real estate developer, who nearly toppled him (he won 54 to 46 percent). The models in chapter 2 suggest that newspapers publish more articles when elections are competitive, and the two Chicago papers did publish an above-average number of campaign articles (table 7.6). But these articles were not particularly informative about the candidates. Horse race journalism, which was not common in most other papers, was probably a better fit for politics Chicago-style.

San Francisco Papers

The *San Francisco Chronicle* and the *San Francisco Examiner* painted remarkably similar portraits of Ronald Dellums. The convergence in coverage for these newspapers was closer than for any of the other paired newspapers. No matter which San Francisco paper citizens happened to read, they would learn that Ronald Dellums took liberal positions on most issues, was active in constituency service, chaired the House Armed Services Committee, and worked hard to protect the bases in his district from the indignities proposed by the Base Closure and Realignment Commission. No matter which paper they happened to read, they would learn little about the 1994 campaign or his electoral opponent.

Although the messages in the two papers were similar, the papers were distinctive in several respects. The *Examiner* regularly published lists of how Dellums and other San Francisco area representatives voted on roll calls. The *Chronicle*, rather than publishing lists, incorporated the various positions that Dellums took into its coverage of specific issues. Put differently, the *Examiner* published more facts about roll-call voting, the *Chronicle* more interpretative material. Overall, the *Examiner* published more articles that mentioned Dellums, but the articles in the *Chronicle* were considerably more informative. For example, both newspapers covered the government's plan to close four military installations in his district, employing eighteen thousand people, but it was the *Chronicle* that covered the irony of having Dellums, long a critic of military spending, working to preserve spending in his district, or the oddity of Dellums, having reached the pinnacle of congressional power over military affairs, powerless to do anything more than plead his case before an independent commission.

Explanations

What can these six paired comparisons tell us about the factors that affect newspaper coverage of representatives? It helps to recognize that although the differences between coverage in the paired newspapers are real and noticeable, the differences are small compared to the differences in coverage from city to city. Put differently, the within-city variation is relatively small compared to the between-city variation. What might account for this pattern?

One possibility is that newspaper coverage was largely driven by the flow of a representative's press releases. Similar coverage in competing papers would be a consequence of reporters responding to identical flows of press releases from a local representative, while differential coverage between cities would be a consequence of differing flows of press releases from various representatives. Although press release journalism is surely part of the explanation for media coverage of any issue, the coverage in these newspapers does not have the tell-tale signs of excessive reliance on press releases. Nowhere in these six pairs of newspapers do we find anything like the similarities of coverage that one finds in Princeton's competing papers — the *Princeton Packet* and *Town Topics* — where, for example, articles that focus on Princeton University are virtually indistinguishable from each

other and from the press releases on the University's Web-site. Although the
articles in the six paired newspapers were sometimes on the same subjects,
they seldom shared the same structure, details, and quotations. It may well
be that press releases, whether from representatives, their supporters, or their
opponents, stimulated journalists to write these stories, but the stories in
competing newspapers were sufficiently different in subject matter, in the
level of detail, in political sophistication, and in tone, that press release
journalism is only a part—and probably a small part—of the explanation.

A second possibility is that one newspaper in each city took the lead and
originated most of the stories about a local representative, while the other
newspaper was more reactive and published articles a day or two later on
the same subject. This is surely what happens with coverage of many complicated national issues, where respected journalists at the *New York Times*,
Wall Street Journal, and *Washington Post* help frame how other journalists
cover these issues (Cook 1998, 79). This also happens at the local level,
where local newspapers frame how local television and radio stations cover
political campaigns (Mondak 1995; McManus 1990). In contrast, the coverage patterns in the paired newspapers do not suggest that one newspaper
was regularly setting the agenda for the other. To be sure, journalists at one
paper were probably reading what their crosstown colleagues were writing,
so it is likely that each group prodded the other to cover particular issues.
But there is no evidence that one newspaper regularly led while the other
regularly followed.

A third possibility is that the similarities in coverage were largely rooted in
the objective reality of what a representative says and does. Journalists may
pick and choose what to cover about a representative, but they pick and
choose from a relatively short list of positions and behaviors. Moreover, the
positions and behaviors they choose to cover are probably the ones that
journalistic norms suggest are most newsworthy. The two Seattle papers focused on Jim McDermott's role in health care reform rather than on his
chairing the House Ethics Committee because, by the standards of journalism, the intense conflict surrounding health care reform was more newsworthy than the ethical lapses of distant representatives. The two Washington
papers provided scant coverage of Albert Wynn's legislative activities because his almost complete lack of action—however relevant this lack might
have been to Wynn's constituents—would make for a deadly series of stories. The two Chicago papers focused more on William Lipinski's role in
local politics than in national politics because battles among the titans of
Chicago politics—Daley, Rostenkowski, Lipinski—provided much more
drama and excitement for Chicagoans than distant debates that involved the
skilled and productive chair of the Merchant Marine Subcommittee.

The objective reality of what a representative said and did, supplemented
by a flow of press releases that emphasized particular positions and actions,

provided the basic ingredients for what editors and reporters published about representatives. As any good chef knows, however, the supply of ingredients shapes — it does not dictate — the menu for dinner. Journalists had considerable freedom in deciding what to do with the basic ingredients about each representative's behavior. Editors and reporters at competing newspapers emphasized different things.

Sometimes the tone of coverage in competing newspapers diverged. The *Boston Globe* portrayed Joe Moakley in a favorable light, both on its opinion pages and in its news stories, while the *Boston Herald* was highly critical on its opinion pages and much more balanced than the *Globe* in its news stories. The *Chicago Sun-Times* portrayed William Lipinski very positively; the *Chicago Tribune* offered a more balanced view. The tone of coverage was affected both by the choice of subjects that reporters featured — obtaining constituency benefits was almost always portrayed positively — and by the extent to which reporters emphasized the views of a representative's supporters or critics in their stories.

Sometimes journalists emphasized different types of behaviors. The *Washington Post* covered the reelection campaign of Albert Wynn much more frequently than did the *Washington Times*. The *Chicago Sun-Times*, *San Francisco Examiner*, *Seattle Post-Intelligencer*, and *Washington Times* reported the position-taking activities of William Lipinski, Ronald Dellums, Jim McDermott, and Albert Wynn much more frequently than did the *Chicago Tribune*, *San Francisco Chronicle*, *Seattle Times*, or *Washington Post* (table 7.4). The types of behavior that newspapers cover are affected more by the decisions of editors than reporters. Editors decide when to assign reporters to cover campaigns. and they determine which campaigns deserve special attention. Editors also decide whether to publish lists of roll-call votes regularly.

The most striking difference between competing newspapers concerned how informative each paper was about the local representative. Although informativeness is not something that is easily measured with a single metric, my assistants had no trouble judging some newspapers as more informative than others. Informativeness depends on several factors, including the volume of coverage, the breadth of issues covered, the level of detail offered about particular issues, and the extent to which journalists explained complicated matters. The *Arizona Daily Star*, *Chicago Tribune*, and *Seattle Post-Intelligencer* were much more informative than their competitors. The *Boston Herald* and the *San Francisco Chronicle* were somewhat more informative than their competitors. The *Washington Post* was marginally more informative than the *Washington Times*.

How did these papers compare with other papers in the first data set? The informativeness of these twelve papers was relatively low compared with that of the other nineteen newspapers examined in chapters 3 through 6. None of the twelve newspapers were as informative as the five best newspapers in the sample, the *Las Vegas Review-Journal, Los Angeles Times, Tulsa World, Hartford Courant,* or *San Diego Union-Tribune.* Although a case could be made that one of them, the *Seattle Post-Intelligencer,* was above the median, more or less comparable to the *Buffalo News, Lewiston Morning Tribune,* or *Rock Hill Herald,* none of the other eleven papers with same-city competitors were above the median in informativeness.

Summary of Empirical Findings

- A newspaper with at least one competing daily paper published 72 fewer articles about a local representative than did an otherwise similar monopoly newspaper.
- Competing newspapers provided similar amounts of information about representatives. Competition induced a convergence in coverage levels, and convergence at a low level.
- The two tabloid newspapers provided comparable amounts of information about local representatives as their two broadsheet competitors.
- Despite their convergence in overall levels of coverage, competing newspapers reported position-taking activities in diverse ways.
- Competing newspapers gave representatives' lawmaking activities similar amounts of coverage.
- The volume of campaign coverage was comparable in four pairs of competing papers, but divergent in the other two.
- The differences between competing newspapers appeared to be the result of differing editorial practices.
- The differences between newspapers with local competition and newspapers with local monopolies appeared to be the result of market pressures.

Discussion

Two kinds of evidence support Zaller's hypothesis that competitive market pressures diminish the quality of news about politics and public affairs. The quantitative analysis of the third data set shows that competitive newspapers publish fewer articles about local representatives than do otherwise similar monopoly papers. The qualitative analysis of the second data set and the comparison with the other papers in the first data set demonstrate that competitive newspapers are much less informative than most other papers. Competition among newspapers does not enhance coverage of local representatives; it diminishes both the quantity and quality of newspaper coverage.

Economists teach that monopolies tend to produce several evils, including higher prices, less variety, and inferior service. Competition helps insure that firms produce what consumers want and at the lowest prices. In recent decades, efforts to introduce competition into previously regulated industries, for example airlines and trucking, have produced lower prices, greater variety, and better service. All the consequences of competition, however, are not necessarily good. For example, the deregulation of electricity markets, even when it is well designed, seems to produce less reliable service, since no firm has an incentive to invest in the spare generating and transmission capacity that is necessary for year-round reliability.

Monopoly newspapers tend to cover polities and public affairs better than newspapers that compete directly with each other. A cynic might argue that journalists at monopolistic newspapers are providing citizens with something that they clearly do not want, for if citizens wanted it, competitive newspapers would supply it. But the truth is that we don't know enough about the dynamics that create monopoly newspapers. We know that once a newspaper gains an advantage in advertising and circulation over its rival, both advertising and circulation at the weaker paper tend to spiral downward. At a certain point, the weaker paper is doomed, unless it serves a specialized niche. How the stronger paper first gains its advantage is not clear, although some studies suggest that supplying a higher-quality editorial product is what helps a paper attract a larger audience in the first place (Lacy and Simon, 1993, 91–129).

It is probably a mistake to think of local newspapers as monopolies anyway. Even if a newspaper has no competitor that owns a large printing press, it competes vigorously with local radio and television stations for audiences and advertising dollars. Once a dominant newspaper eliminates its print rival, it still needs to differentiate itself from radio and television newscasts. Concentrating on politics and public affairs may be its comparative advantage, just as fires, protests, and car chases appear to be the comparative advantage of local television stations that prefer great visuals to taking heads.

8

Effects of Newspaper Coverage on Citizens

DOES IT MATTER that newspapers differ so much in how they cover representatives? Are citizens who live in districts where newspapers carefully cover representatives better informed than citizens who live in districts where newspapers provide superficial coverage? Does higher quality campaign coverage increase the chances that citizens will learn useful things about challengers as well as incumbents? Do representatives behave differently depending on whether newspapers regularly cover their actions in office? These are questions about whether differences in the informational environment have consequences for citizens' and representatives' behavior.

Scholars have had only limited success in determining how variations in the informational environment affect what citizens know and believe. Michael Delli Carpini and Scott Keeter found that newspapers in Virginia's capital city covered state politics more thoroughly than newspapers in northern Virginia, and as a result Richmond area residents were better informed about state politics than residents of northern Virginia (Delli Carpini and Keeter 1996, 211–13). Marion Just and her coauthors analyzed media messages and citizens' attitudes during the 1992 presidential campaign in Boston, Los Angeles, Winston-Salem, and Moorhead Minnesota, and concluded that citizens were better informed about the candidates and more interested in the electoral contests in cities where the informational environment was richer (Just et al. 1996, 12, 153, 183). Edie Goldenberg and Michael Traugott analyzed the content of newspapers in forty-three congressional districts during three weeks of the 1978 campaign and found that the more frequently a local newspaper mentioned a candidate, the more likely local residents recognized that candidate (Goldenberg and Traugott 1984, 124, 139). Wendy Schiller analyzed newspaper coverage in ten states and found that the volume of coverage in each state affected the ability of citizens to express opinions about their senators (Schiller 2000, 99). Jeffrey Mondak found that Pittsburgh-area residents, who were deprived of local newspapers during a long newspaper strike in 1992, were less interested in local House races, less informed about the candidates, and less likely to discuss House campaigns with family and friends than were Cleveland-area residents, where local newspapers published throughout the 1992 campaign (Mondak 1995).[1]

---

[1] There is also experimental evidence on the topic. Shanto Iyengar and Donald Kinder report evidence from an experiment that shows that messages on television about congressional

Although these studies support the notion that greater news coverage is associated with greater awareness of candidates, it is far from clear that heavy coverage causes greater awareness among citizens. Goldenberg and Traugott found that both newspaper readers and people who were not regular newspaper readers were more likely to recognize candidates when news coverage was heavy (1984, 139). What might account for the effect among nonreaders? One possibility is that both heavy newspaper coverage and greater awareness of candidates are the consequence of intense, hard-fought campaigns, where incumbents and challengers use their talents and financial resources to create campaigns that both citizens and journalists notice (Westlye 1991). A second possibility is that political information is transmitted in stages, first to a phalanx of interested newspaper readers, and later to a group of less attentive citizens through discussions and interactions among family, friends, and coworkers (Huckfeldt and Sprague 1995; Mondak 1995).[2]

A second limitation of these studies is that most authors do not estimate the impact of varying amounts of media coverage on what citizens know and believe.[3] Mondak's superb study shows how the absence of newspaper coverage in Pittsburgh affected citizens' awareness of candidates and their interest in and discussion of House campaigns. But the comparison of newspaper-rich Cleveland with newspaper-absent Pittsburgh does not allow one to estimate the consequences of varying amounts of news coverage. If news coverage in Cleveland doubled, would citizens know 2 percent, 20 percent, or 200 percent more about the candidates? Would the effects be the same for citizens' knowledge of incumbents and challengers? How much coverage does it take to reach less-aware citizens?

The aim for future studies should be to move beyond crude measures of the volume of coverage to precise measures of the content of coverage.[4]

---

candidates affected what citizens knew about those candidates (Iyengar and Kinder 1987, 98–105). Stephanie Larson interviewed newspaper subscribers and their nonsubscriber neighbors before and after a weekly newspaper ran six articles that Larson had written about a representative's issue positions. She found that the two groups were equally well informed about the representative's positions at the start of the seven-week experiment, but that newspaper subscribers were substantially better informed at the end of the experiment (Larson 1992, 93–114).

[2] In a recent poll, 10 percent of respondents claimed that they get most of their information about Congress from personal conversations with people they know rather than directly from the media (Povich 1996, 149). The question was about Congress, not congressional candidates.

[3] Wendy Schiller is an exception. She notes that "media coverage exerts a substantive and significant effect on the total number of like and dislike mentions for senators; for every additional twenty-five newspaper articles in which a senator is mentioned, respondents named one additional mention about the senator" (Schiller 2000, 99).

[4] A recent study does this nicely, showing that when Senate candidates and the news media focus on a particular issue — the economy, education, the environment, health care — citizens are more likely to recognize that issue as a campaign theme (Kahn and Kenney 2001). A

Then we can estimate the impact of specific types of coverage on citizens' knowledge and beliefs. If we want to learn how citizens learn about representatives' votes on critical bills like NAFTA, crime control, or the budget, we need both measures of how local media sources cover these votes and measures of how much citizens know. If we want to understand how citizens learn about challengers — the political newcomers — we need measures of what local newspapers have been publishing about them.

Merged Data Set

The data set that I have assembled to explore the impact of newspaper coverage on citizens' knowledge and opinions is far from ideal. The foundation for the analysis is the autumn 1994 survey conducted by the National Election Studies. This biennial survey of American citizens is the gold standard for information about what citizens know about candidates for the House, Senate, and presidency. The problem is finding an appropriate way to link the NES data set with my own data on newspaper coverage.

Ideally, one would like to know which newspaper each respondent read and then link information about how that newspaper covered a representative with information about the respondent's opinions. Unfortunately, although the NES survey asked how many times a week a respondent read a newspaper, it did not ask the name of the newspaper. So, I have been forced to assume that the local newspaper for which I have data is the same paper that a citizen read.[5] It is not a crazy assumption. In many districts, there was a single dominant paper that most newspaper readers read. The *Los Angeles Times* has no major competitors, so it is highly likely that a Los Angeles resident who claimed to read a newspaper was actually reading the *Times*.[6] Errors in matching are more common in cities with competing newspapers and in far-flung districts that encompass several media markets.

---

similar study shows that when representatives used their newsletters to emphasize their stands on the 1991 Persian Gulf War Resolution or the 1993 Budget Reconciliation Conference Report citizens were better informed about their representatives' positions on these issues (Lipinski 2001).

[5] If two newspapers served the same media market, I assume that a respondent read the larger one. The assumption is arbitrary, but it captures the fact that a citizen is more likely to read the larger paper.

[6] The *Los Angeles Times* has nearly six times the circulation of its central-city competitor, the *Los Angeles Daily News*. The *Times* faces greater competition in the suburbs, where, for example, the *Orange County Register* competes with the Orange County edition of the *Times*. My practice was to assume that suburban residents read whatever large suburban paper circulates in their communities (specifically, the *Orange County Register*, New Jersey's *Bergen Record*, and Long Island's *Newsday*), not the Los Angeles or New York newspapers that also circulate in those suburbs. The aim was to include the dominant paper in each district. All these decisions were made when I created the third data set, long before it was merged with the NES data to create the fourth data set (see chapter 1 for complete details).

The inevitable errors in linking my data with NES data introduce noise into the merged data set. Although the noise will surely mask weak signals in the data, it should not overpower strong signals. One reason is that competing same-city newspapers do not cover local representatives that differently (see chapter 7). Incorrectly coding a respondent as a reader of the *San Francisco Chronicle* rather than the *San Francisco Examiner* does not introduce a great deal of noise. In any event, the noise works against confirming hypotheses about the impact of newspaper coverage on what citizens know about representatives. Appropriately, the assumption about newspaper readership, essential to linking the two data sets, is scientifically conservative.

The 1994 survey asked respondents numerous questions about their ability to recall or recognize their representative; their contacts with a representative, including meeting the representative in person, receiving mail from him or her, or noticing a representative in three kinds of media; their willingness to mention something they liked or disliked about a representative; their ability to rate a representative on various scales, including a feeling thermometer and an ideological scale; their knowledge of various factual details, including how many years a representative had served in the House and how the representative had voted on the crime bill; and their overall evaluation of a representative's performance in office. The survey also asked respondents a similar but shorter list of questions about challengers, including questions about recall, recognition, contacts, likes and dislikes, and ratings of challengers on ideological and other scales.

The original NES survey had 1,795 respondents. Ideally, one would link these data with my first data set, the comprehensive one that contained detailed information about how 25 newspapers covered 25 representatives, including information about how newspapers covered challengers. Unfortunately, only 41 NES respondents were located in any of the districts represented in the first data set, and only 26 respondents were in districts where an incumbent was running in a contested race.[7] That data set would be too small for analysis. The linkage with the third data set, which contains information about the volume of coverage for 187 representatives, was more successful. One hundred of these representatives were located in districts where NES interviewed citizens.

The merged data set contains 675 respondents in 100 congressional districts. Nine representatives in these districts did not run for reelection and nine representatives ran unopposed, so the analysis focuses on a reduced data set with 559 respondents in 82 congressional districts.[8] The unit of

---

[7] The 41 respondents were distributed among nine districts. Eleven respondents were in a district where the incumbent ran for the Senate. Four respondents were in a district where incumbent ran unopposed.

[8] The eighteen representatives included two who retired (9 cases), two who lost a primary (7

analysis is the individual respondent. The fourth data set contains all information that NES collected about each respondent and all information from
the third data set about how the dominant newspaper in the respondent's
district covered the local representative. The newspaper information is about
the volume of coverage in 33 newspapers, not about the content of the
coverage.[9] We know how many articles per month mentioned a local representative; we know nothing about what messages those articles conveyed.

The fourth data set was created to test hypotheses about the impact that
newspaper coverage of a representative has on a citizen's awareness, knowledge, and opinions of that representative. As it happens, the data set is also
appropriate for testing similar hypotheses about challengers. It is appropriate
for the second task, even though it has no direct measure of how each
newspaper covered a challenger, because it has an excellent proxy.

We know from the first and second data sets that newspaper coverage of
representatives during peak campaign season — September, October, and
early November — is an excellent predictor of how newspapers cover challengers. If one combines the first and second data sets, one finds that the
number of articles in each newspaper that mentioned a local representative
explains 81 percent of the variance in the number of articles that mentioned
the challenger. An additional 10 articles mentioning an incumbent result
in an additional 6.7 articles mentioning the challenger. Similarly, the total
mentions of each representative in these articles explains 88 percent of the
variance in the total mentions of challengers. An additional 10 mentions of
a representative result in an additional 8 mentions of the challenger.[10] With

---

cases), four who ran for the Senate (60 cases), one who ran for governor (3 cases), and nine
who ran unopposed (37 cases). These 116 cases were too disparate and too few to support
systematic analysis.

[9] The 33 newspapers that covered the 82 representatives were the *Arizona Republic, Atlanta
Journal and Constitution, Baltimore Sun, Baton Rouge Advocate, Bergen Record, Buffalo News,
Chicago Tribune, Dallas Morning News, Denver Post, Des Moines Register, Detroit News,
Fresno Bee, Fort Worth Star-Telegram, Houston Chronicle, Kansas City Star, Los Angeles Times,
Minneapolis Star Tribune, New York Times, Newark Star-Ledger, Newsday, Orange County Reg-
ister, Orlando Sentinel Tribune, Richmond Times-Dispatch, Riverside Press Enterprise, Sacra-
mento Bee, Salt Lake Tribune, San Diego Union-Tribune, San Francisco Chronicle, Seattle
Times, St. Louis Post Dispatch, Tacoma Morning News Tribune, Washington Post, Worcester
Telegram Gazette.*

[10] Both regressions are estimated for the 27 newspapers in the first and second data sets that
covered contested elections involving an incumbent (i.e., not Archer, Goodling, McCollum, or
Mazzoli). The regression equations, with standard errors in parentheses, are:

Articles Mentioning Challenger = .669 * Articles Mentioning Representative − 12.167
$\qquad\qquad\qquad\qquad\qquad\quad$ (.063) $\qquad\qquad\qquad\qquad\qquad\qquad\qquad\qquad\qquad$ (3.912)

Total Challenger Mentions = .800 * Total Representative Mentions − 45.169
$\qquad\qquad\qquad\qquad\qquad\quad$ (.059) $\qquad\qquad\qquad\qquad\qquad\qquad\qquad\qquad$ (15.605)

only one outlier among 27 newspapers, it seems clear that coverage of representatives during September, October, and early November is an excellent proxy for coverage of challengers during the same period.[11]

Examining the impact of newspaper coverage on citizens' opinions about challengers is not only possible with the fourth data set, it offers one advantage over examining the impact of coverage on citizens' opinions about representatives. Most challengers enter the campaign period as relative unknowns. As a consequence, most of what citizens learn about challengers they learn during the campaign period. Although the sources of that learning are several, including newspaper coverage, television coverage, and paid advertising, the sources are heavily concentrated during the period under investigation. In contrast, most incumbent representatives enter the campaign period relatively well known. Some representatives have been in office for many years and are household names in their districts. Others, who are relative newcomers, have nevertheless survived one or more hard-fought campaigns. All representatives have spent their time in office burnishing their images. As a consequence, a large portion of what some citizens know about incumbents they learned prior to the campaign period. Put differently, it is easier to estimate the effects of newspaper coverage on citizens' opinions about challengers than about incumbents because we are more likely to observe substantial opinion changes for challengers than for incumbents during the period under investigation.[12]

Reading about Candidates

The NES interviewer asked respondents eight questions about any contacts they may have had with each of the House candidates. Among these questions were three about media contact, including whether a respondent had

---

The results are virtually the same if the two Senate elections (Inhofe, Kyl) are dropped and the equations are estimated for the remaining 25 newspapers, although the adjusted R^2 is slightly smaller for each equation (.75 instead of .81 for articles and .83 instead of .88 for mentions).

[11] The scatterplot shows only one outlier, the *Cleveland Plain Dealer*'s coverage of Louis Stokes and his challenger, James Sykora. We know from chapter 6 that the incumbent was safe, the challenger weak, and campaign coverage minimal. The outlier was a consequence of the *Plain Dealer* continuing its heavy coverage of Stokes's policy-making activities during campaign season.

[12] Larry Bartels captures this nicely: "The logic of Bayesian opinion change pursued here also suggests that media exposure is most likely to be consequential (in the sense of producing large observable opinion changes) when prior opinions are weak, most notably for new candidates or issues. For this reason, simply as a matter of efficiency, analysts of media effects would do well to focus upon new or uncrystallized opinions, even if they are atypical or intrinsically less significant than opinions that are better established and more firmly held" (Bartels 1993, 275).

read about a candidate in a newspaper, had heard him on the radio, or had seen him on television.[13] Of the 559 respondents who lived in a district where an incumbent faced a challenger, 45 percent claimed to have read about the incumbent and 19 percent about the challenger.

How much did the volume of newspaper coverage affect the likelihood that a citizen would read about the challenger or the incumbent? The top section of table 8.1 takes a first cut at the question by sorting respondents into quintiles according to the volume of newspaper coverage during the campaign period. Where newspaper coverage was scant, respondents were unlikely to notice challengers. Only 9 percent of citizens noticed coverage of challengers when newspapers published fewer than twenty articles. Where newspaper coverage was relatively generous, however, respondents were far more likely to notice challengers. Thirty-nine percent of respondents noticed coverage of challengers when newspapers published more than 56 articles, and 49 percent noticed coverage when they published more than 95 articles. The relationship for incumbents was also positive, but the slope was much less steep. Thirty-three percent of respondents in the first quintile noticed coverage of incumbents, compared with 59 percent in the top quintile.

The bottom section of table 8.1 adjusts the coverage data for the fact that some respondents read a newspaper daily while others read one rarely or not at all. The logic that underlies this section is that a citizen cannot learn things about a candidate from a local newspaper unless the paper actually covers the campaign and the citizen actually reads the newspaper. The measure of media coverage in this section is the number of days that a respondent claimed to have read a daily newspaper in the past week (0 to 7) times the number of articles published during the campaign period (3 to 240). The new measure has a range from zero, for the 109 respondents who did not read a daily newspaper, to 1,680 for one respondent who confessed a seven-day-a-week habit and who lived in Newt Gingrich's district, where the local newspaper published 240 articles mentioning Gingrich. The adjusted data show even more powerful media effects. Six percent of respondents in the first quintile noticed newspaper coverage of challengers, compared with 44 percent in the top quintile and 57 percent in the top decile. Twenty-five

[13] Actually, the interviewer handed respondents a list of eight types of contact while saying: "There are many ways in which congressional candidates can have contact with the people from their districts. On this page are some of these ways. Think of (name of one candidate) who ran for the U.S. House of Representatives from this district in the last election. Have you come into contact with or learned anything about him (or her) through any of these ways?" The list included: (a) met him personally, (b) attended a meeting or gathering where he spoke, (c) talked to a member of his staff or someone in his office, (d) received something in the mail from him, (e) read about him in a newspaper or magazine, (f) heard him on the radio, (g) saw him on TV, or (h) any other contact (NES variables 503–10, 514–21).

TABLE 8.1
Effects of Newspaper Coverage and Newspaper Readership

Quintile	Articles Mentioning Incumbent 9/1/94–11/8/94	Percentage of Respondents Who Reported Reading about Challenger	Percentage of Respondents Who Reported Reading about Incumbent
First	3–19	9	33
Second	20–26	16	45
Third	27–36	17	51
Fourth	37–56	16	38
Fifth	57–240	39	59
Top Decile	96–240	49	54
All 559 Respondents	3–240	19	45

Quintile	Articles 9/1/94–11/8/94 Times Days Newspaper Read (0–7)	Percentage of Respondents Who Reported Reading about Challenger	Percentage of Respondents Who Reported Reading about Incumbent
First	0–6	6	25
Second	7–55	11	41
Third	56–140	15	41
Fourth	141–251	19	57
Fifth	252–1,680	44	62
Top Decile	399–1,680	57	67
All 559 Respondents	0–1,680	19	45

Note: Results are from the fourth data set (559 citizens, 33 newspapers, 82 representatives, 82 challengers).

percent of respondents in the first quintile noticed coverage of incumbents, compared with 62 percent in the top quintile and 67 percent in the top decile.

The evidence in table 8.1 shows the magnitude of the advantage that incumbents have in news coverage. It also reveals how much coverage it takes before citizens notice challengers. In the middle quintile, representing average levels of readership and average levels of coverage, 41 percent of respondents reported reading about incumbents, compared with 15 percent who reported reading about challengers. The incumbent advantage at this level is derived not from excessive campaign coverage, for we know from chapter 6 that most newspapers cover incumbents and challengers fairly during campaign season, but from the regular coverage of representatives that newspapers provide between elections. Challengers do not make a dent in the incumbent advantage at average levels of campaign coverage. The top decile, however, shows the incumbent advantage narrowing. This is the decile populated by dedicated readers who live in districts where newspapers covered campaigns heavily. In this group, 57 percent of respondents claimed to have read about challengers, compared with 67 percent who read about incumbents.

Although the evidence in table 8.1 supports the view that the volume of newspaper coverage matters, it does not clinch the argument. Perhaps what citizens were noticing in newspapers and reporting in interviews was not news coverage but campaign advertising. Perhaps citizens were reacting to the general intensity of campaigns and not merely to the intensity of news-paper coverage. Table 8.2 sorts out these rival explanations with a multivari-ate model. Here I unpack the combined variable about newspaper reader-ship and newspaper coverage into three variables: the number of days a citizen claimed to have read a newspaper during the previous week, the number of articles in the local newspaper that mentioned the incumbent during the campaign period, and the product of the two. The table also includes two new variables, campaign expenditures by the incumbent and campaign expenditures by the challenger. These are the best available mea-sures of campaign intensity and campaign advertising.

Table 8.2 demonstrates that the volume of newspaper coverage affected the likelihood that a citizen would read about the challenger, even after controlling for campaign expenditures. Several aspects of equation 8.1 sup-port the basic argument that I have been developing. First, the volume of newspaper coverage, by itself, explains nothing. When a citizen doesn't read the newspaper, heavy coverage goes unnoticed. Second, the regularity of newspaper readership, by itself, explains nothing. Not even the most dedi-cated newspaper reader profits from nonexistent campaign articles. It is the combination of the two variables — newspaper coverage times newspaper readership — that affects the likelihood that a citizen would read about the challenger. Third, although both incumbent's expenditures and challenger's expenditures affected the likelihood that a citizen would read about the challenger, the impact of campaign expenditures did not diminish the im-pact of news coverage. In short, the relationship first reported in the bottom of table 8.1 was not spurious. The intensity of campaigns matters, but so too does how frequently newspapers cover campaigns.

Turning next to incumbents, the evidence also supports the hypothesis that the volume of coverage matters. The coefficients for both the volume of coverage and volume times readership are positive (equation 8.2). Although the individual coefficients are not statistically significant, the chi-square test shows that the two variables together are highly significant ($p = .02$). Cam-paign spending does not matter. Neither incumbents' nor challengers' ex-

TABLE 8.2
Did a Citizen Read about the Incumbent or the Challenger?

	Equation	
	8.1 *Did Citizen Read* *about Challenger?*	8.2 *Did Citizen Read* *about Incumbent?*
A. Number of Days Citizen Claimed to Have Read Newspaper during Past Week	.0754 (.0753)	.0964* (.0531)
B. Number of Articles Mentioning Incumbent between 9/1/94 and 11/8/94	−.0061 (.0063)	.0024 (.0046)
C. Days Newspaper Read Times Number of Articles Mentioning Incumbent (A × B)	.0033*** (.0013)	.0017 (.0011)
D. Campaign Expenditures by Challenger, 1993–94 (in millions)	2.0956*** (.4878)	−.0747 (.4032)
E. Campaign Expenditures by Incumbent, 1993–94 (in millions)	.6210** (.2979)	−.0291 (.2601)
Constant	−3.0207*** (.3887)	−.8762*** (.2484)
−2 Times Log of Likelihood Ratio	445.813	730.417
Chi-Square (entire model)	102.938	39.489
Addition to Chi-Square (variables B and C)	8.829	8.075
Number of Cases	559	559

Notes: Results are from the fourth data set (559 citizens, 33 newspapers, 82 representatives, 82 challengers).

Dependent variables are dichotomous (yes = 1, no = 0).

Entries are unstandardized logistic regression coefficients (standard errors in parentheses).

* $p < .10$ ** $p < .05$ *** $p < .01$

penditures help explain readership patterns for incumbents. Scholars have long known that heavy spending benefits challengers more than incumbents, so this finding is further evidence of the differential effects of spending by challengers and incumbents (Jacobson 1980; Green and Krasno 1988).

These two multivariate models allow one to estimate the impact of newspaper coverage on the probability of citizens reading about the incumbent or the challenger, while controlling for the effects of campaign intensity. Table 8.3 displays the probabilities for varying levels of newspaper readership and newspaper coverage. The probabilities were calculated by setting campaign expenditures at their mean values, newspaper readership at zero, one, four, and seven days a week, and newspaper coverage at the 10th percentile, the median, and the 90th percentile (13, 30, and 96 articles). Looking first at challengers, one sees that the impact of newspaper coverage depends on how frequently citizens read newspapers. The volume of coverage does not matter when citizens claim to read a paper once a week or not at all. The volume of coverage is more important when citizens read a paper four days a week, with the probability of reading about the challenger rising from .14 for papers that published 13 articles during the campaign period, to .22 when they published 96 articles, an increase of more than 50 percent. Volume is even more important for daily readers, rising from .19 to .48, an increase of more than 150 percent. For incumbents, the impact is small for infrequent readers, ranging from .32 at low levels of coverage to .40 at high levels (an increase of 25 percent). The impact is much greater for frequent readers and daily readers, with citizens 50 percent more likely to read about incumbents at high levels of coverage than at low levels.

The evidence in these three tables supports the notion that the actions of both readers and publishers matter. Citizens are more likely to recall seeing coverage of candidates when they regularly read newspapers and when publishers regularly feature campaign coverage. The evidence also gives a sense of how much newspaper coverage is required before citizens notice challengers. It takes nearly 100 articles during campaign season before a majority of daily newspaper readers recall reading about the challenger, whereas it takes only 13 articles during campaign season before the same group of readers recalls reading about the incumbent (table 8.3). This is a consequence of the newspaper coverage that representatives receive prior to the campaign, not of any special advantage that incumbents enjoy during campaign season.

Learning about Challengers

Citizens were more likely to read about challengers when newspapers covered campaigns heavily. That much has been established. But what did citizens learn about challengers when they encountered them in newspapers? Did they profit from these encounters, learning valuable things about challengers, or did they receive, process, and remember little information of political relevance? Table 8.4 explores the effects of newspaper coverage by examining how respondents answered three questions that interviewers asked about challengers. The questions ranged from relatively easy to relatively hard.

TABLE 8.3
Probability of a Citizen Reading about the Candidates

Probability of a Citizen	Number of Days Citizen Read Newspaper in Past Week	Total Articles Mentioning Incumbent during Campaign Season		
		13	30	96
Reading about Challenger	0	.09	.08	.06
	1	.10	.10	.08
	4	.14	.15	.22
	7	.19	.23	.48
Reading about Incumbent	0	.29	.30	.34
	1	.32	.33	.40
	4	.40	.44	.59
	7	.49	.55	.75

Notes: Probabilities are calculated with the equations in table 8.2. Campaign expenditures are set at their mean values. The other three variables take the values indicated above. Total articles are calculated at the 10th percentile (13 articles), the median (30 articles), and the 90th percentile (96 articles).

The most basic fact that each new candidate seeks to convey is his or her name. The first question in table 8.4 was designed to see how successful challengers were at this fundamental task by identifying which respondents recognized challengers' names.[14] Forty-four percent of respondents recognized challengers. As the table makes clear, newspaper coverage and newspaper readership were strongly correlated with citizens' ability to recognize challengers, although the slope was much less steep than it was for the relationships displayed in table 8.1. Thirty-five percent of respondents in the first quintile—most of whom did not read a daily newspaper—recognized challengers, compared with 63 percent in the top quintile and 78 percent in the top decile. Clearly, those who did not read newspapers had other sources of information about challengers. Even so, citizens who were regu-

[14] A respondent's ability to recognize a name was established by combining answers to two questions. Early in the survey, respondents were asked if they could recall from memory the names of the House candidates. Eleven percent correctly recalled the challenger's name. Later they were asked to rate on a feeling thermometer more than thirty politicians and groups, including the House candidates. Respondents were told: "If we come to a person whose name you don't recognize, you don't need to rate that person. Just tell me and we'll move on to the next one." Forty-three percent of respondents rated (and therefore recognized) the challenger. The two variables combined produce a recognition rate of 44 percent because six respondents correctly recalled, though chose not to rate, the challenger (NES variables 211, 215, 219, 238, 239).

TABLE 8.4
Effects of Newspaper Coverage on Information about Challengers

Quintile	Articles 9/1/94–11/8/94 Times Days Newspaper Read (0–7)	Percentage of Respondents Who Recognized Challenger	Percentage Who Rated Challenger on Ideology Scale	Percentage Who Reported Something They Liked or Disliked about Challenger
First	0–6	35	26	14
Second	7–55	32	31	9
Third	56–140	43	43	12
Fourth	141–251	46	31	21
Fifth	252–1,680	63	51	35
Top Decile	399–1,680	78	52	46
All 559	0–1,680	44	37	18

Note: Results are from the fourth data set (559 citizens, 33 newspapers, 82 challengers).

lar newspaper readers and who lived in areas where newspaper coverage was heavy were more than twice as likely to recognize challengers as those who were not regular readers.

The second question in table 8.4 asked a respondent to place the challenger on a seven-point ideological scale.[15] This is a somewhat tougher question, for it asks citizens what they know about a candidate, and not simply whether they recognize the candidate. Of course, it is a multiple choice question, with no penalty for guessing, so it is not as difficult as the third question. Thirty-seven percent of respondents were able to place the challenger on the ideological scale. Again, table 8.4 shows the effects of newspaper coverage. Twenty-six percent of respondents in the first quintile were able to rate challengers on the ideological scale, compared with 51 percent in the top quintile and 52 percent the top decile.

The third question asked whether there was anything in particular that the respondent liked or disliked about the challenger.[16] By the standards of survey research, this is a tough question. It asks the respondent to report something that he or she liked or disliked about a candidate without any

[15] The question occurred shortly after the respondent was asked to place herself on the same ideological scale. Seventeen percent of respondents accepted the interviewer's opt-out invitation ("or haven't you thought much about this?") and declined to rate themselves, although a third of these did place the challenger on the ideological scale (NES variables 839, 843, 845).

[16] Actually, the interviewer asked: (a) "Was there anything in particular that you liked about (name of one candidate) the (Democratic or Republican) candidate for the U.S. House of Representatives?" and (b) "Was there anything in particular that you didn't like about (name of one candidate)?" Table 8.3 reports an affirmative response to either question (NES variables 401, 407, 413, 419).

further prompting by the interviewers — no list of acceptable answers, no menu of possibilities, no hints of any kind. It is the essay question of survey research, set in the midst of a multiple choice examination. Only 18 percent of respondents could think of a single like or dislike, less than half of those who claimed to recognize the challenger. Once again, table 8.4 shows the effects of newspaper coverage. Fourteen percent of respondents in the first quintile (and 9 percent in the second) were able to mention at least one like or dislike, compared with 35 percent in the top quintile and 46 percent in the top decile.

Table 8.5 examines with a multivariate model the effects of newspaper coverage on a citizen's knowledge of challengers. Again the aim is to separate the effects of newspaper coverage from the effects of campaign intensity, as measured by campaign spending. The first thing to notice is that challenger's spending is important in all three equations. The more challengers spent, the more likely citizens were to recognize their names, rate them on an ideological scale, and express one or more likes or dislikes about them. Not surprisingly, incumbents' expenditures did nothing to make citizens more knowledgeable about challengers. Even with campaign expenditures controlled, newspaper coverage was positively related to what citizens knew about challengers, although statistically significant in only the first two equations.

These three equations were then used to estimate the impact of newspaper coverage on the probability of a citizen recognizing the challenger, rating the challenger on the ideology scale, or expressing one or more likes or dislikes about the challenger (table 8.6). As expected, citizens were more knowledgeable about challengers when they read newspapers regularly and when newspapers covered campaigns heavily. The oddity in this table is that the volume of newspaper coverage was equally important for citizens no matter how frequently they read a newspaper. Even those who did not happen to read a paper in the previous week were better informed when newspaper coverage was heavy than when it was light.

The most likely explanation for the overall importance of newspaper coverage, even among infrequent readers, is that newspaper coverage during the campaign period is a good proxy for how other media outlets were covering the campaign. As Mondak (1995) shows, local newspapers often set the news agenda for local electronic media. A campaign that is attracting nearly 100 articles in the local newspaper is probably also attracting extensive coverage on radio and television. Newspaper coverage, therefore, is a measure of the flow of information in the so-called free media, just as campaign expenditures are a measure of the flow of information in the paid media.

The findings in this section are not as decisive as were the findings in the previous section. The very best indicator of media effects — the interaction of newspaper readership and newspaper coverage — is unimportant in table

TABLE 8.5
What Did a Citizen Know about the Challenger?

	Equation		
	8.3 Did Citizen Recognize Name of Challenger?	8.4 Able to Rate Challenger on Ideology Scale?	8.5 Like or Dislike Something about Challenger?
A. Number of Days Citizen Claimed to Have Read Newspaper during Past Week	.0592 (.0616)	.0608 (.0549)	.1107 (.0685)
B. Number of Articles Mentioning Incumbent between 9/1/94 and 11/8/94	.0170*** (.0062)	.0107** (.0052)	.0068 (.0060)
C. Days Newspaper Read Times Number of Articles Mentioning Incumbent (A × B)	−.0002 (.0014)	−.0009 (.0010)	.0002 (.0012)
D. Campaign Expenditures by Challenger, 1993–94 (in millions)	2.8972*** (.5417)	1.5615*** (.4367)	2.7310*** (.5223)
E. Campaign Expenditures by Incumbent, 1993–94 (in millions)	−.0468 (.2763)	.1013 (.2641)	−.7603* (.4372)
Constant	−1.6329*** (.2978)	−1.4616*** (.2689)	−2.4934*** (.3620)
−2 Times Log of Likelihood Ratio	667.606	693.783	472.462
Chi-Square (entire model)	99.283	40.956	61.706
Addition to Chi-Square (variables B and C)	18.334	5.830	3.583
Number of Cases	559	559	559

Notes: Results are from the fourth data set (559 citizens, 33 newspapers, 82 challengers).
Dependent variables are dichotomous (yes = 1, no = 0).
Entries are unstandardized logistic regression coefficients (standard errors in parentheses).
* $p < .10$ ** $p < .05$ *** $p < .01$

8.5, whereas it was relatively powerful in table 8.2. The next best measure, the volume of newspaper coverage, is important in explaining citizens' knowledge of challengers. Of course, this variable could reflect the intensity of campaigns rather than the direct effects of newspaper coverage, despite my attempts to control for intensity with two expenditure variables. In short, although the findings support the notion that the volume of newspaper coverage affected how knowledgeable citizens were about challengers, the evi-

TABLE 8.6
Probability of a Citizen Knowing Things about the Challenger

Probability of a Citizen	Number of Days Citizen Read Newspaper in Past Week	Total Articles Mentioning Incumbent during Campaign Season		
		13	30	96
Recognizing Name	0	.30	.36	.64
of Challenger	1	.31	.38	.65
	4	.35	.42	.67
	7	.39	.45	.70
Rating Challenger	0	.28	.32	.48
on Ideology Scale	1	.29	.33	.48
	4	.32	.35	.46
	7	.35	.37	.44
Expressing a Like or	0	.10	.11	.17
Dislike about Challenger	1	.11	.13	.19
	4	.15	.17	.26
	7	.20	.23	.34

Notes: Probabilities are calculated with the equations in table 8.5. Campaign expenditures are set at their mean values. The other three variables take the values indicated above. Total articles are calculated at the 10th percentile (13 articles), the median (30 articles), and the 90th percentile (96 articles).

dence is less compelling than the evidence about the effects of newspaper coverage on the likelihood that citizens would read about challengers.

Learning about Representatives

Did newspaper readership and newspaper coverage affect what citizens knew about their representatives? The analysis for representatives is similar to the analysis for challengers. Since the NES survey contained many more questions about representatives than about challengers, including several questions about factual knowledge, the analysis is potentially much richer. Moreover, for representatives we have evidence about the volume of coverage for the entire two-year period, not just for the campaign period. Offsetting these two advantages, however, is one substantial disadvantage. As previously noted, most of what citizens know about challengers they learn during campaign season, whereas some of what citizens know about representatives they learned during representatives' previous campaigns and during previous years in the House. Since we have no measures of news coverage prior to January 1, 1993, and no measures of citizens' opinions at the start of the study period, we are at a considerable disadvantage in isolating the effects of newspaper coverage on citizens' opinions about their representatives.

Testing various models that included the volume of newspaper coverage for the entire two-year period, I found evidence of media effects for only one type of knowledge, whether a citizen recognized the name of the incumbent. Table 8.7 shows that both newspaper readership and newspaper coverage were important in explaining recognition levels, although the interaction term was not important (equation 8.6). The top section of table 8.8 then uses this equation to calculate the probability of a citizen recognizing the representative for varying levels of newspaper readership and newspaper coverage. Once again, the effects of newspaper readership and newspaper coverage are clear, although again there is the oddity that even citizens who did not read a newspaper appeared to profit from heavy coverage.

The previous explanation for this oddity — that local newspaper coverage may be a proxy for coverage by other local media outlets — continues to be a possible explanation for why nonreaders appear to profit from newspaper coverage. Two other explanations are also plausible. First, the measurement of newspaper readership is not very precise. How often a citizen happened to read a paper during the week prior to an autumn 1994 interview is a poor guide to readership patterns over the entire two-year period. Indeed, how respondents answered the readership question in autumn 1992 explains only 40 percent of the variance in how the same respondents answered the same question in 1994.[17] So, it is not correct to consider that the first category is composed exclusively of perpetual nonreaders. Second, the respondents at the lowest level of readership were also the ones with the most to learn. Nearly 500 articles over a two-year period may be just what it takes to communicate a representative's name to the occasional readers in this category. At the top level of readership, citizens were already so well informed — 88 percent recognized their representative when newspapers published only one article per week — that there was not much room for improvement.

I have also estimated models that are similar to equation 8.6 for all other questions that respondents answered about their representatives, using data about newspaper coverage for the entire two-year period. None of these models showed any evidence that the volume of coverage affected citizens'

---

[17] Fewer than half the respondents who claimed to be nonreaders in 1992 made the same claim in 1994; four percent switched from one extreme to the other (0 days to 7, or 7 days to 0). Only 44 percent of respondents answered the question identically in 1992 and 1994. These calculations are based on 255 respondents, among the 559, who were interviewed in both years (NES variables 125 and 3203).

TABLE 8.7
What Did a Citizen Know about the Incumbent?

	Equation		
	8.6 Did Citizen Recognize Name of Incumbent?	8.7 Did Citizen Dislike Something about Incumbent?	8.8 Did Citizen Know Incumbent's Years in Office?
A. Number of Days Citizen Claimed to Have Read Newspaper during Past Week	.2193*** (.0820)	.1814*** (.0660)	.2070*** (.0537)
B. Number of Articles Mentioning Incumbent between 1/1/93 and 11/8/94	.0024** (.0011)		
C. Number of Articles Mentioning Incumbent between 9/1/94 and 11/8/94		.0117** (.0055)	.0105** (.0049)
D. Days Newspaper Read Times Number of Articles Mentioning Incumbent (A × B)	−.0002 (.0003)		
E. Days Newspaper Read Times Number of Articles Mentioning Incumbent (A × C)		−.0004 (.0011)	−.0009 (.0010)
F. Campaign Expenditures by Challenger, 1993–94 (in millions)	.4911 (.6017)	.4797 (.4289)	.5487 (.4034)
G. Campaign Expenditures by Incumbent, 1993–94 (in millions)	.1573 (.4080)	.3580 (.2841)	−.0630 (.2629)
Constant	.1568 (.3507)	−2.8695*** (.3462)	−1.6102*** (.2676)
−2 Times Log of Likelihood Ratio	510.079	524.131	705.934
Chi-Square (entire model)	27.052	44.078	43.477
Addition to Chi-Square (B and D or C and E)	5.648	7.869	6.071
Number of Cases	559	559	559

Notes: Results are from the fourth data set (559 citizens, 33 newspapers, 82 representatives).
Dependent variables are dichotomous (yes = 1, no = 0).
Entries are unstandardized logistic regression coefficients (standard errors in parentheses).
* $p < .10$ ** $p < .05$ *** $p < .01$

TABLE 8.8
Probability of a Citizen Knowing Things about the Incumbent

Probability of a Citizen	Number of Days Citizen Read Newspaper in Past Week	Total Articles Mentioning Incumbent during Study Period		
		98 (13)	241 (30)	458 (96)
Recognizing Name	0	.64	.71	.81
of Incumbent	1	.69	.75	.83
	4	.80	.83	.87
	7	.88	.89	.91
Disliking Something	0	.08	.10	.19
about Incumbent	1	.10	.11	.21
	4	.15	.18	.29
	7	.23	.26	.38
Knowing Incumbent's	0	.21	.24	.39
Years in Office	1	.24	.28	.42
	4	.37	.40	.51
	7	.51	.53	.60

Notes: Probabilities are calculated with the equations in table 8.7. The first equation is for the full sample (1/1/93 to 11/8/94); the second and third equations are for campaign season (9/1/94 to 11/8/94). Campaign expenditures are set at their mean values. The other three variables take the values indicated above. Total articles are calculated at the 10th percentile (98 or 13 articles), the median (241 or 30 articles), and the 90th percentile (458 or 96 articles).

attitudes or beliefs.[18] When coverage was heavy, respondents were no more likely to rate the representative on the ideological, health services, or government services scales; no more likely to know the representative's vote on the crime bill or know how often the representative supported President Clinton's legislative proposals; no more likely to recall anything special the representative had done for the district; and no more likely to express something they liked or disliked about the representative.

These findings suggest something about the limitations of voluminous coverage for educating citizens. Heavy coverage may be sufficient to communicate simple things like a representative's name, for repetition is the key to name recognition. But volume by itself does little to educate readers about the finer points of legislative life. Content matters as much as sheer volume when the question is how did a representative vote, what has he done for the district, or where does he stand ideologically. And we know from chapters 3, 4, and 5 that newspapers differed greatly in what aspects of

[18] By no evidence, I do not mean that the coefficients merely failed to meet some arbitrary level of statistical significance; I mean that the standard errors were often larger than the coefficients.

legislative life they chose to cover. Newspapers that published hundreds of articles about a representative without ever mentioning his vote on the crime bill did nothing to educate citizens about that vote.

Turning next to the campaign period, there is some evidence that voluminous coverage during campaign season may have affected what citizens knew about their representatives. Equations 8.7 and 8.8 show that when newspaper coverage was heavy respondents were more likely to mention things they disliked about the incumbent and more likely to know how many years the incumbent had served in Congress (table 8.7). We know from chapter 6 that if coverage is heavy during the campaign period it is usually because there is a very active challenger. We also know that challengers work hard to give citizens reasons to dislike the incumbent, and sometimes they emphasize how long a representative has served in office. It follows that citizens would be more likely to express a dislike and know how many years a representative had served in Congress when newspaper coverage was heavy. Table 8.8 shows that heavy newspaper coverage doubled the probability that a citizen would mention something he or she disliked about the incumbent. The effects on knowing how many years the incumbent had served in office were somewhat smaller.[19]

I have also used coverage data from the campaign period to estimate models for all other questions that respondents answered about representatives. None of the models showed any evidence that the volume of coverage mattered. Although heavy coverage was associated with citizens mentioning things they disliked about incumbents, it was not associated with citizens mentioning things they liked about incumbents. Presumably this is because heavy coverage during the campaign period indicates an incumbent in trouble, not an incumbent attracting unusually positive newspaper coverage. During intense campaigns, challengers try to sully representatives' reputations, so it is not an easy time for citizens to discover new reasons to like incumbents. Citizens are more likely to discover new reasons to like representatives long before the start of campaign season, when representatives have no one to challenge their explanations for all the good things they have been doing. Put in the vernacular of campaign managers, when representatives are already well known and well liked, intense campaigns are more likely to increase representatives' "negatives" than their "positives."

Although one might imagine that heavy coverage during campaign season would help educate citizens about how their representatives voted on

---

[19] Respondents who claimed they knew how many years a representative had been in office (NES variable 641) were reasonably accurate. In a simple regression, respondents' estimates of how many years representatives had been in the House (NES variable 642) explained 66 percent of the variance in representatives' actual years in office. When respondents were encouraged to guess (less than 12 years, about 12 years, or more than 12 years), they were much less accurate (NES variable 643).

the crime bill or about how frequently they supported President Clinton's legislative proposals, these consequences would follow only if challengers chose to emphasize these votes. In some races, challengers probably did emphasize the crime vote or a representative's excessive support for the president, but adopting such a strategy required that the representative cooperate by creating a voting record that could be used against them. The lack of any general effects suggests that challengers did not adopt such a strategy commonly or, if they did, that they were not very successful.

Extensions

The NES data set is very rich. It is tempting to use this richness to explore more complicated models about the impact of newspaper coverage on what citizens know and believe, perhaps by incorporating additional interaction terms, perhaps by looking at particular types of races. Unfortunately, the richness of the NES data is not matched by a similar richness in information about newspaper coverage.[20] All that is available is information about the volume of coverage, not about the content of articles. Moreover, the measure of volume is for representatives only. Although that measure is a reasonable proxy for how newspapers cover challengers during campaign season, it is far from ideal. Finally, of course, the linking of the NES data set with the third data set is based on an assumption about which newspaper a respondent happened to read, not on any firm evidence. In short, the merged data set is noisy and imperfect. Before we answer more interesting and more complicated questions about the impact of newspaper coverage on what citizens know and believe, we need better data.

   What would truly be helpful is to have information about the content of newspaper coverage, as in the first and second data sets, rather than information about the volume of newspaper coverage, as in the third and fourth data sets. Knowing what newspaper a respondent had been reading would also be very helpful. Additionally, it would be valuable to have panel data about citizens, so that one could explore how citizens changed their opinions during a period in which they were exposed to different flows of information. Panel data is not really required for studying the impact of news coverage on what citizens know about challengers, because it is a safe bet that most respondents know very little about challengers before campaign season. But the same assumption cannot be made for representatives.

[20] I did test models that incorporated in two additive scales everything that citizens knew about incumbents and everything they knew about challengers. Indeed, this was my initial approach. Eventually, I learned the age-old lesson about apples and oranges. There is a big difference between recognizing a candidate and knowing specific details about that candidate, and it does no good to score each as equivalent bits of knowledge in an additive scale.

Prospects for the future are more promising. If NES were to add a single question to the hundreds that their interviewers already ask, it would be possible to link their superb opinion data with high-quality data that other scholars could collect about newspaper coverage. NES last tried this in 1978, asking which newspaper each respondent read. The only problem was the lack of an appropriate technology in 1978 for collecting information about newspaper coverage. The clipping service that was supposed to collect newspaper articles missed about two-thirds of the articles. As this book makes clear, the technology is now available to collect and code substantial amounts of high-quality information about how local newspapers cover representatives and candidates. Moreover, hundreds of newspapers now have electronic archives available for searching, and more newspapers are coming on-line each year. To give a sense of the possibilities, the budget that I spent collecting and coding articles for the first data set (25 representatives, 8,125 articles, 68 variables) would probably support a project of similar scope that focused on how newspapers covered 100 to 150 representatives and their challengers during several months of the campaign season.

Alternative Evidence

An alternative way to determine if the way local newspapers cover representatives affects what citizens know about representatives is to focus on election returns. Here the aim is to see whether or not citizens' actual behavior is consistent with findings about local newspapers. Gary Jacobson offers an explanation of the 1994 House elections that is perfectly consistent with the findings reported in chapter 4. His aggregate analysis of the 1994 House elections shows that Democratic representatives' votes on crime control, NAFTA, and the budget affected their electoral margins, whereas how they voted on the Brady bill had no effects. Democratic incumbents who supported President Clinton's position on these three bills did significantly worse at the polls than those who opposed the president's position (Jacobson 1996).[21]

There are two explanations for why votes on crime, NAFTA, and the budget affected citizens' choices, while votes on the Brady bill did not. The first possibility is that Democratic representatives were more skilled in choosing their positions on gun control than on the other three issues. Perhaps very few representatives gave challengers a good campaign issue on

---

[21] Jacobson's regression equation explaining the vote for Democratic incumbents in 1994 controls for the 1992 election results, district partisanship, challenger's experience, challenger's spending, and incumbent's spending. The regression coefficients for NAFTA and the budget were significant at the .05 level, while the coefficient for the crime bill fell just short of statistical significance.

gun control, while many representatives cast votes on the other three issues that were difficult to defend. The second possibility is that the media covered the four issues in different ways and that those differences affected what citizens knew about representatives' votes. The first explanation centers on representatives' own behavior, the second on differences in the informational environment.

The evidence in this books suggests that the informational environment was very different for the Brady bill. The 25 newspapers published a total of 744 articles about representatives' positions on the three big issues, compared with 35 stories about their positions on the Brady bill. Moreover, virtually every newspaper covered position taking on NAFTA, crime control, and the budget, whereas 40 percent of all newspapers failed to mention representatives' positions on the Brady bill.[22] How much these differences in the informational environment affected what citizens knew about representatives is impossible to say. The best one can say is that Jacobson's analysis is consistent with what one would expect if citizens were exposed to vastly different amounts of information about representatives' positions. Given these findings about newspaper coverage, it would be very surprising if representatives' votes on the Brady bill did affect how citizens voted in 1994.

[22] Over the two-year period, 25 newspapers published 239 articles that mentioned representatives' positions on NAFTA, 24 papers published 257 articles about crime control, 24 papers published 248 articles about the FY94 budget, and 15 papers published 35 articles about the Brady bill.

9

The Press and Political Accountability

A BASIC PREMISE of this book is that the nature of the informational environment affects the prospects for accountable government. More and better information about what elected officials are doing in office increases both the chances that citizens will notice the information and the likelihood that the information will affect citizens' decisions about whether elected officials deserve to be reelected or removed. A rich informational environment also affects how elected officials behave in office. When officials know that what they do will be reported to citizens, they behave differently than when they believe that their actions will be forever hidden. Assessing the consequences of the various informational environments described in this book requires that one first recognize various differences among both representatives and citizens.

Representatives

Representatives differ in the kinds of things they do. Some representatives do things that most journalists find intrinsically newsworthy; other representatives blend into the background of legislative life. Consider the number of articles in which a representative was mentioned in the *Congressional Quarterly Weekly Report*, the journal of legislative happenings that serves as my benchmark for newsworthiness on Capitol Hill. Among the 187 representatives in the third data set, the range was from 3 articles for Jerry Costello (D-IL) to 226 articles for Dan Rostenkowski (D-IL).[1] As chair of the Ways and Means Committee, Rostenkowski was centrally involved in policy decisions about health care reform, Medicare, NAFTA, unemployment benefits, and every type of federal taxes. He also became embroiled in a sensational scandal. His 1994 indictment for embezzlement and fraud led to his defeat by a Republican novice in what was once the safest of Democratic districts. In contrast, Costello, a member of the Budget and Public Works Committees, was not senior enough to chair a subcommittee. Nothing he did on Capitol Hill was covered by *CQWR*, although he did get three district-oriented mentions, one each for his 1992 election, 1994 primary, and 1994 election.

[1] The range for the 25 representatives in the first data set was from 7 *CQWR* articles for Thomas Ewing to 94 articles for Ronald Dellums.

Most representatives were covered for some of their legislative activities. The median representative in the third data set appeared in 20 articles.[2]

Although representatives vary in how deeply they are involved in particular policies or scandals that journalists find newsworthy, the differences are much smaller for other activities. The differences are minuscule for one major Capitol Hill activity, roll-call voting. The average voting rate for all representatives was 96 percent for the 597 roll-call votes in 1993 and 95 percent for the 497 roll-call votes in 1994. Although some representatives have made it their life's work to show up for every roll-call vote, and some representatives have scores that dip below 90 percent when they run for higher office, most representatives have participation rates within two or three points of the mean (CQA93, 31C–35C; CQA94, 11C–12C, 46C–47C). Not only are all representatives repeatedly asked to take positions on the exact same issues, they have little choice about voting on these hundreds of issues if they are to avoid charges of absenteeism.

Even the least active legislator from the safest of districts, then, provides lots of things for journalists to cover. How has a legislator voted on the various issues of the day? What bills has she introduced? From whom has she raised campaign funds? What has she done to transform her campaign promises into realities? These kinds of questions, which can be asked of all legislators, are relevant to citizens' evaluations of their representatives. On top of this common base, some legislators do even more to attract the interest of journalists and citizens. Representatives who play major roles in important policy conflicts (Kennelly), work to protect endangered federal installations in their district (McCollum), campaign hard for reelection against talented challengers (LaRocco), or run for higher office (Inhofe) provide even more grist for the journalistic mill.

Citizens

Citizens differ in their attentiveness to the mass media and in the regularity with which they read a local newspaper. According to the 1994 NES survey, 20 percent of respondents never read a newspaper during the week prior to the interview, while 23 percent claimed to have read a paper one or two days, 13 percent three or four days, 6 percent five or six days, and 38 percent every day (National Elections Studies 1995, variable 125). Even these responses may overreport actual readership, since newspaper reading is the socially desirable response. Citizens also differ in the thoroughness with which they read newspapers. Reading habits range from a quick skim of the

---

[2] The median representative in the first data set appeared in 24 CQWR articles. Mean coverage was 28 articles in the first data set and 31 in the third; the standard deviation was 20 articles in the first set and 30 in the third.

sports page to a thorough reading of every section. In short, citizens differ widely in the likelihood that they might encounter even extensive coverage of representatives in their local newspapers. Some citizens are highly likely to see at least some coverage of their representatives. Others have virtually no chance of ever seeing any of it.

Citizens also differ enormously in their interest and knowledge about politics (Delli Carpini and Keeter 1996). Political interest affects the likelihood that citizens will notice and choose to read articles about their representative. Political knowledge affects the likelihood that citizens will understand the significance of new information about their representative and that any new information will affect their attitudes toward their representative (Zaller 1992). The range is from completely apolitical and ignorant citizens to those who devour political news.

Even citizens who rarely read local newspapers can acquire information indirectly from them because newspapers pump information into the broader system. Local newspapers help set the agenda for other local media, including television and radio, so some of what citizens hear in the electronic media was first gathered by print journalists (Mondak 1995, 65–66; McManus 1990). Similarly, newspapers provide raw materials for discussion among all sorts of citizens. In the 1994 NES survey, 77 percent of respondents said that they sometimes discuss politics with family or friends. To be sure, regular newspapers readers are more likely to discuss politics with others — 83 percent of seven-day-a-week readers claim that they do — but the rates are not that much lower for those who do not read a paper regularly. Sixty-three percent of those who never read a paper and 71 percent of those who read a paper one or two days a week claim that they discuss politics with family or friends (National Election Studies 1994, variables 125 and 128). The raw materials for these conversations must come from somewhere, and some of it — perhaps lots of it — originates in local newspapers.

Rich Informational Environments

Some local newspapers create rich informational environments about local representatives' performance in office. Rich informational environments are the consequence of newspapers covering representatives frequently, thoroughly, and accessibly. Accessibility refers to whether coverage appears helpful to a broad range of readers and not just well-informed experts. The *Las Vegas Review-Journal*, *Los Angeles Times*, and *Tulsa World* created the richest informational environments among the 31 newspapers in the first and second data sets; the *Hartford Courant* and *San Diego Union-Tribune* were almost as informative. These five papers painted rich and comprehensive portraits of James Bilbray, Anthony Beilenson, James Inhofe, Barbara Kennelly, and Bob Filner. Two small-town newspapers that were nearly as good were the *Lewiston Morning Tribune* and *Rock Hill Herald*. Although their coverage of Larry LaRocco and John Spratt was frequent, informative, and accessible, it was not as comprehensive as coverage in the five larger papers.

What are the consequences of the relatively rich informational environments created by these seven newspapers? One consequence is that a district's most politically interested citizens are likely to be aware of some of the things a representative has been doing in office. When a representative attends a local meeting of an environmental group, union, religious organization, or the Rotary Club, he is almost certain to find that some members of the audience are aware of his recent positions, votes, or actions, and that these members are able to ask penetrating questions. Their questions and a representative's responses help to inform other audience members and create the raw materials for additional discussions among citizens. A related consequence is that a representative is likely to anticipate how he will handle such questions when he is deciding what to do about some potentially controversial issue. He may even adjust his decisions to make subsequent explanations easier (Kingdon 1973, 46–53; Fenno 1978, 136–70).

The richer the informational environment, the more likely information about a representative's performance penetrates into the next few strata of constituents—those who are less interested in politics than citizens in the upper stratum are but interested enough to read occasional articles about a local representative. One can imagine several consequences of this increased penetration. One is that more citizens become knowledgeable about a representative's performance, and this new knowledge may affect their evaluations of a representative's continued fitness for office. A second is that more citizens initiate or participate in discussions about a representative's performance. A third is that more citizens write letters to the representative, praising or criticizing his positions and actions or urging him to do things differently. A fourth consequence is that more constituents write letters to the editor, commenting on a representative's performance.

It is unlikely that any of these seven informational environments were rich enough to ensure that large majorities of citizens were knowledgeable about representatives' positions and actions. Reaching the least politically aware strata is no easy task. Perhaps the saturation coverage in Chicago's two papers of Dan Rostenkowski's indictment for using $724,000 in public and campaign funds to pay ghost employees and purchase automobiles created this kind of broad-based awareness. With the exception of major scandals, most issues are not so naturally appealing to journalists and citizens that large majorities will ever hear particular messages about a local representative.[3]

---

[3] The best known exception is from 1958, when voters in Little Rock were unusually well

All of these points, however, are merely hypotheses. We don't know for sure if richer informational environments produce all these effects. We don't know how much information it takes to penetrate various strata of citizens. Although chapter 8 provides some support for the notion that richer informational environments are associated with citizens knowing more about both representatives and challengers, the limitations of that chapter are severe. The informational environments are measured only by the volume of coverage that mentioned a representative, not by the content or accessibility of coverage. Moreover, the sample of citizens is small and the matching of newspapers with respondents is imperfect.

We also don't know if it takes more information about some kinds of behavior to create a given level of awareness among citizens than it does about other behaviors. Is it easier to inform citizens about a representative's indictment for embezzlement than to inform citizens about her vote on NAFTA? Is it easier to inform citizens about a representative's vote on NAFTA than about her votes on banking reform, global warming, or dredging the local harbor? These are all researchable questions. Political scientists have developed good techniques for measuring what citizens know about elected officials. What remains is to link high-quality studies of citizens' knowledge and behavior with high-quality studies of how the mass media cover representatives' specific positions and actions.

Meager Informational Environments

Other local newspapers do not create these kinds of rich informational environments. They fall short of the standards set by the Las Vegas Review-Journal, Los Angeles Times, and Tulsa World in various ways. Some newspapers do not publish many articles about local representatives. Some newspapers focus on only one or two aspects of representatives' behavior, typically position taking, while ignoring other important activities. Some newspapers provide coverage that, although helpful to well-informed experts, is largely inaccessible to ordinary citizens who lack the contextual knowledge to appreciate it. Some newspapers are deficient in all three respects, failing to provide frequent, thorough, and accessible coverage about local representatives.

The Washington Times was the least informative of the 31 newspapers. It

---

informed about both the incumbent representative, Brooks Hays, and the write-in challenger, Dale Alford. All twenty-three local citizens interviewed in a national study claimed to have heard or read something about both candidates (compared with 24 percent of citizens who knew about both candidates in other districts). This high level of awareness was the consequence of the federal government sending troops to Little Rock to force the integration of a local high school (Miller and Stokes, 1966, 369–70).

published fewer articles that mentioned a local representative than any other newspaper. Fifty-nine percent of its articles focused on Albert Wynn's position taking. Moreover, most of these articles lacked an explanation of the basic conflict, so they were not particularly useful for citizens who had not followed the policy debate. The newspaper excelled only in its frequent use of photographs, making Albert Wynn the most photographed representative in the study.

What are the consequences of this meager coverage? First, it is difficult to imagine that many readers learned very much about Albert Wynn from the *Washington Times*. The infrequency of the coverage — one article every five days — meant that only the most careful newspaper readers were likely to notice the coverage. Second, the concentration of coverage on a single subject — position taking — and the failure to explain the controversy behind particular roll-call votes, made coverage helpful only to readers who were already well informed. Perhaps the frequent appearance of photographs helped some citizens recognize their representative. The best that can be said for the *Times* is that it allowed local opinion leaders to monitor his roll-call votes. But it seemed not to provide a forum for opinion leaders to inform ordinary citizens about Wynn's shortcomings. In short, the *Times* did little to contribute to an informed citizenry.

The *Washington Times* was not the only media outlet that could have provided information about Albert Wynn's performance in office. Unfortunately, the other outlets had their own problems. The *Washington Post*, which had a much larger circulation than the *Times*, provided only marginally better coverage. Actually, the volume of coverage in the two papers was virtually the same, but the *Post* was better at explaining position taking, covering Wynn's role in local politics, and reporting about the campaign. Two suburban newspapers circulated in Wynn's district, the *Montgomery Journal* and the *Prince George's Journal*, each published five times a week. Even if their coverage had been superb (no information is available), their combined circulations amounted to less than 5 percent of the populations of Montgomery and Prince George's counties, so they could not have informed many of Wynn's constituents about his performance. Overall, it was a meager informational environment that left citizens ill-prepared to monitor Albert Wynn's performance in office.

Although no other newspapers were as uninformative as the *Washington Times*, several papers were better by only a smidgen, including the *Boston Globe*, *Newsday*, *Phoenix Gazette*, and *Tucson Citizen*. The informational environments created by these papers were deficient in diverse ways. The problem with the *Boston Globe* was not the volume of coverage but its excessive focus on Joe Moakley's obtaining constituency benefits; it largely ignored his important policy-making activities in the House. The problem with the *Phoenix Gazette* was not its coverage of Jon Kyl's race for the

Senate, which was frequent, thorough, and accessible, but rather its superficial coverage of Kyl during the year before the Senate campaign. Long Island's *Newsday* was shallow in all aspects of its coverage of Peter King. The lack of informative coverage of King's 1994 campaign was particularly surprising, since he faced a strong challenger. In most other papers, competitive races attracted extra coverage. The *Tucson Citizen* covered Jim Kolbe infrequently and cursorily, especially compared to its local competitor, the *Arizona Daily Star*.

What are the consequences of the meager informational environments created by these six newspapers? The most serious consequence is that not even the most politically interested citizens are likely to be aware of the range of things a representative is doing in office. They may have a hazy sense of what a representative has done, but they are less well equipped to monitor his overall behavior, ask penetrating questions, or sound the alarm when they observe disagreeable actions. They may do some of these things, but they necessarily do so for a limited range of activities. These meager informational environments offer even less help for the next few strata of constituents. The infrequency and inaccessibility of coverage make it much less likely that less politically interested citizens will notice what newspapers happen to publish about representatives.

Typical Informational Environments

The best newspapers provide a wealth of information about where representatives stand on the issues and some information about their lawmaking activities. They also cover campaigns relatively well, although only when there is a strong, well-funded challenger. The least informative papers offer much less frequent, less thorough, and less accessible coverage of position taking, lawmaking, and campaigning. Other newspapers occupy the wide expanse between the least and the most informative newspapers.

What is a typical informational environment? Statistically, the median newspaper in the first data set published about 15 articles per month that mentioned the local representative. More than half of these articles focused on a representative's participation in policy making. The typical newspaper covered representative's position taking extensively, but coverage of bill introductions, committee activities, and leadership was less careful. Competitive elections were covered reasonably well; noncompetitive elections were covered cursorily. The *Baton Rouge Advocate, Bloomington Pantagraph, Orlando Sentinel Tribune*, and *York Daily Record* were typical newspapers.

What are the consequences of these typical informational environments? The most politically interested citizens are likely to notice lots of things about representatives. An article every other day is a lot of coverage for careful newspaper readers. The problem is that typical newspapers tend to cover representatives' lawmaking activities — bills introduced, committee activities, leadership activities — much less thoroughly than do the best papers. Only 6 percent of the articles in the *Baton Rouge Advocate, Bloomington Pantagraph, Orlando Sentinel Tribune*, and *York Daily Record* focused on these lawmaking activities (21 articles on average), compared with 10 percent of the articles in the seven best papers (48 articles on average).[4] As a consequence, the most politically interested citizens are less well-informed about representatives' lawmaking activities, less likely to ask representatives questions about these activities in public meetings, and less likely to monitor representatives' performance in office than are citizens who dwell in richer informational environments.

A second consequence is that even less information is likely to penetrate into the next few strata of constituents. The frequency of coverage is key to informing citizens who are less regular or less careful newspaper readers. Although most readers of the *Orlando Sentinel Tribune* probably missed the four articles in two years that discussed Bill McCollum's committee activities, many readers probably noticed at least some of the 25 articles that focused on his three-month campaign to stop the closing of the Orlando Naval Training Center and the Orlando Naval Hospital.

Citizens and Political Accountability

Are citizens exposed to the kinds of information they need to hold representatives accountable for their performance in office? As the preceding discussion shows, it depends partly on how rich is the informational environment where citizens happen to live, and partly on how interested citizens are in politics, since interest affects the chances that they will notice, read, and comprehend what information newspapers make available. Citizens who regularly read the best newspapers are exposed to a rich diet of information about representatives' positions and actions. Citizens who infrequently read the weakest papers learn very little about what representatives are doing.

How much accountability can one expect in a system with such vast disparities in the information available to citizens? First, one must recognize that newspapers and other media outlets are only part of the informational environment in which citizens dwell. Especially during the campaign period, alternative channels for information exist, including campaign events

---

[4] According to my benchmark of legislative newsworthiness, the representatives who were featured in the four typical newspapers were actually more newsworthy than the representatives who were featured in the seven best papers. The *Congressional Quarterly Weekly Report* published an average of 33 articles that mentioned the four representatives, compared with 25 articles that mentioned the seven (the medians were 33 and 20 articles).

for incumbents and challengers; direct mail sent by incumbents, challengers, political parties, and interest groups; and campaign advertisements created by incumbents and challengers that appear on radio, television, billboards, and newspapers. Information transmitted through any of these channels can also jump-start conversations among citizens about their representatives' performance. Outside the campaign period, there are fewer alternative channels for information, and representatives tend to dominate what channels exist. For example, most representatives regularly send newsletters to their constituents and appear at community meetings throughout their districts.

Second, accountability does not depend on each citizen carefully monitoring every position and action taken by his or her representative. A cadre of individuals who regularly monitor what a representative is doing in office and who inform other citizens when they see something out of line can also serve citizens' interests in accountable government. These opinion leaders need not be a large fraction of a representative's constituency. Careful newspaper readers who write letters to the editor to protest a representative's actions, local talk show hosts who search for topics to spark debates on the radio, local pundits who seek fresh topics for their opinion columns, and potential challengers who seek to impair a representative in advance of a formal campaign are examples of the wide variety of opinion leaders who act as watchdogs for the many citizens who do not regularly monitor what a representative is doing. No obvious advantages would flow from making every citizen a front-line sentry. Much more important is that information regularly flows to those who act as watchdogs, that these watchdogs reflect the diversity of interests in a constituency, and that watchdogs have easy ways to communicate with citizens when they discover a representative doing disagreeable things.

These two points actually widen the disparities between the prospects for accountable government in the richest and the most meager informational environments. The best newspapers satisfy both the Full News and the Burglar Alarm Standards. They not only provide local opinion leaders with the kinds of information they need to monitor representatives' positions and actions; they also provide opinion leaders with easy ways to communicate with citizens when they find representatives doing disagreeable things. These opportunities include coverage of their objections in news stories as well as plentiful opportunities for them to voice their objections on the opinion pages. The weakest papers satisfy neither the Full News nor the Burglar Alarm Standards. They fail to provide local opinion leaders with the range of information necessary for monitoring representatives; they fail to give local critics easy ways to communicate their objections to ordinary citizens. The seven best papers, for example, published an average of 49 letters to the editor about local representatives, while the six weakest papers published an average of 6 letters to the editor.[5]

The existence of alternative informational channels during the campaign period is comforting, but the reality is that these channels are used extensively only when well-funded challengers emerge. Weak challengers cannot afford large campaign events, massive direct mail campaigns, or expensive advertising. In short, the problems endemic in weak informational environments are overcome only when talented challengers raise lots of money and employ these alternative channels creatively and extensively. Most challengers never cross that threshold.

Does the entire informational system provide average citizens with adequate information to evaluate their representatives' performance in office? Ordinarily it does not. The average newspaper does not publish enough information about a representative's positions and actions for the average citizen to notice, read, and comprehend very much of the information. The average challenger is not well-enough funded to communicate directly with citizens during the campaign period or to overcome the inherent advantages that a representative has in communicating with citizens during non-campaign periods. Ordinarily, then, the average citizen does not learn a great deal about a representative's performance. This can change quite quickly, however, if a representative does something to attract the attention of journalists, opinion leaders, or well-funded challengers and if these individuals find ways to communicate with citizens, whether by generating heavy media coverage or by running effective advertisements.

Representatives and Political Accountability

In what ways do coverage patterns in local newspapers affect representatives' own behavior? Do representatives who observe newspapers covering them heavily behave differently from those who observe newspapers covering them lightly? Does it matter what types of behavior newspapers choose to cover? Scholars have yet to examine these questions empirically. At their theoretical extremes, it seems likely that the volume of coverage would greatly affect a representative's behavior. A representative who found that journalists reported every position, action, and utterance — imagine, say, if journalists covered a representative as heavily as they cover an American president — would probably be much more cautious when speaking or acting than a representative who worked without any public scrutiny. What is

---

[5] The median was 33 letters for the best papers and 2 letters for the weakest ones.

not known is how much the narrower differences reported in this study matter.

Some things that representatives do are recorded for posterity even if they are not reported contemporaneously in the newspapers. For example, the government maintains public records of campaign contributions, bills introduced, speeches on the House floor, and roll-call votes. Since challengers regularly scrutinize these records, searching for positions, actions, statements, or contributions that they can use to tarnish representatives' reputations, the question is whether representatives behave differently when local newspapers cover these things contemporaneously. I believe that they do. If all that a representative fears is that some future challenger might unearth a roll-call vote and use it against her, then the electoral risk associated with most individual votes is relatively low. The appropriate consideration for a representative is whether, a year or more from now, a challenger could make a compelling thirty-second television advertisement attacking her for voting a particular way. When a newspaper covers a representative's roll-call votes contemporaneously, however, coverage can affect how constituents view their representative, even if it would be difficult to make a good television spot a year from now. Coverage that emphasizes how a representative is opposing a popular president, or that suggests she is seriously out of line with the rest of the state delegation, or that informs readers she won't budge despite the strong views of local editorialists, columnists, or letter writers can affect how some citizens perceive her. Coverage that regularly emphasizes these things can gradually erode a representative's local reputation, even if the individual votes would not make compelling campaign advertisements. Most representatives do their best to avoid such erosion.

The situation is quite different for other types of behavior. There are no publicly available records that show whether a representative commands the respect of her colleagues, whether she is a workhorse or a show horse, whether she has done anything to build a supporting coalition for a bill she has introduced, or even whether she attends committee hearings or markup sessions. These things need to be observed and reported contemporaneously. When journalists do not cover these things, a representative need not worry that a challenger will later uncover reliable records that can be featured in advertisements against her. The lack of regular coverage of hearings, markups, and coalition building makes it much easier for representatives to avoid the heavy lifting that is required to make things happen on Capitol Hill. They can be talkers, rather than doers, and their constituents will be unable to observe the difference.

It is ironic that most newspapers cover position taking heavily, despite the existence of alternative informational sources, while they tend to cover leadership activities lightly. Representatives already have good electoral reasons to be cautious when the roll is called; heavy newspaper coverage merely encourages them to choose their positions more carefully. Representatives have few electoral incentives to be diligent committee members, skilled legislative drafters, or active leaders. The lack of extensive newspaper coverage of these entrepreneurial activities helps guarantee that these activities continue to be undersupplied on Capitol Hill. What incentives are there to work hard if those who evaluate one's performance never notice? Of course, entrepreneurial activities can mobilize one's opponents as well as one's supporters, so heavy coverage may sometimes increase the risks of becoming a leader. Certainly the two representatives whose lawmaking activities were most heavily covered — Bilbray and LaRocco — profited little from their investments. Both representatives faced challengers who emphasized the negative consequences of the issues they championed. Both were defeated.

When representatives observe local newspapers covering them thoroughly, they need to be especially careful about their positions and actions. But even haphazard coverage can keep a representative on his toes. Police officers don't line the highways with radar guns to control speeding; sporadic radar traps provide sufficient incentives to keep most drivers from excessive speeding. Presumably a representative, who has more at stake than mere speeding tickets, calculates similarly. A newspaper that thoroughly covers a random third of a representative's roll-call votes may have as great an effect on how a representative calculates the electoral consequences of particular votes as a newspaper that throughly covers them all. The crucial point is that a representative decides first, and only then learns whether a newspaper will feature his vote.

Representatives probably have most to fear when newspapers publish lots of editorials, opinion columns, or letters that directly criticize what they are doing. A simple factual account of how a representative voted on some complicated regulatory matter does not have the same bite as a stinging editorial that argues that a representative ignored the people he claims to represent when he voted to advance the interests of out-of-state bankers who contributed heavily to his campaign. Whether heavy coverage on the opinion pages — especially coverage in advance of when a representative makes a final decision — affects how a representative decides is not known. It is a hypothesis worth testing.

Opinion Coverage

One-sixth of the articles in the first data set were opinion items — editorials, columns, or letters to the editor. How informative are these opinion items compared with news stories? Would citizens who read lots of opinion items learn more about their representative than those who read lots of news stories? Would citizens be more likely to alter their views of their representative after reading opinion items or news stories? These questions are important because the differences between how newspapers covered representatives on the opinion pages were even more pronounced than the differences on the news pages. Some newspapers featured representatives in editorials and columns; other papers rarely mentioned them in these opinion items. The top five newspapers averaged 69 editorials and columns; the bottom five averaged 7. The variance was even greater for letters to the editor. The top five papers averaged 79 letters; the bottom five averaged 1.

Opinion items can be enormously informative for citizens because they help citizens evaluate policy proposals and politicians.[6] Factual accounts of what representatives have been doing can be helpful for those citizens who already know a fair amount about politics, policies, and politicians. Most citizens, however, do not even have firm preferences about most of the issues that come before Congress. Citizens often need help in understanding what is at stake in a particular conflict before they can know whether their representative is doing good or evil. Opinion coverage often does a better job than news coverage at explaining what is at stake. For example, the typical editorial, column, or letter that reported a representative's policy position was much more likely to explain something about the basic policy conflict than was the typical news story that reported a representative's position. Although individual opinion items were often one-sided, collectively they tended to be balanced between those favoring and those opposing a representative's position.

Opinion items are also more likely than news stories to include criticisms of a representative's policy-making activities. I don't mean to suggest that boundless criticism is a virtue, but a representative has so many opportunities to tout all the wonderful things he has been doing that it is surely a sign of political health when those who don't agree with a representative have opportunities to communicate their own views to citizens. Forty percent of the letters and 26 percent of the editorials and columns contained criticism of the local representative, compared with only 6 percent of news stories. Opinion items were also more likely to contain praise of a representative's policy-making activities. Indeed, the balance between praise and criticism was much more evenly balanced in opinion items than in news stories.

The principal virtue of opinion coverage is that it dovetails nicely with citizens' two evaluative tasks. Citizens are asked to evaluate a representa-

---

[6] One experimental study has shown that articles from newsmagazines tend to be more informative for citizens than similar articles from newspapers. The authors suggest this may be because newsmagazines provide more contextual and evaluative information than do newspapers on their news pages (Neuman, Just, and Crigler 1992, 58–59, 78–83). Experimental researchers have yet to examine whether the same is true for newspapers' opinion coverage compared with their news coverage.

tive's continued fitness for office, not to describe what a representative has been doing. Citizens are asked to evaluate the relative merits of incumbent and challenger, not to describe each candidate's positions. The best opinion coverage focuses directly on these evaluative tasks. The best opinion coverage gives readers a sense of what is at stake, rather than merely summarizing what the candidates have done and where they stand. A second virtue of opinion coverage is that it tends to be more vivid and memorable than news coverage. None of this is to suggest that newspapers should substitute opinion coverage for news coverage. But newspapers that published frequent editorials, columns, and letters about a representative seemed more informative than those that seldom published opinion items.

Of course, we do not know for sure whether heavy coverage on the opinion pages allows citizens to learn more about their representative than they would learn from just news stories. It is merely a hypothesis. Unfortunately, it is not a hypothesis that can be examined in this project because the fourth data set, which connects local newspaper coverage with citizens' knowledge and attitudes, is based on the volume of newspaper coverage, not on the content, quality, location, or format of coverage.[7]

Models of Accountability

The discussion in this chapter recognizes a division of labor between journalists, local opinion leaders, and ordinary citizens. Disinterested journalists report what a representative is doing in office. These journalists must be selective; they could not possibly cover everything a representative does. Ideally, they choose to report a range of positions and actions that are important to various segments of a representative's constituency. Local opinion leaders monitor journalists' accounts of what a representative is doing. They usually monitor activities related to issues about which they care. Ideally, opinion leaders reflect the diversity of interests in a constituency, so that no interest goes unmonitored. Ordinary citizens pay attention when opinion leaders sound the alarm. Ideally, these leaders have easy ways to communicate with citizens, so when they sound the alarm, citizens have a reasonable chance of hearing it.

According to this tripartite division, disinterested journalists practice broad-based police-patrol-style oversight, local opinion leaders scrutinize journalists' reports about particular policy precincts, and ordinary citizens listen for alarms. Of course, newspapers are not the only sources of information for opinion leaders. Washington-based interest groups and party leaders

[7] The relative efficacy of news coverage and opinion coverage has not been the subject of much scholarly research, but see Dalton, Beck, and Huckfeldt 1998; Beck, Dalton, Greene, and Huckfeldt 2002; and Kahn and Kenney 2002.

also monitor what a representative is doing. But the existence of Washington-based monitoring is not the same as having local opinion leaders—a representative's own constituents—monitor a representative. Washington-based interest groups are known to underrepresent many interests. Careful reporting by newspapers allows local champions of underrepresented interests to monitor what a representative is doing.

Some newspapers also facilitate communications among constituents by welcoming on their editorial and op-ed pages messages about a representative's performance. They provide free platforms for local opinion leaders to communicate with other citizens about a representative's accomplishments and shortcomings. Of course, opinion leaders have other ways to sound the alarm besides writing columns or letters to the editor, including organizing protest meetings, mailing newsletters, and buying campaign advertisements. But opinion coverage in local newspapers has several virtues. It is freely available to anyone who wishes to voice an objection. The objections are displayed in a public forum where others can endorse or dispute them. Individuals can lodge their objections before a representative makes a decision or immediately after a representative announces a decision. When local newspapers welcome and regularly publish objections, the disgruntled need not wait for campaign season to sound the alarm.

The point of this discussion is to clarify the role of the press in helping citizens engage in burglar-alarm-style oversight of their representative. Burglar-alarm-style oversight works only if other individuals, groups, or organizations practice police-patrol-style oversight. Someone must monitor what a representative is doing and sound the alarm. Although local media outlets are not the only organizations that can monitor a representative's actions in Washington, they are the only monitorial organizations that are staffed by disinterested individuals. Other monitorial organizations are designed to protect specific interests. Burglar-alarm-style oversight also requires that local opinion leaders have opportunities to inform ordinary citizens when they find a representative doing disagreeable things. Although local media outlets are not the only means by which these messages can be transmitted, they are the only organizations that transmit messages for free. These two points suggest that careful reporting by local newspapers helps level the playing field. In its absence, well-funded interest groups dominate the important functions of monitoring and alarm sounding.

An alternative way for citizens to hold representatives accountable is to focus on their performance as members of party teams. Political scientists often speak fondly of strong, disciplined parties because such parties provide powerful incentives for representatives to work together before they are judged together. If citizens seek to reward or punish their representative in this fashion, they need to know whether or not their representative is a loyal team member. Unfortunately, local newspapers convey little information about representatives as members of party teams. Representatives seldom claim to be either party supporters or party opponents; they seldom invoke party as a reason for their roll-call votes. Challengers and other opponents are a bit more likely to accuse representatives of being strong party supporters, although the number of instances is small.[8] Of course, well-informed citizens who know where the parties stand on various issues can still make inference about a representative's party loyalty by studying his or her voting record. But newspapers do virtually nothing to facilitate this kind of evaluation by ordinary citizens. Indeed, on their editorial pages they regularly praise representatives for their independence and for standing firm against party leaders.

Yet another way for citizens to hold representatives accountable is to focus on their connection to the incumbent president. Citizens who strongly support or oppose the president can choose to reward or punish their representative depending on whether he or she seems to be aiding or thwarting the president. Some local newspapers facilitate this kind of evaluation. Newspapers provided more than three times as many references to a representative's support for the president as they did to a representative's support for his or her party. Given President Clinton's unpopularity, representatives were somewhat more likely to portray themselves as presidential opponents than as supporters, while challengers and other critics were much more likely to accuse representatives of being strong presidential supporters, although both patterns varied from district to district.[9] At least in 1993 and 1994, newspapers emphasized the presidential connection more than the party connection.

Most of the time, however, local newspapers portray representatives as individuals, not as members of party or presidential teams. This is exactly how David Mayhew argued most representatives seek to be portrayed (Mayhew 1974). Representatives run for office as individuals; they defend their records as individuals; they seek to show that they are the best individuals for the job. And we now know that they are largely criticized for their fail-

[8] A total of 157 articles (out of 8,003) referred to a representative's party support (113) or opposition (44). Representatives portrayed themselves as party supporters in 18 articles and as party opponents in 4. Challengers and other critics portrayed representatives as party supporters in 38 articles and as opponents in 3. Most other references were by neutral sources. Among the 244 articles where a representative explained a policy position, only one explanation emphasized party loyalty or party leadership as a reason for taking a particular position.

[9] A total of 536 articles referred to a representative's presidential support (275) or opposition (261). Representatives portrayed themselves as presidential supporters in 102 articles and as presidential opponents in 158. Challengers and other critics portrayed representatives as presidential supporters in 92 articles and as opponents in 18. Most other references were by neutral sources (although the president portrayed three representatives as supporters on three occasions). Among the 244 articles where a representative explained a policy position, only three explanations emphasized the role of the president as a reason for taking a particular position.

ures as individuals. Ten percent of all articles included someone criticizing a representative's individual performance as a policy maker.

Future Research

This book is the first large-scale study of how local media outlets cover members of Congress. My hope is that it stimulates other scholars to join the parade, for there is still much to learn. What are the remaining puzzles? We should investigate how other media outlets, including small daily newspapers, weekly newspapers, radio, television, wire services, and Web-based media, cover representatives.[10] My sense is that local newspapers cover representatives more carefully than other media outlets do, but intuition is no substitute for research. In any event, many citizens obtain their information from these outlets, so we need to determine how they cover representatives. We should also explore how media coverage patterns have changed over time. Are the coverage patterns in 1993 and 1994 typical or are they distinctive in some respects? How does coverage of a single representative change over time?[11] We should investigate more deeply how local media outlets cover representatives and challengers during campaign season. How do they cover open seats, the most competitive races of all? We should also study more carefully the nature of opinion coverage. If I had known that opinion coverage would constitute one-sixth of all coverage, I would have designed lots of special codes for editorials, columns, and letters, rather than using coding rules that were designed for news stories.[12]

A second line of research should investigate why journalists cover representatives as they do. This book first established how frequently newspapers covered representatives and then used quantitative methods to analyze various newspaper-centered and representative-centered explanations for variations in the volume of coverage. Future quantitative studies could explore the impact of other factors, including ownership patterns, a representative's press releases, coverage by the wire services, and coverage by other local and

[10] With random samples, please. It is shocking that few scholars choose random samples of local media outlets, even when doing so would not increase the difficulty or cost of their studies.

[11] Richard Fenno suggests that the *Cleveland Plain Dealer's* favorable coverage of Louis Stokes in 1993 and 1994 was not typical of how the paper covered Stokes early in his career, when coverage was much more negative. Indeed, the paper opposed Stokes in the 1968 Democratic primary (Fenno 2003).

[12] Local newspapers appear to be increasing the space devoted to opinion coverage. Two surveys of editorial page editors, conducted eight years apart, revealed growth in the use of op-ed pages and in the number of letters published. According to the second survey, editors considered letters to be the best-read item on the editorial page (Hynds 1984).

regional outlets. Future studies should also attempt to explain variations in the content of coverage. Someone should interview editors and reporters to learn why they make the choices they do. Such interviews tend to be more productive, however, when scholars already know what are the patterns of coverage. Interviewing in advance of content analysis requires that journalists generalize about both the patterns and the causes of those patterns. Journalists have no comparative advantage in the first task; indeed, they are often unaware of the patterns that they collectively produce.[13]

A third line of research should investigate the consequences of various coverage patterns for what citizens know about representatives and challengers. Chapter 8 reports my own fledgling attempts at this type of research, but my data are far from ideal and the results are inconclusive. Those who do content analysis of the media need to coordinate with those who do survey research to make sure that their data sets can be linked. Experimental researchers should also examine the relative efficacy of news coverage and opinion coverage. My sense is that editorials, opinion columns, and letters to the editor were often more informative than news stories, but this assertion needs to be investigated, both in the laboratory and in the field.[14]

Excellence in Journalism

Books on politics and the press often close with exhortations about how journalists should do better. It makes no difference whether scholars or journalists write these books; the reformist impulse is nearly universal. At this point, I may disappoint readers, since I lack the reformist gene. Although I enjoy discovering how and why political actors behave as they do, I have no expertise in reforming institutions or changing behavior. Moreover, I lack experience in writing news stories, attracting readers, retaining advertisers, or managing newspapers. If reform is the aim, experts on journalism need to draft the plans.

Journalists aspire to cover politics and public affairs in ways that are useful to citizens. Bill Kovach and Tom Rosenstiel distilled the basic principles

[13] The interviews that Martin Gilens conducted with photo editors at *Time* and *Newsweek* were most revealing because Gilens had already discovered racial patterns in the photos that the editors had selected to illustrate news stories about welfare, patterns of which the editors were unaware (Gilens 1999, 140–50).

[14] There is a literature on the effects of newspaper endorsements on presidential elections but no corresponding literature for congressional elections. It should not be difficult to identify the endorsement decisions for hundreds of papers and then determine what impact these endorsements have on election outcomes. For studies of presidential elections, see Erikson 1976; Hurd and Singletary 1985.

of journalism by interviewing hundreds of journalists to discover what values they shared. Journalists agreed overwhelmingly that "the purpose of journalism is to provide people with the information they need to be free and self-governing." To fulfill this task, journalists agreed that (*a*) journalism's first obligation is to the truth; (*b*) its first loyalty is to citizens; (*c*) it must serve as an independent monitor of power; (*d*) it must provide a forum for public criticism; and (*e*) it must strive to make the significant interesting and relevant (Kovach and Rosenstiel 2001, 12–13).[15]

My surprise in this study was to discover that some newspapers achieved these five goals admirably. The best papers were wonderfully informative. They provided frequent, thorough, and accessible coverage about local representatives. Their news stories were interesting and relevant. Their opinion pages provided forums for public criticism of representatives and challengers. They provided citizens with the kinds of information they needed to hold their representatives accountable. These newspapers offered excellent models for other newspapers — models produced by successful journalists, not armchair critics.

What makes the best papers so distinctive? What lessons do they offer for editors and reporters at other newspapers? First, the best newspapers explained what was at stake in particular disputes and they found interesting and informative ways to report roll-call votes. Most of the decisions that politicians face are not about choosing appropriate means or ends; they are about making trade-offs among conflicting goals. Can we afford to spend more to improve health, education, transportation, or the environment? If we must spend more on defense, should we cut domestic programs, increase taxes, or tolerate larger deficits? Would more stringent environmental or safety regulations make firms less competitive and cost workers their jobs? The best newspapers found ways to inform readers about these kinds of trade-offs, even when they reported roll-call votes. The model paper was one where reporters offered a brief synopsis of a bill and the legislative situation, summarized the arguments on each side by quoting from at least one proponent and at least one opponent, and then reported the positions of area representatives.[16] The best papers also incorporated coverage of representatives' positions into news stories about what was happening on major national issues.

The best newspapers also reported representatives' participation in legisla-

[15] Journalists also agreed that (*a*) the essence of journalism is a discipline of verification; (*b*) its practitioners must maintain an independence from those they cover; (*c*) it must keep the news comprehensive and proportional; and (*d*) its practitioners must be allowed to exercise their personal conscience.

[16] Individual newspapers need not write these synopses or identify pithy quotations. These tasks could be performed by an independent organization, such as Congressional Quarterly or the Associated Press.

tive activities. They reported what legislators were doing besides taking positions on roll-call votes. When representatives were involved in the major
issues of the day, they included coverage of local representatives in their
front-page stories on these national issues. When representatives were involved in less salient issues, they informed readers about what representatives were doing to advance or block particular proposals. If they happened
to have reporters based in Washington, the best newspapers used them to
cover representatives' legislative activities. If they lacked Washington-based
reporters, the best papers found other ways to cover these activities.

The best newspapers featured representatives on their editorial and op-ed
pages. Editors and opinion columnists regularly evaluated what representatives were doing in Washington, sometimes in conjunction with editorials or
columns on particular issues, sometimes in pieces that focused on individual representatives. The best newspapers welcomed and published letters to
the editor that praised or critiqued representatives' positions and actions.
They also offered representatives opportunities to respond to their critics.
During campaign season, the best newspapers created public forums where
politicians, opinion leaders, and ordinary citizens could debate the strengths
and weaknesses of representatives and challengers.

The best newspapers covered competitive races extensively. They were
scrupulously fair to incumbents and challengers on their news pages. They
offered analysis and guidance on their editorial pages. They welcomed and
published letters and opinion columns from diverse viewpoints. Although
the best papers did not cover less competitive races particularly well, it is not
clear whether the challengers in these few campaigns were too weak to
create compelling messages, or whether newspapers simply refuse to cover
challengers who fail to raise mountains of cash.

The best newspapers sought to satisfy both the Full News Standard and
the Burglar Alarm Standard. They acted as if the two standards were not
rivals, but complements. They published lots of specialized articles, so that
their most attentive readers could monitor representatives' positions and actions on a wide range of issues. They also published lots of accessible information for less attentive readers, especially when local opinion leaders, challengers, and other critics were unhappy with what representatives were
doing in office.

The best newspapers were a diverse lot, ranging from the largest paper in
the sample to the smallest. Some of these papers covered many representatives; some covered one. Some employed many Washington reporters; some
employed none. Some were rich; most were not. The best papers were
distinctive principally in their commitment to covering representatives frequently, thoroughly, and fairly. The smallest newspapers were often creative
in finding ways to stretch their resources. It was no accident that the smallest newspapers covered representatives more extensively on their opinion

pages than did their larger cousins, for welcoming and publishing letters and opinion columns is an inexpensive strategy for covering representatives and campaigns. That this opinion coverage was also wonderfully informative reminds us that quality journalism is more about taste and commitment than about resources.

References

Alvarez, R. Michael, and Paul Gronke. 1996. Citizens and Legislators: Learning about the Persian Gulf War Resolution. *Legislative Studies Quarterly* 21:105–28.

Arnold, R. Douglas. 1979. *Congress and the Bureaucracy: A Theory of Influence*. New Haven: Yale University Press.

———. 1981. The Local Roots of Domestic Policy. In *The New Congress*, edited by Thomas E. Mann and Norman J. Ornstein. Washington, DC: American Enterprise Institute.

———. 1990. *The Logic of Congressional Action*. New Haven: Yale University Press.

———. 1993. Can Inattentive Citizens Control Their Elected Representatives? In *Congress Reconsidered*, 5th ed., edited by Lawrence C. Dodd and Bruce I. Oppenheimer. Washington, DC: CQ Press.

Bacon. 1993. *Bacon's Newspaper Directory, 1994*. Chicago: Bacon's Information.

Bagdikian, Ben H. 1987. *The Media Monopoly*. 2nd ed. Boston: Beacon Press.

Bartels, Larry M. 1988. *Presidential Primaries and the Dynamics of Public Choice*. Princeton: Princeton University Press.

———. 1993. Messages Received: The Political Impact of Media Exposure. *American Political Science Review* 87:267–85.

Beck, Paul A., Russell J. Dalton, Steven Greene, and Robert Huckfeldt. 2002. The Social Calculus of Voting: Interpersonal, Media, and Organizational Influences on Presidential Choices. *American Political Science Review* 96:57–73.

Bogart, Leo. 1981. *Press and Public: Who Reads What, When, Where, and Why in American Newspapers*. Hillsdale, NJ: Erlbaum.

———. 1984. The Public's Use and Perception of Newspapers. *Public Opinion Quarterly* 48:709–19.

Broder, David S. 1987. *Behind the Front Page: A Candid Look at How the News Is Made*. New York: Simon and Schuster.

Campbell, James E. 1982. Cosponsoring Legislation in the U.S. Congress. *Legislative Studies Quarterly* 7:415–22.

Census, Bureau of the. 1994. *Statistical Abstract of the United States, 1994*. Washington, DC: Government Printing Office.

Clarke, Peter, and Susan H. Evans. 1983. *Covering Campaigns: Journalism in Congressional Elections*. Stanford, CA: Stanford University Press.

Compaine, Benjamin M. 1982. *Who Owns the Media? Concentration of Ownership in the Mass Communications Industry*. White Plains, NY: Knowledge Industry Publications.

Congressional Quarterly. 1991. *Congressional Quarterly's Guide to Congress*. 4th ed. Washington, DC: Congressional Quarterly.

———. 1993a. *Congressional Districts in the 1990s*. Washington, DC: Congressional Quarterly.

———. 1993b. *Politics in America, 1994*. Washington, DC: Congressional Quarterly.

Congressional Quarterly. 1994. *Congressional Quarterly Almanac, 1993*. Washington, DC: Congressional Quarterly.

———. 1995a. *Congressional Quarterly Almanac, 1994*. Washington, DC: Congressional Quarterly.

———. 1995b. *Politics in America, 1996*. Washington, DC: Congressional Quarterly.

Cook, Timothy E. 1986. House Members as Newsmakers: The Effects of Televising Congress. *Legislative Studies Quarterly* 11:203–26.

———. 1989. *Making Laws and Making News: Media Strategies in the U.S. House of Representatives*. Washington, DC: Brookings Institution.

———. 1998. *Governing with the News: The News Media as a Political Institution*. Chicago: University of Chicago Press.

Dahl, Robert A. 1989. *Democracy and Its Critics*. New Haven: Yale University Press.

———. 1998. *On Democracy*. New Haven: Yale University Press.

Dalton, Russell J., Paul A. Beck, and Robert Huckfeldt. 1998. Partisan Cues and the Media: Information Flows in the 1992 Presidential Election. *American Political Science Review* 92:111–26.

Deering, Christopher J. 1996. Congress, the President, and Automatic Government: The Case of Military Base Closures. In *Rivals for Power: Presidential-Congressional Relations*, edited by James A. Thurber. Washington, DC: CQ Press.

Delli Carpini, Michael X., and Scott Keeter. 1996. *What Americans Know about Politics and Why It Matters*. New Haven: Yale University Press.

Downs, Anthony. 1957. *An Economic Theory of Democracy*. New York: Harper and Row.

Editor & Publisher. 1993. *The International Yearbook*. New York: Editor & Publisher.

Entman, Robert M. 1989. *Democracy without Citizens: Media and the Decay of American Politics*. Oxford University Press.

Erikson, Robert S. 1976. The Influence of Newspaper Endorsements in Presidential Elections: The Case of 1964. *American Journal of Political Science* 20:207–33.

Everett, Shu-Ling, and Stephen E. Everett. 1989. How Readers and Advertisers Benefit from Local Newspaper Competition. *Journalism Quarterly* 66:76–79.

Fan, David P. 1988. *Predictions of Public Opinion from the Mass Media: Computer Content Analysis and Mathematical Modeling*. New York: Greenwood Press.

Fan, David P., and Lois Norem. 1992. The Media and the Fate of the Medicare Catastrophic Extension Act. *Journal of Health Politics, Policy, and Law* 17:39–70.

Fenno, Richard F., Jr. 1973. *Congressmen in Committees*. Boston: Little, Brown.

———. 1978. *Home Style: House Members in Their Districts*. Boston: Little, Brown.

———. 1996. *Senators on the Campaign Trail: The Politics of Representation*. Norman: University of Oklahoma Press.

———. 2003. *Going Home: Black Representatives and Their Constituencies*. Chicago: University of Chicago Press.

Fiorina, Morris P. 1981. *Retrospective Voting in American National Elections*. New Haven: Yale University Press.

Gans, Herbert J. 1979. *Deciding What's News*. New York: Random House.

Gilens, Martin. 1999. *Why Americans Hate Welfare: Race, Media, and the Politics of Antipoverty Programs*. Chicago: University of Chicago Press.

Gimpel, James G. 1996. *Fulfilling the Contract: The First 100 Days*. Boston: Allyn and Bacon.

Goldenberg, Edie N. and Michael Traugott. 1978. *Congressional Campaign Study, 1978*. Computer file. Study Number 8431. Ann Arbor, MI: Interuniversity Consortium for Political and Social Research.

———. 1984. *Campaigning for Congress*. Washington, DC: CQ Press.

———. 1987. Mass Media Effects on Recognizing and Rating Candidates in U.S. Senate Elections. In *Campaigns in the News: Mass Media and Congressional Elections*, edited by Jan P. Vermeer. New York: Greenwood Press.

Graber, Doris A. 1993. *Processing the News: How People Tame the Information Tide*. 2nd ed. Lanham, MD: University Press of America.

Green, Donald Philip, and Jonathan S. Krasno. 1988. Salvation for the Spendthrift Incumbent: Reestimating the Effects of Campaign Spending in House Elections. *American Journal of Political Science* 32:884–907.

Green, Mark J., James M. Fallows, and David R. Zwick. 1972. *Who Runs Congress?* New York: Bantam Books.

Hale, Jon F. 1987. The Scribes of Texas: Newspaper Coverage of the 1984 U.S. Senate Campaign. In *Campaigns in the News: Mass Media and Congressional Elections*, edited by Jan P. Vermeer. New York: Greenwood Press.

Hall, Richard L. 1996. *Participation in Congress*. New Haven: Yale University Press.

Hart, Roderick P. 2000. *Campaign Talk: Why Elections Are Good for Us*. Princeton: Princeton University Press.

Hastie, Reid, and Nancy Pennington. 1988. Notes on the Distinction between Memory-Based and On-Line Judgments. In *On-Line Cognition in Person Perception*, edited by John N. Bassili. Hillsdale, NJ: Erlbaum.

Herrnson, Paul S. 2000. *Congressional Elections: Campaigning at Home and in Washington*. 3rd ed. Washington, DC: CQ Press.

Hess, Stephen. 1981. *The Washington Reporters*. Washington, DC: Brookings Institution.

———. 1991. *Live from Capitol Hill: Studies of Congress and the Media*. Washington, DC: Brookings Institution.

Hill, David B. 1981. Letter Opinion on the ERA: A Test of the Newspaper Bias Hypothesis. *Public Opinion Quarterly* 45:384–92.

Huckfeldt, Robert, and John Sprague. 1995. *Citizens, Politics, and Social Communication: Information and Influence in an Election Campaign*. Cambridge: Cambridge University Press.

Hunt, Gaillard, and James Brown Scott, eds. 1920. *The Debates in the Federal Convention of 1787 which Framed the Constitution of the United States of America, as Reported by James Madison*. New York: Oxford University Press.

Hurd, Robert E., and Michael W. Singletary. 1985. Newspaper Influence on the 1980 Presidential Election Vote. *Journalism Quarterly* 61:332–38.

Hynds, Ernest C. 1984. Editorials, Opinion Pages Still Have Vital Roles at Most Newspapers. *Journalism Quarterly* 61:634–39.

Iyengar, Shanto, and Donald R. Kinder. 1987. *News That Matters: Television and American Opinion*. Chicago: University of Chicago Press.

Jacobson, Gary C. 1980. *Money in Congressional Elections*. New Haven: Yale University Press.

———. 1996. The 1994 House Elections in Perspective. *Political Science Quarterly* 111:203–23.

Jacobson, Gary C. 1997. *The Politics of Congressional Elections*. 4th ed. New York: Longman.

Just, Marion R., Ann N. Crigler, Dean E. Alger, Timothy E. Cook, Montague Kern, and Darrell M. West. 1996. *Crosstalk: Citizens, Candidates, and the Media in a Presidential Campaign*. Chicago: University of Chicago Press.

Kahn, Kim F. 1991. Senate Elections in the News: Examining Campaign Coverage. *Legislative Studies Quarterly* 16:349–74.

Kahn, Kim F., and Patrick J. Kenney. 1999. *The Spectacle of U.S. Senate Campaigns*. Princeton: Princeton University Press.

———. 2001. The Importance of Issues in Senate Campaigns: Citizens' Reception of Issue Messages. *Legislative Studies Quarterly* 26:573–97.

———. 2002. The Slant of the News: How Editorial Endorsements Influence Campaign Coverage and Citizens' Views of Candidates. *American Political Science Review* 96:381–94.

Kaniss, Phyllis. 1991. *Making Local News*. Chicago: University of Chicago Press.

Kingdon, John W. 1973. *Congressmen's Voting Decisions*. New York: Harper and Row.

Koger, Gregory. 2003. Position-Taking and Cosponsorship in the U.S. House. *Legislative Studies Quarterly* 28:225–46.

Kovach, Bill, and Tom Rosenstiel. 2001. *The Elements of Journalism: What Newspeople Should Know and the Public Should Expect*. New York: Crown Publishers.

Lacy, Stephen. 1990. Newspaper Competition and Number of Press Services Carried. *Journalism Quarterly* 67:79–83.

Lacy, Stephen, and Todd F. Simon. 1993. *The Economics and Regulation of United States Newspapers*. Norwood, NJ: Ablex Publishing.

Larson, Stephanie Greco. 1992. *Creating Consent of the Governed: A Member of Congress and the Local Media*. Carbondale: Southern Illinois University Press.

Levy, Dena, and Peverill Squire. 2000. Television Markets and the Competitiveness of U.S. House Elections. *Legislative Studies Quarterly* 25:313–25.

Lichter, S. Robert, Stanley Rothman, and Linda S. Lichter. 1990. *The Media Elite: America's New Powerbrokers*. Mamaroneck, NY: Hastings House.

Lipinski, Daniel. 2001. The Effect of Messages Communicated by Members of Congress: The Impact of Publicizing Votes. *Legislative Studies Quarterly* 26:81–100.

Lodge, Milton, Kathleen M. McGraw, and Patrick Stroh. 1989. An Impression-Driven Model of Candidate Evaluation. *American Political Science Review* 83: 399–419.

Lodge, Milton, Marco R. Steenbergen, and Shawn Brau. 1995. The Responsive Voter: Campaign Information and the Dynamics of Candidate Evaluation. *American Political Science Review* 89:309–26.

Manheim, Jarol B. 1974. Urbanization and Differential Press Coverage of the Congressional Campaign. *Journalism Quarterly* 51:649–53, 669.

Mann, Thomas E., and Norman J. Ornstein, eds. 1994. *Congress, the Press, and the Public*. Washington, DC: American Enterprise Institute and Brookings Institution.

Martin, Paul. 1996. Over the Wire and Then What? Presented at the Annual Meeting of the Midwest Political Science Association, Chicago.

Mayer, William G. 1993. The Polls: Trends in Media Usage. *Public Opinion Quarterly* 57:593–611.

Mayhew, David R. 1974. *Congress: The Electoral Connection*. New Haven: Yale University Press.

———. 1991. *Divided We Govern: Lawmaking, Investigations, and Party Control, 1946–1990*. New Haven: Yale University Press.

———. 1998. Clinton, the 103rd Congress, and Unified Party Control: What Are the Lessons? In *Politicians and Party Politics*, edited by John G. Geer. Baltimore: Johns Hopkins University Press.

McCombs, Maxwell. 1987. Effect of Monopoly in Cleveland on Diversity of Newspaper Content. *Journalism Quarterly* 64:740–44.

McCubbins, Mathew D., and Thomas Schwartz. 1984. Congressional Oversight Overlooked: Police Patrols versus Fire Alarms. *American Journal of Political Science* 28:165–79.

McManus, John. 1990. How Local Television Learns What Is News. *Journalism Quarterly* 67:672–83.

Miller, Warren E., and Donald E. Stokes. 1966. Constituency Influence in Congress. In *Elections and the Political Order*, edited by Angus Campbell, Philip E. Converse, Warren E. Miller, and Donald E. Stokes. New York: John Wiley.

Mondak, Jeffery. 1995. *Nothing to Read: Newspapers and Elections in a Social Experiment*. Ann Arbor: University of Michigan Press.

Monitor Publishing. 1993. *News Media Yellow Book of Washington and New York*. New York: Monitor Publishing.

National Election Studies. 1995. *American National Election Study, 1994 Postelection Survey*. Computer file. Study Number 6507. Ann Arbor, MI: Interuniversity Consortium for Political and Social Research.

Neuman, W. Russell, Marion R. Just, and Ann N. Crigler. 1992. *Common Knowledge: News and the Construction of Political Meaning*. Chicago: University of Chicago Press.

Nixon, Raymond B. and Robert L. Jones. 1956. The Content of Non-competitive vs. Competitive Newspapers. *Journalism Quarterly* 33:299–314.

Orman, John. 1985. Media Coverage of the Congressional Underdog. *PS: Political Science and Politics* 18:754–59.

Ornstein, Norman J., Thomas E. Mann, and Michael J. Malbin, eds. 1996. *Vital Statistics on Congress, 1995–1996*. Washington, DC: Congressional Quarterly.

Page, Benjamin I. 1996. *Who Deliberates? Mass Media in Modern Democracy*. Chicago: University of Chicago Press.

Patterson, Thomas E. 1980. *The Mass Media Election: How Americans Choose Their President*. New York: Praeger.

Picard, Robert G. 1989. *Media Economics: Concepts and Issues*. Newbury Park, CA: Sage Publications.

Povich, Elaine S. 1996. *Partners and Adversaries: The Contentious Connection between Congress and the Media*. Arlington, VA: Freedom Forum.

Prinz, Timothy S. 1995. Media Markets and Candidate Awareness in House Elections, 1978–1990. *Political Communication* 12:305–25.

Robinson, Michael J. 1981. Three Faces of Congressional Media. In *The New Congress*, edited by Thomas E. Mann and Norman J. Ornstein. Washington, DC: American Enterprise Institute.

Robinson, Michael J., and Margaret A. Sheehan. 1983. *Over the Wire and On TV*. New York: Russell Sage Foundation.

Rozell, Mark J. 1994. Press Coverage of Congress, 1946–1992. In *Congress, the Press, and the Public*, edited by Thomas E. Mann and Norman J. Ornstein. Washington, DC: American Enterprise Institute and Brookings Institution.

———. 1996. *In Contempt of Congress: Postwar Press Coverage on Capitol Hill*. Westport, CT: Praeger.

Schiller, Wendy J. 2000. *Partners and Rivals: Representation in U.S. Senate Delegations*. Princeton: Princeton University Press.

Schudson, Michael. 1998. *The Good Citizen: A History of American Civic Life*. Cambridge: Harvard University Press.

Snider, J. H., and Kenneth Janda. 1998. Newspapers in Bytes and Bits: Limitations of Electronic Databases for Content Analysis. Presented at the Annual Meeting of the American Political Science Association.

Takeda, Okiyoshi. 2000. Bill Passage in the United States House of Representatives. Ph.D. diss., Princeton University.

Thomas, Scott, and Bernard Grofman. 1993. The Effects of Congressional Rules about Bill Cosponsorship on Duplicate Bills: Changing Incentives for Credit Claiming. *Public Choice* 75:93–98.

Tidmarch, Charles M., and Brad S. Karp. 1983. The Missing Beat: Press Coverage of Congressional Elections in Eight Metropolitan Areas. *Congress and the Presidency* 10:47–61.

Tidmarch, Charles M., Lisa J. Hyman, and Jill E. Sorkin. 1984. Press Issue Agendas in the 1982 Congressional and Gubernatorial Election Campaigns. *Journal of Politics* 46:1226–42.

Tidmarch, Charles M., and John J. Pitney, Jr. 1985. Covering Congress. *Polity* 17: 463–83.

U.S. Congress. 1993. *Congressional Directory, 103rd Congress*. Washington, DC: Government Printing Office.

———. 1993–94. *Congressional Record*. Washington, DC: Government Printing Office.

Vanderbilt Television News Archive. 1992–94. *Television News Index and Abstracts*. Nashville, TN: Vanderbilt Television News Archive.

Vermeer, Jan P. 1982. *For Immediate Release: Candidate Press Releases in American Political Campaigns*. Westport, CT: Greenwood Press.

———. 1987. Congressional Campaign Coverage in Rural Districts. In *Campaigns in the News: Mass Media and Congressional Elections*, edited by Jan P. Vermeer. New York: Greenwood Press.

———. 2002. *The View from the States: National Politics in Local Newspaper Editorials*. Lanham, MD: Rowman and Littlefield.

Vinson, C. Danielle. 2003. *Local Media Coverage of Congress and Its Members: Through Local Eyes*. Cresskill, NJ: Hampton Press.

Weaver, David H., and L. E. Mullins. 1975. Content and Format Characteristics of Competing Daily Newspapers. *Journalism Quarterly* 52:257–64.

Westlye, Mark C. 1991. *Senate Elections and Campaign Intensity*. Baltimore: Johns Hopkins University Press.

White, H. Allen, and Julie Andsager. 1990. Winning Newspaper Pulitzer Prizes: The (Possible) Advantage of Being a Competitive Paper. *Journalism Quarterly* 67: 912–19.

Wilson, J. Matthew, and Paul Gronke. 2000. Concordance and Projection in Citizen Perceptions of Congressional Roll-Call Voting. *Legislative Studies Quarterly* 25: 445–67.

Wilson, Woodrow. [1885] 1981. *Congressional Government*. Baltimore: Johns Hopkins University Press.

Zaller, John R. 1992. *The Nature and Origins of Mass Opinion*. Cambridge: Cambridge University Press.

———. 1999. "A Theory of Media Politics: How the Interests of Politicians, Journalists, and Citizens Shape the News." Book manuscript, October 24.

———. 2003. A New Standard of News Quality: Burglar Alarms for the Monitorial Citizen. *Political Communication* 20:109–30.

Citations for Newspaper Stories and Congressional Sources

ADS	*Arizona Daily Star*
BG	*Boston Globe*
BH	*Boston Herald*
BN	*Buffalo News*
BP	*Bloomington Pantagraph*
BRA	*Baton Rouge Advocate*
CPD	*Cleveland Plain Dealer*
CST	*Chicago Sun-Times*
CT	*Chicago Tribune*
HCH	*Houston Chronicle*
HCO	*Hartford Courant*
IFPR	*Idaho Falls Post Register*
LAT	*Los Angeles Times*
LCJ	*Louisville Courier-Journal*
LMT	*Lewiston Morning Tribune*
LVRJ	*Las Vegas Review-Journal*
NDAY	*Newsday* (Long Island)
NLS	*Norfolk Ledger-Star*
OST	*Orlando Sentinel Tribune*
PG	*Phoenix Gazette*
RHH	*Rock Hill Herald*
SDUT	*San Diego Union-Tribune*
SFC	*San Francisco Chronicle*
SFE	*San Francisco Examiner*
SPI	*Seattle Post-Intelligencer*
ST	*Seattle Times*
TC	*Tucson Citizen*
TW	*Tulsa World*

WP   *Washington Post*
WT   *Washington Times*
YDR   *York Daily Record*

CQA93   *Congressional Quarterly Almanac, 1993*
CQA94   *Congressional Quarterly Almanac, 1994*
CQWR   *Congressional Quarterly Weekly Report*
CR   *Congressional Record*

Newspaper stories and congressional sources are cited in the text with a minimalist citation: source abbreviation, date, section, and page (e.g., *SDUT* 1/1/94 B12).

Index